W9-BCM-434

THE UNFINISHED NATION

A Concise History of the American People
Volume I: To 1877

Fourth Edition

ALAN BRINKLEY
Columbia University

Boston   Burr Ridge, IL   Dubuque, IA   Madison, WI   New York
San Francisco   St. Louis   Bangkok   Bogotá   Caracas   Kuala Lumpur
Lisbon   London   Madrid   Mexico City   Milan   Montreal   New Delhi
Santiago   Seoul   Singapore   Sydney   Taipei   Toronto

Higher Education

THE UNFINISHED NATION: A CONCISE HISTORY OF THE AMERICAN PEOPLE
VOLUME I: TO 1877
Published by McGraw-Hill, a business unit of The McGraw-Hill Companies, Inc., 1221 Avenue
of the Americas, New York, NY, 10020.

This book is printed on acid-free paper.

1 2 3 4 5 6 7 8 9 0 DOC/DOC 0 9 8 7 6 5 4 3

ISBN   0-07-256562-4

Publisher: *Lyn Uhl*
Senior sponsoring editor: *Steve Drummond*
Senior developmental editor: *Jim Strandberg*
Editorial assistant: *Kimberly McGrath*
Marketing manager: *Katherine Bates*
Senior media producer: *Sean Crowley*
Lead project manager: *Susan Trentacosti*
Production supervisor: *Carol A. Bielski*
Freelance design coordinator: *Gino Cieslik*
Supplement associate: *Kathleen Boylan*
Supplement developmental editor: *Kate Scheinman*
Associate photo research coordinator: *Natalia Peschiera*
Associate art editor: *Cristin Yancey*
Photo researcher: *PhotoSearch, Inc.*
Cover and interior design: *Maureen McCutcheon*
Typeface: *10.5/12 Janson*
Compositor: *Shepherd Inc.*
Printer: *R.R. Donnelley and Sons, Inc.*

Library of Congress Cataloging-in-Publication Data

Brinkley, Alan.
    The unfinished nation : a concise history of the American people / Alan Brinkley.—4th ed.
        p. cm.
    Includes bibliographical references and index.
    Contents: v. 1. To 1877 — v. 2. From 1865.
    ISBN 0-07-256554-3 (softcover : alk. paper) — ISBN 0-07-256562-4 (v. 1 : softcover :
    alk. paper) — ISBN 0-07-256563-2 (v. 2 : softcover : alk. paper)
        1. United States—History. I. Title
E178.1B827 2004
973—dc21   2003046457

www.mhhe.com

About the Author

ALAN BRINKLEY is the Allan Nevins Professor of History at Columbia University. He is the author of *Voices of Protest: Huey Long, Father Coughlin, and the Great Depression*, which won the 1983 National Book Award; *American History: A Survey; The End of Reform: New Deal Liberalism in Recession and War*; and *Liberalism and Its Discontents*. He was educated at Princeton and Harvard, and he has taught at Harvard (where he was awarded the Joseph R. Levenson Memorial Teaching Award), Princeton, the City University of New York Graduate School, and Oxford University, where he was the Harmsworth Professor of American History. He is a member of the American Academy of Arts and Sciences, a member of the board of the New York Council for the Humanities, and chairman of the board of the Century Foundation.

Brief Contents

Contents

Chapter Fourteen

The Civil War   *360*

List of Illustrations

LIST OF ILLUSTRATIONS

List of Maps and Charts

LIST OF MAPS AND CHARTS

Preface

The story of the American past, which is the subject of this book, has undergone many transformations in recent decades. The past itself has not changed, of course, but the way Americans understand it has changed dramatically. And in the wake of those changes have come both new forms of presentation and bitter controversies.

In one sense, American history is thriving as almost never before as a part of American popular culture. Historical museums and exhibitions have multiplied and have attracted large audiences. Popular writing on history—both nonfiction and novels—has grown in popularity. History is a continuing presence on television, in films, and increasingly on the Internet. The popular appetite for American history seems to be almost boundless. At the same time, however, historical scholarship has become the source of increasing debate—among historians themselves, among the various publics historians try to reach, and among politicians, some of whom attack the historical profession for what they claim is an excessively critical view of the past.

Both the growing popularity of history and the growing controversies surrounding it reflect the character of our time. Ours is an era of rapid and bewildering change, which encourages people—particularly in the aftermath of the attacks of September 11, 2001—to look to the past for guidance, reassurance, and for reminders of what many believe were simpler, stabler times. But the turbulence of our age has also encouraged historians to ask new questions of the past—and thus to reinterpret it—in an effort to understand the tensions and contests that preoccupy us today. As the population of the United States has become more diverse and as groups that once stood outside the view of scholarship have thrust themselves into its center, historians have labored to reveal the immense complexity of their country's past. As America's economy and culture and power become more deeply involved in the life of the rest of the world, historians struggle to see the ways in which global forces have shaped the nation's development. Historical narratives once recounted little beyond the experiences of great men and the unfolding of great public events. Today, they attempt to tell a more complicated story—one that includes private as well as public lives, ordinary people as well as celebrated ones, differences as well as unity, international phenomena as well as national ones. This newer history seems fragmented at times, because it attempts to embrace so many more areas of human experience than the older narratives. It is often disturbing, because it reveals failures and injustices as well as triumphs. But it is also richer, fuller, and better suited to helping us understand our own diverse and contentious world.

I have tried in this book to consider both the diversity and the unity that have characterized the American experience. The United States is, and has always been, a nation of many cultures. To understand its history, we must understand the experiences of the many groups who have shaped American society—the many worlds that have developed within it based on region, religion, class, ideology, race, gender, and ethnicity.

But the United States is not simply a collection of different cultures. It is also a great nation. And as important as understanding its diversity is understanding the forces that have drawn it together and allowed it to survive and flourish despite division. The United States has constructed a remarkably stable and enduring political system, which touches the lives of all Americans. It has developed an immense and highly productive national economy that affects the working and consuming lives of virtually everyone and reaches all across the globe. It has created a mass popular culture that colors the experiences and assumptions of almost all Americans, and of the people of much of the rest of the world as well. One can admire these unifying forces for their contributions to America's considerable success as a nation, or condemn them for creating—or failing to address—injustices. But no one proposing to understand the history of the United States can afford to ignore them.

In this fourth edition of *The Unfinished Nation*, I have tried to tell the complicated and fascinating story of America for students of history and for general readers. Those familiar with earlier editions will find a thorough editing and updating of all chapters, reflecting recent scholarship. Beyond that, there are three areas of special emphasis in this revision:

1. Greater attention to the global context of United States history, including a new feature called "America in the World."
2. Expanded coverage of science and technology.
3. Extensive new material on environmental history.

In addition, new chapter introductions and marginal notes throughout the text should make it more accessible to readers. And the most visible change is the introduction of full color maps, images, and other graphics to the book—and an expanded map and illustration program to take advantage of this change.

I trust that this edition will introduce readers to enough different aspects of American history to make them aware of its extraordinary richness and complexity. But I hope, too, that it will provide readers some sense of the shared experiences of Americans and of the forces that have sustained the United States as a nation.

My thanks to Kevin Murphy for his assistance on this edition. I am, as always, grateful to the many people at McGraw-Hill who have helped with the editing and production of this book: Lyn Uhl, Steve Drummond, Jim Strandberg, Susan Trentacosti, Gino Cieslik, Kim McGrath, Carol Bielski, Holly Rudelitsch, Natalia Peschiera, and Cristin Yancey. I am also grateful to the teachers and scholars who reviewed the manuscript and offered suggestions for revision: S. Charles Bolton, *University of Arkansas,*

Preface

The story of the American past, which is the subject of this book, has undergone many transformations in recent decades. The past itself has not changed, of course, but the way Americans understand it has changed dramatically. And in the wake of those changes have come both new forms of presentation and bitter controversies.

In one sense, American history is thriving as almost never before as a part of American popular culture. Historical museums and exhibitions have multiplied and have attracted large audiences. Popular writing on history—both nonfiction and novels—has grown in popularity. History is a continuing presence on television, in films, and increasingly on the Internet. The popular appetite for American history seems to be almost boundless. At the same time, however, historical scholarship has become the source of increasing debate—among historians themselves, among the various publics historians try to reach, and among politicians, some of whom attack the historical profession for what they claim is an excessively critical view of the past.

Both the growing popularity of history and the growing controversies surrounding it reflect the character of our time. Ours is an era of rapid and bewildering change, which encourages people—particularly in the aftermath of the attacks of September 11, 2001—to look to the past for guidance, reassurance, and for reminders of what many believe were simpler, stabler times. But the turbulence of our age has also encouraged historians to ask new questions of the past—and thus to reinterpret it—in an effort to understand the tensions and contests that preoccupy us today. As the population of the United States has become more diverse and as groups that once stood outside the view of scholarship have thrust themselves into its center, historians have labored to reveal the immense complexity of their country's past. As America's economy and culture and power become more deeply involved in the life of the rest of the world, historians struggle to see the ways in which global forces have shaped the nation's development. Historical narratives once recounted little beyond the experiences of great men and the unfolding of great public events. Today, they attempt to tell a more complicated story—one that includes private as well as public lives, ordinary people as well as celebrated ones, differences as well as unity, international phenomena as well as national ones. This newer history seems fragmented at times, because it attempts to embrace so many more areas of human experience than the older narratives. It is often disturbing, because it reveals failures and injustices as well as triumphs. But it is also richer, fuller, and better suited to helping us understand our own diverse and contentious world.

I have tried in this book to consider both the diversity and the unity that have characterized the American experience. The United States is, and has always been, a nation of many cultures. To understand its history, we must understand the experiences of the many groups who have shaped American society—the many worlds that have developed within it based on region, religion, class, ideology, race, gender, and ethnicity.

But the United States is not simply a collection of different cultures. It is also a great nation. And as important as understanding its diversity is understanding the forces that have drawn it together and allowed it to survive and flourish despite division. The United States has constructed a remarkably stable and enduring political system, which touches the lives of all Americans. It has developed an immense and highly productive national economy that affects the working and consuming lives of virtually everyone and reaches all across the globe. It has created a mass popular culture that colors the experiences and assumptions of almost all Americans, and of the people of much of the rest of the world as well. One can admire these unifying forces for their contributions to America's considerable success as a nation, or condemn them for creating—or failing to address—injustices. But no one proposing to understand the history of the United States can afford to ignore them.

In this fourth edition of *The Unfinished Nation*, I have tried to tell the complicated and fascinating story of America for students of history and for general readers. Those familiar with earlier editions will find a thorough editing and updating of all chapters, reflecting recent scholarship. Beyond that, there are three areas of special emphasis in this revision:

1. Greater attention to the global context of United States history, including a new feature called "America in the World."
2. Expanded coverage of science and technology.
3. Extensive new material on environmental history.

In addition, new chapter introductions and marginal notes throughout the text should make it more accessible to readers. And the most visible change is the introduction of full color maps, images, and other graphics to the book—and an expanded map and illustration program to take advantage of this change.

I trust that this edition will introduce readers to enough different aspects of American history to make them aware of its extraordinary richness and complexity. But I hope, too, that it will provide readers some sense of the shared experiences of Americans and of the forces that have sustained the United States as a nation.

My thanks to Kevin Murphy for his assistance on this edition. I am, as always, grateful to the many people at McGraw-Hill who have helped with the editing and production of this book: Lyn Uhl, Steve Drummond, Jim Strandberg, Susan Trentacosti, Gino Cieslik, Kim McGrath, Carol Bielski, Holly Rudelitsch, Natalia Peschiera, and Cristin Yancey. I am also grateful to the teachers and scholars who reviewed the manuscript and offered suggestions for revision: S. Charles Bolton, *University of Arkansas,*

Little Rock; Steven Boyd, *University of Texas, San Antonio;* Mike Haridopolos, *Brevard Community College;* Mark D. Van Ells, *Queensborough Community College;* B. R. Burg, *Arizona State University;* Yolanda Chávaz Leyva, *University of Texas, El Paso;* Gregory Wilson, *University of Akron;* Beverly Garrison, *Oral Roberts University;* Kenneth W. Townsend, *Coastal Carolina University;* Joanne Kropp, *University of Texas, El Paso;* Anita Ashendel, *Texas A & M University;* Donald Rakestraw, *Georgia Southern University;* Josh Rothman, *University of Alabama;* David Freligh, *Phillips Community College;* Victor Triary, *Middlesex Community College;* Alex Wellek, *Quinnipiac University;* Margaret Orelup, *Keene State College;* Dr. Robert Tracy McKenzie, *University of Washington;* Jeffrey A. Kaufmann, *Muscatine Community College;* Jack Hammersmith, *West Virginia University;* Wendy Gunderson, *Collin County Community College;* Elizabeth Osborn, *Indiana University;* Alexander Knott, *University of Northern Colorado;* William Virden, *University of Northern Colorado;* and David Cullin, *Collin County Community College.*

I am grateful, finally, to those readers of the book who have offered me unsolicited comments, criticisms, and corrections. I hope they will continue to do so. Suggestions can be sent to me at the Department of History, Columbia University, New York, NY 10027, or by e-mail at ab65@columbia.edu.

Alan Brinkley

THE UNFINISHED NATION

A Concise History of the American People

Frobisher and the Eskimos   In 1577, the English explorer Martin Frobisher embarked on an elusive search that enchanted a generation of Europeans—the search for the "Northwest Passage," a waterway through North America to the Pacific. He sailed into the Arctic regions of eastern Canada, deep into Baffin Bay, before finding his route blocked by impassable ice. Along the way, he encountered groups of Baffinland Eskimos, who—as this John White drawing (repainted by his contemporary Hans Sloan) shows—attacked his party. Even outnumbered, the Frobisher party had the advantage of firearms and escaped serious harm.   *(British Museum, London/The Bridgeman Art Library, NY)*

TIME LINE

16,000-14,000 B.C.	1492	1497	1502	1518-1530	1519-1522	
Asians migrate to North America	Columbus discovers America	Cabot explores North America	African slaves arrive in Spanish America	Smallpox ravages Indians	Magellan circumnavigates globe	

CHAPTER ONE

⤌❧⤍

THE MEETING
OF CULTURES

America before Columbus
Europe Looks Westward
The Arrival of the English

he discovery of America did not begin with Christopher Columbus. It
started many thousands of years earlier when human beings first crossed
an ancient land bridge from eastern Siberia across the Bering Strait into
what is now Alaska. These early migrants, thought to be mostly of Mongolian
stock, were truly the first Americans. Humans never developed in the Americas; the people had to find it. The early arrivals from Siberia began the first
of two great migrations that would make the western hemisphere eventually
the site of some of the largest and most important civilizations in the world.

Over the course of many centuries, migrants from Russia and probably
also from other areas of Asia and from the Pacific Islands spread out through
the lands of North and South America and created great civilizations. But beginning in the fifteenth century A.D., Europeans began to encounter the
Americas as well—and began to launch their own great migrations into what
they called the New World. This early period of contact between American
and European civilization was sometimes friendly and sometimes mutually
beneficial. But mostly, it was catastrophic for the American natives (or "Indians," as Europeans called them), both because they were not able to match
European technologies in battle and because they were highly vulnerable to
European diseases. Plagues from Europe decimated the native population in
many parts of the Americas and made the European conquest of the continents much easier. By the late sixteenth century, Europeans had established
a claim to all the lands of the Americas and actual control over much of it.

1558	1565	1587	1603	1607	1608	1609	
Elizabeth I becomes English queen	St. Augustine, Florida, founded	"Lost Colony" established on Roanoke Island	James I becomes English king	Jamestown founded	French establish Quebec	Spanish found Santa Fe	

AMERICA BEFORE COLUMBUS

No one is certain when the first migrations into the Americas began; recent estimates suggest that they started between 14,000 and 16,000 years ago. They were probably a result of the development of stone-tipped spears and other hunting implements that made it possible for humans to pursue large animals from Asia into North America. Year after year, a few at a time, these nomadic peoples entered the new continent and moved deeper into its heart. Perhaps as early as 8,000 B.C., the migrations reached the southern tip of South America. By the end of the fifteenth century A.D., when the first important contact with Europeans occurred, America was the home of many millions of men and women. Scholars estimate that well over 50 million people—and perhaps as many as 75 million—lived in the Americas by 1500 and that perhaps 10 million lived in the territory that now constitutes the United States.

The Civilizations of the South

Elaborate societies emerged in South and Central America and in Mexico. In Peru, the Incas created a powerful empire of perhaps 6 million people. They developed a complex political system and a large network of paved roads that welded together the populations of many tribes under a single government. In Central America and on the Yucatan Peninsula of Mexico, *Incan and Aztec Empires* the Mayas built a sophisticated culture with a written language, a numerical system similar to the Arabic, an accurate calendar, and an advanced agricultural system. They were succeeded by the Aztecs, a once-nomadic warrior tribe from the north. In the late thirteenth century, the Aztecs established a precarious rule over much of central and southern Mexico and built elaborate administrative, educational, and medical systems. They also developed a harsh religion that required human sacrifice. Their Spanish conquerors discovered the skulls of 100,000 victims in one location when they arrived in 1519.

The economies of these societies were based primarily on agriculture, but there were also substantial cities. Tenochtitlán, the Aztec capital built on the site of present-day Mexico City, had a population of over 100,000 in 1500. The Mayas (at Mayapan and elsewhere) and the Incas (in such cities as Cuzco and Machu Picchu) produced elaborate settlements with striking religious and ceremonial structures. These civilizations accomplished all this without some of the important technologies that Asian and European civilizations possessed. As late as the sixteenth century, no American society had yet developed wheeled vehicles.

INDIANS OF NEW FRANCE The drawing is by the cartographer Charles Bécard de Granville, who was employed by the French government to make maps of its territories in North America. Granville also produced drawings of the flora and fauna of the region and of the natives he encountered. This depiction of Indian hunters traveling by river dates from approximately 1701. *(Codex Canadiensis, by Louis Nicolas, from the Collection of Gilcrease Museum, Tulsa)*

The Civilizations of the North

The peoples north of Mexico developed less elaborate but still substantial civilizations. Inhabitants of the northern regions of the continent subsisted on some combination of hunting, gathering, and fishing. They included the Eskimos of the Arctic Circle, who fished and hunted seals; the big-game hunters of the northern forests, who led nomadic lives based on pursuit of moose and caribou; the tribes of the Pacific Northwest, whose principal occupation was salmon fishing and who created substantial permanent settlements along the coast; and a group of tribes spread through relatively arid regions of the Far West, who developed successful communities based on fishing, hunting small game, and gathering edible plants.

Hunting and Gathering

Other societies in North America were agricultural. Among the most developed were those in the Southwest. The people of that arid region built large irrigation systems, and they constructed towns of stone and adobe structures. In the Great Plains region, too, most tribes were engaged in sedentary farming (corn and other grains) and lived in large permanent settlements.

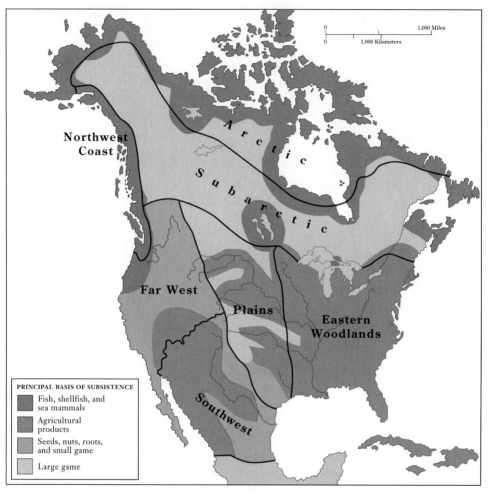

HOW THE EARLY NORTH AMERICANS LIVED This map shows the various ways in which the native tribes of North America supported themselves before the arrival of European civilization. Like most precommercial peoples, the native Americans survived largely on the resources available in their immediate surroundings. Note, for example, the reliance on the products of the sea of the tribes along the northern coastlines of the continent, and the way in which tribes in relatively inhospitable climates in the North—where agriculture was difficult—relied on hunting large game. Most native Americans were farmers. ◆ *What different kinds of farming would have emerged in the very different climates of the agricultural regions shown on this map?*

 For an interactive version of this map go to www.mhhe.com/unfinishednation4ch1maps

The eastern third of what is now the United States—much of it covered with forests and inhabited by the Woodland Indians—had the greatest food resources of any area of the continent. Most of the many tribes of the region engaged in farming, hunting, gathering, and fishing simultaneously. In the South there were permanent settlements and large trading networks based on the corn and other grains grown in the rich lands of the

Mississippi River valley. Cahokia, a trading center located near present-day St. Louis, had a population of 40,000 at its peak in A.D. 1200.

Cahokia

The agricultural societies of the Northeast were more mobile. Farming techniques there were designed to exploit the land quickly rather than to develop permanent settlements. Many of the tribes living east of the Mississippi River were linked together loosely by common linguistic roots. The largest of these language groups consisted of the Algonquin tribes, which lived along the Atlantic seaboard from Canada to Virginia; the Iroquois Confederacy, which was centered in what is now upstate New York; and the Muskogean tribes, which consisted of the tribes in the southernmost region of the eastern seaboard. Alliances among the various Indian societies (even among those with common languages) were fragile.

Religion was usually closely linked with the natural world on which the tribes depended. Native Americans worshipped many gods, whom they associated variously with crops, game, forests, rivers, and other elements of nature.

All tribes assigned women the jobs of caring for children, preparing meals, and gathering certain foods. But the allocation of other tasks varied from one society to another. Some tribal groups reserved farming tasks almost entirely for men. Among other groups, women tended the fields, while men engaged in hunting, warfare, or clearing land. Because women and children were often left alone for extended periods while men were away hunting or fighting, women in some tribes tended to control the social and economic organization of the settlements.

Gender Relations

EUROPE LOOKS WESTWARD

Europeans were almost entirely unaware of the existence of the Americas before the fifteenth century. A few early wanderers—Leif Eriksson, an eleventh-century Norse seaman, and others—had glimpsed parts of the New World on their voyages. But even if their discoveries had become common knowledge (and they did not), there would have been little incentive for others to follow. Europe in the Middle Ages (roughly A.D. 500–1500) was too divided and decentralized to inspire many great ventures. By the end of the fifteenth century, however, conditions in Europe had changed, and the incentive for overseas exploration had grown.

Commerce and Nationalism

Two changes in particular encouraged Europeans to look toward new lands. One was a result of the significant growth in Europe's population in the fifteenth century. The

European Population Growth

Black Death, a catastrophic epidemic of the bubonic plague that began in Constantinople in 1347, had killed (according to some estimates) more than a third of the people of the continent. But a century and a half later, the population had rebounded. With that growth came a reawakening of commerce. A new merchant class was emerging to meet the rising demand for goods from abroad. As trade increased, and as advances in navigation made long-distance sea travel more feasible, interest in expanding trade even further grew quickly.

The second change was the emergence of new governments that were more united and powerful than the feeble political entities of the feudal past. In the western areas of Europe in particular, strong new monarchs were eager to enhance the commercial development of their nations.

Ever since the early fourteenth century, when Marco Polo and other adventurers had returned from Asia bearing exotic spices, cloths, and dyes, and even more exotic tales, Europeans who craved commercial glory had dreamed above all of trade with the East. For two centuries, that trade had been limited by the difficulties of the long overland journey to the Asian courts. But in the fourteenth century, as the maritime talents of several western European societies increased, talk of finding a faster, safer sea route to East Asia began.

Portuguese Exploration The Portuguese were the preeminent maritime power in the fifteenth century largely because of Prince Henry the Navigator, who devoted much of his life to the promotion of exploration. In 1486, after Henry's death, the Portuguese explorer Bartholomeu Dias rounded the southern tip of Africa (the Cape of Good Hope); and in 1497–1498, Vasco da Gama proceeded all the way around the cape to India. But the Portuguese were not the first to encounter the New World.

Christopher Columbus

Christopher Columbus was born and reared in Genoa, Italy, and spent his early seafaring years in the service of the Portuguese. By the time he was a young man, he had developed great ambitions. He believed he could reach East Asia by sailing west, across the Atlantic, rather than east, around Africa. Columbus thought the world was far smaller than it actually is. He also believed that the Asian continent extended farther eastward than it actually does. Most important, he did not realize that anything lay to the west between Europe and the lands of Asia.

Columbus failed to enlist the leaders of Portugal behind his plan, so he turned instead to Spain. The marriage of Spain's two most powerful regional rulers, Ferdinand of Aragon and Isabella of Castile, had produced the strongest and most ambitious monarchy in Europe. Columbus appealed to Queen Isabella for support for his proposed westward voyage, and in 1492, she agreed. Commanding ninety *Columbus's First Voyage* men and three ships—the *Niña*, the *Pinta*, and the

EUROPEAN EXPLORATION AND CONQUEST, 1492–1583 This map shows the many voyages of exploration to and conquest of North America launched by Europeans in the late fifteenth and sixteenth centuries. Note how Columbus and the Spanish explorers who followed him tended to move quickly into the lands of Mexico, the Caribbean, and Central and South America, while the English and French explored the northern territories of North America. ◆ *What factors might have led these various nations to explore and colonize these different areas of the New World?*

 For an interactive version of this map go to www.mhhe.com/unfinishednation4ch1maps

Santa María—Columbus left Spain in August 1492 and sailed west into the Atlantic. Ten weeks later, he sighted land and assumed he had reached an island off Asia. In fact, he had landed in the Bahamas. When he pushed on and encountered Cuba, he assumed he had reached China. He returned to Spain, bringing with him several captured natives as evidence of his achievement. (He called the natives "Indians" because he believed they were from the East Indies in the Pacific.)

But Columbus did not, of course, bring back news of the great khan's court in China or any samples of the fabled wealth of the Indies. And so a year later, he tried again, this time with a much larger expedition. As before, he headed into the Caribbean, discovering several other islands and leaving a small and short-lived colony on Hispaniola. On a third voyage, in 1498, he finally reached the mainland and cruised along the northern coast of South America. He then realized, for the first time, that he had encountered not a part of Asia but a separate continent.

Columbus's celebrated accomplishments made him a popular hero for a time, but he ended his life in obscurity. Ultimately, he was even unable to give his name to the land he had revealed to the Europeans. That distinction went instead to a Florentine merchant, Amerigo Vespucci, who wrote a series of vivid descriptions of the lands he visited on an expedition to the New World and helped popularize the idea that the Americas were new continents.

Partly as a result of Columbus's initiative, Spain began to devote greater resources and energy to maritime exploration. In 1513 the Spaniard Vasco de Balboa crossed the Isthmus of Panama and became the first known European to gaze westward upon the great ocean that separated America from China. Seeking access to that ocean, Ferdinand Magellan, a Portuguese in Spanish employ, found the strait that now bears his name at the southern end of South America, struggled through the stormy narrows and into the ocean (so calm by contrast that he christened it the *Pacific*), and then proceeded to the Philippines. There Magellan died in a conflict with the natives, but his expedition went on to complete the first *Circumnavigation of the Globe* known circumnavigation of the globe (1519–1522). By 1550, Spaniards had explored the coasts of North America as far north as Oregon in the west and Labrador in the east.

The Spanish Empire

In time, Spanish explorers in the New World stopped thinking of America simply as an obstacle to their search for a route to the East and began instead to consider it a possible source of wealth in itself. The Spanish claimed for themselves the whole of the New World, except for a piece of it (today's Brazil) that was reserved by a papal decree for the Portuguese.

The early Spanish colonists settled on the islands of the Caribbean. But then, in 1518, Hernando Cortés, who had been an unsuccessful Spanish government official in Cuba for fourteen years, decided to lead a small military expedition (about 600 men) against the Aztecs in Mexico and their powerful emperor, Montezuma, after hearing stories of great treasures there. His first assault on Tenochtitlán, the Aztec capital, failed. But Cortés and his army had unwittingly exposed the natives to smallpox. An epidemic of that deadly disease, to which the natives, unlike the Europeans, had developed no immunity, decimated the Aztec population and made it possible for the Spanish to triumph in their second attempt at conquest. Through his ruthless suppression of the surviving natives, Cortés established himself as one of the most bru- *"Conquistadores"* tal of the Spanish "conquistadores" (conquerors). Twenty years later, Francisco Pizarro conquered the Incas in Peru and opened the way for other advances into South America.

The conquistadores had cleared the way for the first Spanish settlers in America. They were interested only in exploiting the American stores of gold and silver, and they were fabulously successful. For 300 years, beginning in the sixteenth century, the mines of Spanish America yielded more than ten times as much gold and silver as the rest of the world's mines together. After the first wave of conquest, however, most Spanish settlers in America traveled to the New World for other reasons. Many went in hopes of profiting from agriculture, and they helped establish elements of European civilization permanently in America. Other Spaniards—priests, friars, and missionaries—went to America to spread the Christian religion; through their efforts, the influence of the Catholic Church ultimately extended throughout South and Central America and Mexico.

THE MEXICANS STRIKE BACK In this vivid scene from the Duran Codex, Mexican artists illustrate a rare moment in which Mexican warriors gained the upper hand over the Spanish invaders. Driven back by native fighters, the Spanish have taken refuge in a room in the royal palace in Tenochtitlán while brightly attired Mexican warriors besiege them. Although the Mexicans gained a temporary advantage in this battle, the drawing illustrates one of the reasons for their inability to withstand the Spanish in the longer term. The Spanish soldiers are armed with rifles and crossbows, while the Indians carry only spears and shields. *(Oronoz Archivo)*

By the end of the sixteenth century, the Spanish Empire included the Caribbean islands, Mexico, and southern North America. It also spread into South America and included what is now Chile, Argentina, and Peru. In 1580, when the Spanish and Portuguese monarchies temporarily united, Brazil came under Spanish jurisdiction as well.

Northern Outposts

St. Augustine and Santa Fe   In 1565, the Spanish established the fort of St. Augustine in Florida, their first permanent settlement north of Mexico. But it was little more than a small military outpost. A more substantial colonizing venture began in the Southwest in 1598, when Don Juan de Onate traveled north from Mexico with a party of 500, claimed for Spain some of the lands of the Pueblo Indians in what is now New Mexico, and began to establish a colony. Onate granted *encomiendas* (the right to exact tribute and labor from the natives on large tracts of land) to favored Spaniards. In 1609, Spanish colonists founded Santa Fe. By 1680, there were over 2,000 Spanish colonists living among about 30,000 Pueblos. The economic heart of the colony was cattle and sheep, raised on the *ranchos* that stretched out around the small towns Spanish settlers established.

In 1680, the colony was nearly destroyed when the Pueblos rose in revolt. Despite widespread conversions to Catholicism, most natives (including the converts) continued to practice their own religious rituals. In 1680, Spanish priests and the colonial government were trying to suppress these rituals. In response, Pope, an Indian religious leader, led an uprising that killed hundreds of European settlers, captured Santa Fe, and drove the Spanish from the region. Twelve years later the Spanish returned, resumed seizing Pueblo lands, and crushed a last revolt in 1696.

After the revolts, many Spanish colonists seemed to understand that they could not hope to prosper in New Mexico in constant conflict with a native population that greatly outnumbered them. Although the Spanish intensified their efforts to assimilate the Indians, they also now permitted the Pueblos to own land. They stopped commandeering Indian labor, and they tacitly tolerated the survival of tribal religious rituals. There was significant intermarriage between Europeans and Indians. By 1750, the Spanish population had grown modestly to about 4,000. The Pueblo population had declined (through disease, war, and migration) to about 13,000—less than half what it had been in 1680. New Mexico had by then become a reasonably stable but still weak and isolated outpost of the Spanish Empire.

Assimilation and Accommodation

Biological and Cultural Exchanges

European and native cultures never entirely merged in the Spanish Empire. Nevertheless, the arrival of whites launched a process of interaction between different peoples that left no one unchanged.

SPANISH AMERICA From the time of Columbus's initial voyage in 1492 until the mid-nineteenth century, Spain was the dominant colonial power in the New World. From the southern regions of South America to the northern regions of the Pacific northwest, Spain controlled one of the world's vastest empires. Note how much of the Spanish empire was simply grafted upon the earlier empires of native peoples—the Incas in what is today Chile and Peru, and the Aztecs across much of the rest of South America, Mexico, and the Southwest of what is now the United States. ◆ *What characteristics of Spanish colonization would account for their preference for already settled regions?*

 For an interactive version of this map go to www.mhhe.com/unfinishednation4ch1maps

THE AMERICAN POPULATION BEFORE COLUMBUS

No one knows how many people lived in the Americas in the centuries before Columbus. But scholars, and others, have spent more than a century debating the question. Interest in this question survives because the debate over the pre-Columbian population is closely connected to the much larger debate over the consequences of European settlement of the Western Hemisphere.

Throughout the nineteenth century, Native Americans spoke often of the great days before Columbus when there were many more people in their tribes. The painter and ethnographer George Catlin, who spent much time among the tribes in the 1830s, listened to these oral legends and estimated that there had been 16 million Indians in North America before the Europeans came. Other white Americans dismissed such claims as preposterous, insisting that Indian civilization was far too primitive ever to have sustained a population even as large as a million.

In 1928, James Mooney, an ethnologist at the Smithsonian Institution, drawing from early accounts of soldiers and missionaries in the sixteenth century, came up with the implausibly precise figure of 1.15 million natives who lived north of Mexico in the early sixteenth century. That was a larger figure than nineteenth-century writers had suggested, but still much smaller than the Indians themselves claimed. A few years later, the anthropologist Alfred Kroeber used some of Mooney's methods to come up with an estimate considerably larger than Mooney's, but much lower than Catlin's. He concluded in 1934 that there were 8.4 million people in the Americas in 1492, half in North America and half in the Caribbean and South America.

These low early estimates reflected an assumption that the arrival of the Europeans did not much reduce the native population. But in the 1960s and 1970s, scholars discovered that the early tribes had been catastrophically decimated by European plagues not long after the arrival of Columbus—that the numbers Europeans observed even in the late 1500s were already dramatically smaller than the numbers in 1492. Historians such as William McNeill in 1976 and Alfred Crosby a decade later produced powerful accounts of the near extinction of some tribes and the dramatic depopulation of others in a pestilential holocaust with few parallels in history.

The belief that the native population was much larger in 1492 than it was a few decades later has helped spur much larger estimates of how many people were in America before Columbus. Henry Dobyns, an anthropologist, claimed in 1966 that there were between 10 and 12 million people north of Mexico in 1492, and between 90 and 112 million in all of the Americas. No subsequent scholar has made so high a claim, but most subsequent estimates have been much closer to Dobyns's than to Kroeber's. The geographer William M. Denevan, for example, argued in 1976 that the American population in 1492 was around 55 million and that the population north of Mexico was under 4 million. These are among the lowest of modern estimates, but still dramatically higher than the nineteenth-century numbers.

The vehemence with which scholars, and at times the larger public, have debated these figures does not stem solely from the difficulty inherent in the effort to determine population size. It is also because the debate over the population is part of the debate over whether the arrival of Columbus—and the millions of Europeans who followed him—was a great advance in the history of civilization or an unparalleled catastrophe that virtually exterminated a large and flourishing native population. How to balance the many achievements of European civilization in the New World after 1492 against the terrible destruction of native peoples that accompanied it is, in the end, less a historical question, perhaps, than a moral one.

(text continued from page 12)

Beneficial and Catastrophic Exchanges

That Europeans were exploring the Americas at all was a result of their early contacts with the natives, from whom they had learned of the rich deposits of gold and silver. From then on, the history of the Americas became one of increasing levels of exchanges—some beneficial, some catastrophic—among different peoples and cultures. The first and perhaps most profound result of this exchange was the importation of European diseases to the New World. It would be difficult to exaggerate the consequences of the exposure of Native Americans to such illnesses as influenza, measles, typhus, and above all smallpox. Millions died. In some areas, native populations were virtually wiped out within a few decades of their first contact with whites. On Hispaniola, where Columbus had landed in the 1490s, the native population quickly declined from approximately 1 million to about 500. In the Mayan areas of Mexico, as much as 95 percent of the population perished within a few years of the natives' first contact with the Spanish. Many (although not all) of the tribes north of Mexico, whose contact with European settlers came later and was often less intimate, were spared the worst of the epidemics. But for other areas of the New World, this was a catastrophe at least as grave as, and in some places far worse than, the Black Death that had killed over a third of the population of Europe two centuries before. Europeans, watching this biological catastrophe, saw it as evidence of God's will that they should dominate the New World—and its native population.

The decimation of native populations in the southern regions of the Americas was not, however, purely a result of exposure to infection. It was also a result of the conquistadores' deliberate policy of subjugation and extermination. Their brutality was in part a reflection of the ruthlessness with which Europeans waged war in all parts of the world. It was also a result of their conviction that the natives were "savages"—uncivilized peoples who could be treated as somehow not fully human. By the 1540s, the combined effects of European diseases and European military brutality had all but destroyed the empires of Mexico and South America.

Deliberate Subjugation and Extermination

Not all aspects of the exchange were so disastrous to the Indians. The Europeans introduced to America important new crops (among them sugar and bananas), domestic livestock (cattle, pigs, and sheep), and, perhaps most significant, the horse, which gradually became central to the lives of many natives and transformed their societies.

The exchange was at least as important (and more beneficial) to the Europeans. In both North and South America, the arriving white peoples learned from the natives new agricultural techniques appropriate to the

New World Crops   demands of the new land. They discovered new crops—above all maize (corn), which Columbus took back to Europe from his first trip to America. Such foods as squash, pumpkins, beans, sweet potatoes, tomatoes, peppers, and potatoes all found their way into European diets.

In South America, Central America, and Mexico, a society in which Europeans and natives lived in intimate, if unequal, contact with one another emerged. Many natives gradually came to speak Spanish or Portuguese, but they created a range of dialects fusing the European languages with elements of their own. European men outnumbered European women by at least ten to one. As a result, male Spanish immigrants had substantial sexual contact with native women. Intermarriage—often forcible—became frequent. Before long, the population of the colonies came to be dominated (numerically, at least) by people of mixed race, or mestizos.

Virtually all the enterprises of the Spanish and Portuguese colonists depended on an Indian workforce. In some places, Indians were sold into slav-

Coercive Wage System   ery. More often, colonists used a coercive (or "indentured") wage system, under which Indians worked in the mines and on the plantations under duress for fixed periods. That was not, in the end, enough to meet the labor needs of the colonists. As early as 1502, therefore, European settlers began importing slaves from Africa.

Africa and America

Over half of all the immigrants to the New World between 1500 and 1800 were Africans, virtually all of them sent to America against their will. Most came from a large region below the Sahara Desert, known as Guinea.

Europeans and white Americans came to portray African society as primitive and uncivilized. But most Africans were, in fact, civilized peoples with well-developed economies and political systems. The residents of upper Guinea had substantial commercial contact with the Mediterranean

Trade States of West Africa   world—trading ivory, gold, and slaves for finished goods—and, largely as a result, became early converts to Islam. After the collapse of the ancient kingdom of Ghana around A.D. 1100, they created the even larger empire of Mali, whose trading center at Timbuktu became fabled as a center of education and a meeting place of the peoples of many lands.

Farther south, Africans were more isolated from Europe and the Mediterranean and were more politically fragmented. The central social unit was the village, which usually consisted of members of an extended family group. Some groups of villages united in small kingdoms. But no large empires emerged in the south. Nevertheless, these southern societies developed extensive trade, both among themselves and, to a lesser degree, with the outside world.

African civilizations developed economies that reflected the climates and resources of their lands. In upper Guinea, fishing and rice cultivation, supplemented by the extensive trade with Mediterranean lands, were the foundation of the economy. Farther south, Africans grew wheat and other food crops, raised livestock, and fished. There were some more nomadic tribes in the interior, who subsisted largely on hunting and gathering. But most Africans were sedentary, farming people.

As in many Indian societies in America, African families tended to be matrilineal: They traced their heredity through *Matrilineal Societies* and inherited property from their mothers. Women played a major role, often the dominant role, in trade. In many areas, they were the principal farmers (while the men hunted, fished, and raised livestock), and everywhere, they managed child care and food preparation. Most tribes also divided political power by gender, with men choosing leaders to manage male affairs and women choosing parallel leaders to handle female matters.

In those areas of west Africa where indigenous religions had survived the spread of Islam, people worshiped many gods, whom they associated with various aspects of the natural world and whose spirits they believed lived in trees, rocks, forests, and streams. Most Africans also developed forms of ancestor worship and took great care in tracing family lineage; the most revered priests were generally the oldest people.

Small elites of priests and nobles stood at the top of many African societies. Most people belonged to a large middle group of farmers, traders, crafts workers, and others. At the bottom of society *African Slavery* were slaves—men and women who were put into bondage after being captured in wars, because of criminal behavior, or as a result of unpaid debts. African people were generally in bondage for a fixed term, and in the meantime retained certain legal protections (including the right to marry). Children did not inherit their parents' condition of bondage.

The African slave trade long preceded European settlement in the New World. As early as the eighth century, west Africans began selling small numbers of slaves to traders from the Mediterranean and later to the Portuguese. In the sixteenth century, however, the mar- *Sugar and the Slave Trade* ket for slaves increased dramatically as a result of the growing European demand for sugar cane. The small areas of sugar cultivation in the Mediterranean could not meet the demand, and production soon spread to new areas: to the island of Madeira off the African coast, which

Most Americans understand that our nation has recently become intimately bound up with the rest of the world—that we live in a time sometimes called the "age of globalization." Until recently, however, most historians have examined the nation's past in relative isolation. Among the first areas of American history to re-examine the past in an international perspective is the earliest period of European settlement of the Americas. Many scholars of early American history now examine what happened in the "New World" in the context of what has become known as the "Atlantic World."

The idea of an "Atlantic World" rests in part on the obvious connections between western Europe and the Spanish, British, French, and Dutch colonies in North and South America. All the early European civilizations of the Americas were part of a great imperial project launched by the major powers of Europe. The massive European immigration to the Americas beginning in the sixteenth century, the defeat and devastation of native populations, the creation of European agricultural and urban settlements, and the imposition of imperial regulations on trade, commerce, landowning, and political life—all of these forces reveal the influence of Old World imperialism on the history of the New World.

But the creation of empires is only one part of the creation of the Atlantic World. At least equally important—and closely related—is the expansion of commerce from Europe to the Americas. Although some Europeans traveled to the New World in search of religious freedom, or to escape oppression, or to search for adventure, the great majority of European immigrants were in search of economic opportunity. Not surprisingly, therefore, the European settlements in the Americas were almost from the start intimately connected to Europe through the growth of commerce between them—commerce that grew more extensive and more complex with every passing year. The commercial relationship between America and Europe was responsible not just for the growth of trade, but also for the increases in migration over time—as the demand for labor in the New World drew more and more settlers from the Old World. Commerce was also the principal reason for the rise of slavery in the Americas, and for the growth of the slave trade between European America and Africa. The Atlantic World, in other words, included not just Europe and the Americas, but Africa as well.

Religion was another force binding together the Atlantic World. The vast majority of people of European descent were Christians, and most of them maintained important religious ties to Europe. Catholics, of course, were part of a hierarchical church based in Rome and maintained close ties with the Vatican. But the Protestant faiths that predominated in North America were intimately linked to their European counterparts as well. New religious ideas and movements spread back and forth across the Atlantic with astonishing speed. Great revivals that began in Europe moved quickly to America. The "Great Awakening" of the mid-eighteenth century, for example, began in Britain and traveled to America in large part through the efforts of the English evangelist George Whitefield. American evangelists later carried religious ideas from the New World back to the Old.

The early history of European America was also closely bound up with the intellectual life of Europe. The Enlightenment—the cluster of ideas that emerged in Europe in the seventeenth and eighteenth centuries emphasizing the power of human reason—moved quickly to the Americas, producing considerable intellectual ferment throughout the New World, but particularly in the British colonies in North America and the Caribbean. The ideas of the British philosopher John Locke, for example, helped shape the founding of Georgia. The English Constitution, and the idea of the "rights of Englishmen," shaped the way North Americans shaped their own concepts of politics. Many of the ideas that lay behind the American Revolution were products of British and continental philosophy that had traveled across the Atlantic. The reinterpretation of those ideas by Americans to help justify their drive to independence—by, among others, Thomas Paine—moved back to Europe and helped, among other things, to inspire the French Revolution. Scientific and technological knowledge—another product of the Enlightenment—traveled constantly across the Atlantic and back. Americans borrowed industrial technology from Britain. Europe acquired much of its early knowledge of electricity from experiments done in America. But the Enlightenment was only one part of the continuing intellectual connections within the Atlantic World, connections that spread artistic, scholarly, and political ideas widely through the lands bordering the ocean.

Instead of thinking of the early history of what became the United States simply as the story of the growth of thirteen small colonies along the Atlantic seaboard of North America, the idea of the "Atlantic World" encourages us to think of early American history as a vast pattern of exchanges and interactions—trade, migration, religious and intellectual exchange, and many other relationships—among all the societies bordering the Atlantic: western Europe, western Africa, the Caribbean, and North and South America.

(text continued from page 17)

became a Portuguese colony, and not long thereafter (still in the sixteenth century) to the Caribbean islands and Brazil. Sugar was a labor-intensive crop, and the demand for African workers in these new areas of cultivation was high. At first the slave traders were overwhelmingly Portuguese. By the seventeenth century, the Dutch had won control of most of the market. In the eighteenth century, the English dominated it. (Despite some recent claims, Jews were never significantly involved in the slave trade.) By 1700, slavery had spread well beyond its original locations in the Caribbean and South America and into the English colonies to the north.

THE ARRIVAL OF THE ENGLISH

England's first documented contact with the New World came only five years after Spain's. In 1497, John Cabot (like Columbus, a native of Genoa) sailed to the northeastern coast of North America on an expedition sponsored by King Henry VII, in an unsuccessful search for a northwest passage through the New World to the Orient. But nearly a century passed before the English made any serious efforts to establish colonies in America.

Incentives for Colonization

Interest in colonization grew in part as a response to social and economic problems in sixteenth-century England. The English people suffered from frequent and costly European wars, and they suffered from almost constant religious strife within their own land. Many suffered, too, from harsh economic changes in their countryside. Because the worldwide demand for wool was growing rapidly, landowners were converting their land from

Scarce Land

fields for crops to pastures for sheep. The result was a reduction in the amount of land available for growing food. England's food supply declined at the same time that the English population was growing—from 3 million in 1485 to 4 million in 1603. To some of the English, the New World began to seem attractive because it offered something that was growing scarce in England: land.

At the same time, new merchant capitalists were prospering by selling the products of England's growing wool-cloth industry abroad. At first, most exporters did business almost entirely as individuals. In time, however, merchants formed companies, whose charters from the king gave them monopolies for trading in particular regions. Investors in these companies often made fantastic profits, and they were eager to expand their trade.

Central to this trading drive was the emergence of a new concept of economic life known as mercantilism. Mercantilism rested on the belief that one person or nation could grow rich only at the expense of another, and that a nation's economic health depended, therefore, on selling as much as possible to foreign lands and buying as little as possible from

Mercantilism

them. The principles of mercantilism spread throughout Europe in the sixteenth and seventeenth centuries. One result was the increased attractiveness of acquiring colonies, which could become the source of raw materials and a market for the colonizing power's goods.

In England, the mercantilistic program thrived at first on the basis of the flourishing wool trade with the European continent, and particularly with the great cloth market in Antwerp. In the 1550s, however, that glutted market began to collapse, and English merchants had to look elsewhere for overseas trade. Some English believed colonies would solve their problems. They would create markets, alleviate poverty, and siphon off the surplus population. Perhaps most important, colonial commerce would allow England to acquire products for which the nation had previously been dependent on foreigners—products such as lumber, naval stores, and silver and gold.

Religious Motives of Colonization

There were also religious motives for colonization—a result of the Protestant Reformation. It had began in Germany in 1517, when Martin Luther challenged some of the basic practices and beliefs of the Roman Catholic Church. Luther quickly won a wide following among ordinary men and women in northern Europe. When the pope excommunicated him in 1520, Luther began leading his followers out of the Catholic Church entirely.

The Swiss theologian John Calvin went even further than Luther had in rejecting the Catholic belief that human behavior could affect an individual's prospects for salvation. Calvin introduced the doctrine of predestination. God "elected" some people to be saved and condemned others to damnation; each person's destiny was determined before birth, and no one could change that predetermined fate. But those who accepted Calvin's teachings came to believe that the way they led their lives might reveal to them their chances of salvation. A wicked or useless existence would be a sign of damnation; saintliness, diligence, and success could be signs of grace. Calvinism created anxieties among its followers, but it also produced a strong incentive to lead virtuous, productive lives. The new creed spread rapidly throughout northern Europe and produced (among other groups) the Huguenots in France and the Puritans in England.

The English Reformation was at first more a *The English Reformation* result of a political dispute between the king and the pope than of these doctrinal revolts. In 1529 King Henry VIII, angered by the refusal of the pope to grant him a divorce from his Spanish wife, broke England's ties with the Catholic Church and established himself as the head of the Christian faith in his country. After Henry's death, his Catholic daughter, Queen Mary, restored England's allegiance to Rome and persecuted those who resisted. But when Mary died in 1558, her half-sister, Elizabeth I, became England's sovereign and once again severed the nation's connection with the Catholic Church, this time for good.

To many English people, however, the new Church of England was not reformed enough. Some had been affected by the teachings of the European Reformation, and they clamored for reforms that would "purify" the church. As a result, they became known as Puritans.

The most radical Puritans, known as Sepa- *Puritan Separatists* ratists, were determined to worship in their own independent congregations, despite English laws that required all subjects to attend regular Anglican services. But most Puritans did not wish to leave the Church of England. They wanted, rather, to simplify Anglican forms of worship and reform the leadership of the church. Like the Separatists, they grew increasingly frustrated by the refusal of political and ecclesiastical authorities to respond to their demands.

Puritan discontent grew rapidly after the death of Elizabeth, the last of the Tudors, and the accession of James I, the first of the Stuarts, in 1603. Convinced that kings ruled by divine right, James quickly antagonized the Puritans by resorting to illegal and arbitrary taxation, by favoring English Catholics in the granting of charters and other favors, and by supporting "high-church" forms of ceremony. By the early seventeenth century, some religious nonconformists were beginning to look for places of refuge outside the kingdom.

England's first experience with colonization came not in the New World but in neighboring Ireland. The English had long laid claim to the island, but only in the late sixteenth century did serious efforts at colonization

Lessons of Irish Colonization begin. The long, brutal process by which the English attempted to subdue the Irish led to an important assumption about colonization that the English would take with them to America: the belief that settlements in foreign lands must retain a rigid separation from the native populations. Unlike the Spanish in America, the English in Ireland tried to build a separate society of their own, peopled with emigrants from England itself. They would take that concept with them to the New World.

The French and the Dutch in America

English settlers in North America were to encounter not only natives but also other Europeans who were, like them, driven by mercantilist ideas. There were scattered North American outposts of the Spanish Empire and, more important, there were French and Dutch settlers who were also vying for a stake in the New World.

France founded its first permanent settlement in America at Quebec in 1608, less than a year after the English started their first at Jamestown. The colony's population grew very slowly, but the French exercised an influence in the New World disproportionate to *Disproportionate French Influence* their numbers, because of their relationships with Native Americans. Unlike the early English settlers, the French forged close ties with natives deep inside the continent. French Jesuit missionaries established some of the first contacts between the two peoples. More important were the *coureurs de bois*—adventurous fur traders and trappers—who also penetrated far into the wilderness and developed an extensive trade that became one of the underpinnings of the French colonial economy. The French traders formed partnerships with the Indians. They often lived among the natives and married Indian women. The fur trade helped open the way for French agricultural estates (or *seigneuries*) along the St. Lawrence River and for the development of trade and military centers at Quebec and Montreal.

New Amsterdam The Dutch, too, were establishing a presence in North America. Holland in the early seventeenth century was one of the leading trading nations of the world. In 1609 an English explorer in the employ of the Dutch, Henry Hudson, sailed up the river that was to be named for him in what is now New York State. His explorations led to a Dutch claim on that territory. In 1624, not long after the first two permanent English colonies took root in Jamestown and Plymouth, the Dutch created a wedge between them when the Dutch West India Company established a series of permanent trading posts on the Hudson, Delaware, and Connecticut Rivers that soon became the colony of New Netherland. Its principal town, New Amsterdam, was on Manhattan Island.

The First English Settlements

The first permanent English settlement in the New World was established at Jamestown, in Virginia, in 1607. But for nearly thirty years before that, English merchants and adventurers had been engaged in a series of failed efforts to create colonies in America.

Through much of the sixteenth century, the English had harbored mixed feelings about the New World. They were intrigued by its possibilities, but they were also leery of Spain, which remained the dominant force in America. In 1588, however, King Philip II of Spain sent one of the largest military fleets in the history of warfare—the *The Spanish Armada* Spanish Armada—across the English Channel to attack England itself. The smaller English fleet, taking advantage of its greater maneuverability, defeated the armada and, in a single stroke, ended Spain's domination of the Atlantic. This great shift in naval power caused interest in colonizing the New World to grow quickly.

The pioneers of English colonization were Sir *Gilbert and Raleigh* Humphrey Gilbert and his half-brother Sir Walter Raleigh—both veterans of earlier colonial efforts in Ireland. In 1578 Gilbert obtained from Queen Elizabeth a six-year patent granting him the exclusive right "to inhabit and possess any remote and heathen lands not already in the possession of any Christian prince." Five years later, after several setbacks, he led an expedition to Newfoundland looking for a good place to build a profitable colony. But a storm sank his ship, and he was lost at sea. The next year, Sir Walter Raleigh secured his own six-year grant from the queen and sent a small group of men on an expedition to explore the North American coast. When they returned, Raleigh named the region they had explored Virginia, in honor of Elizabeth, who was known as the "Virgin Queen."

In 1585 Raleigh recruited his cousin, Sir Richard Grenville, to lead a group of men to the island of Roanoke, off the coast of what is now North Carolina, to establish a colony. Grenville deposited the settlers on the island, destroyed an Indian village as retaliation for a minor theft, and returned to England. The following spring, with supplies and reinforcements from England long overdue, Sir Francis Drake unexpectedly arrived in Roanoke. The dispirited colonists boarded his ships and left.

Raleigh tried again in 1587, sending an expedition to Roanoke carrying ninety-one men, seventeen women, and nine children. The settlers attempted to take up where the first group of colonists had left off. (Shortly after arriving, one of the women gave birth to a daughter, Virginia Dare, the first American-born child of English parents.) John White, the commander of the expedition, returned to England after several weeks, in search of supplies and additional settlers. Because of a war with Spain, he was unable to return to Roanoke for three years. When he did, in 1590, he found the island utterly deserted, with no clue to the fate of the *Failed Colony of Roanoke* settlers other than the cryptic inscription "Croatoan" carved on a post.

ROANOKE A drawing by one of the English colonists in the ill-fated Roanoke expedition of 1585 became the basis for this engraving by Theodore DeBry, published in England in 1590. A small European ship carrying settlers approaches the island of Roanoke, at left. The wreckage of several larger vessels farther out to sea and the presence of Indian settlements on the mainland and on Roanoke itself suggest some of the perils the settlers encountered. *(New York Public Library)*

The Roanoke disaster marked the end of Sir Walter Raleigh's involvement in English colonization of the New World. No later colonizer would receive grants of land in America as vast or undefined as those Raleigh and Gilbert had acquired. Yet the colonizing impulse remained very much alive. In the early years of the seventeenth century, a group of London merchants to whom Raleigh had assigned his charter rights decided to renew the attempt at colonization in Virginia. A rival group of merchants, from the area around Plymouth, was also interested in American ventures and was sponsoring voyages of exploration farther north. In 1606 James I issued a new charter, which divided North America between the two groups. The London group got the exclusive right to colonize in the south, and the Plymouth merchants received the same right in the north. Through the efforts of these and other companies, the first enduring English colonies would be established in America.

CONCLUSION

The lands that Europeans eventually named the Americas were the home of many millions of people before the arrival of Columbus. Having migrated from Asia thousands of years earlier, the pre-Columbian Americans spread throughout the Western Hemisphere and eventually created great civilizations. Among the most notable of them were the Incas in Peru, and the Mayas and Aztecs in Mexico. In the regions north of what was later named the Rio Grande, the human population was smaller and the civilizations less advanced than they were further south. Even so, North American natives created a cluster of civilizations that thrived and expanded.

In the century after European contact, these native populations suffered a series of catastrophes that all but destroyed the civilizations they had built: brutal invasions by Spanish and Portuguese conquistadores and a series of plagues inadvertently imported by Europeans. By the middle of the sixteenth century, the Spanish and Portuguese—no longer faced with effective resistance from the native populations—had established colonial control over all of South America and much of North America.

In the parts of North America that would eventually become the United States, the European presence was for a time much less powerful. The Spanish established an important northern outpost in what is now New Mexico, a society in which Europeans and Indians lived together intimately, if unequally. On the whole, however, the North American Indians remained largely undisturbed by Europeans until English, French, and Dutch migrations began in the early seventeenth century.

FOR FURTHER REFERENCE

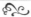

Alvin M. Josephy, ed., *America in 1492: The World of the Indian Peoples Before the Arrival of Columbus* (1993) and Brian M. Fagan, *The Great Journey: The Peopling of Ancient America* (1987) provide introductions to pre-Columbian history. William M. Denevan, ed., *The Native Population of the Americas in 1492* (1976) and Russell Thornton, *American Indian Holocaust and Survival: A Population History since 1492* (1987) are important contributions to the debate over the size and character of the American population before Columbus. Alfred Crosby, *The Columbian Exchange: Biological and Cultural Consequences of 1492* (1972) explores the results of European-Indian contact both in the Americas and Europe. D. W. Meinig, *The Shaping of America, Vol I: Atlantic America, 1492–1800* (1986) is an account of the early contacts between Europeans and the New World. Gary Nash, *Red, White and Black: The Peoples of Early America* (1982) provides a brief, multiracial survey of colonial America. Philip Curtin, *The Atlantic Slave Trade: A Census* (1969) has become the indispensable starting point for understanding African forced migration to the Americas. An outstanding collection of essays that summarizes modern scholarship on colonial America is Jack P. Green and J. R. Pole, eds., *Colonial British America: Essays in the New History of the Early Modern Era* (1984). *Columbus and the Age of Discovery* (1991) is a seven-part documentary film series on Christopher Columbus, his era, and his legacy.

For quizzes, Internet resources, references to additional books and films, and more, consult this book's Online Learning Center at www.mhhe.com/unfinishednation4.

THE INCONVENIENCIES

THAT HAVE HAPPENED TO SOME PERSONS WHICH HAVE TRANSPORTED THEMSELVES

from *England* to *Virginia*, without prouisions necessary to sustaine themselues, hath greatly hindred the Progresse of that noble Plantation: For preuention of the like disorders heereafter, that no man suffer, either through ignorance or misinformation; it is thought requisite to publish this short declaration: wherein is contained a particular of such necessaries, as either priuate families or single persons shall haue cause to furnish themselues with, for their better support at their first Landing in Virginia; whereby also greater numbers may receiue in part, directions how to prouide themselues.

Apparrell.	li.	s.	d.
One Monmouth Cap	00	01	10
Three falling bands	—	01	03
Three shirts	—	07	06
One waste-coate	—	02	02
One suite of Canuase	—	07	06
One suite of Frize	10	00	
One suite of Cloth	15	00	
Three paire of Irish stockins	04	—	
Foure paire of shooes	08	08	
One paire of garters	00	10	
One doozen of points	00	03	
One paire of Canuase sheets	08	00	
Seuen ells of Canuase, to make a bed and boulster, to be filled in Virginia 8.s.	08	00	
One Rug for a bed 8.s. which with the bed seruing for two men, halfe is.			
Fiue ells coorse Canuase, to make a bed at Sea for two men, to be filled with straw, iiij.s.	05	00	
One coorse Rug at Sea for two men, will cost vj.s. is for one			
	04	00	00

For a family of 6 persons and so after the rate for more.

Apparrell for one man, and so after the rate for more.

Victuall.			
Eight bushels of Meale	02	00	00
Two bushels of pease at 3.s.	06	00	
Two bushels of Oatemeale 4.s. 6.d.	09	00	
One gallon of Aquauitæ	02	06	
One gallon of Oyle	03	06	
Two gallons of Vineger 1.s.	02	00	
	03	03	00

For a whole yeere for one man, and so for more after the rate.

Armes.			
One Armour compleat, light	—	17	00
One long Peece fiue foot or fiue and a halfe, neere Musket bore	01	02	—
One sword	—	05	—
One belt	—	01	—
One bandaleere	—	01	06
Twenty pound of powder	—	18	00
Sixty pound of shot or lead, Pistoll and Goose shot	—	05	00
	03	09	06

For one man, but if halfe of your men haue armour it is sufficient so that all haue Peeces and swords.

Tooles.	li.	s.	d.
Fiue broad howes at 2.s. a piece	—	10	—
Fiue narrow howes at 16.d. a piece	—	06	08
Two broad Axes at 3.s. 8.d. a piece	—	07	04
Fiue felling Axes at 18.d. a piece	—	07	06
Two steele hand sawes at 16.d. a piece	—	02	08
Two two-hand sawes at 5.s. a piece	—	10	—
One whip-saw, set and filed with box, file, and wrest	—	10	—
Two hammers 12.d. a piece	—	02	00
Three shouels 18.d. a piece	—	04	06
Two spades at 18.d. a piece	—	03	00
Two augers 6.d. a piece	—	01	00
Sixe chissels 6.d. a piece	—	03	00
Two percers stocked 4.d. a piece	—	00	08
Three gimlets 2.d. a piece	—	00	06
Two hatchets 21.d. a piece	—	03	06
Two froues to cleaue pale 18.d.	—	03	00
Two hand bills 20. a piece	—	03	04
One grindlestone 4.s.	—	04	00
Nailes of all sorts to the value of	02	00	—
Two Pickaxes	—	03	—
	06	02	08

For a family of 6 persons and so after for more or lesse after the rate.

Houshold Implements.			
One Iron Pot	—	07	—
One kettle	—	06	—
One large frying pan	—	02	06
One gridiron	—	01	06
Two skillets	—	05	—
One spit	—	02	—
Platters, dishes, spoones of wood	—	04	—
	01	08	00

For Sugar, Spice, and fruit, and at Sea for 6 men | 00 | 12 | 06 |

So the full charge of Apparrell, Victuall, Armes, Tooles, and houshold stuffe, and after this rate for each person, will amount vnto about the summe of | 12 | 10 | — |

The passage of each man is | 06 | 00 | — |

The fraight of these prouisions for a man, will bee about halfe a Tun, which is | 01 | 10 | — |

So the whole charge will amount to about | 20 | 00 | 00 |

Nets, hookes, lines, and a tent must be added, if the number of people be greater, as also some kine, &c.

And this is the usuall proportion that the Virginia Company doe bestow vpon their Tenants which they send.

Whosoeuer transports himselfe or any other at his owne charge vnto *Virginia*, shall for each person so transported before Midsummer 1625. haue to him and his heires for euer fifty Acres of Land vpon a first, and fifty Acres vpon a second diuision.

Imprinted at London by FELIX KYNGSTON. 1622.

ADVICE TO MIGRANTS This 1622 handbill by the Virginia Company of London provides a detailed list of items that people contemplating a voyage to America should plan to take with them. The list reflects the company's awareness of how few finished goods were yet available in America (and also their realization that they themselves could profit from selling such goods to their passengers). *(Rare Books Division, New York Public Library, Astor, Lenox and Tilden Foundations)*

TIME LINE

1607	1619	1620	1622	1624	1630	1634	1636	1637
Jamestown founded	First African workers in Virginia	Pilgrims found Plymouth Colony	Powhatan Indians attack Virginia	Dutch settle Manhattan	Puritans establish Massachusetts Bay Colony	Maryland founded	Roger Williams founds Rhode Island	Anne Hutchinson expelled from Massachusetts Bay Colony
	Virginia House of Burgesses meets							Pequot War

TRANSPLANTATIONS AND BORDERLANDS

The Early Chesapeake
The Growth of New England
The Restoration Colonies
Borderlands and Middle Grounds
The Development of Empire

T he Roanoke fiasco dampened colonization enthusiasm in England for a time. But the lures of the New World were too strong to be suppressed for very long. By the early seventeenth century, the effort to establish permanent English colonies in the New World had resumed.

The new efforts were much like the earlier, failed ones: private ventures, with little planning or direction from the English government; small, fragile enterprises led by people unprepared for the hardships they were to face. Unlike the Roanoke experiment, they survived, but not before experiencing a series of disastrous setbacks.

Several things shaped the character of these English settlements. First, the colonies were business enterprises, and one of their principal concerns was to produce a profit for their corporate sponsors. Second, because the colonies were tied only indirectly to the crown, they began from the start to develop their own political and social institutions. Third, the English tried to isolate themselves from the Indians and created communities that would be entirely their own: "transplantations" of societies from the Old World to the New. And fourth, almost nothing worked out as they had planned—largely because the English could not effectively isolate themselves from the world around them—a world populated by Native Americans, by colonists, explorers, and traders from Spain, France, the Netherlands, and other parts of Europe, and by forced immigrants from Africa.

1663	1664	1675	1676	1681	1686	1689	1732	
Carolina chartered	English capture New Netherlands	King Philip's War	Bacon's Rebellion	Pennsylvania chartered	Dominion of New England	Glorious Revolution in America	Georgia chartered	

THE EARLY CHESAPEAKE

Once James I had issued his 1606 charters, the London Company moved quickly and decisively to launch a colonizing expedition headed for Virginia—a party of 144 men aboard three ships, the *Godspeed*, the *Discovery*, and the *Susan Constant*, which set sail for America early in 1607.

The Founding of Jamestown

Only 104 men survived the journey. They reached the American coast in the spring of 1607, sailed into Chesapeake Bay and up a river they named the James, and established their colony on a peninsula. They called it Jamestown.

They chose an inland setting that they believed would offer them security from the natives. But they chose poorly. The site was low and swampy. It was surrounded by thick woods and it bordered the territories
Jamestown's Early Ordeal
of powerful local Indians. The result could hardly have been more disastrous. For seventeen years, one wave of settlers after another attempted to make Jamestown a habitable and profitable colony. Every effort failed. All that could be said of Jamestown at the end of this first period of its existence was that it had survived.

The initial colonists ran into serious difficulties from the moment they landed. They had no prior exposure to the infections of the new land and were highly vulnerable to local diseases, particularly malaria. The promoters in London diverted the colonists' energies into futile searches for gold and only slightly more successful efforts to pile up lumber, tar, pitch, and iron for export. These energies would have been better spent on growing food. The promoters also sent virtually no women to Jamestown. Hence, settlers could not establish real households and had no permanent stake in the community.

By January 1608, when ships appeared with additional men and supplies, all but 38 of the first 104 colonists were dead. Jamestown survived
John Smith
largely as a result of the efforts of Captain John Smith, who at age twenty-seven was already a famous world traveler. Leadership in the colony had been bitterly divided until the fall of 1608, when Smith took control. He imposed work and order on the community. He also organized raids on neighboring Indian villages to steal food and kidnap natives. During the colony's second winter, fewer than a dozen died. By the summer of 1609, the colony was showing promise of survival. But Jamestown's ordeal was not over yet.

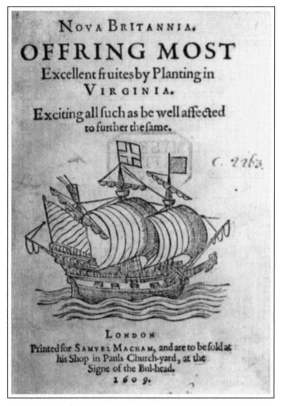

NOVA BRITANNIA.
OFFRING MOST
Excellent fruites by Planting in
VIRGINIA.

Exciting all such as be well affected
to further the same.

LONDON
Printed for SAMVEL MACHAM, and are to be sold at
his Shop in Pauls Church-yard, at the
Signe of the Bul-head.
1609.

RECRUITING FOR THE COLONIES, 1609 This is the title page for a pamphlet that describes the attractions of settlement in the New World. Most accounts of the "excellent fruites" of life in Virginia were, like this one, written by people who had never seen America but who shared the excitement that the colonies inspired among the early-seventeenth-century English. *(Rare Books Division, New York Public Library, Astor, Lenox and Tilden Foundations)*

Reorganization and Expansion

As Jamestown struggled to survive, the London Company (now renamed the Virginia Company) was already dreaming of bigger things. In 1609, it obtained a new charter from the king, which increased its power and enlarged its territory; and it sent Lord De La Warr to be the colony's first governor. It offered stock in the company to planters who were willing to migrate at their own expense. And it provided free passage to Virginia for poorer people who would agree to serve the company for seven years. In the spring of 1609, the Virginia Company dispatched a fleet of nine vessels with about 600 people aboard (including some women and children) to Virginia.

Disaster followed. One of the Virginia-bound ships was lost at sea in a hurricane. Another ran aground on one of the Bermuda islands and was unable to free itself for months. Many of those who reached Jamestown succumbed to fevers before winter came. The winter of 1609–1610 became known as the "starving time." The local Indians killed off the livestock in the woods and kept the colonists barricaded within their palisade. The Europeans lived on what they could find: "dogs, cats, rats, snakes, toadstools, horsehides," and even the "corpses of dead men," as one survivor recalled. When the migrants who had run aground in Bermuda finally arrived in Jamestown the following May, they found only about 60 emaciated people still alive. The new arrivals took the survivors onto their ship and sailed for home. But as the refugees proceeded down the James, they met an English ship coming up the river—part of a fleet bringing supplies and the colony's first governor, Lord De La Warr. The departing settlers agreed to return to Jamestown. New relief expeditions with hundreds of colonists soon began to arrive, and the effort to turn a profit in Jamestown resumed.

The "Starving Time"

Under the leadership of its first governors, Virginia survived and even expanded. New settlements began lining the river above and below Jamestown. That was partly because of the order and discipline the governors at times managed to impose and because of increased military assaults on the local Indian tribes to protect the new settlements. But it was also because the colonists had at last discovered a marketable crop: tobacco.

Europeans had become aware of tobacco soon after Columbus's first return from the West Indies, where he had seen the Cuban natives smoking small cigars *(tabacos)*, which they inserted in the nostril. By the early seventeenth century, tobacco from the Spanish colonies was already in wide use in Europe. Then in 1612, the Jamestown planter John Rolfe began trying to cultivate the crop in Virginia. Tobacco planting soon spread up and down the James.

The Tobacco Economy

Tobacco growers needed large areas of farmland, and because tobacco exhausted the soil very quickly, the demand for land increased rapidly. As a result, English farmers began establishing plantations deeper and deeper in the interior, isolating themselves from Jamestown and penetrating farther into the territory of the native tribes.

The tobacco economy also created a heavy demand for labor. To entice new workers to the colony, the Virginia Company established what it called the "headright" system. Headrights were fifty-acre grants of land. Those who already lived in the colony received two headrights (100 acres) apiece. Each new settler received a single headright for himself or herself. This system encouraged family groups to migrate together, since the more family members who traveled to America, the more land the family would receive. In addition, anyone who paid for the passage of immigrants to Virginia would receive an extra headright for each arrival. As a result, some colonists were able to assemble large plantations.

The "Headright System"

The company also transported ironworkers and other skilled crafts-men to Virginia to diversify the economy. In 1619, it sent 100 English-women to the colony to become the wives of male colonists. It promised the male colonists the full rights of Englishmen (as provided in the origi-nal charter of 1606), an end to strict and arbitrary rule, and even a share in self-government. On July 30, 1619, delegates from the various communi-ties met as the House of Burgesses, the first elected legislature within what was to become the United States.

A month later, Virginia established another important precedent. As John Rolfe recorded, "about the latter end of August" a Dutch ship brought in "20 and odd Negroes." There is some reason to believe that the colonists thought of these first Africans as ser-vants to be held for a term of years and then freed. *Birth of American Slavery* For a time, moreover, the use of black labor remained limited. Although Africans trickled steadily into the colony, planters continued to prefer Eu-ropean indentured servants until at least the 1670s. But the small group of blacks who arrived in 1619 marked the first step toward the enslavement of Africans within what was to be the American republic.

The European settlers in Virginia built their society not only on the coerced labor of imported Africans but also on the effective suppression of the local Indians. For two years in the 1610s, Sir Thomas Dale, De La Warr's successor as governor, led unrelenting assaults against the Powhatan Indians, led by (and named for) their formidable chief, Powhatan. In the process, Dale kidnapped Powhatan's young daughter Pocahontas. Several years earlier, Pocahontas had *Pocahontas* played a role in mediating differences between her people and the Europeans. But now, Powhatan refused to ransom her. Living among the English, Pocahontas gradually adapted to many of their ways. She converted to Christianity and in 1614 married John Rolfe and visited En-gland with him. There she stirred interest among many English in projects to "civilize" the Indians. She died shortly before her planned return to Virginia.

By the time of Pocahontas's marriage, Powhatan had ceased his attacks on the English in the face of overwhelming odds. But after his death sev-eral years later, his brother, Opechancanough, began secretly to plan the elimination of the English intruders. On a March morning in 1622, tribes-men called on the white settlements as if to offer goods for sale; then they suddenly attacked. Not until 347 whites of both sexes and all ages (includ-ing John Rolfe) lay dead were the Indian warriors finally forced to retreat. And not until over twenty years later were the Powhatans finally defeated.

By then, however, the Virginia Company in London was defunct. In 1624, James I revoked the company's charter, and the colony came under the control of the crown where it would remain until 1776. The colony, if not the company, had survived—but at a terrible cost. In Virginia's first seventeen years, more than *Demise of the Virginia Company* 8,500 white settlers had arrived in the colony, and nearly eighty percent of them had died.

Exchanges of Agricultural Technology

The hostility the early English settlers expressed toward their Indian neighbors was in part a result of their conviction that their own civilization was greatly superior to that of the natives. The English, after all, had great ocean-going vessels, muskets and other advanced implements of weaponry, and many other tools that the Indians had not developed. Indeed, when John Smith and other early Jamestown residents grew frustrated at their inability to find gold, they often blamed the backwardness of the natives. The Spanish in South America, Smith once wrote, had grown rich because the natives there had built advanced civilizations and mined much gold and silver. If Mexico and Peru had been as "ill peopled, as little planted, laboured and manured as Virginia," he added, the Spanish would have found no more wealth than the English did.

Yet the survival of Jamestown was, in the end, largely a result of agricultural technologies developed by Indians and borrowed by the English. Native agriculture was far better adapted to the soil and climate of Virginia than the agricultural traditions the English settlers brought with them. The Indians of Virginia were settled farmers whose villages were surrounded by neatly ordered fields in which grew a variety of crops—beans, pumpkins, vegetables, and above all maize (known to us as corn). Some of the Indian farmlands stretched over hundreds of acres and supported substantial populations.

Indian Agricultural Techniques   The English settlers did not adopt all the Indian agricultural techniques. But the English learned a great deal from the Indians about how to grow food in the New World. In particular, they quickly recognized the value of corn, which proved to be easier to cultivate and which produced much larger yields than any of the European grains the English had known at home. The English also learned the advantages of growing beans alongside corn to enrich the soil. An early settler in New England wrote that the Indians had taught the settlers "to cull out the finest seede, to observe the fittest season, to keepe distance for holes, and fit measure for hills, to worme it, and weede it; to prune it, and dresse it as occasion shall require."

Like the natives, the English quickly learned to combine the foods they grew with food for which they hunted and fished, and here, too, Indian techniques proved of great value. Particularly valuable was the canoe, which was much better at navigating the rivers and streams of Virginia (and later New England) than were any English vessels. Canoes could be made by hollowing out a single log (dugouts) or sewing birchbark around a simple frame and sealing it with resin (birchbark canoes, some of which could hold as many as eighty people). John Smith was a particular admirer of the Indian canoes. The "primitive" civilizations of the natives in fact provided the early settlers with some of their most vital agricultural techniques and technologies.

THE GROWTH OF THE CHESAPEAKE, 1607–1750 This map shows the political forms of European settlement in the region of the Chesapeake Bay in the seventeenth and early eighteenth centuries. Note the several different kinds of colonial enterprises: the royal colony of Virginia, controlled directly by the English crown after the failure of the early commercial enterprises there; and the proprietary regions of Maryland, northern Virginia, and North Carolina, which were under the control of powerful English aristocrats. • *Did these political differences have any significant effect on the economic activities of the various Chesapeake colonies?*

Maryland and the Calverts

The Maryland colony ultimately came to look much like Virginia, but its origins were very different from those of its southern neighbor. George Calvert, the first Lord Baltimore, envisioned establishing a colony in America both as a great speculative venture in real estate and as a refuge for English Catholics like himself. Calvert died while still negotiating with the king for a charter to establish a colony in the Chesapeake region. But in 1632 his son Cecilius, the second Lord Baltimore, finally received the charter.

George Calvert

Lord Baltimore named his brother, Leonard Calvert, as governor of the colony. In March 1634, two ships—the *Ark* and the *Dove*—bearing Calvert along with 200 or 300 other colonists, entered the Potomac River, turned into one of its eastern tributaries, and established the village of St. Mary's on a high, dry bluff. Neighboring Indians befriended the settlers and provided them with temporary shelter and with stocks of corn.

The Calverts needed to attract thousands of settlers to Maryland if their expensive colonial venture was to pay. As a result, they had to encourage the immigration of Protestants as well as their fellow English Catholics. The Calverts soon realized that Catholics would always be a minority in the colony, and so they adopted a policy of religious tolera-

"Act Concerning Religion"

tion, embodied in the 1649 "Act Concerning Religion." Nevertheless, politics in Maryland remained plagued for years by tensions, and at times violence, between the Catholic minority and the Protestant majority.

At the insistence of the first settlers, the Calverts agreed in 1635 to the calling of a representative assembly—the House of Delegates. But the proprietor retained absolute authority to distribute land as he wished; and since Lord Baltimore granted large estates to his relatives and to other English aristocrats, a distinct upper class soon established itself. By 1640, a severe labor shortage forced a modification of the land-grant procedure; and Maryland, like Virginia, adopted a headright system—a grant of 100 acres to each male settler, another 100 for his wife and each servant, and 50 for each of his children. But the great landlords of the colony's earliest years remained powerful. Like Virginia, Maryland became a center of tobacco cultivation; planters worked their land with the aid, first, of indentured servants imported from England and then, beginning late in the seventeenth century, of slaves imported from Africa.

Bacon's Rebellion

Sir William Berkeley

For more than thirty years, one man—Sir William Berkeley, the royal governor of Virginia—dominated the politics of the colony. He took office in 1642 at the age of thirty-six and with but one brief interruption remained in control of the government until the 1670s. In his first years as governor, he helped open up the interior of Virginia by sending explorers across the Blue Ridge Mountains and crushing a 1644 Indian uprising. The defeated Indians agreed to a treaty ceding to England most of the territory east of the mountains and establishing a boundary west of which white settlement would be prohibited. But the rapid growth of the Virginia population made this agreement difficult to sustain. Between 1640 and 1660, Virginia's population rose from 8,000 to over 40,000. By 1652, English settlers had established three counties in the territory set aside by the treaty for the Indians.

In the meantime, Berkeley was expanding his own powers. By 1670, the vote for delegates to the House of Burgesses, once open to all white men, was restricted to landowners. Elections were rare, and the same burgesses, representing the established planters of the eastern (or tidewater) region of the colony, remained in office year after year. The more recent settlers on the frontier were underrepresented.

Resentment of the power of the governor and the tidewater aristocrats grew steadily in the newly settled lands of the west (often known as the "backcountry"). In 1676, this resentment helped create a major conflict, led by Nathaniel Bacon. *"Backcountry" Resentment* Bacon had a good farm in the west and a seat on the governor's council. But like other members of the new backcountry gentry, he chafed at the governor's attempts to hold the line of settlement steady so as to avoid antagonizing the Indians. Bacon's rift with Berkeley was also a result of resentment that Berkeley refused to allow him a piece of the Indian fur trade, which the governor himself controlled.

In 1675, a major conflict erupted in the west between whites and natives. As the fighting escalated, Bacon and other concerned landholders demanded that the governor send the militia. When Berkeley refused, Bacon responded by offering to organize a volunteer army of backcountry men who would do their own fighting. Berkeley rejected the offer. Bacon ignored him and launched a series of vicious but unsuccessful pursuits of the Indian challengers. When Berkeley heard of the unauthorized military effort, he proclaimed Bacon and his men to be rebels. Bacon now turned his army against the governor and, in what became known as Bacon's Rebellion, twice led his troops east to Jamestown. The first time he won a temporary pardon from the governor; the second time, after the governor repudiated the agreement, Bacon burned much of the city and drove the governor into exile. But then Bacon died suddenly of dysentery; and Berkeley soon regained control. In 1677, the Indians reluctantly signed a new treaty that opened new lands to white settlement.

Bacon's Rebellion was evidence of the continuing struggle to define the Indian and white *Consequences of Bacon's Rebellion* spheres of influence in Virginia. It also revealed the bitterness of the competition among rival elites, and it demonstrated the potential for instability in the colony's large population of free, landless men. One result was that landed elites in both eastern and western Virginia began to recognize a common interest in quelling social unrest from below. That was among the reasons that they turned increasingly to the African slave trade to fulfill their need for labor. African slaves, unlike white indentured servants, did not need to be released after a fixed term and hence did not threaten to become an unstable, landless class.

THE GROWTH OF NEW ENGLAND

The northern regions of British North America were slow to attract settlers, in part because the Plymouth Company was never able to mount a successful colonizing expedition after receiving its charter in 1606. It did, however, sponsor explorations of the region. Captain John Smith, after his departure from Jamestown, made an exploratory journey for the Plymouth merchants, wrote an enthusiastic pamphlet about the lands he had seen, and called them New England.

Plymouth Plantation

A discontented congregation of Puritan Separatists in England, not the Plymouth Company, established the first enduring European settlement in New England. In 1608, a congregation of Separatists from the hamlet of Scrooby began emigrating quietly (and illegally), a few at a time, to Leyden, Holland, where they could enjoy freedom of worship. But as foreigners in Holland, they had to work at unskilled and poorly paid jobs. They also watched with alarm as their children began to adapt to Dutch society and drift away from their church. Finally, some of the Separatists decided to move again, across the Atlantic, where they hoped to create a stable, protected community where they could spread "the gospel of the Kingdom of Christ in those remote parts of the world."

The Scrooby Separatists

In 1620, leaders of the Scrooby group obtained permission from the Virginia Company to settle in Virginia. The "Pilgrims," as they saw themselves, sailed from Plymouth, England, in September 1620 on the *Mayflower*; thirty-five "saints" (Puritan Separatists) and sixty-seven "strangers" (people who were not part of the congregation) were aboard. In November, after a long and difficult voyage, they sighted land—the shore of what is now known as Cape Cod. That had not been their destination, but it was too late in the year to sail farther south. So the Pilgrims chose a site for their settlement in the area just north of the cape, a place John Smith had labeled "Plymouth" on a map he had drawn during an earlier exploration of New England. Because Plymouth lay outside the London Company's territory, the settlers were not bound by the company's rules. While still aboard ship, the "saints" in the group drew up an agreement, the Mayflower Compact, to establish a government for themselves. Then, on December 21, 1620, they stepped ashore at Plymouth Rock.

Plymouth Founded

The Pilgrims' first winter was a difficult one. Half the colonists perished from malnutrition, disease, and exposure. But the colony survived, in large part because of crucial assistance from local Indians. Trade and other exchanges with the Indians were critical to the settlers and attractive to the natives. The tribes

Pilgrim-Indian Interaction

provided the colonists with furs. They also showed the settlers how to cultivate corn and how to hunt wild animals for meat. After the first autumn harvest, the settlers invited the natives to join them in a festival, the original Thanksgiving. But the relationship between the settlers and the local Indians was not a happy one for long. Thirteen years after the Pilgrims arrived, a devastating smallpox epidemic—a result of natives' exposure to Europeans carrying the disease—wiped out much of the Indian population around Plymouth.

The Pilgrims could not create rich farms on the sandy and marshy soil around Plymouth, but they developed a profitable trade in fish and furs. New colonists arrived from England, and in a decade the population reached 300. The people of Plymouth Plantation chose as their governor the remarkable William Bradford, who governed successfully for many years. The Pilgrims were always poor. As late as the 1640s, they had only one plow among them. But they were, on the whole, content to be left alone to live their lives in what they considered godly ways.

The Massachusetts Bay Experiment

Events in England encouraged other Puritans to migrate to the New World. King James I had pursued repressive policies toward Puritans for years. When he died in 1625, his son and successor, Charles I, was even more hostile to Puritans and imprisoned many of them for their beliefs. The king dissolved Parliament in 1629 (it was not to be recalled until 1640), ensuring that there would be no one in a position to oppose him.

In the midst of this turmoil, a group of Puritan merchants began organizing a new colonial venture in America. They obtained a grant of land in New England for most of the area now comprising Massachusetts and New Hampshire, and they acquired a charter from the king allowing them to create the Massachusetts *Massachusetts Bay Company* Bay Company and to establish a colony in the New World. Some members of the Massachusetts Bay Company wanted to create a refuge in New England for Puritans. They bought out the interests of company members who preferred to stay in England, and the new owners elected a governor, John Winthrop. They then sailed for New England in 1630. With 17 ships and 1,000 people, it was the largest single migration of its kind in the seventeenth century. Winthrop carried with him the charter of the Massachusetts Bay Company, which meant that the colonists would be responsible to no company officials in England.

The Massachusetts migration quickly produced several settlements. The port of Boston became the capital, but in the course of the next decade colonists established several other towns in eastern Massachusetts: Charlestown, Newtown (later renamed Cambridge), Roxbury, Dorchester, Watertown, Ipswich, Concord, Sudbury, and others.

The Massachusetts Puritans were not grim or joyless, as many critics would later come to believe, but they were serious and pious. They strove to lead useful, conscientious lives of thrift and hard work, and they honored material success as evidence of God's favor. Winthrop and the other founders of Massachusetts believed they were founding a holy commonwealth, a model—a "city upon a hill"—for the corrupt world to see and emulate. Colonial Massachusetts was a "theocracy," a society in which the church was almost indistinguishable from the state. Residents had no more freedom of worship than the Puritans themselves had had in England.

Winthrop's "City on a Hill"

Like other new settlements, the Massachusetts Bay colony had early difficulties. During the first winter (1629–1630), nearly 200 people died and many others decided to leave. But the colony soon grew and prospered. The nearby Pilgrims and neighboring Indians helped with food and advice. Incoming settlers brought needed tools and other goods. The dominance of families in the colony helped ensure a feeling of commitment to the community and a sense of order among the settlers, and it also ensured that the population would reproduce itself.

The Expansion of New England

It did not take long for English settlement to begin moving outward from Massachusetts Bay. Some people migrated in search of soil more productive than that the stony land around Boston provided. Others left because of the oppressiveness of the church-dominated government of Massachusetts.

Fundamental Orders of Connecticut

The Connecticut River valley, about 100 miles west of Boston, began attracting English families as early as the 1630s because of the valley's fertile lands and its isolation from Massachusetts Bay. In 1635, Thomas Hooker, a minister of Newtown (Cambridge), defied the Massachusetts government, led his congregation west, and established the town of Hartford. Four years later, the people of Hartford and of two other newly founded towns nearby adopted a constitution known as the Fundamental Orders of Connecticut, which created an independent colony with a government similar to that of Massachusetts Bay but gave a larger proportion of the men the right to vote and hold office. (Women were barred from voting virtually everywhere.)

Another Connecticut colony grew up around New Haven on the Connecticut coast. Unlike Hartford, it reflected unhappiness with what its founders considered the increasing religious laxity in Boston. The Fundamental Articles of New Haven (1639) established a Bible-based government even stricter than that of Massachusetts Bay. New Haven remained independent until 1662, when a royal charter officially gave the Hartford colony jurisdiction over the New Haven settlements.

European settlement in what is now Rhode Island was a result of the religious and political dissent of Roger Williams, a controversial young minister who lived for a time in Salem, Massachusetts. Williams was a confirmed Separatist who

Roger Williams's Dissent

THE GROWTH OF NEW ENGLAND, 1620–1750 The European settlement of New England, as this map reveals, traces its origins primarily to two small settlements on the Atlantic coast. The first was the Pilgrim settlement at Plymouth, which began in 1620 and spread out through Cape Cod, southern Massachusetts, and the islands of Martha's Vineyard and Nantucket. The second, much larger settlement began in Boston in 1630 and spread rapidly through western Massachusetts, north into New Hampshire and Maine, and south into Connecticut. ◆ *Why would the settlers of Massachusetts Bay have expanded so much more rapidly and expansively than those of Plymouth?*

 For an interactive version of this map go to www.mhhe.com/unfinishednation4ch2maps

argued that the Massachusetts church should abandon all allegiance to the Church of England. He also proclaimed that the land the colonists were occupying belonged to the natives. The colonial government voted to deport him, but he escaped before they could do so. During the winter of 1635–1636, he took refuge with Narragansett tribesmen; the following spring he bought a tract of land from them, and with a few followers, created the town of Providence. In 1644, after obtaining a charter from Parliament, he established a government similar to that of Massachusetts but without any ties to the church. For a time, Rhode

Island was the only colony in which all faiths (including Judaism) could worship without interference.

Another challenge to the established religious order in Massachusetts Bay came from Anne Hutchinson, an intelligent *Anne Hutchinson* and charismatic woman from a substantial Boston family. She argued that many clergy were not among the "elect" and were, therefore, entitled to no spiritual authority. Such teachings (known as the Antinomian heresy) were a serious threat to the spiritual authority of the established clergy. Hutchinson also challenged prevailing assumptions about the proper role of women in Puritan society. As her influence grew, and as she began to deliver open attacks on members of the clergy, the Massachusetts hierarchy mobilized to stop her. In 1638, she was convicted of heresy and sedition and was banished. With her family and some of her followers, she moved to a point on Narragansett Bay not far from Providence. Later she moved south into New York, where in 1643 she and her family died during an Indian uprising.

The Hutchinson affair had an important impact on the settlement of the areas north of Massachusetts Bay. New Hamp-*Maine and New Hampshire* shire and Maine were established in 1629 by two English proprietors. But few settlers moved into these northern regions until the religious disruptions in Massachusetts Bay. In 1639, John Wheelwright, a disciple of Anne Hutchinson, led some of his fellow dissenters to Exeter, New Hampshire. Others soon followed. New Hampshire became a separate colony in 1679. Maine remained a part of Massachusetts until 1820.

Settlers and Natives

The first white settlers in New England had generally friendly relations with the natives. Indians taught whites how to grow vital food crops such as corn, beans, pumpkins, and potatoes; they also taught them new agricultural techniques. European farmers also benefited from the extensive lands Indians had already cleared (and either abandoned or sold). White traders used Indians as partners in some of their most important trading activities. Indeed, commerce with the Indians was responsible for the creation of some of the first great fortunes in British North America. Other white settlers attempted to educate the Indians in European religion and culture. Protestant missionaries converted some natives to Christianity, and a few Indians became at least partially assimilated into white society.

But as in other areas of white settlement, tensions soon developed—primarily as a result of the white colonists' insatiable appetite for land. The particular character of those conflicts emerged as well out of Puritan attitudes toward the natives. The religious leaders of New England came to consider the tribes a threat to their hopes of creating a godly community in the New World. Gradually, the image of Indians as helpful neighbors came to be replaced by the image of Indians as "heathens" and barbarians.

A PEQUOT VILLAGE DESTROYED An English artist drew this view of a fortified Pequot village in Connecticut surrounded by English soldiers and their allies from other tribes during the Pequot War in 1637. The invaders massacred more than 600 residents of the settlement. *(Rare Books Division, New York Public Library, Astor, Lenox and Tilden Foundations)*

King Philip's War and the Technology of Battle

In 1637, hostilities broke out between English settlers in the Connecticut Valley and the Pequot Indians of the region, a conflict (known as the Pequot War) in which the natives were almost wiped out. But the bloodiest and most prolonged encounter between whites and Indians in the seventeenth century began in 1675, a conflict that whites called King Philip's War. The Wampanoags, under the leadership of a chieftain known to the white settlers as King Philip and among his own *Metacomet* people as Metacomet, rose up to resist the English. For three years, the natives inflicted terror on a string of Massachusetts towns, killing over a thousand people. But beginning in 1676, the white settlers gradually prevailed, with the help of a group of Mohawk allies who ambushed Metacomet and killed him. Without Metacomet, the fragile alliance among the tribes collapsed, and the white settlers were soon able to crush the uprising.

The character of these and subsequent conflicts between natives and settlers was crucially affected by earlier exchanges of technology between the English and the tribes. In particular, the Indians made effective use of a relatively new weapon introduced to New England by Myles Standish and others: the flintlock rifle. It replaced the earlier staple of colonial musketry, the matchlock rifle, which proved too heavy, cumbersome, and inaccurate to be effective. The matchlock had to be steadied on a fixed object and ignited with a match before firing. The flintlock could be held up without support and fired without a match. Indians using bows and arrows often outmatched settlers using the clumsy matchlocks.

Flintlock Muskets

Many English settlers were slow to give up their matchlocks, but the Indians recognized the advantages of the newer rifles right away and began purchasing them in large quantities. Despite rules forbidding colonists to instruct natives on how to use and repair the weapons, the natives learned to handle the rifles, and even to repair them, very effectively on their own. In King Philip's War, the very high casualties on both sides were a result of the use of these more advanced rifles.

Indians also used more traditional military technologies—especially the construction of forts. The Narragansetts, allies of the Wampanoags in King Philip's War, built an enormous fort in the Great Swamp of Rhode Island in 1675, which became the site of one of the bloodiest battles of the war before English attackers burned it down. After that, a band of Narragansetts set out to build a large stone fort, with the help of a member of the tribe who had learned masonry while working with the English. When English soldiers discovered the stone fort in 1676, after the end of King Philip's War, they killed most of its occupants and destroyed it. In the end, the technological skills of the Indians were no match for the overwhelming advantages of the English settlers in both numbers and firepower.

THE RESTORATION COLONIES

For nearly thirty years after Lord Baltimore received the charter for Maryland in 1632, no new English colonies were established in America. England had to deal with troubles of its own at home.

The English Civil War

After Charles I dissolved Parliament in 1629 and began ruling as an absolute monarch, he steadily alienated a growing number of his subjects. Finally, desperately in need of money, Charles called Parliament back into session in 1640 and asked it to levy new taxes. But he antagonized the members by dismissing them twice in two years; and in 1642, they organized a military force, thus beginning the English Civil War.

The conflict between the Cavaliers (the supporters of the king) and the Roundheads (the forces of Parliament, who were largely Puritans) lasted seven years. In 1649, the Roundheads defeated the king's forces and shocked all of Europe by beheading the monarch. The stern Roundhead leader Oliver Cromwell replaced the king and assumed the position of "protector." But when *Oliver Cromwell* Cromwell died in 1658, his son and heir proved unable to maintain his authority. Two years later, Charles II, son of the executed king, returned from exile and seized the throne, in what became known as the Restoration.

Among the results of the Restoration was the resumption of colonization in America. Charles II rewarded faithful courtiers with grants of land in the New World, and in the twenty-five years of his reign he issued charters for four additional colonies: Carolina, New York, New Jersey, and Pennsylvania.

The Carolinas

In successive charters issued in 1663 and 1665, Charles II awarded eight proprietors joint title to a vast territory stretching south from Virginia to the Florida peninsula and west to the Pacific Ocean. Like Lord Baltimore, they received almost kingly powers over their grant, which they prudently called Carolina (a name derived from the Latin word for "Charles"). They reserved tremendous estates for themselves and distributed the rest through a headright system similar to those in Virginia and Maryland. Although committed Anglicans themselves, the proprietors guaranteed religious freedom to all Christian faiths. They also created a representative assembly. They hoped to attract settlers from the existing American colonies and to avoid the expense of financing expeditions from England.

But their initial efforts to profit from settlement in Carolina failed dismally. A few early attempts at colonization were quickly abandoned, and most of the original proprietors soon gave up the project. Anthony Ashley Cooper, however, persisted. He convinced the other proprietors to finance expeditions to Carolina from England, the first of which set sail with 300 people in the spring of 1670. Only 100 people survived the difficult voyage; those who did established a settlement at Port Royal on the Carolina coast. Ten years later they founded a city at the junction of the Ashley and Cooper Rivers, which in 1690 became the colonial capital. They called it Charles Town (it was later renamed Charleston).

With the aid of the English philosopher John Locke, Cooper (now the earl of Shaftesbury) drew up the Fundamental Constitution for Carolina in *Fundamental Constitution for Carolina* 1669. It divided the colony into counties of equal size and divided each county into equal parcels. It also envisioned a social hierarchy with the proprietors themselves (who were to be known as "seigneurs") at the top, a local aristocracy (consisting of lesser nobles known as "landgraves" or "caciques") below them, and then ordinary settlers ("leet-men"). At the bottom of this stratified society would be poor whites, who would have few political rights, and African slaves. Proprietors, nobles, and other landholders would have a voice in the colonial parliament in proportion to the size of their landholdings.

In reality, Carolina developed along lines quite different from the carefully ordered vision of Shaftesbury and Locke. For one thing, the northern and southern regions of settlement were widely separated and socially and economically distinct from one another. The northern settlers were mainly backwoods farmers. In the south, fertile lands and the good harbor at Charles Town promoted a more prosperous economy and a more stratified, aristocratic society. Settlements grew up rapidly along the Ashley and Cooper Rivers, and colonists established a flourishing trade, particularly (beginning in the 1660s) in rice.

Southern Carolina very early developed close commercial ties to the *Close ties with the Caribbean* large (and overpopulated) European colony on the Caribbean island of Barbados. During the first ten years of settlement, in fact, most of the new residents in Carolina were Barbadians, some of whom established themselves as substantial landlords. African slavery had taken root on Barbados earlier than in any of the mainland colonies, and the white Caribbean migrants—tough, uncompromising profit seekers—established a similar slave-based plantation society in Carolina.

Carolina Divided Carolina was one of the most divided English colonies in America. There were tensions between the small farmers of the Albemarle region in the north and the wealthy planters in the south. And there were conflicts between the rich Barbadians in southern Carolina and the smaller landowners around them. After Lord Shaftesbury's death, the proprietors proved unable to establish order. In 1719, the colonists seized control of the colony from them. Ten years later, the king divided the region into two royal colonies, North Carolina and South Carolina.

New Netherland, New York, and New Jersey

In 1664, Charles II granted his brother James, the duke of York, all the territory lying between the Connecticut and Delaware Rivers. But the grant faced a major challenge from the Dutch, who claimed the entire area.

England and the Netherlands were already commercial rivals in Europe, and that rivalry now extended to America. In 1664, vessels of the *New Amsterdam Seized* English navy, under the command of Richard Nicolls, put in at New Amsterdam, the capital of the Dutch colony of New Netherland, and extracted a surrender from the governor, Peter Stuyvesant. Several years later, in 1673, the Dutch reconquered and briefly held their old provincial capital. But they lost it again, this time for good, in 1674.

The duke of York renamed his territory New York. It contained not only Dutch and English but Scandinavians, Germans, French, and a large number of Africans (imported as slaves by the Dutch West India Company), as well as members of several different Indian tribes. James wisely made no effort to impose his own Roman Catholicism on the colony. He delegated powers to a governor and a council but made no provision for representative assemblies.

Property holding and political power remained *Unequal Wealth and Power* highly divided and highly unequal in New York. In addition to confirming the great Dutch "patroonships" already in existence, James granted large estates to some of his own political supporters. Power in the colony thus remained widely dispersed among wealthy English landlords, Dutch patroons, fur traders, and the duke's political appointees. By 1685, when the duke of York ascended the English throne as James II, New York contained about four times as many people (around 30,000) as it had twenty years before.

Shortly after James received his charter, he gave a large part of the land south of New York to a pair of political allies, both Carolina proprietors, Sir John Berkeley and Sir George Carteret. Carteret named the territory New Jersey. But the *New Jersey Founded* venture in New Jersey generated few profits, and in 1674, Berkeley sold his half interest. The colony was divided into two jurisdictions, East Jersey and West Jersey, which squabbled with one another until 1702, when the two halves of the colony were again joined. New Jersey, like New York, was a colony of enormous ethnic and religious diversity, and the weak colonial government made few efforts to impose strict control over the fragmented society. But unlike New York, New Jersey developed no important class of large landowners.

The Quaker Colonies

Pennsylvania was born out of the efforts of a dissenting English Protestant sect, the Society of Friends, to find a home for their own distinctive social order. The society began in the mid-seventeenth century under the leadership of George Fox, a Nottingham shoemaker, and Margaret Fell. Their followers came to be known as Quakers (from Fox's instruction to them to "tremble at the name of the Lord"). Unlike the Puritans, Quakers rejected the concept of predestination and original sin. All people, they believed, had divinity within themselves and need only learn to cultivate it; all could attain salvation.

The Quakers had no formal church govern- *The Quakers* ment and no paid clergy; in their worship they spoke up one by one as the spirit moved them. Disregarding distinctions of gender and class, they addressed one another with the terms "thee" and "thou," words commonly used in other parts of English society only in speaking to servants and social inferiors. As confirmed pacifists, they would not take part in wars. Unpopular in England, the Quakers began looking to America for asylum. A few migrated to New England or Carolina, but most Quakers wanted a colony of their own. As members of a despised sect, however, they could not get the necessary royal grant without the aid of someone influential at the court.

Fortunately for the Quaker cause, a number of wealthy and prominent men had converted to the faith. One of them was William Penn, who, over his aristocratic father's objections, converted to Quakerism, took up evangelism, and was sent repeatedly to prison. He soon began working with George Fox to create a Quaker colony in America. When his father died in 1681, Charles II paid a large debt he had owed to the older Penn with an enormous grant to the son of territory between New York and Maryland. At the king's insistence, the territory was to be named Pennsylvania, after Penn's late father.

Pennsylvania Established Through his informative and honest advertising, Penn soon made Pennsylvania the best-known and most cosmopolitan of all the English colonies in America. More than any other English colony, Pennsylvania prospered from the outset, because of Penn's successful recruiting, his careful planning, and the region's mild climate and fertile soil. Penn sailed to Pennsylvania in 1682 to oversee the laying out, between the Delaware and Schuylkill Rivers, of the city he named Philadelphia ("Brotherly Love"). Penn recognized Indians' claims to the land in the province, and he was scrupulous about reimbursing them for it. The Indians generally respected Penn, and during his lifetime the colony had no major battles with the natives.

But the colony was not without conflict. By the late 1690s, some residents of Pennsylvania were beginning to resist the nearly absolute power of the proprietor. Pressure from these groups grew to the point that in 1701, shortly before he departed for England for the last time, Penn *Charter of Liberties* agreed to a Charter of Liberties for the colony. The charter established a representative assembly (consisting, alone among the English colonies, of only one house) that greatly limited the authority of the proprietor. The charter also permitted "the lower counties" of the colony to establish their own representative assembly. The three counties did so in 1703 and as a result became, in effect, a separate colony—Delaware—although until the American Revolution it continued to have the same governor as Pennsylvania.

BORDERLANDS AND MIDDLE GROUNDS

The English colonies clustered along the Atlantic seaboard of North America eventually united, expanded, and became the beginnings of a great nation. But in the seventeenth and early eighteenth centuries, their future was not all clear. In those years, they were small, frail settlements surrounded by other, competing societies and settlements. The British Empire in North America was, in fact, a much smaller and weaker one than the great Spanish Empire to the South, and not, on the surface at least, clearly stronger than the enormous French Empire to the North.

The continuing contest for control of North America, and the complex interactions among the diverse peoples populating the continent, were most clearly visible in areas around the borders of English settlement—the Caribbean and along the northern, southern, and western borders of the coastal colonies. In the regions of *Complex Cultural Interactions* the borderlands emerged societies very different from those in the heart of the English seaboard colonies—areas that have been described by recent scholars as "middle grounds," in which diverse civilizations encountered one another and, for a time at least, shaped one another.

The Caribbean Islands

The Chesapeake was the site of the first permanent English settlements in the New World. Throughout the first half of the seventeenth century, however, the most important destinations for English immigrants were the islands of the Caribbean and the northern way station of Bermuda. More than half the English migrants to the New World in the early seventeenth century settled on these islands. The island societies had close ties to English North America.

Before the arrival of Europeans, most of the Caribbean islands had substantial native populations. But beginning with Christopher Columbus's first visit in 1492, and accelerating after 1496, the native population was all but wiped out by European epidemics.

The Spanish Empire claimed title to all the islands in the Caribbean, but created substantial settlement only on the largest of them: Cuba, Hispaniola, and Puerto Rico. English, French, and Dutch traders began settling on some of the smaller islands early in the sixteenth century, despite the Spanish claim to them. After Spain and the Netherlands went to war in 1621 (distracting the Spanish navy and leaving *The English Caribbean* the English in the Caribbean relatively unmolested), the pace of English colonization increased. By mid-century, there were several substantial English settlements on the islands, the most important of them on Antigua, St. Kitts, Jamaica, and Barbados.

In their first years in the Caribbean, English settlers experimented unsuccessfully with tobacco and cotton. But they soon discovered that the most lucrative crop was sugar, for which there was a substantial and growing market in Europe. Sugar cane could also be distilled into rum, for which there was also a booming market abroad. Planters were devoting almost all of their land to sugar cane.

Sugar and Slavery   Because sugar was a labor-intensive crop, English planters quickly found it necessary to import laborers. As in the Chesapeake, they began by bringing indentured servants from England. But the arduous work discouraged white laborers. By mid-century, therefore, the English planters in the Caribbean (like the Spanish colonists) were relying more and more heavily on an enslaved African work force, which soon substantially outnumbered them.

On Barbados and other islands where a flourishing sugar economy developed, the English planters were a tough, aggressive, and ambitious breed. Since their livelihoods depended on their work forces, they expanded and solidified the system of African slavery there remarkably quickly. By the late seventeenth century, there were four times as many African slaves as there were white settlers.

Masters and Slaves in the Caribbean

Fearful of slave revolts, whites in the Caribbean monitored their labor *Harsh Conditions for Slaves*   forces closely and often harshly. Planters paid little attention to the welfare of their workers. Many concluded that it was cheaper to buy new slaves periodically than to protect the well-being of those they already owned, and it was not uncommon for masters literally to work their slaves to death. Few African workers survived more than a decade in the brutal Caribbean working environment—they were either sold to planters in North America or died. Even whites, who worked far less hard than did the slaves, often succumbed to the harsh climate; most died before the age of forty.

Establishing a stable society and culture was extremely difficult for people living in such harsh and even deadly conditions. Those whites who could returned to England with their fortunes and left their estates in the hands of overseers. Europeans in the Caribbean lacked many of the institutions that gave stability to the North American settlements: church, family, community.

Africans in the Caribbean faced much greater difficulties, but because they had no chance of leaving, they created what was in many ways a more elaborate culture than did the white settlers. They started families (although many of them were broken up by death or the slave trade); they *Slave Culture and Resistance*   sustained African religious and social traditions (and resisted Christianity); and within the rigidly controlled world of the sugar plantations, they established patterns of resistance.

The Caribbean settlements were an important part of the Atlantic trading world in which many Americans became involved—a source of sugar and rum and a market for goods made in the mainland colonies and in England. They were the principal source of African slaves for the mainland colonies. And because Caribbean planters established an elaborate plantation system earlier than planters in North America, they provided models that many mainland people copied.

SUGAR PLANTATION IN THE ANTILLES This nineteenth-century engraving shows a sugar plantation in one of the Caribbean islands of the Antilles. Although the picture gives the sense of an idyllic landscape, sugar plantations were notoriously rugged places for the African slaves who worked there (and whose quarters can be seen on the left). (*Explorer/Mary Evans Picture Library*)

The Southwestern Borderlands

By the end of the seventeenth century, the Spanish had established a sophisticated and impressive em- *Spain's New World Empire* pire. Their capital, Mexico City, was the most dazzling metropolis in the Americas. The Spanish residents, well over a million of them, enjoyed much greater prosperity than all but a few English settlers in North America.

But the principal Spanish colonies north of Mexico—Florida, Texas, New Mexico, Arizona, and California—were relatively unimportant economically to the empire. They attracted religious minorities, Catholic missionaries, independent ranchers fleeing the heavy hand of imperial authority, and Spanish troops defending the northern flank of the empire. But they remained weak and peripheral parts of the great empire to their south.

New Mexico was the most prosperous and populous of these Spanish outposts—even if far less *Spanish New Mexico* successful than Spanish settlements in Mexico and South America. By the end of the eighteenth century, New Mexico had a non-Indian population of over 10,000—the largest European settlement west of the Mississippi and north of Mexico—and it was steadily expanding through the region.

The Spanish began to colonize California once they realized that other Europeans—among them English merchants and French and Russian trappers—were beginning to establish a presence in the region. Formal Spanish settlement of California began in the 1760s, when the governor of Baja California was ordered to create outposts of the empire further north. Soon a string of missions, forts (or *presidios*), and trading communities

California were springing up along the Pacific coast: beginning with San Diego and Monterey in 1769 and eventually San Francisco (1776), Los Angeles (1781), and Santa Barbara (1786). The arrival of the Spanish in California had a devastating effect on the native population, which died in great numbers from the diseases the colonists imported. As the new settlements spread, however, the Spanish insisted that the remaining natives convert to Catholicism. That explains the centrality of missions in almost all the major Spanish outposts in California. But the Spanish colonists were also intent on creating a prosperous agricultural economy, and they enlisted Indian laborers to help them do so. California's Indians had no choice but to accede to the demands of the Spanish, although there were frequent revolts by natives against the harsh conditions imposed upon them.

The Spanish considered the greatest threat to the northern borders of their empire to be the growing ambitions of the French. In the 1680s French explorers traveled down the Mississippi Valley to the mouth of the river and claimed the lands for France in 1682. They called the territory Louisiana. Fearful of French incursions further west, the Spanish began to fortify their claim to Texas by establishing new forts, missions, and settlements there, including San Fernando (later San Antonio) in 1731. Much of the region that is now Arizona was also becoming increasingly tied to the Spanish empire and was governed from Santa Fe.

The Spanish colonies in the Southwest were the sparsely populated

Spanish "Middle Grounds" edges of the great Spanish empire to the South— created less to increase the wealth of the empire than to defend it from threats by other European powers in the North. Nevertheless, these Spanish outposts helped create enduring societies that were very unlike those being established by the English along the Atlantic seaboard. The Spanish colonies were not committed to displacing the native populations, but rather to enlisting them. They sought to convert them to Catholicism, to recruit them (sometimes forcibly) as agricultural workers, and to cultivate them as trading partners.

The Southeast Borderlands

A more direct challenge to English ambitions in North America was the Spanish presence in the southeastern areas of what is now the United States. After the establishment of the Spanish claim to Florida in the 1560s, missionaries and traders began moving northward into Georgia and westward into what is now known as the Florida panhandle, and some

ambitious Spaniards began to dream of expanding
their empire still further north, into what became *The Spanish Threat*
the Carolinas, and perhaps beyond. The founding of Jamestown in 1607
dampened those hopes and replaced them with fears. The English
colonies, they believed, could threaten their existing settlements in
Florida and Georgia. As a result, the Spanish built forts in both regions to
defend themselves against the slowly increasing English presence there.
Throughout the eighteenth century, the area between the Carolinas and
Florida was the site of continuing tension, and frequent conflict, between
the Spanish and the English—and, to a lesser degree, between the Spanish
and the French, who were threatening their northwestern borders with
settlements in Louisiana and in what is now Alabama.

There was no formal war between England and Spain in these years,
but that did not dampen the hostilities in the Southeast. English pirates
continually harassed the Spanish settlements and, in 1668, actually sacked
St. Augustine. The English encouraged Indians in Florida to rise up
against the Spanish missions. The Spanish, for their part, offered freedom
to African slaves owned by English settlers in the Carolinas if they agreed
to convert to Catholicism. About 100 Africans accepted the offer, and the
Spanish later organized some to them into a military regiment to defend
the northern border of New Spain. By the early eighteenth century, the
constant fighting in the region had driven almost all the Spanish out of
Florida except for settlers in St. Augustine on the Atlantic coast and Pensacola on the Gulf Coast.

Eventually, after more than a century of conflict in the southeastern
borderlands, the English prevailed—acquiring Florida in the aftermath of
the Seven Years' War (known in America as the French and Indian War)
and rapidly populating it with settlers from their colonies to the North.
Before that point, however, protecting the southern boundary of the
British empire in North America was a continual concern to the English
and contributed in crucial ways to the founding of the colony of Georgia.

The Founding of Georgia

Georgia—the last English colony to be established in what would become
the United States—was founded to create a military barrier between the
Spanish lands on the southern border of English America, and also to provide a refuge for the impoverished, a place where English men and
women without prospects at home could begin anew. Its founders, led by
General James Oglethorpe, served as unpaid trustees of a society created
to serve the needs of the British Empire.

The need for a military buffer between South Carolina and the Spanish settlements in Florida was particularly urgent in the colony's first
years. Oglethorpe, himself a veteran of the most
recent Spanish wars with England, was keenly *Oglethorpe's Philanthropic
Mission*
aware of the military advantages of an English

colony south of the Carolinas. Yet his interest in settlement rested even more on his philanthropic commitments. As head of a parliamentary committee investigating English prisons, he had grown appalled by the plight of honest debtors rotting in confinement. Such prisoners, and other poor people in danger of succumbing to a similar fate, could, he believed, become the farmer-soldiers of the new colony in America.

In 1732, King George II granted Oglethorpe and his fellow trustees control of the land between the Savannah and Altamaha Rivers. Their colonization policies reflected the vital military purposes of the colony. They *Georgia Founded* limited the size of landholdings to make the settlement compact and easier to defend against Spanish and Indian attacks. They excluded Africans, free or slave; Oglethorpe feared slave labor would produce internal revolts, and that disaffected slaves might turn to the Spanish as allies. The trustees strictly regulated trade with the Indians, again to limit the possibility of wartime insurrection. They also excluded Catholics for fear they might collude with their coreligionists in the Spanish colonies to the south.

Oglethorpe himself led the first colonial expedition to Georgia, which built a fortified town at the mouth of the Savannah River in 1733 and later constructed additional forts south of the Altamaha. In the end, only a few debtors were released from jail and sent to Georgia. Instead, the trustees brought hundreds of impoverished tradesmen and artisans from England and Scotland and many religious refugees from Switzerland and Germany. Among the immigrants was a small group of Jews. English settlers made up a lower proportion of the European population of Georgia than of any other English colony.

Georgia's Political Evolution Oglethorpe (whom some residents of Georgia began calling "our perpetual dictator") created almost constant dissensions and conflict through his heavyhanded regulation of the colony. He also suffered military disappointments, such as a 1740 assault on the Spanish outpost as St. Augustine, Florida, which ended in failure. Gradually, as the threats from Spain receded, he lost his grip on the colony, which over time became more like the rest of British North America, with an elected legislature that loosened the restrictions on settlers. Georgia continued to grow more slowly than the other southern colonies, but in other ways it now developed along lines roughly similar to those of South Carolina.

Middle Grounds

The struggle for the North American continent was not just one among competing European empires. It was also a series of contests among the many different peoples who shared the continent—the Spanish, English, French, Dutch, and other colonists, on the one hand, and the many Indian tribes with whom they shared the continent, on the other.

In some parts of the British empire—Virginia and New England, for example—English settlers fairly quickly established their dominance, subjugating and displacing most natives until they had established societies that were dominated almost entirely by Europeans. But in other regions, the balance of power was for many years far more precarious. Along the western borders of English settlement, in particular, Europeans and Indians lived together in regions in which neither side was able to establish clear dominance. In these "middle grounds," as they have been called, the two populations—despite frequent conflicts—carved out ways of living together, with each side making concessions to the other.

These were the peripheries of empires, in which the influence of formal colonial government was virtually invisible. European settlers, and the soldiers scattered in forts throughout these regions to protect them, were unable to displace the Indians. So they had to carve out on their own a relationship with the tribes. In that relationship, the Europeans found themselves obligated to adapt to tribal expectations at least as much as the Indian had to adapt to European ones.

To the Indians, the European migrants were both menacing and appealing. They feared the power of these strange people: their guns, their rifles, their forts. But they also wanted the French and British settlers to behave like "fathers"—to help them mediate their own internal disputes, to offer them gifts, to help them moderate their conflicts. Europeans came from a world in which the formal institutional and military power of a nation or empire governed relationships between societies. But the natives had no understanding of the modern notion of a "nation" and thought much more in terms of cere- *Paternal Expectations* mony and kinship. Gradually, Europeans learned to fulfill at least some of their expectations—to settle disputes among tribes, to moderate conflicts within tribes, to participate solemnly in Indian ceremonies, and to offer gifts as signs of respect.

In the seventeenth century, before many English settlers had entered the interior, the French *"Middle Ground"* were particularly adept at creating successful rela- *Accommodation and Adaptation* tionships with the tribes. French migrants in the interior regions of the continent were often solitary fur traders, and some of them welcomed the chance to attach themselves to—even to marry within—tribes. They also recognized the importance of treating tribal chiefs with respect and channeling gifts and tributes through them. By the mid-eighteenth century, French influence in the interior was in decline, and British settlers gradually became the dominant European group in the "middle grounds." Eventually, the British learned the lessons that the French had long ago absorbed—that simple commands and raw force were ineffective in creating a workable relationship with the tribes; that they too had to learn to deal with Indian leaders through gifts and ceremonies and mediation. In large western regions—especially those around the Great Lakes—they established a precarious peace with the tribes that lasted for several decades.

The Shifting Balance   But as the British (and after 1776) American presence in the region grew, the balance of power between Europeans and natives shifted. Newer settlers had difficulty adapting to the complex rituals that the earlier migrants had developed. The stability of the relationship between the Indians and whites deteriorated. By the early nineteenth century, the "middle ground" had collapsed, replaced by a European world in which Indians were ruthlessly subjugated and eventually removed. Nevertheless, for a considerable period of early American history, the story of the relationship between whites and Indians was not simply a story of conquest and subjugation, but also—in some regions—a story of a difficult but stable accommodation and tolerance.

THE DEVELOPMENT OF EMPIRE

The English colonies in America had begun as separate projects, and for the most part they grew up independent of one another and subject to nominal control from London. Yet by the mid-seventeenth century, the growing commercial success of the colonial ventures was producing pressure in England for a more uniform structure to the empire.

The English government began trying to regulate colonial trade in the 1650s, when Parliament passed laws to keep Dutch ships out of the English colonies. Later, Parliament passed three important Navigation

The Navigation Acts   Acts. The first of them, in 1660, closed the colonies to all trade except that carried by English ships, and it required that tobacco and other items be exported from the colonies only to England or to English possessions. The second act, in 1663, required that all goods sent from Europe to the colonies pass through England on the way, where they would be subject to English taxation. The third act, in 1673, imposed duties on the coastal trade among the English colonies, and it provided for the appointment of customs officials to enforce the Navigation Acts. These acts formed the legal basis of England's regulation of the colonies for a century.

The Dominion of New England

Before the Navigation Acts, all the colonial governments except that of Virginia had operated largely independently of the crown, with governors chosen by the proprietors or by the colonists themselves and with powerful representative assemblies. Officials in London recognized that to increase their control over their colonies they would have to create a center of authority less tied to the independent-minded colonial governments, which were unlikely to enforce the new laws.

Lords of Trade   In 1675, the king created a new body, the Lords of Trade, to make recommendations for imperial reform. In 1679, following their advice, he moved to increase his control over Massachusetts. He stripped it of its authority over New Hampshire and chartered a separate, royal colony there whose governor he would himself appoint. And in 1684, citing the colonial assembly's defiance of the Navigation Acts, he revoked the Massachusetts charter.

Charles II's brother James II, who succeeded him to the throne in 1685, went further. He created a single Dominion of New England, which combined the government of Massachusetts with the governments of the rest of the New England colonies and later with those of New York and New Jersey as well. He appointed a single governor, Sir Edmund Andros, to supervise the entire *Sir Edmund Andros*
region from Boston. Andros's rigid enforcement of the Navigation Acts and his brusque dismissal of the colonists' claims to the "rights of English-men" made him thoroughly unpopular.

The "Glorious Revolution"

James II was not only losing friends in America; he was making powerful enemies in England by attempting to control Parliament and the courts and by appointing his fellow Catholics to high office. By 1688, his popular support had all but vanished, and Parliament invited his Protestant daughter Mary and her husband, William of Orange, ruler of the Netherlands, to assume the throne. James II offered no resistance and fled to France. As a result of this bloodless coup, which the English called the "Glorious Revolution," William and Mary became joint sovereigns.

When Bostonians heard of the overthrow of James II, they arrested and imprisoned the unpopular Andros. The new
sovereigns in England abolished the Dominion of *Dominion of New England*
New England, and restored separate colonial gov- *Abolished*
ernments. In 1691, however, they combined Massachusetts with Plymouth and made it a single, royal colony. The new charter restored the General Court, but it gave the crown the right to appoint the governor. It also replaced church membership with property ownership as the basis for voting and officeholding.

Andros had been governing New York through a lieutenant governor, Captain Francis Nicholson, who enjoyed the support of the wealthy merchants and fur traders of the province. Other, less favored colonists had a long accumulation of grievances against Nicholson and his allies. The leader of the New York dissidents was Jacob
Leisler, a German merchant who had never won *"Leislerians" and*
acceptance as one of the colony's ruling class. In *"Anti-Leislerians"*
May 1689, when news of the Glorious Revolution and the fall of Andros reached New York, Leisler raised a militia, captured the city fort, drove Nicholson into exile, and proclaimed himself the new head of government in New York. For two years, he tried in vain to stabilize his power in the colony amid fierce factional rivalry. In 1691, when William and Mary appointed a new governor, Leisler briefly resisted. He was convicted of treason and executed. Fierce rivalry between what became known as the

"Leislerians" and the "anti-Leislerians" dominated the politics of the colony for many years thereafter.

In Maryland, many people erroneously assumed that their proprietor, the Catholic Lord Baltimore, who was living in England, had sided with the Catholic James II and opposed William and Mary. So in 1689, an old opponent of the proprietor's government, the Protestant John Coode, led a revolt that drove out Lord Baltimore's officials and led to Maryland's establishment as a royal colony in 1691. The colonial assembly then established the Church of England as the colony's official religion and excluded Catholics from public office. Maryland became a proprietary colony again in 1715, after the fifth Lord Baltimore joined the Anglican Church.

The Glorious Revolution of 1688 in England touched off revolutions, mostly bloodless ones, in several colonies. Under the new king and queen, the representative assemblies that had been abolished were revived, and the scheme for colonial unification from above was abandoned. But the Glorious Revolution in America did not stop the reorganization of the empire. The new governments that emerged in America actually increased the crown's potential authority. As the first century of English settlement in America came to its end, the colonists were becoming more a part of the imperial system than ever before.

Growing Participation in the Imperial System

CONCLUSION

The English colonization of North America was part of a larger effort by several European nations to expand the reach of their increasingly commercial societies. Indeed, for many years, the British empire in America was among the smallest and weakest of the imperial ventures there, overshadowed by the French to the North and the Spanish to the South.

In the British colonies along the Atlantic seaboard, new agricultural and commercial societies gradually emerged—in the South centered on the cultivation of tobacco and cotton, and reliant on slave labor; and in the northern colonies centered on more traditional food crops and based mostly on free labor. Substantial trading centers emerged in such cities as Boston, New York, Philadelphia, and Charleston, and a growing proportion of the population became prosperous and settled in these increasingly complex communities. By the early eighteenth century, English settlement had spread from northern New England (in what is now Maine) south into Georgia.

But this growing British empire coexisted with, and often found itself in conflict with, the presence of other Europeans—most notably the Spanish and the French—in other areas of North America. In these borderlands, societies did not assume the settled, prosperous form they were taking in the Tidewater and New England. They were raw, sparsely populated settlements in which Europeans, including over time increasing numbers of English, had to learn to accommodate not only one another but also the still-substantial Indian tribes with whom they shared these interior lands. By the middle of the eighteenth century, there was a significant European presence across a broad swath of North America—from Florida to Maine, and from Texas to Mexico to California—only a relatively small part of it controlled by the British. But changes were underway within the British empire that would soon lead to its dominance through a much larger area of North America.

FOR FURTHER REFERENCE

Alan Taylor, *American Colonies* (2001) is an excellent general history of the colonial era of American history. William Cronon, *Changes in the Land: Indians, Colonists, and the Ecology of New England* (1983) examines the social and environmental effects of English settlement in colonial America. Richard White, *The Middle Ground: Indians, Empires, and Republics in the Great Lakes Region, 1650–1815* (1991) is an important study of the accommodations that Indians and early European settlers made in the continental interior. David Hackett Fischer and James C. Kelly, *Bound Away: Virginia and the Westward Movement* (2000) examines early western migrations from the Chesapeake. James H. Merrell, *The Indians' New World* (1991) and *Into the American Woods: Negotiators on the Pennsylvaina Frontier* (1999) are among the best examinations of the impact of European settlement on eastern tribes. Joyce E. Chaplin, *Subject Matter: Technology, the Body, and Science on the Anglo-American Frontier, 1500–1676* (2001) is an innovative exploration of the way British settlers viewed Native Americans. Daniel K. Richeter, *Facing East from Indian Country: A Native History of Early America* (2001) is an important study of how European settlement appeared to Indians. Allan Kullikoff, *From British Peasants to Colonial American Farmers* (2000) is an account of early American agriculture. Perry Miller, *The New England Mind: From Colony to Province* (1953) is a classic exposition of the Puritan intellectual milieu. Michael Kammen, *Colonial New York* (1975) illuminates the diversity and pluralism of New York under the Dutch and the English. Edmund Morgan, *American Slavery, American Freedom* (1975) is an excellent narrative of political and social development in early Virginia. Peter Wood, *Black Majority* (1974) describes the early importance of slavery in the founding of South Carolina. Richard S. Dunn, *Sugar and Slaves: The Rise of the Planter Class in the English West Indies, 1624–1713* (1972) is important for understanding the origins of British colonial slavery. David J. Weber, *The Spanish Frontier in North America* (1992) examines the northern peripheries of the Spanish empire.

For quizzes, Internet resources, references to additional books and films, and more, consult this book's Online Learning Center at www.mhhe.com/unfinishednation4.

DR. WILLIAM GLEASON The American artist Winthrop Chandler painted this image of a doctor examining a female patient in 1780. The doctor obviously considers it inappropriate to view a woman lying in bed, so he takes her pulse as she slips her hand through the curtain obscuring her. *(Ohio State Historical Society)*

TIME LINE

1636	1662	1685	1692	1697
Harvard founded	Halfway Covenant	Huguenots migrate to America	Salem witchcraft trials	Slave importations increase

SOCIETY AND CULTURE IN PROVINCIAL AMERICA

The Colonial Population
The Colonial Economies
Patterns of Society
Awakenings and Enlightenments

The British colonies were, most people in both England and America believed, outposts of the British world. And it is true that as the colonies grew and became more prosperous, they also became more English. Some of the early settlers had come to America to escape what they considered English tyranny. But by the early eighteenth century, many, perhaps most, colonists considered themselves Englishmen just as much as the men and women in England itself did.

At the same time, however, life in the colonies was diverging in many ways from that in England simply by the nature of the New World. The physical environment was very different—vaster and less tamed. The population was more diverse as well. The area that would become the United States was a magnet for immigrants from many lands other than England: Scotland, Ireland, the European continent, eastern Russia, the Spanish and French empires already established in America. And English North America became as well the destination for thousands of forcibly transplanted Africans. Equally important, Europeans and Africans were interacting constantly with a native population that for many years outnumbered them.

To the degree that the colonists emulated English society, they were becoming more and more like one another. To the degree that they were shaped by the character of their own regions, they were becoming more and more different. Indeed, the pattern of society in some areas of North America resembled that of other areas scarcely at all.

1720	1734	1739	1740s
Cotton Mather starts smallpox inoculations	Great Awakening begins	George Whitefield arrives in America	Indigo production begins
	Zenger Trial	Great Awakening intensifies	
		Stono Slave rebellion	

THE COLONIAL POPULATION

After uncertain beginnings, the non-Indian population of English North America grew rapidly and substantially, through continued immigration and through natural increase. By the late seven-

Immigration and Natural Increase

teenth century European and African immigrants outnumbered the natives along the Atlantic coast.

A few of the early settlers were members of the English upper classes, but the dominant element was English laborers. Some came independently, such as the religious dissenters in early New England. But in the Chesapeake, at least three-fourths of the immigrants in the seventeenth century arrived as indentured servants.

Indentured Servitude

The system of temporary servitude developed out of practices in England. Young men and women bound themselves to masters for fixed terms of servitude (usually four to five years) in exchange for passage to America, food, and shelter. Male indentures were supposed to receive clothing, tools, and occasionally land upon completion of their service. In reality, however, many left service with nothing. Most women indentures—who constituted roughly one-fourth of the total in the Chesapeake—worked as domestic servants and were expected to marry when their terms of servitude expired.

By the late seventeenth century, the indentured servant population had become one of the largest elements of the colonial population and was

Social Problems of Indentured Servitude

creating serious social problems. Some former indentures managed to establish themselves successfully as farmers, tradespeople, or artisans, and some of the women married propertied men. Others (mostly males) found themselves without land, without employment, without families, and without prospects; and there grew up in some areas, particularly the Chesapeake, a large floating population of young single men who served as a source of social unrest.

Growing Reliance on Slavery

Beginning in the 1670s, a decrease in the birth rate in England and an improvement in economic conditions there reduced the pressures on laboring men and women to emigrate, and the flow of indentured servants declined. Those who did travel to America as indentures now generally avoided the southern colonies, where prospects for advancement were slim. In the Chesapeake, therefore, landowners began to rely much more heavily on African slavery as their principal source of labor.

Birth and Death

Although immigration remained for a time the greatest source of population growth, the most important long-range factor in the increase of the colonial population was its ability to reproduce itself. Marked improvement in the reproduction rate began in New England and the mid-Atlantic colonies in the second half of the seventeenth century, and after the 1650s natural increase became the most important source of population growth in those areas. The New England population more than quadrupled through reproduction alone in the second half of the seventeenth century. This rise was a result not only of families having large numbers of children. It was also because life expectancy in New England was unusually high.

Conditions improved much more slowly in the South. The high death rates in the Chesapeake region did not begin to decline to the levels of those elsewhere until the mid-eighteenth century. Throughout the seventeenth *High Death Rate in the South* century, the average life expectancy for European men in the region was just over forty years, and for women slightly less. One in four white children died in infancy, and half died before the age of twenty. Children who survived infancy often lost one or both of their parents before reaching maturity. Widows, widowers, and orphans thus formed a substantial proportion of the white Chesapeake population. Only after settlers developed immunity to local diseases (particularly malaria) did life expectancy increase significantly. Population growth was substantial in the region, but it was largely a result of immigration.

The natural increases in the population in the seventeenth century were in large part a result of steady improvement in the balance between men and women in the *Toward a Balanced Sex Ratio* colonies. In the early years of settlement, more than three-quarters of the white population of the Chesapeake consisted of men. And even in New England, which from the beginning had attracted more families (and thus more women) than the southern colonies, 60 percent of the inhabitants were male in 1650. Gradually, however, more women began to arrive in the colonies; and increasing birth rates contributed to shifting the sex ratio (the balance between men and women) as well. Throughout the colonial period, the population almost doubled every twenty-five years. By 1775, the non-Indian population of the colonies was over 2 million.

Medicine in the Colonies

The very high death rates of women who bore children illustrate the primitive nature of medical knowledge and practice in the colonies. Physicians had little or no understanding of infection and sterilization. As a result, many people died from infections contracted during childbirth or surgery. Because communities were unaware of bacteria, many were plagued with infectious diseases transmitted by garbage or unclean water.

One result of the limited extent of medical knowledge was that it was relatively easy for people to enter the field, even without any professional training. The biggest beneficiaries of this were women, who established themselves in considerable numbers as midwives. *Midwifery* Midwives assisted women in childbirth, but they also dispensed other medical advice. They were popular because they were usually friends and neighbors of the people they treated, unlike physicians, who were few and therefore not often well known to their patients. Male doctors felt threatened by the midwives and struggled continually to drive them from the field, although they did not make substantial progress in doing so until the nineteenth century.

Midwives and doctors alike practiced medicine on the basis of the prevailing assumptions of their time, most of them derived from the theory of "humoralism" popularized by the great second-*"Humoralism"* century Roman physician Galen. Galen argued that the human body was governed by four "humors" that were lodged in four bodily fluids: yellow bile (or "choler"), black bile ("melancholy"), blood, and phlegm. In a healthy body, the four humors existed in balance. Illness represented an imbalance and suggested the need for removing from the body the excesses of whatever fluid was causing the imbalance. That was the rationale that lay behind the principal medical techniques of the seventeenth century: purging, expulsion, and bleeding. Bleeding was practiced mostly by male physicians. Midwives favored "pukes" and laxatives. The great majority of early Americans, however, had little contact with physicians, or even midwives, and sought instead to deal with illness on their own. The assumption that treating illness was the exclusive province of trained professionals, so much a part of the twentieth century and beyond, lay far in the distance in the colonial era.

That seventeenth-century medicine rested so much on ideas produced 1,400 years before is evidence of how little support there was for the scientific method in England and America at the time. Bleeding, for example, had been in use for hundreds of years, during which time there had been no evidence at all that it helped people recover from illness; indeed, if anyone had chosen to look for it, there was considerable evidence that bleeding could do great harm. But what would seem in later eras to be the simple process of testing scientific assumptions was not yet a common part of Western thought. That was one reason that the birth of the Enlightenment in the late seventeenth century— with its faith in human reason and its belief in the capacity of individuals and societies to create better lives—was important not just to politics but to science.

Women and Families in the Colonies

Because there were many more men than women in seventeenth-century America, few women re- *Early Marriages* mained unmarried for long. The average European woman in America married for the first time at twenty or twenty-one years of age. Because of the large numbers of indentured servants who were forbidden to marry until their terms of service expired, premarital sexual relationships were frequent. Children born out of wedlock to indentured women were often taken from their mothers at a young age and themselves bound out as indentured servants.

Women in the Chesapeake could anticipate a life consumed with childbearing. The average wife experienced pregnancies every two years. Those who lived long enough bore an average of eight children apiece (up to five of whom typically died in infancy or early childhood). Since childbirth was one of the most frequent causes of female death, many women did not survive to see their children grow to maturity. Those who did, however, were often widowed, since they were usually much younger than their husbands.

In New England, where many more immigrants arrived with family members and where death rates declined far more quickly, family structure was much more *Stable New England Families* stable than in the Chesapeake. The sex ratio was more balanced than in the Chesapeake, so most men could expect to marry. As in the Chesapeake, women married young, began producing children early, and continued to do so well into their thirties. In contrast to the situation in the South, however, northern children were more likely to survive, and their families were more likely to remain intact. Fewer New England women became widows, and those who did generally lost their husbands later in life.

The longer lives in New England meant that parents continued to control their children longer than did parents in the South. Few sons and daughters could choose a spouse entirely independently of their parents' wishes. Men tended to rely on their fathers for land to cultivate. Women needed dowries from their parents if they were to attract desirable husbands. Stricter parental supervision of children meant, too, that fewer women became pregnant before marriage than was the case in the South.

Puritanism placed a high value on the family, and the position of wife and mother was highly val- *Patriarchal Puritanism* ued in Puritan culture. At the same time, however, Puritanism served to reinforce the idea of nearly absolute male authority. A wife was expected to devote herself almost entirely to serving the needs of her husband and the family economy.

AFRICANS BOUND FOR AMERICA Shown here are the below-deck slave quarters of a Spanish vessel en route to the West Indies. A British warship captured the slaver, and a young English naval officer (Lt. Francis Meynell) made this watercolor sketch on the spot. The Africans seen in this picture appear somewhat more comfortable than prisoners on some other slave ships, who were often chained and packed together so tightly that they had no room to stand or even sit. *(National Maritime Museum, London)*

The Beginnings of Slavery in English America

The demand for African servants to supplement the scarce southern labor force existed almost from the first moments of settlement. For a time, however, black workers were hard to find. Not until the mid-seventeenth century, when a substantial commerce in slaves grew up between the Caribbean islands and the southern colonies, did black workers become generally available in North America.

The demand for slaves in North America helped expand the transatlantic slave trade. And as slave trading grew more extensive and more sophisticated, it also grew more horrible. Before it ended in the nineteenth century, it was responsible for the forced immigration of as many as 11 million Africans to North and South America and the Caribbean. In the flourishing slave marts on the African coast, native chieftains brought captured members of rival tribes to the ports. The terrified victims were then packed into the dark, filthy holds of ships for the horrors of

The "Middle Passage"

the "middle passage"—the long journey to the Americas, during which the prisoners were usually kept chained in the bowels of the slave ships and supplied with only minimal food and water. Many slave traders tried to cram as many Africans as possible into their ships to ensure that enough would survive to yield a profit at journey's end. Those who died en route, and many did, were simply thrown overboard. Upon arrival in the New World, slaves were auctioned off to white landowners and transported, frightened and bewildered, to their new homes.

North America was a less important direct destination for African slaves than were such other parts of the New World as the Caribbean islands and Brazil; fewer than 5 percent of the Africans imported to the Americas arrived first in the English colonies. Through most of the seventeenth century, those blacks who were transported to what became the United States came not directly from Africa but from the West Indies. Not until the 1670s did traders start importing blacks directly from Africa to North America. Even then the flow remained small for a time, mainly because a single group, the Royal African Company of England, monopolized the trade and kept prices high and supplies low.

A turning point in the history of the black population in North America was 1697, the year rival traders broke the Royal African Company's monopoly. With the trade now open to competition, prices fell and the number of Africans greatly increased. In 1700, *Surging Slave Population* about 25,000 African slaves lived in English North America. Because blacks were so heavily concentrated in a few southern colonies, they were already beginning to outnumber whites in some areas. There were perhaps twice as many black men as black women in most areas, but in some places the African-American population grew by natural increase nevertheless. In the Chesapeake more new slaves were being born than were being imported from Africa. In South Carolina, by contrast, the arduous conditions of rice cultivation ensured that the black population would barely be able to sustain itself through natural increase until much later. By 1760, the number of Africans in the colonies had increased to approximately a quarter of a million, the vast majority of whom lived in the South. By then blacks had almost wholly replaced white indentured servants as the basis of the southern work force.

For a time, the legal and social status of the *Ambiguous Legal Status* African laborers remained somewhat fluid. In some areas white and black laborers worked together at first on terms of relative equality. Some blacks were treated much like white hired servants, and some were freed after a fixed term of servitude. By the late seventeenth century, however, a rigid distinction was emerging between blacks and whites. Gradually, the assumption spread that blacks would remain in service permanently and that black children would inherit their parents' bondage. White beliefs about the inferiority of the black race reinforced the growing rigidity of the system, but so did the economic advantages of the system to white slaveowners.

The system of permanent servitude—American slavery—became legal in the early eighteenth century when colonial assemblies began to pass "slave codes" granting white masters almost absolute authority over their slaves. Only one factor determined whether a person was subject to the slave codes: color. In the *Race-based "Slave Codes"* colonial societies of Spanish America, people of mixed race were granted a different (and higher) status than pure Africans. English America recognized no such distinctions.

The debate among historians over how and why white Americans created a system of slave labor in the seventeenth century—and how and why they determined that African Americans and no others should populate that system—has been an unusually lively one. At its center is a debate over whether slavery was a result of white racism, or whether racism was a result of slavery.

In 1950, Oscar and Mary Handlin published an influential article comparing slavery to other systems of "unfreedom" in the colonies. What separated slavery from other conditions of servitude, they argued, was that it was restricted to people of African descent, that it was permanent, and that it passed from one generation to the next. The unique characteristics of slavery, the Handlins argued, were part of an effort by colonial legislatures to increase the available labor force. White laborers needed an incentive to come to America; black laborers, forcibly imported from Africa, did not. The distinction between the conditions of white workers and the conditions of black workers was, therefore, based on legal and economic motives, not on racism.

Winthrop Jordan was one of a number historians who later challenged the Handlins' thesis and argued that white racism, more than economic interests, produced African slavery. In *White Over Black* (1968) and other works, Jordan argued that Europeans had long viewed people of color as inferior beings. Those attitudes migrated with white Europeans to the New World, and white racism shaped the treatment of Africans in America from the beginning. Even without the economic incentives the Handlins described, in other words, whites would have been likely to oppress blacks in the New World.

Peter Wood's *Black Majority* (1974), a study of seventeenth-century South Carolina, was one of a number of works that moved the debate back toward social and economic conditions. Wood demonstrated that blacks and whites often worked together on relatively equal terms in the early years of settlement. But as rice cultivation expanded, it became more difficult to find white laborers willing to do the arduous work. The increase in the forcible importation of African slaves was a response to this growing demand for labor. It was also a response to fears among whites that without slavery it would be difficult to control a labor force brought to America against its will. Edmund Morgan's *American Slavery, American Freedom* (1975) argued similarly that the southern labor system was at first relatively flexible and later grew more rigid. In colonial Virginia, he claimed, white settlers did not at first intend to create a system of permanent bondage. But as the tobacco economy grew and created a high demand for cheap labor, white landowners began to feel uneasy about their dependence on a large group of dependent white workers. Such workers were difficult to recruit and control. Slavery, therefore, was less a result of racism than of the desire for whites to find a reliable and stable labor force.

Robin Blackburn's *The Making of New World Slavery* (1996) argues particularly strenuously that, while race was a factor in making the enslavement of Africans easier for whites to justify to themselves, the real reasons for the emergence of slavery were hardheaded economic decisions by ambitious entrepreneurs who realized very early that a slave-labor system in the labor-intensive agricultural world of the American South and the Caribbean was more profitable than a free-labor system. Slavery served the interests of a powerful combination of groups: planters, merchants, industrialists, and consumers. The most important reason for the creation and continuation of the system, therefore, was not racism, but the pursuit of profit. Slavery was not, Blackburn concludes, an antiquated remnant of an older world. It was a recognizably modern labor system that served the needs of an emerging market economy.

(text continued from page 65)

Changing Sources of European Immigration

The most distinctive and enduring feature of the American population was that it brought together peoples of many different races, ethnic groups, and nationalities. North America was home to a substantial population of natives, to a growing number of English immigrants, to forcibly imported Africans, and to substantial non-English groups from Europe.

The earliest of these continental European im- *Religious Refugees* migrants were about 300,000 French Calvinists, or Huguenots, who left Roman Catholic France for the English colonies of North America after the Edict of Nantes, which had guaranteed them substantial liberties, was revoked in 1685. Many German Protestants emigrated to America to escape similarly arbitrary religious policies and the frequent wars between their principalities and France. The Rhineland of southwestern Germany, known as the Palatinate, was exposed to frequent invasion; more than 12,000 Palatinate Germans fled to England early in the eighteenth century, and approximately 3,000 of them found their way to America. Most settled in Pennsylvania, where they ultimately became known to English settlers as the "Pennsylvania Dutch" (a corruption of the German term for their nationality, *Deutsch*). Other, later German immigrants headed to Pennsylvania as well, among them the Moravians and Mennonites.

The most numerous of the newcomers were *Scotch-Irish* the so-called Scotch-Irish—Scotch Presbyterians who had settled in northern Ireland (in the province of Ulster) in the early seventeenth century. Most of the Scotch-Irish in America pushed out to the edges of European settlement and occupied land without much regard for who actually claimed to own it.

There were also immigrants from Scotland itself and from southern Ireland. Scottish Highlanders, some of them Roman Catholics, mainly immigrated into North Carolina. Scottish Presbyterian Lowlanders, fleeing high rents and unemployment, left for America in large numbers shortly before the American Revolution. The Irish migrated steadily over a long period. Many of them abandoned their Roman Catholic religion and much of their ethnic identity after they arrived in America.

	English
	Scotch-Irish
	German
	Dutch
	African

IMMIGRANT GROUPS IN COLONIAL AMERICA, 1760 Even though the entire Atlantic seaboard of what is now the United States had become a series of British colonies by 1760, the population consisted of people from many nations. As this map reveals, English settlers dominated most of the regions of North America. But note the large areas of German settlement in the western Chesapeake and Pennsylvania; the swath of Dutch settlement in New York and New Jersey; the Scotch-Irish regions in the western regions of the South; and the large areas in which Africans were becoming the majority of the population, even if subjugated by the white minority. ◆ *What aspects of the history of these colonies help explain their ethnic composition?*

 For an interactive version of this map go to www.mhhe.com/unfinishednation4ch3maps

THE COLONIAL ECONOMIES

Farming dominated almost all areas of European and African settlement in North America throughout the seventeenth and eighteenth centuries. Even so, the economies of the different regions varied markedly.

The Southern Economy

A strong European demand for tobacco enabled some planters in the Chesapeake (Maryland and Virginia) to become enormously wealthy and at times allowed the region as a whole to prosper. But throughout the seventeenth and eighteenth centuries, production of tobacco frequently exceeded demand, and as a result the price of the crop sometimes suffered severe declines. The result was a boom-and-bust cycle in the Chesapeake economy, with the first major bust occurring in 1640.

Boom-and-bust Tobacco Economy

South Carolina and Georgia relied on rice production, since the low-lying coastline with its many tidal rivers made it possible to create rice

SELLING TOBACCO This late-seventeenth-century label was used in the sale of American tobacco in England. The drawing depicts Virginia as a land of bright sunshine, energetic slaves, and prosperous, pipe-smoking planters. *(American Heritage Publishing Co./A Division of Forbes, Inc.)*

paddies that could be flooded and drained. Rice cultivation was so difficult and unhealthy that white laborers generally refused to perform it. Hence planters in South Carolina and Georgia were much more dependent on slaves than were their northern counterparts. African workers were adept at rice cultivation, in part because some of them had come from rice-producing regions of west Africa and in part because they were generally more accustomed to the hot, humid climate than were Europeans and had a greater natural immunity to malaria.

The South's Cash-Crop Economy   Because of their dependence on large-scale cash crops, the southern colonies developed less of a commercial or industrial economy than the colonies of the North. The trading in tobacco and rice was handled largely by merchants based in London and, later, in the northern colonies.

Northern Economic and Technological Life

In the North, as in the South, agriculture continued to dominate, but it was agriculture of a more diverse kind. In northern New England, colder weather and hard, rocky soil made it difficult for colonists to develop the kind of large-scale commercial farming system that southerners were creating. Conditions for agriculture were better in southern New England and the middle colonies, where the soil was fertile and the weather more temperate. New York, Pennsylvania, and the Connecticut River valley were the chief suppliers of wheat to much of New England and to parts of the South. Even there, however, a substantial commercial economy emerged alongside the agricultural one.

Almost every colonist engaged in a certain amount of industry at home. Occasionally these home industries provided families with surplus goods they could trade or sell. Beyond these domestic efforts, craftsmen and artisans established themselves in colonial towns as cobblers, black-smiths, riflemakers, cabinetmakers, silversmiths, and printers. In some areas, entrepreneurs har-nessed water power to run small mills for grinding grain, processing cloth, or milling lumber. And in several places, large-scale shipbuilding operations began to flourish.

Colonial Artisans and Entrepreneurs

The first effort to establish a significant metals industry in the colonies was an ironworks established in Saugus, Massachusetts, in the 1640s. The Saugus works used water power to drive a bellows, which controlled the heat in a charcoal furnace. The carbon from the burning charcoal helped remove the oxygen from the ore and thus reduced its melting temperature. As the ore melted, it trickled down into molds or was taken in the form of simple "sow bars" to a nearby forge to be shaped into iron objects such as pots and anvils. There was also a mill suitable for turning the "sow bars" into narrow rods that blacksmiths could cut into nails. The Saugus works was a technological success but a financial failure. It began operations in 1646; in 1668, its financial problems forced it to close its doors.

Metal works, however, gradually became an important part of the colonial economy. The largest industrial enterprise anywhere in English North America was the ironworks of the German *Peter Hasenclever's Ironworks* ironmaster Peter Hasenclever in northern New Jersey. Founded in 1764 with British capital, it employed several hundred laborers. There were other, smaller ironmaking enterprises in every northern colony, and there were ironworks as well in several of the southern colonies. Even so, these and other growing industries did not become the basis for the kind of explosive industrial growth that Great Britain experienced in the late eighteenth century—in part because English parliamentary regulations such as the Iron Act of 1750 restricted metal processing in the colonies. Similar prohibitions limited the manufacture of woolens, hats, and other goods. But the biggest obstacles to industrialization in America were an inadequate labor supply, a small domestic market, and inadequate transportation facilities and energy supplies.

More important than manufacturing were industries that exploited the natural resources of the continent. By the mid-seventeenth century, the flourishing fur trade of earlier years was in decline. Taking its place were lumbering, mining, and fishing. These industries provided commodities that could be exported to England in exchange for manufactured goods. And they helped produce the most distinctive feature of the northern economy: a thriving commercial class.

The Extent and Limits of Technology

Despite the technological progress that was occurring in some parts of America in the seventeenth and eighteenth centuries, much of colonial society was conspicuously lacking in even very basic *Persistent Colonial Poverty* technological capacities. Up to half the farmers in the colonies were so primitively equipped that they did not even own a plow. Substantial numbers of households owned no pots or kettles for cooking. And only about half the households in the colonies owned guns or rifles. The relatively low levels of ownership of these and other elementary tools was not because such things were difficult to make, but because most Americans remained too poor or too isolated to be able to afford them. Many households had few if any candles, because they were unable to afford candle molds or tallow (wax), or because they had no access to commercially produced candles. In the early eighteenth century, very few farmers owned wagons. Most made do with two-wheeled carts, which were not very efficient for transporting crops to market. The most commonly owned tool on American farms was the axe.

Even so, few colonists were self-sufficient in the late seventeenth and early eighteenth centuries. *Myth of Colonial Self-Sufficiency* A popular image of early American households is of people who grew their own food, made their own clothes, and bought little from anyone else. In fact, relatively few colonial families owned spinning wheels or looms, which suggests that most people purchased whatever yarn and cloth they needed. Most farmers who grew grain took it to centralized facilities for processing.

In general, unsurprisingly, people who lived in isolated or poor areas owned fewer tools and had less access to advanced technologies than did those in more populous or affluent areas. But throughout the colonies, the ability of people to acquire manufactured implements lagged far behind the economy's capacity to produce them.

The Rise of Colonial Commerce

Obstacles to Trade Perhaps the most remarkable feature of colonial commerce was that it was able to survive at all. American merchants faced such bewildering obstacles, and lacked so many of the basic institutions of trade, that they managed to stay afloat only with great difficulty. The colonies had almost no gold or silver, and their paper currency was not acceptable as payment for goods from abroad. For many years, colonial merchants had to rely on barter or on money substitutes such as beaver skins.

A second obstacle was lack of information about supply and demand. Traders had no way of knowing what they would find in foreign ports; vessels sometimes stayed at sea for years, journeying from one port to another, trading one commodity for another, attempting to find some way to turn a profit. There was also an enormous number of small, fiercely competitive companies, which made the problem of rationalizing the system even more acute.

Nevertheless, commerce in the colonies survived and grew. There was elaborate trade among the colonies themselves and with the West Indies. The mainland colonies offered their Caribbean trading partners rum, agricultural products, meat, and fish. The islands offered sugar, molasses, and at times slaves in return. There was also trade with England, continental Europe, and the west coast of Africa. This commerce has often been described, somewhat inaccurately, as the "triangular trade," suggesting a neat process by which merchants carried rum and other goods from New England to Africa, exchanged their merchandise for slaves, whom they then transported to the West Indies (hence the term "middle passage" for the dreaded journey—it was the second of the three legs of the voyage), and then exchanged the slaves for sugar and molasses, which they shipped back to New England to be distilled into rum. In reality, the so-called triangular trade in rum, slaves, and sugar was a complicated maze of highly diverse trade routes. Out of this risky trade emerged a group of adventurous entrepreneurs who by the mid-eighteenth century were beginning to constitute

An Emerging Merchant Class a distinct merchant class. The British Navigation Acts protected them from foreign competition in the colonies. They had ready access to the market in England for such colonial products as furs, timber, and American-built ships. But they also

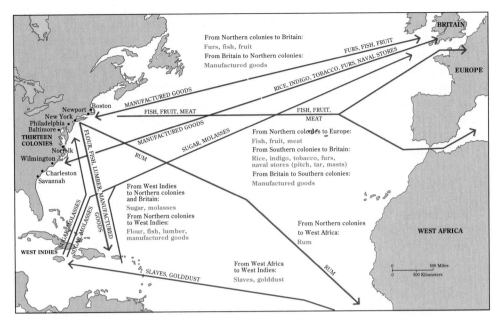

THE "TRIANGULAR TRADE" This map illustrates the complex pattern of trade that fueled the colonial American economy in the seventeenth and eighteenth centuries. A simple explanation of this trade is that the American colonies exported raw materials (agricultural products, furs, and others) to Britain and Europe and imported manufactured goods in return. But while that explanation is accurate, it is not complete, largely because the Atlantic trade was not a simple exchange between America and Europe, but a complex network of exchanges involving the Caribbean, Africa, and the Mediterranean. Note the important exchanges between the North American mainland and the Caribbean islands; the important trade between the American colonies and Africa; and the wide range of European and Mediterranean markets in which Americans were active. Not shown on this map, but also very important to colonial commerce, was a large coastal trade among the various regions of British North America. ◆ *Why did the major ports of trade emerge almost entirely in the northern colonies?*

 For an interactive version of this map go to www.mhhe.com/unfinishednation4ch3maps

developed markets illegally outside the British Empire—in the French, Spanish, and Dutch West Indies—where they could often get higher prices for their goods than in the British colonies.

The Rise of Consumerism

Among relatively affluent residents of the colonies, the growing prosperity and commercialism of British America created both new appetites and new opportunities to satisfy them. The result was a growing preoccupation with the consumption of material goods.

One thing that spurred the growth of the eighteenth-century consumerism was the increasing division of American societies by class. As the

Class Differences and Consumerism

difference between the upper and lower classes became more glaring, people of means became more intent on demonstrating their own membership in the upper ranks of society. The ability to purchase and display consumer goods was an important way of doing so, particularly for affluent people in cities and towns, who did not have large estates with which they could demonstrate their success. But the growth of consumerism was also a product of the early stages of the industrial revolution. Although there was relatively little industry in America in the eighteenth century, England and Europe were making rapid advances and producing more and more affordable goods for affluent Americans to buy.

To facilitate the new consumer appetites, merchants and traders began advertising their goods in journals and newspapers. Agents of urban merchants—the ancestors of the traveling salesman—fanned out through the countryside, attempting to interest wealthy landowners and planters in the luxury goods now available to them. George and Martha Washington, for example, spent considerable time and money ordering elegant furnishings for their home at Mount Vernon, goods that were shipped to them mostly from England and Europe.

One feature of a consumer society is that things that once were considered luxuries quickly come to be seen as necessities once they are readily available. In the colonies, items that became commonplace after having once been expensive luxuries included tea, household linens, glassware, manufactured cutlery, crockery, furniture, and many other things. Another result of consumerism is the association of material goods—of the quality of a person's home and possessions and clothing, for example—with virtue and "refinement." The ideal of the cultivated "gentleman" and the gracious "lady" became increasingly powerful throughout the colonies in the eighteenth century. In part that meant striving to become educated and "refined"—"gentlemanly" or "ladylike" in speech and behavior. Americans read books on manners and fashion. They bought magazines about London society. And they strove to develop themselves as witty and educated conversationalists. They also commissioned portraits of themselves and their families, devoted large portions of their homes to entertainment, built shelves and cases in which they could display fashionable possessions, constructed formal gardens, and lavished attention on their wardrobes and hairstyles.

PATTERNS OF SOCIETY

Although there were sharp social distinctions in the colonies, the well-defined and deeply entrenched class system of England failed to reproduce itself in America. Aristocracies emerged to be sure; but they tended to rely less on landownership than on control of a substantial work force, and they were generally less secure and less powerful than their English counterparts.

More than in England, white people in America faced opportunities for social mobility—both up and down. There were also new forms of community in America, and they varied greatly from one region to another.

Social Mobility

Masters and Slaves on the Plantation

The plantation system of the American South produced one form of community. The first plantations emerged in the tobacco-growing areas of Virginia and Maryland. Some of the early planters became established aristocrats with vast estates. On the whole, however, seventeenth-century colonial plantations were rough and relatively small. In the early days in Virginia, they were little more than crude clearings where landowners and indentured servants worked side by side in conditions so harsh that death was an everyday occurrence. Most landowners lived in rough cabins or houses, with their servants or slaves nearby. The economy of the plantation was a precarious one. Planters could not control their markets, so even the largest of them were constantly at risk. When prices fell, planters faced the prospect of ruin. The plantation economy created many new wealthy landowners, but it also destroyed many.

Precarious Plantation Economy

The enslaved African Americans, of course, lived very differently. On the smaller farms with only a handful of slaves, it was not always possible for a rigid separation to develop between whites and blacks. But by the early eighteenth century, over three-fourths of all blacks lived on plantations of at least ten slaves, and nearly half lived in communities of fifty slaves or more. In those settings, they were able to develop a society and culture of their own. Although whites seldom encouraged formal marriages among slaves, blacks themselves developed a strong and elaborate family structure. There was also a distinctive slave religion, which blended Christianity with African folklore and which became a central element in the emergence of an independent black culture.

Slave Culture

Nevertheless, black society was subject to constant intrusions from and interaction with white society. Black house servants, for example, were isolated from their own community. Black women were subject to usually unwanted sexual advances from owners and overseers and hence to bearing mulatto children, who were rarely recognized by their white fathers. On some plantations, black workers were treated with kindness and sometimes responded to their owners with genuine devotion. On others, they encountered physical brutality and occasionally even sadism, against which they were virtually powerless.

Slaves often resisted their masters, in large ways and small. The most serious example in the colonial period was the Stono Rebellion in South Carolina in 1739, during which about 100 blacks rose up, seized weapons, killed several whites, and

Stono Rebellion

attempted to escape south to Florida. The uprising was quickly crushed, and most participants were executed. A more frequent form of resistance was simply running away, but that provided no real solution either. For most, there was nowhere to go. Resistance more often took the form of subtle, and often undetected, defiance or evasion of their masters' wishes.

Most slaves, male and female, worked as field hands. But on the larger plantations that aspired to genuine self-sufficiency, some slaves learned trades and crafts: blacksmithing, carpentry, shoemaking, spinning, weaving, sewing, midwifery, and others. These skilled crafts workers were at times hired out to other planters. Some set up their own establishments in towns or cities and shared their profits with their owners. A few were able to buy their freedom.

The Puritan Community

The characteristic social unit in New England was not the isolated farm but the town. In the early years of colonization, each new settlement drew

Close-knit Puritan Communities up a "covenant" binding all residents tightly together both religiously and socially. Colonists laid out a village, with houses and a meetinghouse arranged around a central pasture, or "common." Thus families generally lived with their neighbors close by. They divided up the outlying fields and woodlands among the residents; the size and location of a family's field depended on the family's numbers, wealth, and social station.

Once a town was established, residents held a yearly "town meeting" to decide important questions and to choose a group of "selectmen," who

Participatory Democracy ran the town's affairs. Participation in the meeting was generally restricted to adult males who were members of the church. Only those who could give evidence of being among the elect assured of salvation (the "visible saints") were admitted to full church membership, although other residents of the town were required to attend church services.

New Englanders did not adopt the English system of primogeniture—the passing of all property to the firstborn son. Instead, a father divided up his land among all his sons. His control of this inheritance gave him great power over the family. Often a son would reach his late twenties before his father would allow him to move into his own household and work his own land. Even then, sons would usually continue to live in close proximity to their fathers.

The early Puritan community was a tightly knit organism. Yet as the years passed and the communities grew, strains and tensions began to affect this communal structure. This was partly because of the increasing commercialization of New England society, which introduced new forces into the communities of the region. It was also partly because of population growth. As towns grew larger, residents tended to cultivate lands farther and farther from the community center and, by necessity, to live at

THE NEW ENGLAND TOWN: SUDBURY, MASSACHUSETTS, 17TH CENTURY Just as the
plantation was a characteristic social form in the southern colonies, the town was the most
common social unit in New England. This map shows the organization of Sudbury,
Massachusetts, a town just west of Boston, in its early years in the seventeenth century. Note
the location of the houses, which are grouped mostly together around a shared pasture (or
"commons") and near the church. Note, too, the outlying fields, which were divided up among
residents of the town, even though they were often not connected to the land on which they
lived. The map illustrates the holdings of a single resident of Sudbury, John Goodnow, whose
house was on the Common, but whose lands were scattered over a number of areas of Sudbury.
◆ *What aspects of New England life might help explain the clustering of residences at the center of the
town?* (*From Sumner Chilton Powell,* Puritan Village: The Formation of a New England Town. *Copyright ©
1963 by Wesleyan University. Reprinted by permission from Wesleyan University Press*)

*Communal Strains
and Tensions*

increasing distances from the church. The control
of land by fathers also created strains. In the first
generations, fathers generally controlled enough
land to satisfy the needs of all their sons. After several generations, however, there was often too little to go around, particularly in communities
surrounded by other towns, with no room to expand outward. The result
was that in many communities, groups of younger residents broke off and
moved elsewhere to form towns of their own.

The tensions building in Puritan communities could produce bizarre
and disastrous events. One example was the widespread hysteria in the
1680s and 1690s over accusations of witchcraft (the human exercise of sa-
tanic powers) in New England. The most famous outbreak was in Salem,
Massachusetts, where adolescent girls leveled charges of witchcraft against
several West Indian servants steeped in voodoo lore. Hysteria spread

> ## A Modeſt Enquiry
> Into the Nature of
>
> # Witchcraft,
>
> ### AND
>
> How Perſons Guilty of that Crime
> may be *Convicted* : And the means
> uſed for their Diſcovery Diſcuſſed,
> both *Negatively* and *Affirmatively*,
> according to *SCRIPTURE* and
> *EXPERIENCE*.
>
> ## By John Hale,
> Paſtor of the Church of Chriſt in *Beverley*,
> *Anno Domini.* 1 6 9 7.
>
> *When they ſay unto you, ſeek unto them that have
> Familiar Spirits and unto Wizzards, that peep,&c.
> To the Law and to the Teſtimony ; if they ſpeak
> not according to this word, it is becauſe there is no
> light in them,* Iſaiah VIII. 19, 20.
> *That which I ſee not teach thou me,* Job 34. 32.
>
> *BOSTON in N. E.*
> Printed by *B. Green,*, and *J. Allen,* for
> *Benjamin Eliot* under the Town Houſe. 1702

A STUDY OF WITCHCRAFT This pamphlet, originally written in 1697 near the height of the witchcraft phenomenon in New England, was one of many contemporary studies to take the idea of witchcraft seriously. Belief in witches was widespread in early New England society, and many of the charges that seem preposterous to twentieth-century eyes appeared entirely plausible even to educated people of the time. *(Courtesy Peabody Essex Museum, Salem, MA)*

throughout the town, and hundreds of people (most of them women) were accused of witchcraft. Nineteen residents of Salem were put to death before the trials finally ended in 1692; the girls who had been the original accusers later recanted and admitted that their story had been fabricated.

Salem Witch Trials   The Salem experience was not unique. Accusations of witchcraft spread through many New England towns in the early 1690s and centered mostly on women. Research into the background of accused witches reveals that most were middle-aged women, often widowed, with few or no children. Many accused witches were of low social position, were often involved in domestic conflicts, had frequently been accused of other crimes, and were considered abrasive by their neighbors. Others were women who, through inheritance or hard work, had come into possession of substantial property of their own and thus challenged the gender norms of the community.

The witchcraft controversies were also a reflection of the highly religious character of New England societies. New Englanders believed in the power of Satan. Belief in witchcraft was not a marginal superstition rejected by the mainstream. It was a common feature of Puritan religious conviction.

Cities

In the 1770s the two largest colonial ports— *Colonial Cities*
Philadelphia and New York—had populations of
28,000 and 25,000, respectively, which made them larger than most English urban centers of their time. Boston (16,000), Charles Town (later
Charleston), South Carolina (12,000), and Newport, Rhode Island
(11,000), were also substantial communities by the standards of the day.

Colonial cities served as trading centers for the farmers of their regions and as marts for international commerce. Their leaders were generally merchants who had acquired substantial wealth. More than in any
other area of colonial life (except, of course, in the relationship between
masters and slaves), social distinctions were real and visible in urban areas.

Cities were the centers of much of what indus-
try there was in the colonies. They were the loca- *Centers of Industry and*
Education
tions of the most advanced schools and sophisti-
cated cultural activities and of shops where imported goods could be bought.
In addition, they were communities with urban social problems: crime, vice,
pollution, traffic. Unlike smaller towns, cities needed to set up constables' offices and fire departments and develop systems for supporting the urban
poor, whose numbers became especially large in times of economic crisis.

Finally, cities were places where new ideas could circulate and be dis-
cussed. There were newspapers, books, and other publications from
abroad, and hence new intellectual influences. The taverns and coffee-
houses of cities provided forums in which people could gather and debate
the issues of the day. That is one reason why the Revolutionary crisis,
when it began to build in the 1760s and 1770s, began first in the cities.

AWAKENINGS AND ENLIGHTENMENTS

Intellectual life in colonial America revolved around the conflict between
the traditional emphasis on a personal God deeply involved in individual
lives, and the new spirit of the Enlightenment, which stressed the importance of science and human reason. The old views placed a high value on a
stern moral code in which intellect was less important than faith. The Enlightenment suggested that people had substantial control over their own
lives and societies.

The Pattern of Religions

Religious toleration flourished in America to a degree unmatched in any
European nation. Settlers in America brought with them so many different religious practices that it proved impossible to impose a single religious code on any large area.

The Church of England was established as the official faith in Virginia, Maryland, New York, the Carolinas, and Georgia. Except in Virginia and Maryland, however, the laws establishing the Church of England as the official colonial religion were largely ignored. Even in New England, where the Puritans had originally believed that they were all part of a single faith, there was a growing tendency in the eighteenth century for different congregations to affiliate with different denominations. In parts of New York and New Jersey, Dutch settlers had established their

Multiplying Denominations own Calvinist denomination, Dutch Reformed. American Baptists developed a great variety of sects. All Baptists shared the belief that rebaptism, usually by total immersion, was necessary when believers reached maturity. But while some Baptists remained Calvinists (believers in predestination) others came to believe in salvation by free will.

Persistent Anti-Catholicism Protestants extended toleration to one another more readily than they did to Roman Catholics. New Englanders, in particular, viewed their Catholic neighbors in New France (Canada) not only as commercial and military rivals but also as dangerous agents of Rome. In most of the English colonies, however, Roman Catholics were too few to cause serious conflict. They were most numerous in Maryland, and even there they numbered no more than 3,000. Perhaps for that reason they suffered their worst persecution in that colony. After the overthrow of the original proprietors in 1691, Catholics in Maryland not only lost their political rights but also were forbidden to hold religious services except in private houses.

Anti-Semitism Jews in provincial America totaled no more than about 2,000 at any time. The largest community lived in New York City. Smaller groups settled in Newport and Charleston, and there were scattered Jewish families in all the colonies. Nowhere could they vote or hold office. Only in Rhode Island could they practice their religion openly.

Declining Piety By the beginning of the eighteenth century, some Americans were growing troubled by the apparent decline in religious piety in their society. The movement of the population westward and the wide scattering of settlements had caused many communities to lose touch with organized religion. The rise of commercial prosperity created a more secular outlook in urban areas. The progress of science and free thought caused at least some colonists to doubt traditional religious beliefs.

Concerns about weakening piety surfaced as early as the 1660s in New England, where the Puritan oligarchy warned of a decline in the power of the church. Ministers preached sermons of despair (known as "jeremiads"), deploring the signs of waning piety. By the standards of other societies or other eras, the Puritan faith remained remarkably strong. But to New Englanders the "declension" of religious piety seemed a serious problem.

The Great Awakening

By the early eighteenth century, similar concerns were emerging in other regions and among members of other faiths. Everywhere, colonists were coming to believe, religious piety was in decline. The result was the first great American revival: the Great Awakening.

The Great Awakening began in earnest in the 1730s and reached its climax in the 1740s. The revival had particular ap- *Appeal of the Great Awakening* peal to women (who constituted the majority of converts) and to younger sons of the third or fourth generation of settlers—those who stood to inherit the least land and who faced the most uncertain futures. The rhetoric of the revival emphasized the potential for every person to break away from the constraints of the past and start anew in his or her relationship with God. Such beliefs may have reflected in part the desires of many people to break away from their families or communities and start a new life.

Powerful evangelists from England helped spread the revival. John and Charles Wesley, the founders of Methodism, visited Georgia and other colonies in the 1730s. George Whitefield, a powerful open-air preacher, made several evangelizing tours through the colonies and drew tremendous crowds. But the outstanding preacher of the Great Awakening was the New England Congregationalist Jonathan Edwards. From his pulpit in Northampton, Massachusetts, Edwards attacked the new doctrines of easy salvation for all. He preached anew the traditional Puritan ideas of the absolute sovereignty of God, predestination, and salvation by God's grace alone. His vivid descriptions of hell could terrify his listeners.

The Great Awakening led to the division of existing congregations (between "New Light" revivalists and "Old Light" *"New Lights" and "Old Lights"* traditionalists) and to the founding of new ones. It also affected areas of society outside the churches. Some of the revivalists denounced book learning as a hindrance to salvation. But other evangelists saw education as a means of furthering religion, and they founded or led schools for the training of New Light ministers.

The Enlightenment

The Great Awakening caused one great cultural upheaval in the colonies. The Enlightenment caused another, very different one. The Enlightenment was the product of some of the great scientific and intellectual discoveries in Europe in the seventeenth century—discoveries that revealed the "natural laws" that regulated the workings of *"Natural Law"* nature. The new scientific knowledge encouraged many thinkers to begin celebrating the power of human reason and to argue that rational thought, not just religious faith, could create progress and advance knowledge in the world.

In celebrating reason, the Enlightenment encouraged men and women to look to themselves and their own intellect—not just to God—for guidance as to how to live their lives and shape their societies. It helped produce a growing interest in education and a heightened concern with politics and government.

In the early seventeenth century, Enlightenment ideas in America were largely borrowed from Europe—from such great thinkers as Francis Bacon and John Locke of England, Baruch Spinoza of Amsterdam, and René Descartes of France. Later, however, such Americans as Benjamin Franklin, Thomas Paine, Thomas Jefferson, and James Madison made their own important contributions to Enlightenment thought.

Literacy and Technology

White male Americans achieved a high degree of literacy in the eighteenth century. By the time of the Revolution, well over half of all white men could read and write. The literacy rate for women lagged behind the rate for men until the nineteenth century. While opportunities for education beyond the primary level were scarce for men, they were almost nonexistent for women.

The large number of colonists who could read created a market for the first widely circulated publications in America other than the Bible: almanacs. By 1700, there were dozens, perhaps hundreds, of almanacs circulating throughout the colonies and even in the sparsely settled lands to the west. Most families had at least one. Almanacs provided medical advice, navigational and agricultural information, practical wisdom, humor, and predictions about the future—most famously, predictions about weather patterns for the coming year, which many farmers used as the basis of decisions about crops even though the predictions were notoriously unreliable. The most famous almanac in eighteenth-century America was *Poor*

Poor Richard's Almanac
Richard's Almanac, published by Benjamin Franklin in Philadelphia.

The wide availability of reading material in colonial America by the eighteenth century was a result of the spread of printing technology. The first printing press began operating in the colonies in 1639, and by 1695 there were more towns in America with printers than there were in England. At first, many of these presses did not get very much use. Over time, however, the rising literacy of the society created a demand for books, pamphlets, and almanacs that the presses rushed to fill.

Publick Occurrences
The first newspaper in the colonies, *Publick Occurrences*, was published in Boston in 1690 using a relatively advanced printing facility. It was the first step toward what would eventually become a large newspaper industry. One reason the Stamp Act of 1765, which imposed a tax on printed materials, created such a furor was because printing technology had by then become central to colonial life.

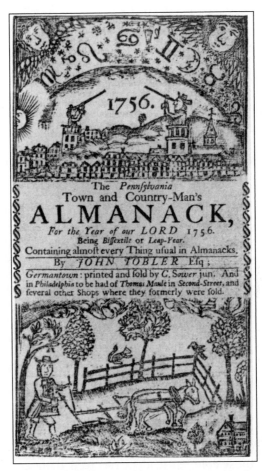

TOWN AND COUNTRY-MAN'S ALMANACK As the population of colonial cities and towns grew, almanacs—originally targeted mainly at farmers—began to appeal to townspeople as well. *(Sinclair Hamilton Collection, Visual Materials Division, Department of Rare Books and Special Collections, Princeton University Library)*

Education

Even before Enlightenment ideas penetrated America, colonists placed a high value on formal education. Some families tried to teach their children to read and write at home, although the heavy burden of work in most agricultural households limited the time available for schooling. In Massachusetts, a 1647 law required that every town support a school; and a modest network of public schools *Growth of Public Education* emerged as a result. The Quakers and other sects operated church schools, and in some communities widows or unmarried women conducted "dame schools" by holding private classes in their homes. In cities, master craftsmen set up evening schools for their apprentices.

African Americans had virtually no access to education. Occasionally a master or mistress would teach slave children to read and write; but as the slave system became more firmly entrenched, strong social (and ultimately legal) sanctions developed to discourage such efforts. Indians, too, remained largely outside the white educational system—to a large degree by choice. Some white missionaries and philanthropists established schools for Native Americans and helped create a small population of Indians literate in spoken and written English.

Harvard, the first American college, was established in 1636 by Puritan theologians who wanted to create a training center for ministers. (The college was named for a Charlestown minister, John Harvard, who had *Colonial Higher Education* left it his library and half his estate.) In 1693, William and Mary College (named for the English king and queen) was established in Williamsburg, Virginia, by Anglicans. And in 1701, conservative Congregationalists, dissatisfied with the growing religious liberalism of Harvard, founded Yale (named for one of its first benefactors, Elihu Yale) in New Haven, Connecticut. Out of the Great Awakening emerged the College of New Jersey, founded in 1746 and known later as Princeton (after the town in which it was located); one of its first presidents was Jonathan Edwards. Despite the religious basis of these colleges, most of them offered curricula that included not only theology but logic, ethics, physics, geometry, astronomy, rhetoric, Latin, Hebrew, and Greek. King's College, founded in New York in 1754 and later renamed Columbia, was specifically devoted to the spread of secular knowledge. The Academy and College of Philadelphia, founded in 1755 and later renamed the University of Pennsylvania, was also a completely secular institution, established by a group of laymen under the inspiration of Benjamin Franklin.

After 1700, most colonial leaders received their entire educations in America (rather than attending university in England, as had once been the case). But higher education remained available only to a few relatively affluent white men.

The Spread of Science

Growing Interest in Science The clearest indication of the spreading influence of the Enlightenment in America was an increasing interest in scientific knowledge. Most of the early colleges established chairs in the natural sciences and introduced some of the advanced scientific theories of Europe, including Copernican astronomy and Newtonian physics, to their students. But the most vigorous promotion of science in these years occurred through the private efforts of amateurs and the activities of scientific societies. Leading merchants, planters, and even theologians became corresponding members of the Royal Society of London, the leading English scientific organization. Benjamin Franklin won international fame through his experiments with electricity. Particularly no-

BENJAMIN FRANKLIN ON ELECTRICITY The discovery of electricity was one of the great scientific events of the eighteenth century, even though large-scale practical use of electrical energy emerged much later. Benjamin Franklin was one of the first Americans, and certainly the most famous American, to experiment with electricity. This is the frontispiece for a book, originally published in 1750 in Philadelphia, that describes his "experiments and observations." The pages shown here are from the London edition, which appeared in 1774. (© *Hulton Getty/Getty Images*)

table was his 1747 theory and his 1752 demonstration, using a kite, that lightning and electricity were the same. (Previously, most scientists had believed that there were several distinct types of electricity.) His research on the way in which electricity could be "grounded" led to the development of the lightning rod, which greatly reduced fires and other damage to buildings during thunderstorms.

The high value that influential Americans were beginning to place on scientific knowledge was clearly demonstrated by the most daring and controversial scientific experiment of the eighteenth century: inoculation against smallpox. The

Smallpox Inoculation

Puritan theologian Cotton Mather had learned of experiments in England by which people had been deliberately infected with mild cases of small-pox in order to immunize them against the deadly disease. Despite strong opposition, he urged inoculation on his fellow Bostonians during an epidemic in the 1720s. The results confirmed the effectiveness of the technique. Other theologians took up the cause, along with many physicians. By the mid-eighteenth century, inoculation had become a common medical procedure in America.

Concepts of Law and Politics

In law and politics, as in other parts of their lives, Americans in the seventeenth and eighteenth centuries believed that they were re-creating in the New World the practices and institutions of the Old. But as in other areas, they in fact created something very different. Although the American legal system adopted most of the essential elements of the English system, including such ancient rights as trial by jury, significant differences developed in court procedures, punishments, and the definition of crimes. In England, for example, a printed attack on a public official, whether true or false, was considered libelous. At the 1734–1735 trial of the New York publisher John Peter Zenger, the courts ruled that criticisms of the government were not libelous if factually true—a verdict that removed some colonial restrictions on the freedom of the press.

More significant for the future of the relationship between the colonies and England were differences emerging between the American and British political systems. Because the royal government was so far *Powerful Colonial Legislatures* away, Americans created a group of institutions of their own that gave them a large measure of self-government. In most colonies, local communities grew accustomed to running their own affairs with minimal interference from higher authorities. The colonial assemblies came to exercise many of the powers that Parliament exercised in England. Provincial governors (appointed by the king after the 1690s) had broad powers on paper, but their actual influence was limited.

The result of all this was that the provincial governments became accustomed to acting more or less independently of Parliament, and a set of assumptions and expectations about the rights of the colonists took hold in America that was not shared by policymakers in England. These differences caused few problems before the 1760s, because the British did little to exert the authority they believed they possessed. But when, beginning in 1763, the English government began attempting to tighten its control over the American colonies, a great imperial crisis resulted.

CONCLUSION

The English colonies in America grew steadily between the 1650s and the 1750s: in population, in the size of their economies, and in the sophistication—and diversity—of their cultures. Although most white Americans in the 1750s still believed that they were fully a part of the British Empire, they were in fact living in a world that had become very different from that of England.

Many distinct societies developed in the colonies, but the greatest distinction was between the colonies of the North and those of the South. In the North, society was dom- *Diverging North and South* inated by relatively small family farms and by towns and cities of growing size. A thriving commercial class was developing, and with it an increasingly elaborate urban culture. In the South, there were many family farms as well. But there were also large plantations cultivating tobacco, rice, indigo, and cotton for export. By the late seventeenth century, these plantations were relying heavily on African workers who had been brought to the colonies forcibly as slaves. There were few significant towns and cities in the South, and little commerce other than the marketing of crops.

The colonies did, however, also have much in common. Most white Americans accepted common assumptions about racial inequality. That enabled them to tolerate the enslavement of African men and women and to justify a campaign of displacement and often violence against Native Americans. Most white Americans (and, in different ways, most nonwhite Americans as well) were deeply religious. The Great Awakening, therefore, had a powerful impact throughout the colonies. And most white colonists shared a belief in certain basic principles of law and politics, which they considered embedded in the English constitution. Their interpretation of that constitution, however, was becoming increasingly different from that of the parliament in England and was laying the groundwork for future conflict.

FOR FURTHER REFERENCE

Edward Countryman, *Americans: A Collision of Histories* (1996) includes a vivid picture of the many cultures that encountered one another in early America. Bernard Bailyn, *Voyagers to the West: A Passage in the Peopling of America on the Eve of the Revolution* (1986) reveals the complexity and scope of European emigration to North America. Bailyn's *The Origin of America Politics* (1968) remains an excellent introduction to colonial politics.

David Hackett Fischer, *Albion's Seed* (1989) suggests four major folkways for English migrants to America. Jack P. Greene, *Pursuits of Happiness: The Social Development of Early Modern British Colonies and the Formation of American Culture* (1986) is a broad portrait of life in early American communities. Laurel Thatcher Ulrich, *Good Wives: Image and Reality in the Lives of Women in Northern New England, 1650–1750* (1982) offers a typology of women's roles in colonial New England. John Demos, *The Unredeemed Captive: A Family Story of Early America* (1994) is a vivid, unconventional account of the experiences of a New England girl captured by Indians. Robin Blackburn, *The Making of New World Slavery: From the Baroque to the Modern, 1492–1800* (1997) includes an important examination of the character of the institution in colonial America. Philip D. Morgan, *Slave Counterpoint: Black Culture in the Eighteenth-Century Chesapeake and Lowcountry* (1998) is a major study of the early history of slavery. Kathleen M. Brown, *Good Wives, Nasty Wenches, and Anxious Patriarchs: Gender, Race and Power in Colonial Virginia* (1996) places gender at the center of the development of slavery in the Chesapeake. Rhys Isaac, *The Transformation of Virginia, 1740–1790* (1982) uses the methods of cultural anthropology in an influential study of the world of the colonial Virginia gentry. Darren Staloff, *The Making of an American Thinking Class: Intellectuals and Intelligentsia in Puritan Massachusetts* (1998) is an intellectual history of early New England.

For quizzes, Internet resources, references to additional books and films, and more, consult this book's Online Learning Center site at www.mhhe.com/unfinishednation4

THE BOSTON MASSACRE (1770), BY PAUL REVERE   This is one of many sensationalized engravings, by Revere and others, of the conflict between British troops and Boston laborers that became important propaganda documents for the Patriot cause in the 1770s. Among the victims of the massacre listed by Revere was Crispus Attucks, probably the first black man to die in the struggle for American independence.   *(Burstein Collection/Corbis)*

TIME LINE

1754	1756	1760	1763	1764	1765	1766	
Beginning of French and Indian War	Seven Years' War begins	George III becomes king	Peace of Paris Proclamation of 1763	Sugar Act	Stamp Act	Stamp Act repealed Declaratory Act	

~❧~

THE EMPIRE IN TRANSITION

Loosening Ties
The Struggle for the Continent
The New Imperialism
Stirrings of Revolt
Cooperation and War

A s late as the 1750s, few Americans objected to their membership in the British Empire. The imperial system provided many benefits to the Americans, and for the most part the English government left the colonies alone. By the mid-1770s, however, the relationship between the American colonies and their British rulers had become so strained that the empire was on the verge of unraveling. And in the spring of 1775, the first shots were fired in a war that would ultimately win America its independence. How had it happened? And why so quickly?

LOOSENING TIES

~❧~

In one sense, it had not happened quickly at all. Ever since the first days of English settlement in North America, the ideas and institutions of the colonies had been diverging from those in Britain. In another sense, however, the Revolutionary crisis emerged in response to relatively sudden

1767	1770	1771	1772	1773	1774	1775
Townshend Duties	Boston Massacre	Regulator movement in North Carolina	Committees of correspondence in Boston	Tea Act, Boston Tea Party	Intolerable Acts	Battles of Lexingon and Concord
	Most Townshend Duties repealed		Gaspée incident		First Continental Congress in Philadelphia	American Revolution begins

changes in the administration of the empire. In 1763 the English government began to enforce a series of policies toward its colonies that brought the differences between the two societies into sharp focus.

A Decentralized Empire

In the fifty years after the Glorious Revolution, the English Parliament established a growing supremacy over the king. Under Kings George I

Decentralized Colonial Administration

(1714–1727) and George II (1727–1760), the prime minister and his cabinet became the nation's real executives. Because they depended politically on the great merchants and landholders of England, they were less inclined than the seventeenth-century monarchs had been to try to tighten control over the empire, which many merchants feared would disrupt the profitable commerce with the colonies. As a result, administration of the colonies remained loose, decentralized, and inefficient.

The character of the royal officials in America contributed further to the looseness of the imperial system. Few governors were able men. Many, perhaps most, had used bribery to obtain their offices and continued to accept bribes once they assumed their offices. Some appointees remained in England and hired substitutes to take their places in America.

Assertive Colonial Assemblies

The colonial assemblies, taking advantage of the weak imperial administration, had asserted their own authority to levy taxes, make appropriations, approve appointments, and pass laws for their respective colonies. The assemblies came to look upon themselves as little parliaments, each practically as sovereign within its colony as Parliament itself was in England.

The Colonies Divided

Even so, the colonists continued to think of themselves as loyal English subjects. Many felt stronger ties to England than they did to the other American colonies. Although the colonies had slowly learned to cooperate with one another on such practical matters as intercolonial trade, road construction, and the creation of a colonial postal service, they remained reluctant to cooperate in larger ways, even when, in 1754, they faced a common threat from their old rivals, the French, and France's Indian allies. Delegates from Pennsylvania, Maryland, New

Albany Plan

York, and New England met in Albany in that year to negotiate a treaty with the Iroquois and tentatively approved a proposal by Benjamin Franklin to set up a "general government" to manage relations with the Indians. War with the French and Indians was already beginning when the Albany Plan was presented to the colonial assemblies. None approved it.

THE STRUGGLE FOR THE CONTINENT

The war that raged in North America through the late 1750s and early 1760s was part of a larger *Seven Years' War* struggle between England and France. The British victory in that struggle, known in Europe as the Seven Years' War, confirmed England's commercial supremacy and cemented its control of the settled regions of North America. In America, however, the conflict, which colonists called the French and Indian War, was also the final stage in a long struggle among the three principal powers in northeastern North America: the English, the French, and the Iroquois.

New France and the Iroquois Nation

By the end of the seventeenth century, the French Empire in America had come to possess a vast territory: the whole length of the Mississippi River and its delta (which they named Louisiana, after their king), and the continental interior as far west as the Rocky Mountains and as far south as the Rio Grande. France claimed, in effect, the entire interior of the continent.

To secure their hold on these enormous claims, *France's Colonial Empire* they founded a string of widely separated communities, fortresses, missions, and trading posts. Would-be feudal lords established large estates *(seigneuries)* along the banks of the St. Lawrence River. On a high bluff above the river stood the fortified city of Quebec. Montreal to the south and Sault Sainte Marie and Detroit to the west marked the northern boundaries of French settlement. On the lower Mississippi emerged plantations much like those in the southern colonies of English America, worked by black slaves and owned by "Creoles" (white immigrants of French descent). New Orleans, founded in 1718 to service the French plantation economy, was soon as big as some of the larger cities of the Atlantic seaboard; Biloxi and Mobile to the east completed the string of French settlement.

Both the French and the English were aware that the battle for control of North America would be determined in part by which group could best win the allegiance of native tribes. The English—with their more advanced commercial economy—could usually offer the Indians better and more plentiful goods. But the French offered tolerance. Unlike the English, the French settlers in the interior generally adjusted their own behavior to Indian patterns. French fur traders frequently married Indian women and adopted tribal ways; Jesuit missionaries interacted comfortably with the natives and converted them to Catholicism by the thousands without challenging most of their social customs. By the mid-eighteenth century, therefore, the French had better and closer relations with most of the Indians of the interior than did the English.

The Powerful Iroquois Confederacy   The most powerful native group, however, had remained aloof from both the British and the French. The Iroquois Confederacy—five Indian nations (Mohawk, Seneca, Cayuga, Onondaga, and Oneida) that had formed a defensive alliance in the fifteenth century—had been the most powerful native presence in the Ohio Valley and a large surrounding region since the 1640s. The Iroquois maintained their autonomy by avoiding too close a relationship with either the French or the English. They traded successfully with both groups and astutely played them against each other. As a result, they maintained precarious power in the Great Lakes region.

Anglo-French Conflicts

As long as England and France remained at peace and as long as the precarious balance in the North American interior survived, English and French colonists coexisted without serious difficulty. But after the Glorious Revolution in England, a series of Anglo-French wars erupted in Europe and continued intermittently for nearly eighty years, creating important repercussions in America.

King William's War (1689–1697) produced only a few, indecisive clashes between the English and the French in northern New England. Queen Anne's War, which began in 1701 and continued for nearly twelve years, generated more substantial conflicts. The Treaty of Utrecht, which brought the conflict to a close in 1713, transferred substantial territory from the French to the English in North America, including Acadia (Nova Scotia) and Newfoundland. Two decades later, disputes over British trading rights in the Spanish colonies produced a conflict between England and Spain that soon grew into a much larger European war. The English colonists in America were drawn into the struggle, which they *King George's War*   called King George's War; and between 1744 and 1748 they engaged in a series of conflicts with the French. New Englanders captured the French bastion at Louisbourg on Cape Breton Island, but the peace treaty that finally ended the conflict forced them to abandon it.

In the aftermath of King George's War, relations among the English, French, and Iroquois in North America quickly deteriorated. The Iroquois (in what appears to have been a major blunder) granted trading concessions in the interior to English merchants for the first time. The French, fearful (probably correctly) that the English were using the concessions as a first step toward expansion into French lands, began in 1749 to construct new fortresses in the Ohio Valley. The English began building up their military forces and building fortresses of their own. The balance of power that the Iroquois had carefully and successfully maintained for so long rapidly disintegrated.

For the next five years, tensions between the English and the French increased. In the summer of 1754 the governor of Virginia sent a militia force (under the command of an inexperienced young colonel, George Washington) into the Ohio Valley to challenge French expansion. Washington built a crude stock- *Fort Necessity* ade (Fort Necessity) not far from Fort Duquesne, the larger outpost the French were building on the site of what is now Pittsburgh. After the Virginians staged an unsuccessful attack on a French detachment, the French countered with an assault on Fort Necessity, trapping Washington and his soldiers inside. After a third of them died in the fighting, Washington surrendered. The clash marked the beginning of the French and Indian War.

The Great War for the Empire

The French and Indian War lasted nearly nine years, and it moved through three distinct phases. During the first of these phases, from the Fort Necessity debacle in 1754 until the expansion of the war to Europe in 1756, it was primarily a local, North American conflict. Virtually all the tribes except the Iroquois were now allied with the French; they launched a series of raids on western English settlements. The English colonists fought largely alone to defend themselves against those raids. The Iroquois feared antagonizing the French and remained largely passive in the conflict. By late 1755, many English settlers along the frontier had withdrawn to the east of the Allegheny Mountains to escape the hostilities.

The second phase of the struggle began in 1756, when the Seven Years' War began. The fighting now spread to the West Indies, India, and Europe itself. But the principal struggle remained the one in North America, where so far England had suffered nothing but frustration and defeat. Beginning in 1757, William Pitt, the En- *William Pitt Takes Command* glish secretary of state (and future prime minister), brought the war for the first time fully under British control. Pitt himself planned military strategy, appointed commanders, and issued orders to the colonists. British commanders began forcibly enlisting colonists (a practice known as "impressment"). Officers also seized supplies from local farmers and tradesmen and compelled colonists to offer shelter to British troops—all generally without compensation. The Americans resented these new impositions and firmly resisted them. By early 1758, the friction between the British authorities and the colonists was threatening to bring the war effort to a halt.

Beginning in 1758, therefore, Pitt initiated the third and final phase of the war by relaxing many of the policies that Americans had found obnoxious. He agreed to reimburse the colonists for all supplies requisitioned by the army. He returned control over recruitment to the colonial assemblies. And he dispatched large numbers of additional British troops to America. Finally, the tide of battle began to turn in England's favor. The French had always been outnumbered by the British colonists. After 1756, moreover, they suffered from a series of poor harvests. As a result, they were unable to sustain their early military successes. By mid-1758, British regulars and

ALL thofe who prefer the Glory of bearing Arms to any fervile mean Employ, and have Spirit to ftand forth in Defence of their King and Country, againft the treacherous Defigns of *France* and *Spain*, in the

Suffex Light Dragoons,

Commanded by

Lt. Col. John Baker Holroyd,

Let them repair to

Where they fhall be handfomely Cloathed, moft compleatly Accoutred, mounted on noble Hunters. and treated with Kindnefs and Generofity.

RECUITING FOR THE FRENCH AND INDIAN WAR The extravagant promises in this recruiting poster, distributed to colonists during the French and Indian War, suggest how difficult it sometimes was to persuade Americans to fight in the British army. *(Bettmann/Corbis)*

colonial militias were seizing one French stronghold after another. Two brilliant English generals, Jeffrey Amherst and James Wolfe, captured the fortress at Louisbourg in July 1758; a few months later Fort Duquesne fell without a fight. The next year, at the end of a siege of Quebec, the army of General Wolfe struggled up a hidden ravine under cover of darkness, surprised the larger forces of the Marquis de Montcalm, and defeated them in a battle in which both commanders were killed. The dramatic fall of Quebec on September 13, 1759, marked the beginning of the end of the American phase of the war. A year later, in September 1760, the French army formally surrendered to Amherst in Montreal. Peace finally came in 1763,

Peace of Paris

with the Peace of Paris, by which the French ceded to Great Britain some of their West Indian islands, most of their colonies in India and Canada, and all other French territory in North America east of the Mississippi. They ceded New Orleans and their claims west of the Mississippi to Spain, thus surrendering all title to the mainland of North America.

The French and Indian War greatly expanded England's territorial claims in the New World. At the same time, the cost of the war greatly enlarged Britain's debt and substantially increased British resentment of the Americans. English lead- *British Resentment* ers were contemptuous of the colonists for what they considered American military ineptitude during the war; they were angry that the colonists had made so few financial contributions to a struggle waged, they believed, largely for American benefit; they were particularly bitter that some colonial merchants had been selling food and other goods to the French in the West Indies throughout the conflict. All these factors combined to persuade many English leaders that a major reorganization of the empire giving London increased authority over the colonies would be necessary in the aftermath of the war.

The war had an equally profound but very different effect on the American colonists. It was an experience that forced them, for the first time, to act in concert against a common foe. And the friction of 1756–1757 over British requisition and impressment policies and the 1758 return of authority to the colonial assemblies seemed to many Americans to confirm the illegitimacy of English interference in local affairs.

For the Indians of the Ohio Valley, the British victory was disastrous. Those tribes that had allied themselves with the French had earned the enmity of the victorious English. The Iroquois Confederacy, which had allied itself with Britain, fared only slightly better. English officials saw the passivity of the Iroquois during the war as evidence of duplicity. In the aftermath of the peace settlement, the Iroquois alliance with the British quickly unraveled. The tribes *Disastrous Consequences* would continue to contest the English for control *for Native Americans* of the Ohio Valley for another fifty years; but increasingly divided and increasingly outnumbered, they would seldom again be in a position to deal with their European rivals on terms of military or political equality.

THE NEW IMPERIALISM

With the treaty of 1763, England found itself truly at peace for the first time in more than fifty years. As a result, the British government could now turn its attention to the organization of its empire. Saddled with enormous debts from the many years of fighting, England was desperately in need of new revenues from its empire. Responsible for vast new lands in the New World, the imperial government believed it must increase its administrative capacities in America. The result was a dramatic and, for England, disastrous redefinition of the colonial relationship.

Burdens of Empire

The experience of the French and Indian War should have suggested that increasing imperial control over the colonies would not be easy. Not only

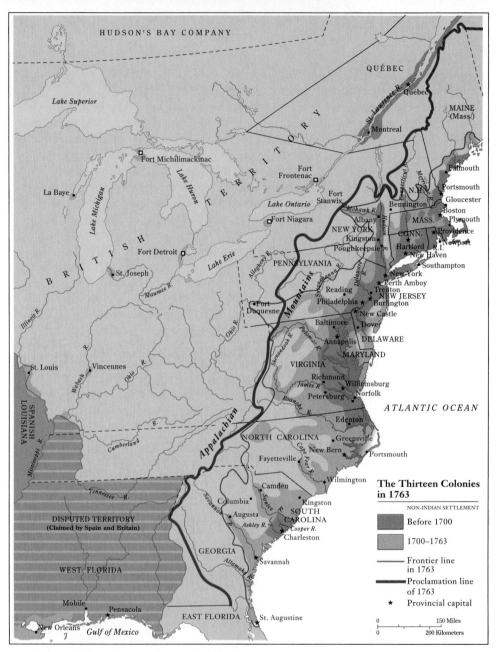

Map labels:

HUDSON'S BAY COMPANY

QUÉBEC

Lake Superior

Fort Michilimackinac

La Baye

Lake Michigan

Lake Huron

Fort Detroit

St. Joseph

Maumee R.

Illinois R.

B R I T I S H   T E R R I T O R Y

Fort Frontenac

Lake Ontario

Fort Niagara

Lake Erie

Allegheny R.

Fort Duquesne

Ohio R.

St. Lawrence R.

Québec

Montreal

Fort Stanwix

Mohawk R.

Albany

NEW YORK

Kingston

Poughkeepsie

Hudson R.

Merrimac R.

Connecticut R.

MAINE
(Mass.)

Falmouth

Portsmouth

N.H.

Bennington

Gloucester

Boston

MASS.

Plymouth

CONN.

Hartford

New Haven

R.I.

Providence

Newport

Southampton

St. Louis

Vincennes

Wabash R.

Ohio R.

Cumberland

Tennessee R.

Mississippi R.

SPANISH LOUISIANA

DISPUTED TERRITORY
(Claimed by Spain and Britain)

WEST FLORIDA

Mobile

Pensacola

New Orleans

Gulf of Mexico

EAST FLORIDA

St. Augustine

PENNSYLVANIA

Susquehanna R.

Mountains

Reading

Philadelphia

Baltimore

Annapolis

MARYLAND

Delaware R.

New York

Perth Amboy

Trenton

NEW JERSEY

Burlington

New Castle

Dover

DELAWARE

Shenandoah R.

Potomac R.

VIRGINIA

Richmond

James R.

Williamsburg

Petersburg

Norfolk

Roanoke R.

Edenton

ATLANTIC OCEAN

Appalachian Mountains

NORTH CAROLINA

Greensville

New Bern

Cape Fear R.

Fayetteville

Portsmouth

Wilmington

Camden

Columbia

Saluda R.

Augusta

Santee R.

Kingston

SOUTH CAROLINA

Ashley R.

Cooper R.

Charleston

Savannah R.

GEORGIA

Altamaha R.

Savannah

The Thirteen Colonies in 1763

NON-INDIAN SETTLEMENT

Before 1700

1700–1763

——— Frontier line in 1763

▬▬ Proclamation line of 1763

★ Provincial capital

0   150 Miles
0   200 Kilometers

THE THIRTEEN COLONIES IN 1763 This map is a close-up of the thirteen colonies at the end of the Seven Years' War. It shows the line of settlement established by the Proclamation of 1763 (the red line), as well as the extent of actual settlement in that year (the thin green line). Note that in the middle colonies (North Carolina, Virginia, Maryland, and southern Pennsylvania), settlement had already reached the red line—and in one small area of western Pennsylvania moved beyond it—by the time of the Proclamation of 1763. Note also the string of forts established beyond the Proclamation line. ◆ *How do the forts help to explain the efforts of the British to restrict settlement? And how does the extent of actual settlement help explain why it was so difficult for the British to enforce their restrictions?*

 For an interactive version of this map go to www.mhhe.com/unfinishednation4ch4maps

had the colonists proved so resistant to British control that Pitt had been forced to relax his policies in 1758, but the colonial assemblies had continued after that to chart a course different from, and often in conflict with, the desires of the government in London. Defiance of imperial trade regulations and other British demands continued. But the most immediate problem for London was its staggering war debt. Landlords and merchants in *Britain's Staggering War Debt* England were objecting strenuously to any further tax increases, and the colonial assemblies had repeatedly demonstrated their unwillingness to pay for the war effort. Many officials in England believed that only by taxing the Americans directly from London could the empire effectively meet its financial needs.

At this crucial moment in Anglo-American relations, the government of England was thrown into turmoil by the accession to the throne of George III, who assumed power in 1760. He *George the Third* brought two particularly unfortunate qualities to the office. First, he was determined to reassert the authority of the monarchy. He removed from power the relatively stable coalition of Whigs that had governed the empire for much of the century and replaced it with a new and very unstable coalition of his own. The new ministries that emerged as a result of this change each lasted in office an average of only about two years.

The king also had serious intellectual and psychological limitations. He suffered, apparently, from a rare mental disease that produced intermittent bouts of insanity. (Indeed, in the last years of his long reign he was, according to most accounts, unable to perform any official functions.) Yet even when George III was lucid and rational, which was most of the time in the 1760s and 1770s, he was painfully immature and insecure. The king's personality, therefore, contributed both to the instability and to the rigidity of the British government during these critical years.

More directly responsible for the problems that soon emerged with the colonies, however, was George Grenville, whom the king made prime minister in 1763. *George Grenville* Grenville shared the prevailing opinion within Britain that the colonists should be compelled to obey the laws and to pay a part of the cost of defending and administering the empire.

The British and the Tribes

With the defeat of the French, frontiersmen from the English colonies had begun immediately to move over the mountains and into tribal lands in the upper Ohio Valley. An alliance of Indian tribes, under the Ottawa chieftain Pontiac, struck back. Fearing that an escalation of the fighting might threaten western trade, the British government—in the Proclamation of 1763—forbade settlers to advance beyond the mountains that divided the Atlantic coast from the interior.

Many Indian groups supported the Proclamation as the best bargain available to them. The Cherokee, in particular, worked actively to hasten the drawing of the boundary, hoping finally to put an end to white movements into their lands. Relations between the western tribes and the British improved for a time, partly as a result of the work of the Indian superintendents the British appointed, who were sympathetic to tribal needs.

In the end, however, the Proclamation of 1763 was ineffective. White settlers continued to swarm across the boundary and continued to claim lands farther and farther into the Ohio Valley. The British authorities failed repeatedly to enforce limits to the expansion. In 1768, new agreements with the western tribes pushed the boundary further west in another effort to create a permanent western boundary for European settle-

Failure of the Proclamation of 1763

ment. But these treaties also failed to stop the white advance. Within a few years, the 1768 agreements were replaced with new ones, which pushed the line of settlement still farther west.

Battles over Trade and Taxes

The Grenville ministry tried to increase its authority in the colonies in other ways as well. Regular British troops were stationed permanently in America, and under the Mutiny Act of 1765 the colonists were required to help provision and maintain the army. Ships of the British navy patrolled American waters to search for smugglers. The customs service was reorganized and enlarged. Royal officials were required to take up their colonial posts in person instead of sending substitutes. Colonial manufacturing was restricted, so that it would not compete with rapidly expanding industries in Great Britain.

Sugar, Stamp, and Currency Acts

The Sugar Act of 1764 raised the duty on sugar while lowering the duty on molasses. It also established new vice-admiralty courts in America to try accused smugglers—thus cutting them off from sympathetic local juries. The Currency Act of 1764 required that the colonial assemblies stop issuing paper money. Most momentously, the Stamp Act of 1765 imposed a tax on every printed document in the colonies: newspapers, almanacs, pamphlets, deeds, wills, licenses. British officials were soon collecting more than ten times as much annual revenue in America as they had been before 1763.

It was difficult for the colonists to resist these unpopular new laws. For one thing, Americans continued to harbor as many grievances against one another as they did against the authorities in London. In 1763, for example, a band of Pennsylvania frontiersmen known

Paxton Boys

as the Paxton Boys descended on Philadelphia to demand tax relief and financial support for their defense against Indians.

Bloodshed was averted only by concessions from the colonial assembly. In 1771, a small-scale civil war broke out in North Carolina when the Regulators, farmers of the Carolina upcountry, organized and armed themselves to resist the high taxes that local sheriffs (appointed by the colonial governor) collected. An army of militiamen, most of them from the eastern counties, crushed the revolt.

But the Grenville program helped the colonists overcome their internal conflicts and recognize that the policies from London were a threat to all Americans. Northern merchants would suffer from restraints on their commerce, from the closing of the West to land speculation and fur trading, and from the restriction of opportunities for manufacturing. Southern planters, in debt to English merchants, would be unable to ease their debts by speculating in western land. Small farmers would suffer from the abolition of paper money, which had been the source of most of their loans. Workers in towns faced the prospect of narrowing opportunities, particularly because of the restraints on manufacturing and currency. Everyone stood to suffer from increased taxes.   *Persistent Colonial Grievances*

Most Americans soon found ways to live with the new British laws without terrible economic hardship. But their political grievances remained. Americans were accustomed to wide latitude in self-government. They believed that colonial assemblies had the sole right to control appropriations for the costs of government within the colonies. By attempting to raise extensive revenues directly from the public, the British government was challenging the basis of colonial political power.

STIRRINGS OF REVOLT

By the mid-1760s, a hardening of positions had begun in both England and America. The result was a progression of events that, more rapidly than imagined, destroyed the British Empire in America.

The Stamp Act Crisis

Grenville could not have devised a better method for antagonizing and unifying the colonies than   *Effects of the Stamp Act* the Stamp Act of 1765. Unlike the Sugar Act of a year earlier, which affected only a few New England merchants, the tax on printed documents fell on everyone. More alarming than the relatively light taxes, however, was the precedent they seemed to create. In the past, taxes and duties on colonial trade had always been designed to regulate commerce. The Stamp Act, however, was clearly an attempt by England to raise revenue in the colonies without the consent of the colonial assemblies.

"Virginia Resolves" Few colonists believed that they could do anything more than grumble until the Virginia House of Burgesses aroused Americans to action. Patrick Henry made a dramatic speech to the House in May 1765, concluding with a vague prediction that if present policies were not revised, George III, like earlier tyrants, might lose his head. There were shocked cries of "Treason!" But Henry introduced a set of resolutions (only some of which the assembly passed) declaring that Americans possessed the same rights as the English, especially the right to be taxed only by their own representatives; that Virginians should pay no taxes except those voted by the Virginia assembly; and that anyone advocating the right of Parliament to tax Virginians should be deemed an enemy of the colony. Henry's resolutions were printed and circulated as the "Virginia Resolves."

In Massachusetts at about the same time, James Otis persuaded his fellow members of the colonial assembly to call an intercolonial congress to take action against the new tax. And in October 1765, the Stamp Act Congress, as it was called, met in New York with delegates from nine colonies. In a petition to the British government, the congress denied that the colonies could rightfully be taxed except through their own provincial assemblies.

In the summer of 1765, meanwhile, mobs were rising up in several colonial cities against the Stamp Act. The largest of them was in Boston, where men belonging to the newly organized Sons of Liberty terrorized stamp agents and burned stamps. The mob also attacked such supposedly pro-British aristocrats as the lieutenant governor, Thomas Hutchinson (who had privately opposed passage of the Stamp Act but who felt obliged to support it once it became law). Hutchinson's elegant house was pillaged and virtually destroyed.

The crisis finally subsided largely because England backed down. The authorities in London were less affected by the political protests than by economic pressure. Many New Englanders had stopped buying English

Stamp Act Repealed goods to protest the Sugar Act of 1764, and the Stamp Act caused the boycott to spread. Under pressure from English merchants concerned about the loss of much of their colonial market, Parliament—under a new prime minister, the Marquis of Rockingham—repealed the unpopular law on March 18, 1766. To satisfy his strong and vociferous opponents, Rockingham also pushed through the Declaratory Act, which confirmed parliamentary authority over the colonies "in all cases whatsoever." In their rejoicing over the Stamp Act repeal, most Americans paid little attention to this ominous declaration of Parliament's power.

The Townshend Program

When the Rockingham government's policy of appeasement met substantial opposition in England, the king dismissed the Rockingham ministry and replaced it with a new government led by the aging but still powerful William Pitt, who was now Lord Chatham. Chatham had in the past been sympathetic toward American interests. Once in office, however, he was at times so incapacitated by mental illness that the actual leadership of his administration fell to the chancellor of the exchequer, Charles Townshend.

Townshend had to deal with colonial grievances left over from the Grenville ministry. With the Stamp Act repealed, the greatest American grievance involved the Mutiny (or *Mutiny Act* Quartering) Act of 1765, which required the colonists to provide shelter and supplies for British troops. The colonists objected not so much to quartering or supplying the troops but to being required by London to do so. The Massachusetts and New York assemblies went so far as to refuse to vote the mandated supplies to the troops.

Townshend responded in 1767 by disbanding the New York Assembly until the colonists agreed to obey the Mutiny Act. By singling out New York, he believed, he would avoid antagonizing all the colonies at once. He also imposed new taxes (known as the *Townshend Duties* Townshend Duties) on various goods imported to the colonies from England—lead, paint, paper, and tea. Townshend assumed that since these were taxes purely on "external" transactions (imports from overseas), as opposed to the internal transactions the Stamp Act had taxed, the colonists would not object. But all the colonies resented the suspension of the New York Assembly, believing it to be a threat to every colonial government. And all the colonies rejected Townshend's careful distinction between external and internal taxation.

Townshend also established a board of customs *Nonimportation Agreement* commissioners in America. The new commissioners virtually ended smuggling in Boston, where they established their headquarters, although smugglers continued to carry on a busy trade in other colonial seaports. The Boston merchants—angry that the new commission was diverting the lucrative smuggling trade elsewhere—helped organize a boycott of British goods that were subject to the Townshend Duties. Merchants in Philadelphia and New York joined them in a nonimportation agreement in 1768, and later some southern merchants and planters also agreed to cooperate. Throughout the colonies, American homespun and other domestic products became suddenly fashionable.

Late in 1767, Charles Townshend died. In March 1770, the new prime minister, Lord North, hoping to end the American boycott, repealed all the Townshend Duties except the tea tax.

The Boston Massacre

Before news of the repeal reached America, an event in Massachusetts electrified colonial opinion. The harassment of the new customs commissioners in Boston had grown so intense that the British government had placed four regiments of regular *Rebellious Boston*

"THE TORY'S DAY OF JUDGMENT" A mob of American Patriots hoists a Loyalist neighbor up a flagpole in this woodcut, which is obviously sympathetic to the victim. The crowd is shown as fat, rowdy, and drunken. Public humiliations of Tories were not infrequent during the war. More common, however, was seizure of their property. *(The Library of Congress)*

troops in the city. Many of the poorly paid British soldiers looked for jobs in their off-duty hours and thus competed with local workers. Clashes between the two groups were frequent.

On the night of March 5, 1770, a mob of dockworkers, "liberty boys," and others began pelting the sentries at the customs house with rocks and snowballs. Hastily, Captain Thomas Preston of the British regiment lined up several of his men in front of the building to protect it. There was some scuffling; one of the soldiers was knocked down; and in the midst of it all, apparently, several British soldiers fired into the crowd, killing five people.

This murky incident, almost certainly the result of panic and confusion, was quickly transformed by local resistance leaders into the "Boston Massacre." The event became the subject of such lurid (and inaccurate) accounts as the widely circulated pamphlet *Innocent Blood Crying to God from the Streets of Boston.* A famous engraving by Paul Revere portrayed the massacre as a calculated assault on a peaceful crowd. The British soldiers, tried before a jury of Bostonians, were found guilty only of manslaughter and given token punishment. But colonial pamphlets and newspapers convinced many Americans that the soldiers were guilty of official murder.

The leading figure in fomenting public outrage over the Boston Massacre was Samuel Adams. England, he argued, had become a morass of sin and corruption; only in America did public virtue survive. In 1772, he proposed the creation of a "committee of correspondence" in Boston to publicize the grievances against England. *"Committee of Correspondence"* Other colonies followed Massachusetts's lead, and a loose intercolonial network of political organizations was soon established that kept the spirit of dissent alive through the 1770s.

The Philosophy of Revolt

Although a superficial calm settled on the colonies after the Boston Massacre, the crises of the 1760s had helped arouse enduring ideological challenges to England and had produced powerful instruments for publicizing colonial grievances. Gradually a political outlook gained a following in America that would ultimately serve to justify revolt.

The ideas that would support the Revolution emerged from many sources. Some were drawn *Sources of Revolutionary Ideology* from religious (particularly Puritan) sources or from the political experiences of the colonies. Others came from abroad. Most important, perhaps, were the "radical" ideas of those in Great Britain who stood in opposition to their government. Some were Scots, who considered the English state tyrannical. Others were embittered "country Whigs," who felt excluded from power and considered the existing system corrupt and oppressive. Drawing from some of the great philosophical minds of earlier generations—most notably John Locke—these English dissidents framed a powerful argument against their government.

Central to this emerging ideology was a new concept of what government should be. Because humans were inherently corrupt and selfish, government was necessary to protect individuals from the evil in one another. But because any government was run by corruptible people, the people needed safeguards against its possible abuses of power. Most people in both England and America considered the English constitution the best system ever devised to meet these necessities. By distributing power among the three elements of society—the monarchy, the aristocracy, and the common people—the English political system ensured that no individual or group could exercise authority unchecked by another. Yet by the mid-seventeenth century, dissidents in both England and America had become convinced that the constitution was in danger. A single center of power—the king and his ministers—was becoming so powerful that it could not be effectively checked.

Such arguments found little sympathy in most of England. The English constitution was not a written document or a fixed set of unchangeable rules. It was a general sense of the "way things are done," and most people in England were willing to accept changes in it. Americans, by contrast, drew from their experience with colonial charters, in which the shape and powers of government were permanently inscribed on paper. They resisted the idea of a flexible, changing set of basic principles.

One basic principle, Americans believed, was the right of people to be taxed only with their own consent—a belief that gradually took shape in *"No Taxation without Representation"* the widely repeated slogan, "No taxation without representation." Whatever the nature of a tax, it could not be levied without the consent of the colonists themselves.

This clamor about "representation" made little sense to the English. According to English constitutional theory, members of Parliament did not represent individuals or particular geographical areas. Instead, each member represented the interests of the whole nation and indeed the whole empire. The many boroughs of England that had no representative in Parliament, the whole of Ireland, and the colonies thousands of miles away—all were thus represented in the Parliament at London, even *"Virtual" and "Actual" Representation* though they elected no representatives of their own. This was the theory of "virtual" representation. But Americans, drawing from their experiences with their town meetings and their colonial assemblies, believed in "actual" representation. Every community was entitled to its own representative, elected by the people of that community. Since the colonists had none of their own representatives in Parliament, it followed that they were not represented there. Americans believed that the colonial assemblies played the same role within the colonies that Parliament did within England. The empire, the Americans argued, was a sort of federation of commonwealths, each with its own legislative body, all tied together by loyalty to the king.

Such ideas illustrated a fundamental difference of opinion between England and America over the question of where ultimate power lay. By arguing that Parliament had the right to legislate for the empire as a whole, but that only the provincial assemblies could legislate for the individual colonies, Americans were in effect arguing for a division of sovereignty. Parliament would be sovereign in some *Sovereignty Debated* matters, the assemblies in others. To the British, such an argument was absurd. In any system of government there must be a single, ultimate authority. And since the empire was, in their view, a single, undivided unit, there could be only one authority within it: the English government of king and Parliament.

Sites of Resistance

The apparent calm in America in the first years of the 1770s hid a growing sense of frustration and resentment about the continued enforcement of the Navigation Acts. Popular anger was visible in occasional acts of rebellion. At one point, colonists seized a British revenue ship on the lower Delaware River. In 1772, angry residents of Rhode Island boarded the British schooner *Gaspée*, set it afire, and sank it.

Colonists kept the growing spirit of resistance alive in many ways, but most of all through writing and talking. Dissenting leaflets, pamphlets, and books circulated widely through the colonies. In towns and cities, men gathered in churches, schools, town squares, and above all in taverns to discuss politics. Indeed, the tavern culture of the colonies was crucial to the growth of Revolutionary sentiment. Taverns were appealing, of course, because they provided alcoholic drinks in a culture where the craving for alcohol was very high. But taverns were also among the few public spaces were people could meet and talk openly. The tavern was a mostly male institution, just as politics was considered a mostly male concern. The combination of male companionship and political conversation emerged naturally out of the tavern culture.

As the Revolutionary crisis deepened, taverns and pubs became the central meeting places for discussions of ideas about resistance. Taverns were *Political Importance of Colonial Taverns* also places were resistance pamphlets and leaflets could be distributed, and the settings for meetings for the planning of protests and demonstrations. Massachusetts had the most elaborately developed tavern culture, which was perhaps one reason why the spirit of resistance grew more quickly there than anywhere else.

The Tea Excitement

The Revolutionary fervor of the 1760s revived, finally, as a result of a new act of Parliament—one that involved the business of selling tea. In 1773, Britain's East India Company was sitting on large stocks of tea that it could not sell in England. It *The Tea Act* was on the verge of bankruptcy. In an effort to save it, the government passed the Tea Act of 1773, which gave the company the right to export its merchandise directly to the colonies without paying any of the regular taxes that were imposed on the colonial merchants, who had traditionally served as the middlemen in such transactions. With these privileges, the company could undersell American merchants and monopolize the colonial tea trade.

The act angered influential colonial merchants, who feared being replaced by a powerful monopoly. More important, however, the Tea Act revived American passions about the issue of taxation without representation. The law provided no new tax on tea. But the original Townshend duty on the commodity survived; and the East India Company was now exempt from paying it. Lord North had assumed that most colonists would welcome the new law because it would reduce the price of tea to consumers by removing the middlemen. But resistance leaders in America argued that the law, in effect, represented an unconstitutional tax on American merchants. The colonists responded by boycotting tea.

Unlike earlier protests, most of which had involved relatively small numbers of people, the tea boycott mobilized large segments of the population. It also helped link the colonies together in a common experience of mass popular protest. Particularly important to the movement were the *Daughters of Liberty* activities of colonial women, who led the boycott. The Daughters of Liberty—a women's patriotic organization that was committed to agitating against British policies— proclaimed, "rather than Freedom, we'll part with our Tea."

In the last weeks of 1773, with strong popular support, leaders in various colonies made plans to prevent the East India Company from landing its cargoes in colonial ports. In Philadelphia and New York, determined colonists kept the tea from leaving the company's ships, and in Charleston, they stored it away in a public warehouse. In Boston, local patriots staged a spectacular drama. On the evening of December 16, 1773, three companies of fifty men each, masquerading as Mohawk Indians, went aboard three ships, broke open the tea chests, and heaved them into *The Boston "Tea Party"* the harbor. As the electrifying news of the Boston "tea party" spread, colonists in other seaports staged similar acts of resistance.

Parliament retaliated in four acts of 1774: closing the port of Boston, drastically reducing the powers of self-government in Massachusetts, permitting royal officers in America to be tried in other colonies or in England when accused of crimes, and providing for the quartering of troops by the colonists. These Coercive Acts—or, as they were more widely known in America, "Intolerable Acts"—were followed by the Quebec Act, which extended the boundaries of Quebec to include the French communities between the Ohio and Mississippi Rivers. It also granted political rights to Roman Catholics and recognized the legality of the Roman Catholic Church within the enlarged province. Many colonists feared that a plot was afoot in London to subject Americans to the authority of the pope.

Consequences of the Coercive Acts The Coercive Acts, far from isolating Massachusetts, made it a martyr in the eyes of residents of other colonies and sparked new resistance up and down the coast. Colonial legislatures passed a series of resolves supporting Massachusetts. Women's groups mobilized to extend the boycotts of British goods and to create substitutes for the tea, textiles, and other commodities they were shunning. In Edenton, North Carolina, fifty-one women signed an agreement in October 1774 declaring their "sincere adherence" to the anti-British resolutions of their provincial assembly and proclaiming their duty to do "every thing as far as lies in our power" to support the "publick good."

COOPERATION AND WAR

Beginning in 1765, colonial leaders developed a variety of organizations for converting popular discontent into action—organizations that in time formed the basis for an independent government.

New Sources of Authority

The passage of authority from the royal government to the colonists themselves began on the local level. In colony after colony, local institutions responded to the resistance movement by simply seizing authority. At times, entirely new institutions emerged.

The most effective of these new groups were the committees of correspondence. Virginia established the first intercolonial committees of correspondence, which helped make possible continuous cooperation among the colonies. After the royal governor dissolved the assembly in 1774, a rump session met in the Raleigh Tavern at Williamsburg, declared that the Intolerable Acts menaced the liberties of every colony, and issued a call for a Continental Congress.

Delegates from all the colonies except Georgia were present when, in September 1774, the First Continental Congress *The First Continental Congress* convened in Philadelphia. They made five major decisions. First, they rejected a plan for a colonial union under British authority. Second, they endorsed a relatively moderate statement of grievances, which addressed the king as "Most Gracious Sovereign," but which also included a demand for the repeal of all oppressive legislation passed since 1763. Third, they approved a series of resolutions recommending that military preparations be made for defense against possible attack by the British troops in Boston. Fourth, they agreed to a series of boycotts that they hoped would stop all trade with Great Britain, and they formed a "Continental Association" to see that these agreements were enforced. Finally, the delegates agreed to meet again the following spring.

During the winter, the Parliament in London debated proposals for conciliating the colonists, and early in 1775 Lord North finally won approval for a series of measures known as the Conciliatory Propositions. Parliament proposed that the colonies would tax themselves at Parliament's demand. With this offer, Lord North hoped to separate the American moderates, whom he believed represented the views of the majority, from the extremist minority. But his offer was too little and too late. It did not reach America until after the first shots of war had been fired.

THE ALTERNATIVES OF WILLIAM BURG In the aftermath of the Boston Tea Party, and in response to the Coercive Acts Great Britain enacted to punish the colonists, the First Continental Congress called on Americans to boycott British goods until the Acts were repealed. In this drawing, a prosperous Virginia merchant is seen signing a pledge to honor the nonimportation agreement—unsurprisingly given the alternative, visible in the background of the picture: tar and feathers hanging from a post labeled "A Cure for the Refractory." *(Colonial Williamsburg Foundation)*

Lexington and Concord

For months, the farmers and townspeople of Massachusetts had been gathering arms and ammunition and training as "minutemen," preparing to fight on a minute's notice. The Continental Congress had approved preparations for a defensive war, and the citizen-soldiers waited only for an aggressive move by the British regulars in Boston.

"Minutemen"

In Boston, General Thomas Gage, commanding the British garrison, considered his army too small to do anything without reinforcements. He resisted the advice of

General Thomas Gage

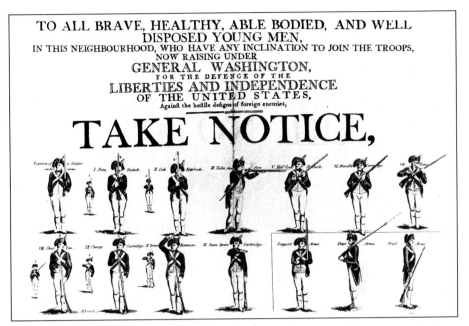

RECRUITING PATRIOTS This Revolutionary War recruiting poster tries to attract recruits by appealing to their patriotism (asking them to defend "the liberties and independence of the United States"), their vanity (by showing the "handsome clothing" and impressive bearing of soldiers), and their greed (by offering them "a bounty of twelve dollars" and "sixty dollars a year"). *(The Library of Congress)*

less cautious officers, who assured him that the Americans would back down quickly before any show of British force. When General Gage received orders to arrest the rebel leaders Sam Adams and John Hancock, known to be in the vicinity of Lexington, he still hesitated. But when he heard that the minutemen had stored a large supply of gunpowder in Concord (eighteen miles from Boston), he decided to act. On the night of April 18, 1775, he sent a detachment of about 1,000 men out toward Lexington. He hoped to surprise the colonials and seize the illegal supplies without bloodshed.

But patriots in Boston were watching the British movements closely, and during the night two horsemen, William Dawes and Paul Revere, rode out to warn the villages and farms. When the redcoats arrived in Lexington the next day, several dozen minutemen awaited them on the town common. Shots were fired and minutemen fell; eight were killed and ten wounded. Advancing to Concord, the British discovered that the Americans had hastily removed most of the powder supply. All along the road back to Boston, the British were harassed by the gunfire of farmers hiding behind trees, rocks, and stone walls. By the end of the day, the British had lost almost three times as many men as the Americans.

THE BATTLES OF LEXINGTON AND CONCORD, 1775 This map shows the fabled series of events that led to the first battle of the American Revolution. On the night of April 18, 1775, Paul Revere and William Dawes rode out from Boston to warn the outlying towns of the approach of British troops. Revere was captured just west of Lexington, but Dawes escaped and returned to Boston. The next morning, British forces moved out of Boston toward Lexington, where they met armed American minutemen on the Lexington common and exchanged fire. The British dispersed the Americans in Lexington. But they next moved on to Concord, where they encountered more armed minutemen, clashed again, and were driven back toward Boston. All along their line of march, they were harassed by riflemen. ◆ *What impact did the battles of Lexington and Concord (and the later battle of Bunker Hill, also shown on this map) have on colonial sentiment toward the British?*

The first shots—the "shots heard 'round the world," as Americans later called them—had been fired. But who had fired them first? According to one of the minutemen at Lexington, the British commander, Major Thomas Pitcairn, had shouted to the colonists on his arrival, "Disperse, ye rebels!" When they ignored him, he ordered his troops to fire. British officers and soldiers claimed that the minutemen had fired first. Whatever the truth, the rebels succeeded in circulating their account well ahead of the British version, adorning it with tales of British atrocities. The effect was to rally thousands of colonists to the rebel cause.

The War for Independence Begins

It was not immediately clear that the skirmishes at Lexington and Concord were the first battles of a war. But whether people recognized it at the time or not, the War for Independence had begun.

CONCLUSION

When the French and Indian War ended in 1763, it might have seemed reasonable to expect that relations between the English colonists in America and Great Britain itself would have been cemented more firmly than ever. But in fact the end of the French and Indian War altered the imperial relationship forever, in ways that ultimately drove Americans to rebel against English rule and begin a war for independence. To the British, the lesson of the war was that the colonies in America needed firmer control from London. The empire was now much bigger, and it needed better administration. The war had produced great debts, and the Americans—among the principal beneficiaries of the war—should help pay them. And so for more than a decade after the end of the fighting, the British tried one strategy after another to tighten control over and extract money from the colonies.

To the colonists, this effort to tighten imperial rule appeared both a betrayal of the sacrifices they had made in the war and a challenge to their long-developing assumptions about the rights of English people to rule themselves. Gradually, white Americans came to see in the British policies evidence of a conspiracy to establish tyranny in the New World. And so throughout the 1760s and 1770s, the colonists developed ever more overt and effective forms of resistance. By the time the first shots were fired in the American Revolution in 1775, Britain and America had come to view each other as two very different societies. Their differences, which came to seem irreconcilable, propelled them into a war that would change the course of both countries' history.

FOR FURTHER REFERENCE

Fred Anderson, *The Crucible of War: The Seven Years' War and the Fate of Empire in British North America, 1754–1766* (2000) is an excellent account of the critical years in which the British Empire transformed itself through its colonial wars in America. David Armitage, *The Ideological Origins of the British Empire* (2000) examines the ideas of those who promoted and sought to justify Britain's imperial ambitions. Francis Jennings, *The Ambiguous Iroquois Empire* (1984) examines the critical role of the Iroquois in the conflicts over empire in North America. Karen Ordahl Kupperman, *Indians and English: Facing Off in Early America* (2000) is an important study of the complex relationships between settlers and natives. Richard Bushman, *King and People in Colonial Massachusetts* (1987) traces the fracture between Massachusetts colonists and the imperial government. Gary Nash, *The Urban Crucible: The Northern Seaports and the Origins of the American Revolution* (1979) argues that increasing class stratification in northern cities contributed to the coming of the American Revolution. Robert R. Palmer, *The*

Age of Democratic Revolution: Vol. 1, The Challenge (1959) and J. G. A. Pocock, *The Machiavellian Moment* (1975) both place the American Revolution in the context of a transatlantic political culture. Jon Butler, *Becoming America: The Revolution Before 1776* (2000) examines social, religious, and intellectual changes in the American self-image. Bernard Bailyn, *The Ideological Origins of the American Revolution* (1967) was one of the first works by an American historian to emphasize the importance of English republican political thought for the revolutionary ideology of the American colonists.

For quizzes, Internet resources, references to additional books and films, and more, consult this book's Online Learning Center site at www.mhhe.com/unfinishednation4.

THE BRITISH SURRENDER This comtemporary drawing depicts the formal surrender of British troops at Yorktown on October 19, 1781. Columns of American troops and a large French fleet flank the surrender ceremony, suggesting part of the reason for the British defeat. General Cornwallis, the commander of British forces in Virginia, did not himself attend the surrender. He sent a deputy in his place. *(Hulton/Archive/Getty Images)*

TIME LINE

1775	1776	1777	1778	1781	
Second Continental Congress	Paine's *Common Sense*	Articles of Confederation adopted	French-America alliance	Articles of Confederation ratified	
Washington commands American forces	Declaration of Independence	British defeat at Saratoga		Cornwallis surrenders at Yorktown	
	Battle of Trenton				

THE AMERICAN REVOLUTION

The States United
The War for Independence
War and Society
The Creation of State Governments
The Search for a National Government

T wo struggles occurred simultaneously during the seven years of war that began in April 1775. One was the military conflict with Great Britain. The second was a political conflict within America.

The military conflict was, by the standards of later wars, a relatively modest one. By the standards of its own day, however, it was an unusually savage conflict, pitting not only army against army but the civilian population against a powerful external force. The shift of the war from a traditional, conventional struggle to a new kind of conflict—a revolutionary war for liberation—is what made it possible for the United States to defeat the more powerful British.

At the same time, Americans were wrestling with the great political questions that the conflict necessarily produced: first, whether to demand independence from Britain; then, how to structure the new nation they had proclaimed.

1783	1784	1786	1787
Treaty of Paris	Postwar depression begins	Shays's Rebellion	Northwest Ordinance

THE STATES UNITED

❧

Although some Americans had long been expecting a military conflict with Britain, the actual beginning of hostilities in 1775 found the colonies generally unprepared for war against the world's greatest armed power.

Defining American War Aims

Three weeks after the battles of Lexington and Concord, when the Second Continental Congress met in Philadelphia, delegates from every colony (except Georgia, which had not yet sent a representative) agreed to support the war. But they disagreed about its purpose. At one extreme was a group led by the Adams cousins (John and Samuel), Richard Henry Lee of Virginia, and others, who already favored independence; at the other extreme was a group led by such moderates as John Dickinson of Pennsylvania, who hoped for a quick reconciliation with Great Britain.

Divergent American War Aims

Most Americans believed at first that they were fighting not for independence but for a redress of grievances within the British Empire. During the first year of fighting, however, many of them began to change their minds. The costs of the war were so high that the original war aims began to seem too modest to justify them. Many colonists were enraged when the British began trying to recruit Indians, African slaves, and German mercenaries (the hated "Hessians") against them. When the British government blockaded the colonial ports and rejected all efforts at conciliation, many colonists concluded that independence was the only remaining option.

An impassioned pamphlet crystallized these feelings in January 1776: Thomas Paine's *Common Sense*. Paine, who had emigrated from England to America less than two years before, wanted to turn the anger of Americans away from particular parliamentary measures and toward what he considered the root of the problem—the English constitution itself. It was simple common sense, he wrote, for Americans to break completely with a political system that could inflict such brutality on its own people. *Common Sense* sold more than 100,000 copies in only a few months. It helped create a rapid growth of support for the idea of independence in the early months of 1776.

Common Sense

The Declaration of Independence

In the meantime, the Continental Congress in Philadelphia was moving toward a complete break with England. At the beginning of the summer, it appointed a committee to draft a formal declaration of independence; and on July 2, 1776, it adopted a

Independence Declared

resolution: "That these United Colonies are, and, of right, ought to be, free and independent states; that they are absolved from all allegiance to the British crown, and that all political connexion between them and the state of Great Britain is, and ought to be, totally dissolved." Two days later, on July 4, Congress approved the Declaration of Independence itself, which provided formal justifications for the actions the delegates had taken two days earlier.

The Declaration launched a period of ener-   *Articles of Confederation*
getic political innovation, as one colony after an-
other reconstituted itself as a "state." By 1781, most states had produced written constitutions for themselves. At the national level, however, the process was more uncertain. In November 1777, finally, Congress adopted a plan for union, the Articles of Confederation. The document confirmed the existing weak, decentralized system.

Thomas Jefferson, a thirty-three-year-old Virginian, wrote most of the Declaration, with help from Benjamin Franklin and John Adams. The Declaration expressed concepts that had been circulating throughout the colonies over the previous few months in the form of at least ninety other, local "declarations of independence"—declarations
drafted up and down the coast by town meetings,   *Thomas Jefferson*
artisan and militia organizations, county officials, grand juries, Sons of Liberty, and colonial assemblies. Jefferson borrowed heavily from these texts.

The final document was in two parts. In the first, the Declaration restated the familiar contract theory of John Locke: the theory that governments were formed to protect what Jefferson called "life, liberty and the pursuit of happiness." In the second part, it listed the alleged crimes of the king, who, with the backing of Parliament, had violated his contract with the colonists and thus had forfeited all claim to their loyalty.

Mobilizing for War

Financing the war was difficult, because Congress lacked the authority and the states generally lacked the inclination to impose taxes on the public. Congress had no authority to levy taxes on its own, and when it requisitioned money from the state governments, none contributed more than a small part of its expected share. Congress had little success borrowing from the public, since few Americans could afford to buy bonds. In the end, there was no alternative but to issue paper money. Printing presses turned out enormous amounts of "Continental currency," and the states printed currencies of their own. The result, predictably, was soaring inflation, and Congress soon found that the Continental currency was virtually worthless. Ultimately, it financed the war mostly by borrowing from other nations.

After a first surge of patriotism in 1775, volunteer soldiers were scarce. States had to pay bounties or use a draft to recruit the needed men.

THE AMERICAN REVOLUTION

The longstanding debate over the origins of the American Revolution has intended to reflect two broad schools of interpretation. One sees the Revolution largely as a political and intellectual event, the other as a social and economic phenomenon.

The Revolutionary generation itself portrayed the conflict as a struggle over ideals, and this interpretation prevailed through most of the nineteenth century. But in the early twentieth century, historians influenced by the reform currents of the progressive era began to identify social and economic forces that they believed had contributed to the rebellion. Carl Becker, for example, wrote in a 1909 study of New York that two questions had shaped the Revolution: "The first was the question of home rule; the second was the question . . . of who should rule at home." The colonists were not only fighting the British; they were also engaged in a kind of civil war, a contest between radicals and conservatives.

Other "progressive" historians elaborated on Becker's thesis. J. Franklin Jameson, writing in 1926, argued, "Many economic desires, many social aspirations, were set free by the political struggle, many aspects of society profoundly altered by the forces thus let loose." Arthur M. Schlesinger maintained in a 1917 book that colonial merchants, motivated by their own interest in escaping the restrictive policies of British mercantilism, aroused American resistance in the 1760s and 1770s.

Beginning in the 1950s, a new generation of scholars began to reemphasize the role of ideology and de-emphasize the role of economic interests. Robert E. Brown (in 1955) and Edmund S. Morgan (in 1956) both argued that most eighteenth-century Americans shared common political principles and that the social and economic conflicts the progressives had identified were not severe. The rhetoric of the Revolution, they suggested, was not propaganda but a real reflection of the ideas of the colonists. Bernard Bailyn, in *The Ideological Origins of the American Revolution* (1967), demonstrated the complex roots of the ideas behind the Revolution and argued that this carefully constructed political stance was not a disguise for economic interests but a genuine ideology, rooted in deeply held convictions about rights and power. The Revolution, he exclaimed, "was above all an ideological, constitutional, political struggle and not primarily a controversy between social groups undertaken to force changes in the organization of the society or the economy."

By the late 1960s, a new generation of historians—many influenced by the New Left—were reviving economic interpretations of the Revolution by exploring the social and economic tensions that they claimed shaped the Revolutionary struggle. Historians cited the actions of mobs in colonial cities, the economic pressures on colonial merchants, the growing climate of economic distress in colonial cities, and other changes in the character of American culture and society as critical prerequisites for the growth of the Revolutionary movement. Gary Nash, attempting to reconcile the emphasis on economic interests with the role of ideology, argued that the two things were not incompatible. "Everyone has economic interests," he claimed, "and everyone . . . has an ideology." Exploring the relationship between the two, he argues, is critical to historians' ability to understand either. Also, as Linda Kerber and others have argued, the newer social interpretations have raised increasing interest in the experience of workers, slaves, women, Native Americans, and other groups previously considered marginal to public life as part of the explanation of the Revolutionary struggle.

Finally, Gordon Wood, in *The Radicalism of the American Revolution* (1992) revived an idea once popular and recently unfashionable: that the Revolution was a genuinely radical event that led to the breakdown of such longstanding characteristics of society as deference, patriarchy, and traditional gender relations. Class conflict may not have caused the Revolution, he argues, but the Revolution had a profound, even radical, effect on society nevertheless.

(text continued from page 119)

REVOLUTIONARY SOLDIERS Jean Baptist de Verger, a French officer serving in America during the Revolution, kept an illustrated journal of his experiences. Here he portrays four American soldiers carrying different kinds of arms: a black infantryman with a light rifle, a musketman, a rifleman, and an artilleryman. *(Anne S.K. Brown Military Collection, Brown University Library)*

At first, the militiamen remained under the control of their respective states. But Congress recognized the need for a centralized military command, and it created a Continental army with a single commander in chief: George Washington. Washington had considerable military experience and was an early advocate of independence; he was admired, respected, and trusted by nearly all Patriots. He took command of the new army in June 1775. With the *Washington Takes Charge* aid of foreign military experts such as the Marquis de Lafayette from

121

France and the Baron von Steuben from Prussia, he built a force that prevailed against the mightiest power in the world. Even more important, perhaps, Washington's steadiness, courage, and dedication to his cause provided the army—and the people—with a symbol of stability around which they could rally.

THE WAR FOR INDEPENDENCE

The British seemed to have overwhelming advantages as the War for Independence began: the greatest navy and the best-equipped army in the world, the resources of an empire, a coherent structure of command. Yet the United States had advantages, too. Americans were fighting on their own ground. They were more committed to the conflict than were the British. And, beginning in 1777, they received substantial aid from abroad.

But the American victory was also a result of a series of blunders and miscalculations by the British in the early stages of the fighting, when England could (and probably should) have won. And it was, finally, a result of the transformation of the war—through three distinct phases—into a new kind of conflict that the British military, for all its strength, was unable to win.

The First Phase: New England

For the first year of the conflict—from the spring of 1775 to the spring of 1776—many English authorities thought that British forces were not fighting a real, but simply quelling pockets of rebellion in the contentious area around Boston. After the redcoats withdrew from Lexington *Bunker Hill* and Concord in April, American forces besieged them in Boston. In the Battle of Bunker Hill (actually fought on Breed's Hill) on June 17, 1775, the Patriots suffered severe casualties and withdrew. But they inflicted even greater losses on the enemy. The siege continued. Early in 1776, finally, the British decided that Boston was a poor place from which to fight. It was in the center of the most anti-British part of America and tactically difficult to defend because it was easily isolated and surrounded. And so, on March 17, 1776, the redcoats evacuated Boston for Halifax, Nova Scotia, with hundreds of Loyalist refugees.

In the meantime, a band of southern Patriots, at Moore's Creek Bridge in North Carolina, crushed an uprising of Loyalists (Americans still loyal to England and its king) on February 27, *Invasion of Canada* 1776. And to the north, the Americans began an invasion of Canada. Generals Benedict Arnold and Richard Montgomery unsuccessfully threatened Quebec in late 1775 and early 1776 in a battle in which Montgomery was killed and Arnold wounded.

THE REVOLUTION IN THE NORTH, 1775–1776 After initial battles in and around Boston, the British forces left Massachusetts and (after a brief stay in Halifax, Canada) moved south to New York. ◆ *Why would the British have considered New York a better base than Boston?* In the meantime, American forces moved north in an effort to capture British strongholds in Montreal and Quebec, with little success.

For an interactive version of this map go to www. mhhe.com/unfinishednation4ch5maps

By the spring of 1776, it had become clear to the British that the conflict was not just a local phenomenon. The American campaigns in Canada, the agitation in the South, and the growing evidence of colonial unity all suggested that England must prepare to fight a much larger conflict.

The Second Phase: The Mid-Atlantic Region

During the next phase of the war, which lasted from 1776 until early 1778, the British were in a good position to win. Indeed, had it not been for a series of mistakes and misfortunes, they probably would have crushed the rebellion.

The British regrouped quickly after their retreat from Boston. During the summer of 1776, hundreds of British ships and 32,000 British soldiers arrived in New York, under the command of General William Howe. He offered Congress a choice between surrender with royal pardon and a battle against apparently overwhelming odds. To op-pose Howe's great force, Washington could muster only about 19,000 soldiers; he had no navy at all. Even so, the Americans

General William Howe

rejected Howe's offer. The British then pushed the Patriot forces off Long Island, forced them to abandon Manhattan, and then drove them in slow retreat over the plains of New Jersey, across the Delaware River, and into Pennsylvania.

The British settled down for the winter in northern and central New Jersey, with an outpost of Hessians at Trenton, on the Delaware River. But Washington did not sit still. On Christmas night 1776, he daringly re-

Trenton and Princeton

crossed the icy Delaware River, surprised and scattered the Hessians, and occupied Trenton. Then he advanced to Princeton and drove a force of redcoats from their base in the college there. But Washington was unable to hold either Princeton or Trenton and finally took refuge for the rest of the winter in the hills around Morristown. The campaign of 1776 came to an end with the Americans having triumphed in two minor battles and with their main army still intact.

For the campaigns of 1777 the British devised a strategy to divide the United States in two. Howe would move from New York up the Hudson to Albany, while another force would come down from Canada to meet him. John Burgoyne, commander of the northern force, began a two-pronged attack to the south along both the Mohawk and the upper Hudson approaches to Albany. But having set the plan in motion, Howe abandoned his part of it. Instead of moving north to meet Burgoyne, he went south and captured Philadelphia, hoping that his seizure of the rebel capital would bring the war to a speedy conclusion. Philadelphia fell with little resistance—and the Continental Congress moved into exile in York, Pennsylvania. After launching an unsuccessful Patriot attack against the British on October 4 at Germantown (just outside Philadelphia), Washington went into winter quarters at Valley Forge.

Howe's move to Philadelphia left Burgoyne to carry out the campaign in the north alone. He sent Colonel Barry St. Leger up the St. Lawrence

Patriot Victory at Saratoga

River toward Lake Ontario. Burgoyne himself advanced directly down the upper Hudson Valley and easily seized Fort Ticonderoga. But Burgoyne soon experienced two staggering defeats. In one of them—at Oriskany, New York, on August 6—Patriots held off a force of Indians and Tories commanded by St. Leger. That allowed Benedict Arnold to close off the Mohawk Valley to St. Leger's advance. In the other battle—at Bennington, Vermont, on August 16—New England militiamen mauled a detachment that Burgoyne had sent to seek supplies. Short of materials, with all help cut off, Burgoyne fought several costly engagements and then withdrew to Saratoga, where General Horatio Gates surrounded him. On October 17, 1777, Burgoyne surrendered.

The campaign in upstate New York was not just a British defeat. It was a setback for the ambitious efforts of several Iroquois leaders. Although the Iroquois Confederacy had declared its neutrality in the Revolutionary War in 1776, some of its members allied themselves with the

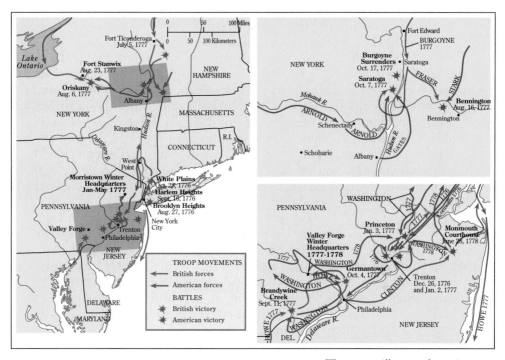

THE REVOLUTION IN THE MIDDLE COLONIES, 1776–1778 These maps illustrate the major campaigns of the Revolution in the middle colonies—New York, New Jersey, and Pennsylvania—between 1776 and 1778. The large map on the left shows the two prongs of the British strategy: first, a movement of British forces south from Canada into the Hudson Valley; and second, a movement of other British forces, under General William Howe, out from New York. The strategy was designed to trap the American army in between the two British movements. ◆ *What movements of Howe helped thwart the plan?* The two smaller maps on the right show a more detailed picture of some of the major battles. The upper one reveals the surprising American victory at Saratoga. The lower one shows a series of inconclusive battles between New York and Philadelphia in 1777 and 1778.

 For an interactive version of this map go to www.mhhe.com/unfinishednation4ch5maps

British, among them a Mohawk brother and sister, Joseph and Mary Brant. This ill-fated alliance further divided the already weakened Iroquois Confederacy, because only three of the Iroquois nations (the Mohawk, the Seneca, and the Cayuga) followed the Brants in support of the British. A year after the defeat at Oriskany, Iroquois forces joined British troops in a series of raids on white settlements in upstate New York. Patriot forces under the command of General John Sullivan harshly retaliated, wreaking such destruction on Indian settlements that large groups of Iroquois fled north into Canada to seek refuge. Many never returned.

Securing Aid from Abroad

The leaders of the American effort knew that victory would not be likely without aid from abroad. And their most promising allies, they realized, were the French, who believed they had much to gain from seeing Britain lose a crucial part of its empire. At first, France provided the United States with badly needed supplies but remained reluctant to grant formal diplomatic recognition to the new nation. After the Declaration of Independence, Benjamin Franklin himself went to France to lobby for aid and diplomatic recognition. Franklin quickly became a hero to the French, but France's foreign minister, the Count de Vergennes, wanted evidence that the Americans had a real chance of winning. The British defeat at Saratoga, he believed, offered that evidence.

French Diplomatic Recognition When the news from Saratoga arrived in London and Paris in early December 1777, a shaken Lord North made a new peace offer: complete home rule within the empire for Americans if they would quit the war. Vergennes feared the Americans might accept the offer and thus destroy France's opportunity to weaken Britain. Encouraged by Franklin, he agreed on February 6, 1778, to give formal recognition to the United States and to provide it with greatly expanded military assistance.

France's decision made the war an international conflict, which over the years pitted France, Spain, and the Netherlands against Great Britain. That helped reduce the resources available for the English effort in America. France was America's most important ally. It furnished the new nation with most of its money and munitions, and it provided a navy and an expeditionary force that were vital to the final, successful phase of the Revolutionary conflict.

The Final Phase: The South

Britain's Southern Strategy The American victory at Saratoga and the intervention of the French transformed the war. Instead of mounting a full-scale military struggle against the American army, the British now tried to enlist the support of those elements of the American population who were still loyal to the crown. And since Loyalist sentiment was thought to be strongest in the South, and since the English also hoped slaves would rally to their cause, the main focus of the British effort shifted there.

The new strategy was a dismal failure. British forces spent three years (from 1778 to 1781) moving through the South. But they had badly overestimated the extent of Loyalist sentiment. And they had underestimated the logistical problems they would face. Patriot forces could move at will throughout the region, blending in with the civilian population and leaving the British unable to distinguish friend from foe. The British, by contrast, suffered all the disadvantages of an army in hostile territory.

It was this phase of the conflict that made the war "revolutionary"—not only because it introduced a new kind of warfare, but because it had the

"Revolutionary" Conflict in the South

effect of mobilizing and politicizing large groups of the population. With the war expanding into previously isolated communities, with many civilians forced to involve themselves whether they liked it or not, the political climate of the United States grew more heated than ever. And support for independence, far from being crushed, greatly increased.

In the North, the fighting settled into a stalemate. Sir Henry Clinton replaced the unsuccessful William Howe in May 1778 and moved what had been Howe's army from Philadelphia back to New York. There the British troops stayed for more than a year. In the meantime, George Rogers Clark led a Patriot expedition over the Appalachian Mountains and captured settlements in the Illinois country from the British and their Indian allies. On the whole, however, there was relatively little military activity in the North after 1778. There was, however, considerable intrigue. In the fall of 1780, American forces were shocked by the exposure of treason on the part of General Benedict Arnold. Convinced that the American cause was hopeless, Arnold conspired with British agents to betray the Patriot stronghold at West Point on the Hudson River. When the scheme was exposed and foiled, Arnold fled to the safety of the British camp, where he spent the rest of the war.

The British did have some significant military successes during this period. On December 29, 1778, they captured Savannah, Georgia. On May 12, 1780, they took the port of Charleston, South Carolina, and advanced into the interior. But although the British were able to win conventional battles, they were constantly harassed by Patriot guerrillas led by such resourceful fighters as Thomas Sumter, Andrew Pickens, and Francis Marion, the "Swamp Fox." Penetrating to Camden, South Carolina, Lord Cornwallis (whom Clinton named British commander in the South) met and crushed a Patriot force under Horatio Gates on August 16, 1780. Congress recalled Gates, and Washington replaced him with Nathanael Greene, one of the ablest of all the American generals of the time.

Even before Greene arrived in the South, the tide of battle had begun to turn against Cornwallis. At King's Mountain (near the North Carolina–South Carolina border) on October 7, 1780, a band of Patriot riflemen from the backwoods killed, wounded, or captured every man in a force of 1,100 New York and South Carolina Tories, upon whom Cornwallis had depended as auxiliaries. Once Greene arrived, he confused and exasperated Cornwallis by dividing the American forces into fast-moving contingents while avoiding open, conventional battles. One of the contingents inflicted what Cornwallis admitted was "a very unexpected and severe blow" at Cowpens on January 17, 1781. Finally, after receiving reinforcements, Greene combined all his forces and maneuvered to meet the British at Guilford Court House, North Carolina. After a hard-fought battle there on March 15, 1781,

Guilford Court House

THE REVOLUTION IN THE SOUTH, 1778–1781 The final phase of the American Revolution occurred largely in the South, which the British thought would be a more receptive region for their troops. ◆ *Why did they believe that?* This map reveals the many, scattered military efforts of the British and the Americans in those years, none of them conclusive. It also shows the final chapter of the Revolution around the Chesapeake Bay and the James River. ◆ *What errors led the British to their surrender at Yorktown?*

 For an interactive version of this map go to www.mhhe.com/unfinishednation4ch5maps

Greene was driven from the field; but Cornwallis had lost so many men that he decided to abandon the Carolina campaign. Instead, he moved north, hoping to carry on raids in the interior of Virginia. But Clinton, fearful that the southern army might be destroyed, ordered him to take up a defensive position at Yorktown.

At that point, American and French forces de- *Yorktown*
scended on Yorktown. Washington and the Count
de Rochambeau marched a French-American army from New York to join
the Marquis de Lafayette in Virginia, while Admiral de Grasse took a
French fleet with additional troops up Chesapeake Bay to the York River.
These joint operations caught Cornwallis between land and sea. After a
few shows of resistance, he surrendered on October 17, 1781. Two days
later, he surrendered his whole army of more than 7,000.

Winning the Peace

Cornwallis's defeat provoked outcries in England against continuing the
war. Lord North resigned as prime minister; Lord Shelburne emerged
from the political wreckage to succeed him; and British emissaries appeared in France to talk informally with the American diplomats there, of
whom the three principals were Benjamin Franklin, John Adams, and
John Jay.

The Americans were under instructions to co- *Franklin's Skillful Diplomacy*
operate with France in their negotiations with En-
gland. But Vergennes, the French foreign minister, insisted that France
could not agree to any settlement of the war with England until its ally
Spain had achieved its principal war aim: winning back Gibraltar from the
British. There was no real prospect of that happening soon, and the
Americans began to fear that the alliance with France might keep them at
war indefinitely. As a result, the Americans began proceeding on their
own, without informing Vergennes, and soon drew up a preliminary treaty
with Great Britain, which was signed on November 30, 1782. Benjamin
Franklin, in the meantime, skillfully pacified Vergennes and avoided an
immediate rift in the French-American alliance.

The final treaty was signed September 3, 1783. The agreement was,
on the whole, remarkably favorable to the United States. It provided a
clear-cut recognition of independence and a large, though ambiguous,
cession of territory to the new nation—from the southern boundary of
Canada to the northern boundary of Florida and from the Atlantic to the
Mississippi. The American people had good reason to celebrate as the last
of the British occupation forces embarked from New York.

WAR AND SOCIETY

Historians have long debated whether the American Revolution was a social as well as a political revolution. But whatever the intention of those
who launched and fought the war, the conflict had important effects on
the nature of American society.

The American Revolution was a result of specific tensions and conflicts between imperial Britain and its colonies along the Atlantic coast of North America. But it was also both a part, and a cause, of what historians have come to call an "age of revolutions," which spread through much of the world in the last decades of the eighteenth century and the first decades of the nineteenth.

The modern idea of revolution—the overturning of old systems and regimes and the creation of new ones—was a product to a large degree of the ideas of the Enlightenment. Among those ideas was the notion of popular sovereignty, articulated by, among others, the English philosopher John Locke. It introduced the idea that political authority did not derive from the divine right of kings or the inherited authority of aristocracies but from the consent of the governed. A related Enlightenment idea was the concept of individual freedom, which challenged the traditional belief that governments had the right to prescribe the way people act, speak, and even think. Champions of individual freedom in the eighteenth century—among them the French philosopher Voltaire—advocated religious toleration (an end to discrimination against those who did not embrace a nation's dominant or official religion) and freedom of thought and expression. The Enlightenment also helped spread the idea of political and legal equality for all people—the end of special privileges for aristocrats and elites, the right of all citizens to participate in the formation of policies and laws. Jean Jacques Rousseau, a Swiss-French theorist, helped define these new ideas of equality. Together, these Enlightenment ideas formed the basis for challenges to existing social orders in many parts of the western world, and eventually beyond it.

The American Revolution was the first and in many ways most influential of the Enlightenment-derived uprisings against established orders. It served as an inspiration to people in other lands who were trying to find a way to oppose unpopular regimes. In 1789, a little over a decade after the beginning of the American Revolution, revolution began in France—at first through a revolt by the national legislature against the king, and then through a series of increasingly radical challenges to established authority. The monarchy was abolished (and the king and queen publicly executed in 1793), the authority of the Catholic church was challenged and greatly weakened, and at the peak of revolutionary chaos during the Jacobin period (1793–1794), over 40,000 suspected enemies of the revolution were executed and hundreds of thousands of others imprisoned. The radical phase of the revolution came to an end in 1799, when Napoleon Bonaparte, a young general, seized power and began to build a new French empire. But France's *ancien regime* of king and aristocracy never wholly revived.

Together, the French and American revolutions helped inspire uprisings in many other parts of the Atlantic world. In 1791, a major slave uprising began in Haiti and soon attracted over 100,000 rebels. The slave army defeated both the white settlers of the island and the French colonial armies sent to quell their rebellion. Under the leadership of Toussaint L'ouverture, they began to agitate for independence and on January 1, 1804, a few months after Toussaint's death, Haiti established its independence.

The ideas of these revolutions spread next into Spanish and Portuguese colonies in the Americas, particularly among the so-called *creoles*, people of European ancestry born in America. In the late eighteenth century, they began to resist the continuing authority of colonial officials sent from Spain and Portugal and to demand a greater say in governing their own lands. When Napoleon's French armies invaded Spain and Portugal in 1807, they weakened the ability of the European regimes to sustain authority over their American colonies. In the years that followed, revolutions swept through much of Latin America and established independent nations throughout the New World. Mexico became an independent nation in 1821, and provinces of Central America that had once been part of Mexico (Guatemala, El Salvador, Honduras, Nicaragua, and Costa Rica) established their independence three years later. Simon Bolivar, modeling his efforts on those of George Washington, led a great revolutionary movement that won independence for Brazil in 1822 and also helped lead revolutionary campaigns in Venezuela, Ecuador, and Peru—all of which won their independence in the 1820s. At about the same time, Greek patriots—drawing from the examples of other revolutionary nations—launched a movement to win their independence from the Ottoman empire, which finally succeeded in 1830.

The age of revolutions left many new, independent nations in its wake. It did not, however, succeed in establishing the ideals of popular sovereignty, individual freedom, and political equality in all the nations it affected. Slavery survived in the United States and in many areas of Latin America. New forms of aristocracy and even monarchy emerged in France, Mexico, Brazil, and elsewhere. Women—many of whom had hoped the revolutionary age would win new rights for them—made few legal or political gains in this era. But the ideals that the revolutionary era introduced to the western world continued to shape the histories of nations throughout the nineteenth century and beyond.

(text continued from page 129)

Loyalists and Minorities

Estimates differ as to how many Americans remained loyal to England during the Revolution, but it is clear that there were many—at least a fifth (and some estimate as much as a third) of the white population. Some were officeholders in the imperial government. Others were merchants whose trade was closely tied to the imperial system. Still others were people who lived in relative isolation and had simply retained their traditional loyalties. And there were those who, expecting the British to win the war, were simply currying favor with the anticipated victors.

Many of these Loyalists were hounded by Patriots in their communities and harassed by legislative and judicial actions. Up to 100,000 fled the country. Those who could afford to moved to England. Others moved to Canada, establishing the first English-speaking community in the province of Quebec. Some returned to America after the war and gradually managed to reenter the life of the nation.

The Loyalists' Plight

The war weakened other groups as well. The Anglican Church, many of whose members were Loyalists, lost its status as the official religion of Virginia and Maryland. By the time the fighting ended, many Anglican parishes could no longer even afford clergymen. Also weakened were the Quakers, whose pacifism won them widespread unpopularity when they refused to support the war.

Other Protestant denominations, however, grew stronger. Presbyterian, Congregational, and Baptist churches successfully tied themselves to the Patriot cause. And most American Catholics also supported the Patriots and won increased popularity as a result. Shortly after the peace treaty was signed, the Vatican provided the United States with its own hierarchy and, in 1789, its first bishop.

The War and Slavery

For the largest of America's minorities—the African-American population—the war had limited, but nevertheless profound, significance. For some, it meant freedom, because the British enabled many escaped slaves to leave the country as a way of disrupting the American war effort. In South Carolina, for example, nearly a third of all slaves defected during the war.

For other African Americans, the Revolution meant an increased exposure to the concept, although seldom to the reality, of liberty. Most black Americans could not read, but few could avoid exposure to the new and exciting ideas circulating through the towns and cities, and even at times on the plantations, where they lived. In several communities, slaves exposed to revolutionary ideas engaged in open resistance to white control. In Charleston, South Carolina, for example, Thomas Jeremiah, a free black, was executed after white authorities learned of elaborate plans for a slave uprising.

Exposure to Liberty

Slaveowners opposed British efforts to emancipate their slaves, but they also feared that the revolution itself would foment slave rebellions. Although the ideals of the Revolution produced occasional challenges to slavery by white southerners (including laws in Virginia and Maryland permitting slaveowners to free—"manumit"—their slaves if they wished), white support for slavery survived. Southern churches, some of which flirted briefly with voicing objections to the system, quickly rejected the antislavery ideas of the North and worked instead to reinforce ideas about white superiority.

In much of the North, by contrast, the combination of revolutionary sentiment and evangelical Christian fervor helped spread antislavery sentiments widely through society. The first target was the slave trade, which was prohibited by several states (Pennsylvania, Rhode Island, and Connecticut among them). The next target was state laws forbidding owners from freeing their slaves. Quakers and other antislavery activists succeeded in pressuring legislatures to allow legal manumission in all the northern states before the end of the Revolution, and even in Kentucky and Tennessee. The final step was emancipation of slaves. Pennsylvania was the first state to declare slavery illegal within its borders—again in part because of the influence of the fiercely antislavery Quakers—in 1780. One by one, all the northern states except New York and New Jersey abolished slavery before the end of the Revolution. New York followed in 1799 and New Jersey in 1804.

The Revolution exposed the continuing tension between the nation's commitment to liberty and its commitment to slavery. To people in our time, and *Tension between Liberty and Slavery* even to some people in revolutionary times, it seems obvious that liberty and slavery are incompatible with one another. But to many white Americans in the eighteenth century, especially in the South, that did not seem obvious. Many white southerners believed, in fact, that enslaving Africans—whom they considered inferior and unfit for citizenship—was the best way to ensure liberty for white people. They feared that without slaves, it would be necessary to recruit a servile white work force in the South, and that the resulting inequalities would jeopardize the survival of liberty. One of the ironies of the American Revolution was that white Americans were fighting both to secure freedom for themselves and to preserve slavery for others.

Native Americans and the Revolution

Indians viewed the American Revolution with considerable uncertainty. Most tribes ultimately chose to stay out of the war. But many Indians feared that the Revolution would replace a ruling group in which they had developed at least some measure of trust (the British, who had tried to limit the expansion of white settlement into tribal land) with one they considered generally hostile to them (the Patriots, who had spearheaded the expansion). Thus some Indians chose to join the English cause. Still others took advantage of the conflict to launch attacks of their own.

In the western Carolinas and Virginia, Cherokee led by Chief Dragging Canoe launched a series of attacks on outlying white settlements in the summer of 1776. Patriot militias responded in great force, ravaging Cherokee lands and forcing the chief and many of his followers to flee west across the Tennessee River. Those Cherokee who remained behind agreed to a new treaty by which they gave up still more land. Some Iroquois, despite the setbacks at Oriskany, continued to wage war against Americans in the West and caused widespread destruction in agricultural areas of New York and Pennsylvania. The retaliating American armies inflicted heavy losses on the Indians, but the attacks continued.

In the end, the Revolution generally weakened the position of Native Americans in several ways. *Native Americans Weakened* The Patriot victory increased white demand for western lands. Many whites resented the assistance such nations as the Mohawk had given the British and insisted on treating them as conquered people. Others drew from the Revolution a paternalistic view of the tribes. Thomas Jefferson, for example, came to view the Indians as "noble savages," uncivilized in their present state but redeemable if they were willing to adapt to the norms of white society.

Women's Rights and Women's Roles

New Roles for Women The long Revolutionary War had a profound effect on American women. The departure of so many men to fight in the Patriot armies left women in charge of farms and businesses. Often, women handled these tasks with great success. But in other cases, inexperience, inflation, the unavailability of male labor, or the threat of enemy troops led to failure. Some women whose husbands or fathers were called away to war did not have even a farm or shop to fall back on. Cities and towns had significant populations of impoverished women, who on occasion led protests against price increases or rioted and looted for food. On several other occasions, women launched attacks on occupying British troops, whom they were required to house and feed at considerable expense.

Not all women stayed behind when the men went off to war. Many joined their male relatives in the camps of the Patriot armies. These female "camp followers" increased army morale and provided a ready source of volunteers to do cooking, laundry, nursing, and other necessary tasks. In the rough environment of the camps, traditional gender distinctions proved difficult to maintain. Considerable numbers of women became involved, at least intermittently, in combat. A few women even disguised themselves as men so as to be able to fight.

The emphasis on liberty and the "rights of man" led some women to begin to question their own position in society. "By the way," Abigail Adams wrote to her husband John Adams in 1776, "in the new code of laws which I suppose it will be necessary for you to make, I desire you would remember the ladies and be more generous and favorable to them than your ancestors." Adams was calling simply for new protections against abusive and tyrannical men. A few women, however, went further. Judith Sargent Murray, one of the leading essayists of the late eighteenth century, wrote in 1779 that women's minds were as good as those of men and that girls as well as boys therefore deserved access to education.

But little changed as a result. Under English common law, an unmarried woman had some legal rights, but a married woman had virtually no rights at all. Everything she owned and everything *Patriarchy Strengthened* she earned belonged to her husband. Because she had no property rights, she could not engage in any legal transactions on her own. She could not vote. She had no legal authority over her children. Nor could she initiate a divorce; that, too, was a right reserved almost exclusively to men. After the Revolution, it did become easier for women to obtain divorces in a few states. Otherwise, there were few advances and some setbacks—including the loss of the right of widows to regain their dowries from their husbands' estates. The Revolution, in other words, did not really challenge, but actually confirmed and strengthened, the patriarchal legal system.

But the Revolution did encourage people of both sexes to reevaluate the contribution of women to the family and society. As the new republic searched for a cultural identity for itself, it attributed a higher value to the role of women as mothers. The new nation was, many Americans liked to believe, producing a new kind of citizen, steeped in the principles of liberty. Mothers had a particularly important task, therefore, in instructing their children in the virtues that the republican citizenry now was expected to possess.

The War Economy

The Revolution also produced important changes in the structure of the American economy. After more than a century of dependence on the British imperial system, American commerce suddenly found itself on its own. English ships no longer protected American vessels, but tried to drive them from the seas. British imperial ports *New Patterns of Trade* were closed to American trade. But this disruption in traditional economic patterns served in the long run to strengthen the American economy. Enterprising merchants in New England and elsewhere began to develop new commerce in the Caribbean and South America. By the mid-1780s, American merchants were also developing an important trade with Asia.

When English imports to America were cut off, there were desperate efforts throughout the states to stimulate domestic manufacturing of certain necessities. No great industrial expansion resulted, but there was a modest increase in production and an even greater increase in expectations. There was also a substantial increase in trade among the American states.

THE CREATION OF STATE GOVERNMENTS

At the same time that Americans were struggling to win their independence on the battlefield, they were also struggling to create new institutions of government to replace the British system they had repudiated.

The Assumptions of Republicanism

If Americans agreed on nothing else when they began to build new governments for themselves, they agreed that those governments would be republican. To them, that meant a political system in which all power came from the people, rather than from some supreme authority (such as a king). The success of such a government depended on the nature of its citizenry. If the population consisted of sturdy, independent property owners imbued with civic virtue, then the republic could survive. If it consisted of a few powerful aristocrats and a great mass of dependent workers, then it would be in danger. From the beginning, therefore, the ideal of the small freeholder (the independent landowner) was basic to American political ideology.

Another crucial part of that ideology was the concept of equality. The Declaration of Independence had given voice to that idea in its most ringing phrase: "All men are created equal." The innate *Rhetoric of Equality* talents and energies of individuals, not their positions at birth, would determine their roles in society. Some people would inevitably be wealthier and more powerful than others. But all people would have to earn their success. There would be no equality of condition, but there would be equality of opportunity.

In reality, of course, the United States was *Reality of Inequality* never a nation in which all citizens were independent property holders. From the beginning, there was a sizable dependent labor force, white and black. American women remained both politically and economically subordinate. Native Americans were systematically exploited and displaced. Nor was there ever full equality of opportunity. American society was more open and more fluid than that of most European nations, but the condition of a person's birth was almost always a crucial determinant of success.

Nevertheless, in embracing the assumptions of republicanism, Americans were adopting a powerful, even revolutionary, ideology, and their experiment in statecraft became a model for many other countries.

The First State Constitutions

Two states—Connecticut and Rhode Island—already had governments that were republican in all but name. They simply deleted references to England and the king from their charters and adopted them as constitutions. The other eleven states, however, produced new documents.

The first and perhaps most basic decision was that the constitutions were to be written down, because Americans believed the vagueness of England's unwritten constitution had produced corruption. The second decision was that the power of the executive, which *Curbing Executive Power* Americans believed had grown too great in England, must be limited. Pennsylvania eliminated the executive altogether. Most other states inserted provisions limiting the power of governors over appointments, reducing or eliminating their right to veto bills, and preventing them from dismissing the legislature. Most important, every state forbade the governor or any other executive officer from holding a seat in the legislature, thus ensuring that, unlike in England, the two branches of government would remain wholly separate.

But most new constitutions did not embrace direct popular rule. In Georgia and Pennsylvania, the legislature consisted of one popularly elected house. But in every other state, there was an upper and a lower chamber, and in most cases, the upper chamber was designed to represent the "higher orders" of society. There were property requirements for voters—some modest, some substantial—in all states.

Revising State Governments

By the late 1770s, Americans were growing concerned about the apparent instability of their new state governments. Many believed the problem was one of too much democracy. As a result, most of the states began to revise their constitutions to limit popular power. Massachusetts was the first to act on the new concerns. By waiting until 1780 to ratify its first constitution, Massachusetts allowed these changing ideas to shape its government.

Two changes in particular differentiated the Massachusetts and later constitutions from the earlier ones. The first was a change in the process of constitution writing itself. Most of the first documents had been written by state legislatures and thus could easily be amended (or violated) by them. Massachusetts created the constitutional *Massachusetts's Constitution* convention: a special assembly of the people that would meet only for the purpose of writing the constitution.

The second change was a significant strengthening of the executive. The 1780 Massachusetts constitution made the governor one of the strongest in any state. He was to be elected directly by the people; he was to have a fixed salary (in other words, he would not be dependent on the good will of the legislature each year for his wages); he would have significant appointment powers and a veto over legislation. Other states followed. Those with weak or nonexistent upper houses strengthened or created them. Most increased the powers of the governor. Pennsylvania, which had no executive at all at first, now produced a strong one. By the late 1780s, almost every state had either revised its constitution or drawn up an entirely new one in an effort to produce stability in government.

Toleration and Slavery

Most Americans continued to believe that religion should play some role in government, but they did not wish to give special privileges to any particular denomination. The privileges that churches had once enjoyed were now largely stripped away. In 1786, Virginia enacted the *Statute of Religious Liberty* Statute of Religious Liberty, written by Thomas Jefferson, which called for the complete separation of church and state.

More difficult to resolve was the question of slavery. In areas where slavery was already weak—in New England, where there had never been many slaves, and in Pennsylvania, where the Quakers opposed slavery—it was abolished. Even in the South, there were some pressures to amend or even eliminate the institution; every state but South Carolina and Georgia prohibited further importation of slaves from abroad, and South Carolina banned the slave trade during the war. Virginia passed a law encouraging manumission (the freeing of slaves).

Reasons for Slavery's Persistence   Nevertheless, slavery survived in all the southern and border states. There were several reasons: racist assumptions among whites about the inferiority of blacks; the enormous economic investments many white southerners had in their slaves; and the inability of even such men as Washington and Jefferson, who had moral misgivings about slavery, to envision any alternative to it. If slavery were abolished, what would happen to the black people in America? Few whites believed blacks could be integrated into American society as equals.

THE SEARCH FOR A NATIONAL GOVERNMENT

Americans were much quicker to agree on state institutions than they were on the structure of their national government. At first, most believed that the central government should remain relatively weak and that each state would be virtually a sovereign nation. It was in response to such ideas that the Articles of Confederation emerged.

The Confederation

The Articles of Confederation, which the Continental Congress had adopted in 1777, provided for a national government much like the one already in place. Congress remained the central—indeed the only—institution of national authority. Its powers expanded to give it authority to conduct wars and foreign relations and to appropriate, borrow, and issue money. But it did not have power to regulate trade, draft troops, or levy taxes directly on the people. For troops and taxes it had to make formal requests to the state legislatures, which could—and often did—refuse them. There was no separate executive; the "president of the United States" was merely the presiding officer at the sessions of Congress. Each state had a single vote in Congress, and at least nine of the states had to approve any important measure. All thirteen state legislatures had to approve any amendment of the Articles.

Limited Power of the National Government

During the process of ratifying the Articles of Confederation (which required approval by all thirteen states), broad disagreements over the plan became evident. The small states had insisted on equal state representation, but the larger states wanted representation to be based on population. The smaller states prevailed on that issue. More important, the states claiming western lands wished to keep them, but the rest of the states demanded that all such territory be turned over to the national government. New York and Virginia had to give up their western claims before the Articles were finally approved. They went into effect in 1781.

The Confederation, which existed from 1781 until 1789, was not a complete failure, but it was far from a success. It lacked adequate powers to deal with interstate issues or to enforce its will on the states.

Diplomatic Failures

In the peace treaty of 1783, the British had promised to evacuate American territory; but British forces continued to occupy a string of frontier *Postwar Problems with Britain* posts along the Great Lakes within the United States. Nor did the British honor their agreement to make restitution to slaveowners whose slaves the British army had confiscated. There were also disputes over the northeastern boundary of the new nation and over the border between the United States and Florida. Most American trade remained within the British Empire, and Americans wanted full access to British markets; England, however, placed sharp restrictions on that access.

In 1784, Congress sent John Adams as minister to London to resolve these differences, but Adams made no headway with the English, who were never sure whether he represented a single nation or thirteen different ones. Throughout the 1780s, the British government refused even to send a diplomatic minister to the American capital.

Confederation diplomats agreed to a treaty with Spain in 1786. The Spanish accepted the American interpretation of the Florida boundary. In return the Americans rec- *Regional Differences over Diplomatic Policy* ognized the Spanish possessions in North America and accepted limits on the right of United States vessels to navigate the Mississippi for twenty years. Southern states, incensed at the idea of giving up their access to the Mississippi, blocked ratification.

The Confederation and the Northwest

The Confederation's most important accomplishment was its resolution of some of the controversies involving the western lands. The Confederation had to find a way to include these areas in the political structure of the new nation. The landed states began to yield their claims to the national government in 1781, and by 1784 the Confederation controlled enough land to permit Congress to begin making policy for the national domain.

The Ordinance of 1784, based on a proposal *Ordinances of 1784 and 1785* by Thomas Jefferson, divided the western territory into ten self-governing districts, each of which could petition Congress for statehood when its population equaled the number of free inhabitants of the smallest existing state. Then, in the Ordinance of 1785, Congress created a system for surveying and selling the western lands. The territory

LAND SURVEY: ORDINANCE OF 1785 In the Ordinance of 1785, the Congress established a new system for surveying and selling western lands. These maps illustrate the way in which the lands were divided in an area of Ohio. Note the highly geometrical grid pattern that the Ordinance imposed on these lands. Each of the squares in the larger map on the left was subdivided into 36 sections, as illustrated in the map on the right. ◆ *Why was this grid pattern so appealing to the planners of the western lands?*

north of the Ohio River was to be surveyed and marked off into neat rectangular townships, each divided into thirty-six identical sections. In every township four sections were to be set aside for the United States; the revenue from the sale of one of the other sections was to support creation of a public school.

The precise rectangular pattern imposed on the Northwest Territory—the grid—became a model for all subsequent land policies of the federal government and for many other planning decisions in states and localities. The grid also became characteristic of the layout of many American cities. It had many advantages. It eliminated the uncertainty about property borders that earlier, more informal land systems had produced. It sped the development of the western lands by making land ownership simple and understandable. But it also encouraged a dispersed form of settlement—with each farm family separated from its neighbors—that made the formation of community more difficult. Whatever its consequences, however, the 1785 Ordinance made a dramatic and indelible mark on the American landscape.

The original ordinances proved highly favorable to land speculators and less so to ordinary settlers, many of whom could not afford the price of the land. Congress compounded the problem by selling much of the best land to the Ohio and Scioto Companies before making it available to anyone else. Criticism of these policies led to the passage in 1787 of another law governing western settlement—legislation that became known as the "Northwest Ordinance." The 1787 Ordinance *The Northwest Ordinance* abandoned the ten districts established in 1784 and created a single Northwest Territory out of the lands north of the Ohio; the territory could be divided subsequently into between three and five territories. It also specified a population of 60,000 as a minimum for statehood, guaranteed freedom of religion and the right to trial by jury to residents of the Northwest, and prohibited slavery throughout the territory.

The western lands south of the Ohio River received less attention from Congress. The region that became Kentucky and Tennessee developed rapidly in the late 1770s as slaveowning territories, and in the 1780s began setting up governments and asking for statehood. The Confederation Congress was never able to resolve the conflicting claims in that region successfully.

Indians and the Western Lands

On paper at least, the western land policies of the Confederation created a system that brought order and stability to the process of white settlement in the Northwest. But in reality, order and stability came slowly and at great cost, because much of the land was claimed by the Indians. Congress tried to resolve that problem in 1784, 1785, and 1786 by persuading Iroquois, Choctaw, Chickasaw, and Cherokee leaders to sign treaties ceding lands to the United States. But those agreements proved ineffective. In 1786, the leadership of the Iroquois Confederacy repudiated the treaty it had signed two years earlier. Other tribes had never really accepted the treaties affecting them and continued to resist white movement into their lands.

Violence between whites and Indians on the Northwest frontier reached a crescendo in the early 1790s. In 1790 and again in 1791, the Miami, led by the famed warrior Little Turtle, defeated United States forces in two major battles; in the second of those battles, on November 4, 1791, 630 white Americans died in fighting at the Wabash River. Efforts to negotiate a settlement failed because of the Miami's insistence that no treaty was possible unless it forbade white settlement west of the Ohio River. Negotiations did not resume until after General Anthony Wayne led 4,000 soldiers into the Ohio Valley in 1794 and de- *Battle of Fallen Timbers* feated the Indians in the Battle of Fallen Timbers.

A year later, the Miami signed the Treaty of Greenville, ceding substantial new lands to the United States in exchange for a formal acknowledgment of their claim to the territory they had managed to retain. This was the first time the new federal government recognized the sovereignty of Indian nations; in doing so, it was affirming that Indian lands could be ceded only by the tribes themselves. That hard-won assurance, however, proved a frail protection against the pressure of white expansion.

Debts, Taxes, and Daniel Shays

The postwar depression, which lasted from 1784 to 1787, increased the perennial American problem of an inadequate money supply, a problem that weighed particularly heavily on debtors. The Confederation itself had an enormous outstanding debt that it had accumulated during the Revolu-

Fiscal Crisis

tionary War, and few means with which to pay it. It had sold war bonds that were now due to be repaid; it owed money to its soldiers; it had substantial debts abroad. But it had no power to tax. It could only make requisitions of the states, and it received only about one-sixth of the money it requisitioned. The fragile new nation was faced with the grim prospect of defaulting on its obligations.

This alarming possibility brought to the fore a group of leaders who would play a crucial role in the shaping of the republic for several decades. Robert Morris, the head of the Confederation's treasury; Alexander Hamilton, his young protégé; James Madison of Virginia; and others

"Continental Impost" Rejected

called for a "continental impost"—a 5 percent duty on imported goods to be levied by Congress and used to fund the debt. Many Americans, however, feared that the impost plan would concentrate too much financial power in the hands of Morris and his allies in Philadelphia. Congress failed to approve the impost in 1781 and again in 1783.

The states had war debts, too, and they generally relied on increased taxation to pay them. But poor farmers, already burdened by debt, considered such policies unfair. They demanded that the state governments issue paper currency to increase the money supply and make it easier for them to meet their obligations. Resentment was especially high among farmers in New England, who felt that the states were squeezing them to enrich already wealthy bondholders in Boston and other towns.

Throughout the late 1780s, therefore, mobs of distressed farmers rioted periodically in various parts of New England. Dissidents in the Connecticut Valley and the Berkshire Hills of Massachusetts rallied behind Daniel Shays, a former captain in the Continental army. Shays issued a set of demands that included paper money, tax relief, a moratorium on debts, and the abolition of imprisonment for debt. During the summer of 1786, the Shaysites concentrated on preventing the collection of debts, private or public, and used force to keep courts from sitting and sheriffs from selling confiscated property. In Boston, members of the legislature denounced Shays and his men as rebels and traitors. When winter came, the rebels ad-

DANIEL SHAYS AND JOB SHATTUCK Shays and Shattuck were the principal leaders of the 1786 uprising of poor Massachusetts farmers demanding relief from their indebtedness. Shattuck led an insurrection in the east, which collapsed when he was captured on November 30. Shays organized the rebellion in the west, which continued until it was finally dispersed by state militia in late February 1787. The following year, state authorities pardoned Shays; even before that, the legislature responded to the rebellion by providing some relief to the impoverished farmers. This drawing is part of a hostile account of the rebellion published in 1787 in a Boston almanac. *(The National Portrait Gallery, Smithsonian Institution/Art Resource, NY)*

vanced on Springfield, hoping to seize weapons from the arsenal there. An army of state militiamen set out from Boston to confront them. In January 1787, this army met Shays's band and dispersed his ragged troops.

As a military enterprise, Shays's Rebellion was a failure, although it produced some concessions to the aggrieved farmers. Shays and his lieutenants, at *Consequences of Shays's Rebellion* first sentenced to death, were later pardoned, and Massachusetts offered the protesters some tax relief and a postponement of debt payments. The rebellion had more important consequences for the future of the United States, for it added urgency to the movement to produce a new, national constitution.

CONCLUSION

Between a small, inconclusive battle on a village green in New England in 1775 and a momentous surrender at Yorktown in 1781, the American people fought a great and terrible war against the mightiest military nation in the world. Few would have predicted in 1775 that the makeshift armies of the colonies could withstand the armies and navies of the British empire. But a combination of luck, brilliance, determination, costly errors by the British, and timely aid from abroad allowed the patriots, as they began to call themselves, to make full use of the advantages of fighting on their home soil and to frustrate British designs.

The war was not just a historic military event. It was also a great political one, for it propelled the colonies to unite, to organize, and to declare their independence. Having done so, they fought with even greater determination, defending now not just a set of principles, but an actual, fledgling nation. By the end of the war, they had created new governments at both the state and national level and had begun experimenting with new political forms.

The war was also important for its effects on American society—for the way it shook the existing social order; for the way it caused women to question their place in society; and for the way it spread notions of liberty and freedom throughout a society that in the past had mostly been rigidly hierarchical. Even African-American slaves absorbed some of the ideas of the Revolution, although it would be many years before they would be in any position to make very much use of them.

Victory in the American Revolution solved many of the problems of the new nation, but it also produced others. What should the United States do about its relations with the Indians and with its neighbors to the north and south? What should it do about the distribution of western lands? What should it do about slavery? How should it balance its commitment to liberty with its need for order? These questions bedeviled the new national government in its first years of existence.

FOR FURTHER REFERENCE

Robert Middlekauf, *The Glorious Cause: The American Revolution, 1763–1789* (1985), a volume in the Oxford History of the United States, is a thorough, general history of the Revolution. Edward Countryman, *The American Revolution* (1985) is a useful, briefer overview. Gordon Wood, *The Radicalism of the American Revolution* (1992) emphasizes the profound political change that the Revolution entailed. Charles Royster, *A Revolutionary People at War: The Continental Army and American Character* (1979) suggests the importance of military service for American men. Mary Beth Norton, *Liberty's Daughters: The Revolutionary Experience of American Women, 1750–1800* (1980) demonstrates that the Revolution had a significant impact on the lives of American women as well. Eric Foner, *Tom Paine and Revolutionary America* (1976) connects the leading pamphleteer of the Revolution with urban radicalism in Philadelphia. Pauline Maier, *American Scripture* (1997) is a penetrating study of the making of the Declaration of Independence, and of its impact on subsequent generations of Americans. Colin Calloway, *The American Revolution in Indian Country* (1995) is a new and important study on an often neglected aspect of the war. Sylvia R. Frey, *Water from the Rock: Black Resistance in a Revolutionary Age* (1991) argues that the American Revolution was a major turning point in the history of slavery in the American South. Alfred E.

Young, *The Shoemaker and the Tea Party: Memory and the American Revolution* (1999) examines the role of memory in the making of the revolution. *Liberty* (1997) is a compelling six-hour PBS documentary film history of the American Revolution, from its early origins in the 1760s.

For quizzes, Internet resources, references to additional books and films, and more, consult this book's Online Learning Center site at www.mhhe.com/unfinishednation4.

THE AMERICAN STAR Frederick Kemmelmeyer painted this tribute to George Washington sometime in the 1790s. It was one of many efforts by artists and others to create an iconography for the new republic. *(The Metropolitan Museum of Art, Gift of Edgar William and Bernice Chrysler Barbisch, 1962. (62.256.7) Photograph © 2002 The Metropolitan Museum of Art)*

TIME LINE

1786	1787	1787-1788	1789	1791	1792	
Annapolis Conference	Constitutional Convention; Constitution adopted	States ratify Constitution	Washington becomes first president	First Bank of U.S. chartered	Washington reelected	
			Bill of Rights			
			French Revolution			
			Judiciary Act			

THE CONSTITUTION AND THE NEW REPUBLIC

Framing a New Government
Adoption and Adaptation
Federalists and Republicans
Establishing National Sovereignty
The Downfall of the Federalists

By the late 1780s, many Americans had grown dissatisfied with the Confederation. It was, they believed, ridden with factions, unable to deal effectively with economic problems, and frighteningly powerless in the face of Shays's Rebellion. A decade earlier, Americans had deliberately avoided creating a strong national government. Now they reconsidered. In 1787, the nation produced a new constitution and a much more powerful government with three independent branches. Yet the adoption of the Constitution did not complete the creation of the republic. For, while most Americans came to agree that the Constitution was a nearly perfect document, they often disagreed on what that document meant.

FRAMING A NEW GOVERNMENT

ৎৄৡ

The Confederation Congress had become so unpopular and ineffectual by the mid-1780s that it began to lead an almost waiflike existence. In 1783, its members timidly withdrew from Philadelphia to escape army veterans demanding their back pay. They took refuge for a while in Princeton, New Jersey, then moved on to Annapolis, and in 1785 settled in New York. Delegates

1793	1794	1795	1796	1797	1798–1799	1800
Genet Affair	Whiskey Rebellion	Pinckney's Treaty	John Adams elected president	XYZ Affair	Quasi war with France	Jefferson elected president
	Jay's Treaty			Alien and Sedition Acts	Virginia and Kentucky Resolutions	

were often scarce. Only with great difficulty could Congress produce a quorum to ratify the treaty with Great Britain ending the Revolutionary War.

Advocates of Reform

In the 1780s, some of the wealthiest and most powerful groups in the population began to clamor for a stronger national government. By 1786, such demands had grown so intense that even defenders of the existing system reluctantly agreed that the government needed strengthening at its weakest point—its lack of power to tax.

The most resourceful advocate of a stronger national government was
Alexander Hamilton   Alexander Hamilton, the illegitimate son of a Scottish merchant in the West Indies, who had become a successful New York lawyer. Hamilton now called for a national convention to overhaul the Articles of Confederation. He found an important ally in James Madison of Virginia, who persuaded the Virginia legislature to convene an interstate conference on commercial questions. Only five states sent delegates to the meeting, which took place at Annapolis, Maryland, in 1786; but the conference approved a proposal drafted by Hamilton for a convention of special delegates from all the states to meet in Philadelphia the next year.

At first there seemed little reason to believe the Philadelphia convention would attract any more delegates than had the Annapolis meeting. Then, early in 1787, the news of Shays's Rebellion spread throughout the nation, alarming many previously apathetic leaders. Most important of all, the rebellion aroused George Washington, who promptly made plans to travel to Philadelphia for the Constitutional Convention. His support gave the meeting wide credibility.

A Divided Convention

Fifty-five men, representing all the states except Rhode Island, attended one or more sessions of the convention that sat in the Philadelphia State
The "Founding Fathers"   House from May to September 1787. These "Founding Fathers," as they became known much later, were relatively young men; the average age was forty-four. They were well educated by the standards of their time. Most were wealthy property owners, and many feared what one of them called the "turbulence and follies" of democracy. Yet all retained the Revolutionary suspicion of concentrated power.

The convention unanimously chose Washington to preside over its sessions and then closed its business to the public and the press. It then ruled that each state delegation would have a single vote and that major decisions would require not unanimity, as they did in Congress, but a simple majority. Almost all the delegates agreed that the United States needed a stronger central government. But there agreement ended.

GEORGE WASHINGTON AT MOUNT VERNON Washington was in his first term as president
in 1790 when an anonymous folk artist painted this view of his home at Mount Vernon, Virginia.
Washington appears in uniform, along with members of his family, on the lawn. After he retired
from office in 1797, Washington returned happily to his plantation and spent the two years
before his death in 1799 "amusing myself in agricultural and rural pursuits." He also played host
to an endless stream of visitors from throughout the country and Europe. *(Gift of Edgar William and
Bernice Chrysler Garbisch, © 1998 Board of Trustees, National Gallery of Art, Washington)*

Virginia, the largest state in population, sent a   *Madison's Virginia Plan*
well-prepared delegation to Philadelphia led by
James Madison (thirty-six years old), who had devised in some detail a
plan for a new "national" government. The Virginia Plan shaped the
agenda of the convention from the moment Edmund Randolph of Virginia opened the debate by proposing that "a national government ought
to be established, consisting of a supreme Legislative, Executive, and Judiciary." Even that brief description outlined a government very different
from the Confederation. But the delegates were so committed to fundamental reform that they approved the resolution after only brief debate.

There was less agreement about the details of Madison's Virginia
Plan. It called for a national legislature of two houses. In the lower house,
states would be represented in proportion to their population. Members
of the upper house were to be elected by the lower house under no rigid
system of representation; thus some of the smaller states might at times
have no members at all in the upper house.

The proposal aroused immediate opposition among delegates from
the smaller states. William Paterson of New Jersey   *The New Jersey Plan*
offered an alternative (the New Jersey Plan) that
would have retained the essence of the existing system with its one-house
legislature in which all states had equal representation, but which would
have given Congress expanded powers to tax and to regulate commerce.

The convention rejected Paterson's proposal, but supporters of the Virginia Plan now realized they would have to make concessions to the small states. They agreed to permit members of the upper house to be elected by the state legislatures.

Many questions remained unresolved. Among the most important was the question of slavery. There was no serious discussion of abolishing slavery during the convention. But other issues were debated heatedly. Would slaves be counted as part of the population in determining representation in Congress? Or would they be considered property, not entitled to representation? Delegates from the states with large slave populations wanted to have it both ways. They argued that slaves should be considered persons in determining representation but as property if the new government levied taxes on the states on the basis of population. Representatives from states where slavery had disappeared or was expected soon to disappear argued that slaves should be included in calculating taxation but not representation.

Compromise

The delegates argued for weeks. By the end of June, as both temperature and tempers rose to uncomfortable heights, the convention seemed in danger of collapsing. But the delegates refused to give up. Finally, on July 2, the convention created a "grand committee," chaired by Franklin and with one delegate from each state, which produced a proposal that became

The "Great Compromise"

the basis of the "Great Compromise." It called for a two-house legislature. In the lower house, the states would be represented on the basis of population; each slave would be counted as three-fifths of a free person in determining the basis for both representation and direct taxation. In the upper house, the states would be represented equally with two members apiece. On July 16, 1787, the convention voted to accept the compromise.

In the next few weeks, the convention agreed to another important compromise. To placate southern delegates, who feared the new government would interfere with slavery, the convention agreed to bar the new government from stopping the slave trade for twenty years.

Unresolved Issues

Some significant issues remained unaddressed. Most important was the absence of a list of individual rights, which would restrain the powers of the national government. Madison opposed the idea, arguing that specifying rights that were reserved to the people would, in effect, limit those rights. Others, however, feared that without such protections the national government might abuse its new authority.

The Constitution of 1787

Many people contributed to the creation of the American Constitution, but the most important person in the process was James Madison. Madison had devised the Virginia Plan, and he did most of the drafting of the

Constitution itself. Madison's most important achievement, however, was in helping resolve two important philosophical questions: the question of sovereignty and the question of limiting power.

How could a national government exercise sovereignty concurrently with state governments? *Popular Sovereignty* Where did ultimate sovereignty lie? The answer, Madison and his contemporaries decided, was that all power, at all levels of government, flowed ultimately from the people. Thus neither the federal government nor the state governments were truly sovereign. All of them derived their authority from below. The resolution of the problem of sovereignty made possible one of the distinctive features of the Constitution—its division of powers between the national and state governments. The Constitution and the government it created were to be the "supreme law" of the land. At the same time, however, the Constitution left important powers in the hands of the states.

In addition to solving the question of sovereignty, the Constitution produced a distinctive solution to the problem of concentrated authority. Drawing from the ideas of the French philosopher Baron de Montesquieu, most Americans had long believed that the best way to avoid tyranny was to keep government close to the people. A large nation would breed corruption and despotism because the rulers would be so distant from most of the people that there would be no way to control them.

Madison, however, helped break the grip of these assumptions by arguing that a large republic would be less, not more, likely to produce tyranny because no single group would ever be able to dominate it. The idea of many centers of power "checking each other" and preventing any single, despotic author- *"Checks and Balances"* ity from emerging also helped shape the internal structure of the federal government. The Constitution's most distinctive feature was its "separation of powers" within the government, its creation of "checks and balances" among the legislative, executive, and judicial branches. The forces within the government would constantly compete with one another. Congress would have two chambers, each checking the other, since both would have to agree before any law could be passed. The president would have the power to veto acts of Congress. The federal courts would be protected from both the executive and the legislature, because judges would serve for life.

The "federal" structure of the government was designed to protect the United States from the kind of despotism that Americans believed had emerged in England. But it was also designed to protect the nation from another kind of despotism: the tyranny of the people. Shays's Rebellion, most of the founders believed, had been only one example of what could happen if a nation did not defend itself against the unchecked exercise of popular will. Thus in the new government, only the members of the House of Representatives would be elected directly by the people. On September 17, 1787, thirty-nine delegates signed the Constitution.

ADOPTION AND ADAPTATION

The delegates at Philadelphia had greatly exceeded their instructions from Congress and the states. Instead of making simple revisions in the Articles of Confederation, they had produced a plan for a completely different form of government. They feared that the Constitution would not be ratified under the rules of the Articles of Confederation, which required unanimous approval by the state legislatures. So the convention changed the rules, proposing that the new government come into being when nine of the thirteen states ratified the Constitution and recommending that state conventions, not state legislatures, be called to ratify it.

Federalists and Antifederalists

The Congress in New York accepted the convention's work and submitted it to the states for approval. All the state legislatures except Rhode Island elected delegates to ratifying conventions, most of which began meeting in early 1788. Even before the ratifying conventions adjourned, however, a great national debate on the new Constitution had begun.

Supporters of the Constitution had a number of advantages. They were better organized. They had the support of the two most eminent men in America, Franklin and Washington. And they seized an appealing label for themselves: "Federalists"—a term that op-

The Federalist Papers

ponents of centralization had once used to describe themselves—thus implying that they were less committed to a "nationalist" government than in fact they were. The Federalists also had the support of the ablest political philosophers of their time: Alexander Hamilton, James Madison, and John Jay. Those three men, under the joint pseudonym "Publius," wrote a series of essays—widely published in newspapers throughout the nation—explaining the meaning and virtues of the Constitution. The essays were later issued as a book, and they are known today as *The Federalist Papers*.

The "Antifederalists"

The Federalists called their critics "Antifederalists," which suggested that their rivals had nothing to offer except opposition. But the Antifederalists, too, were represented by distinguished leaders of the Revolution, among them Patrick Henry and Samuel Adams. And they had serious and intelligent arguments of their own. They saw themselves as the defenders of the true principles of the Revolution. The Constitution, they believed, would betray those principles. It would increase taxes, weaken the states, wield dictatorial powers, favor the "well-born" over the common people, and abolish individual liberty. But their biggest complaint was that the Constitution lacked a bill of rights. Only by enumerating the natural rights of the people, they argued, could there be any certainty that those rights would be protected.

CELEBRATING THE CONSTITUTION Perhaps because opposition to the Constitution had been so intense, its champions staged elaborate celebrations at the time of ratification in an effort to enhance its legitimacy. In 1788, supporters of the Constitution organized an elaborate parade down Wall Street, which included the ship on wheels (representing the "ship of state") pictured here. Alexander Hamilton, whose name is emblazoned on the ship's banners, was New York's leading advocate of the Constitution. *(North Wind Picture Archives)*

Despite the efforts of the Antifederalists, ratification proceeded quickly during the winter of 1787–1788. The Delaware convention was the first to act. It ratified the Constitution unanimously, as did New Jersey and Georgia. New Hampshire ratified the document in June 1788—the ninth state to do so. It was now theoretically possible for the Constitution to go into effect. A new government could not hope to succeed, however, without Virginia and New York, whose conventions remained closely divided. But by the end of June, first Virginia and then New York had consented to the Constitution by narrow margins—on the assumption that a bill of rights would be added in the form of amendments to the Constitution. North Carolina's convention adjourned without taking action, waiting to see what happened to the amendments. Rhode Island did not even consider ratification.

Completing the Structure

The first elections under the Constitution were held in the early months of 1789. There was never any doubt about who would be the first president. George Washington had presided at the Constitutional Convention, and many who had favored ratification did so only because they expected him to preside over the new government as well. Washington received the votes of all the presidential electors. John Adams, a leading Federalist, became vice president. After a journey from his estate at Mount Vernon, Virginia, marked by elaborate celebrations along the way, Washington was inaugurated in New York on April 30, 1789.

The first Congress served in many ways as a continuation of the Constitutional Convention. Its most important task was drafting a bill of rights. By early 1789, even Madison had come to agree that some sort of bill of rights would be essential to legitimize the new government in the eyes of its opponents. On September 25, 1789, Congress approved twelve amendments, ten of which were ratified by the states by the end of 1791. These first ten amendments to the Constitution comprise what we know

The Bill of Rights as the Bill of Rights. Nine of them placed limitations on Congress by forbidding it to infringe on certain fundamental rights: freedom of religion, speech, and the press; immunity from arbitrary arrest; trial by jury; and others. The Tenth Amendment reserved to the states or the people all powers except those specifically withheld from them or delegated to the federal government.

On the subject of federal courts, the Constitution said only: "The judicial power of the United States shall be vested in one Supreme Court, and in such inferior courts as the Congress may from time to time ordain and establish." It was left to Congress to determine the number of Supreme Court judges to be appointed and the kinds of lower courts to be organized. In the Judiciary Act of 1789, Congress provided for a Supreme Court of six members and a system of lower district courts and courts of appeal. It also gave the Supreme Court the power to make the final decision in cases involving the constitutionality of state laws.

The Constitution referred indirectly to executive departments but did not specify which ones or how many there should be. The first Congress

Establishing the Executive Departments created three such departments—state, treasury, and war—and also established the offices of the attorney general and postmaster general. To the office of secretary of the treasury Washington appointed Alexander Hamilton of New York. For secretary of war he chose a Massachusetts Federalist, General Henry Knox. As attorney general he named Edmund Randolph of Virginia. As secretary of state he chose another Virginian, Thomas Jefferson.

FEDERALISTS AND REPUBLICANS

The framers of the Constitution had dealt with many controversies by papering them over with a series of vague compromises; as a result, the disagreements survived to plague the new government.

At the heart of the controversies of the 1790s was the same basic difference in philosophy that had been at the heart of the debate over the Constitution. On one side stood a powerful group who believed that America required a strong, national government. *Competing National Visions* They envisioned that the country's mission was to become a genuine nation-state, with centralized authority and a complex commercial economy. On the other side stood another group whose members envisioned a more modest national government. The United States should not, this group believed, aspire to be a highly commercial or urban nation. It should remain predominantly rural and agrarian. The centralizers became known as the Federalists and gravitated to the leadership of Alexander Hamilton. Their opponents acquired the name Republicans and gathered under the leadership of Thomas Jefferson and James Madison.

Hamilton and the Federalists

For twelve years, the Federalists retained firm control of the new government. That was in part because George Washington had always envisioned a strong national government and as president did little to stop those attempting to create one. But the president, Washington believed, should stand above political controversies, and so he avoided personal involvement in the deliberations of Congress. As a result, the dominant figure in his administration *Hamilton's "Funded" Debt Proposal* became Alexander Hamilton. Of all the national leaders of his time, Hamilton was one of the most aristocratic in political philosophy; he believed that a stable and effective government required an elite ruling class. Thus the new government needed the support of the wealthy and powerful; and to get that, it needed to give elites a stake in its success. Hamilton proposed, therefore, that the existing public debt be "funded": that the various certificates of indebtedness that the old Congress had issued during and after the Revolution—many of them now in the possession of wealthy speculators—be called in and exchanged for interest-bearing bonds. He also recommended that the states' Revolutionary debts be "assumed" (taken over by the federal government) to cause state bondholders also to look to the central government for eventual payment. Hamilton wanted to create a permanent national debt, with new bonds being issued as old ones were paid off. The result, he believed, would be that the wealthy classes, who were the most likely to lend money to the government, would always have a reason to want the government to survive.

Hamilton also wanted to create a national bank. It would provide loans and currency to businesses, give the government a safe place for the deposit of federal funds, facilitate the collection of taxes and the disbursement of the government's expenditures, and provide a stable center to the nation's small and feeble banking system. The bank would be chartered by the federal government, but much of its capital would come from private investors.

The funding and assumption of debts would require new sources of revenue. Hamilton recommended two kinds of taxes to complement the receipts anticipated from the sales of public land. One was an excise tax on alcoholic beverages, a tax that would be most burdensome to the whiskey distillers of the backcountry, small farmers who converted part of their corn and rye crops into whiskey. The other was a tariff on imports, which Hamilton saw not only as a way to raise money but as a way to protect domestic industries from foreign competition. In his *"Report on Manufactures"* famous "Report on Manufactures" of 1791, he outlined a plan for stimulating the growth of industry and spoke glowingly of the advantages to society of a healthy manufacturing sector.

The Federalists, in short, offered more than a vision of a stable new government. They offered a vision of the sort of nation America should become—a nation with a wealthy, enlightened ruling class, a vigorous, independent commercial economy, and a thriving manufacturing sector.

Enacting the Federalist Program

Few members of Congress objected to Hamilton's plan for funding the national debt, but many did oppose his proposal to exchange new bonds for old certificates of indebtedness on a dollar-for-dollar basis. Many of *Objections to the Funding Bill* the original holders had been forced to sell during the hard times of the 1780s to speculators, who had bought them at a fraction of their face value. James Madison, now a representative from Virginia, argued for a plan by which the new bonds would be divided between the original purchasers and the speculators. But Hamilton's allies insisted that the honor of the government required a literal fulfillment of its earlier promises to pay whoever held the bonds. Congress finally passed the funding bill Hamilton wanted.

Hamilton's proposal that the federal government assume the state debts encountered greater difficulty. Its opponents argued that if the federal government took over the state debts, the states with few debts would have to pay taxes to service the states with large ones. Massachusetts, for example, owed much more money than did Virginia. Only by striking a bargain with the Virginians were Hamilton and his supporters able to win passage of the assumption bill.

Compromise on the National Capital The deal involved the location of the national capital. The Virginians wanted to create a new capital near them in the South. Hamilton and Jefferson met and agreed to exchange northern support for placing the capital in the South for Virginia's votes for the assumption bill. The bargain called for the construction of a new capital city on the banks of the Potomac River, which divided Maryland and Virginia, on land to be selected by George Washington.

Hamilton's bank bill produced the most heated debates. Madison, Jefferson, Randolph, and others argued that because the Constitution made no provision for a national bank, Congress had no authority to create one. But Congress agreed to Hamilton's bill despite these objections, and Washington signed it. The Bank of the United States began operations in 1791.

Hamilton also had his way with the excise tax, although protests from farmers later forced revisions to reduce the burden on the smaller distillers. He failed to win passage of a tariff as highly protective as he had hoped for, but the tariff law of 1792 did raise the rates somewhat.

Once enacted, Hamilton's program won the support of manufacturers, creditors, and other influential segments of the population. But others *Division over Hamilton Program* found the Hamilton program less appealing. Small farmers complained that they were being taxed excessively. They and others began to argue that the Federalist program served the interests not of the people but of small, wealthy elites. Out of this feeling an organized political opposition arose.

The Republican Opposition

The Constitution made no reference to political parties. Most of the framers believed that organized parties were dangerous and to be avoided. Disagreement was inevitable on particular issues, but they believed that such disagreements need not and should not lead to the formation of permanent factions.

Yet not many years had passed after the ratification of the Constitution before Madison and others became convinced that Hamilton and his *Establishment of the Federalist Party* followers had become a dangerous, self-interested faction. The Federalists had used the powers of their offices to reward their supporters and win additional allies. They were doing many of the same things, their opponents believed, that the corrupt British governments of the early eighteenth century had done.

Because the Federalists appeared to their critics to be creating such a menacing and tyrannical structure of power, there was no alternative but to organize a vigorous opposition. The result was the emergence of an alternative political organization, whose members called themselves "Republicans." *Formation of the Republican Party* (These first Republicans are not institutionally related to the modern Republican Party, which was born in the 1850s.) By the late 1790s, the Republicans were going to even greater lengths than the Federalists to create vehicles of partisan influence. In every state they had formed committees, societies, and caucuses; Republican groups were banding together to influence state and local elections. Neither side was willing to admit that it was acting as a party, nor would either concede the right of the other to exist. This institutionalized factionalism is known to historians as the "first party system."

From the beginning, the preeminent figures among the Republicans were Thomas Jefferson and James Madison. Jefferson became the most prominent spokesman for the cause. He promoted a vision of an agrarian republic, in which most citizens would farm their own land. Jefferson did not scorn commercial or industrial activity. But he believed that the nation should be wary of too much urbanization and industrialization.

Regional and Economic Differences   Although both parties had supporters in all parts of the country and among all classes, there were regional and economic differences. The Federalists were most numerous in the commercial centers of the Northeast and in such southern seaports as Charleston; the Republicans were most numerous in the rural areas of the South and the West. The difference in their philosophies was visible in, among other things, their reactions to the progress of the French Revolution. As that revolution grew increasingly radical in the 1790s, the Federalists expressed horror. But the Republicans applauded the democratic, antiaristocratic spirit they believed the French Revolution displayed.

When the time came for the nation's second presidential election, in 1792, both Jefferson and Hamilton urged Washington to run for a second term. The president reluctantly agreed. But while Washington had the respect of both factions, he was, in reality, more in sympathy with the Federalists than with the Republicans.

ESTABLISHING NATIONAL SOVEREIGNTY

The Federalists consolidated their position by acting effectively in two areas in which the old Confederation had not always been successful: the western territories and diplomacy.

Securing the West

Despite the Northwest Ordinance, the old Congress had largely failed to tie the outlying western areas of the country firmly to the national government. Farmers in western Massachusetts had rebelled; settlers in Vermont, Kentucky, and Tennessee had flirted with seceding from the Union. At first, the new government under the Constitution faced similar problems.

In 1794, farmers in western Pennsylvania raised a major challenge to federal authority when they refused to pay the new whiskey excise tax and began terrorizing tax collectors in the region. But the federal government did not leave settlement of the so-called Whiskey Rebellion *Whiskey Rebellion* to the authorities of Pennsylvania. At Hamilton's urging, Washington called out the militias of three states and assembled an army of nearly 15,000—and he personally accompanied the troops into Pennsylvania. At the approach of the militiamen, the rebellion quickly collapsed.

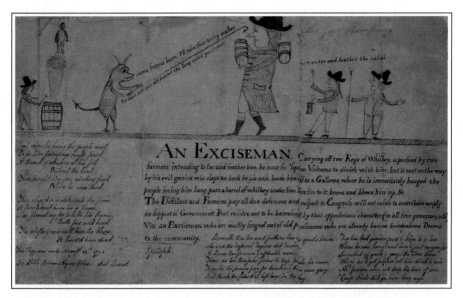

A COMMENT ON THE WHISKEY REBELLION Although Thomas Jefferson and other Republicans claimed to welcome occasional popular uprisings, the Federalists were horrified by such insurgencies as Shays's Rebellion in Massachusetts and, later, the Whiskey Rebellion in Pennsylvania. The Federalist cartoon portrays the rebels as demons who pursue and eventually hang an unfortunate "exciseman" (tax collector), who has confiscated two kegs of rum. *(Courtesy of the Atwater Kent Museum of Philadelphia)*

The federal government won the allegiance of the whiskey rebels through intimidation. It won the loyalties of other western people by accepting new states as members of the Union. The last two of the original thirteen colonies joined the Union once the Bill of Rights had been appended to the Constitution—North Carolina in 1789 and Rhode Island in 1790. Vermont became the fourteenth state in 1791 after New York and New Hampshire agreed to give up their claims to it. Next came Kentucky, in 1792, when Virginia gave up its claim to that region. After North Carolina ceded its western lands to the Union, Tennessee became a state in 1796.

The new government faced a greater challenge in more distant areas of the Northwest and the Southwest. The ordinances of 1784–1787, establishing the terms of white settlement in the West, had produced a series of border conflicts with Indian tribes. The new government inherited these clashes, which continued with few interruptions for nearly a decade.

These clashes revealed another issue the Constitution had done little to resolve: the place of the Indian nations within the new federal structure. The Constitution gave Congress power to "regulate Commerce . . . with the Indian tribes." And it bound the new government to respect treaties *The Indians' Ambiguous Status* negotiated by the Confederation, most of which had been with the tribes. But none of this did very much to clarify the precise legal standing of Indians or Indian nations within the United States. The tribes received no direct representation in the new government. Above all, the Constitution did not address the major issue of land. Indian nations lived within the boundaries of the United States, yet they claimed (and the white government at times agreed) that they had some measure of sovereignty over their own land. But neither the Constitution nor common law offered any clear guide to the rights of a "nation within a nation" or to the precise nature of tribal sovereignty.

Maintaining Neutrality

A crisis in Anglo-American relations emerged in 1793 when the new French government established after the revolution of 1789 went to war with Great Britain. Both the president and Congress took steps to establish American neutrality in the conflict, but that neutrality was severely tested.

Early in 1794, the Royal Navy began seizing hundreds of American ships engaged in trade in the French West Indies. Hamilton was deeply concerned. War would mean an end to imports from England, and most of the revenue for maintaining his financial system came from duties on those imports. Hamilton and the Federalists did not trust the State Department, now in the hands of the ardently pro-French Edmund Randolph, to find a solution to the crisis. So they persuaded Washington to name a special commissioner to go to England and negotiate a solution: the chief justice of the Supreme Court, John Jay. Jay was instructed to secure compensation for the recent British assaults on American shipping, to demand withdrawal of British forces from their posts on the frontier of the United States, and to negotiate a commercial treaty with Britain.

Jay's Treaty   The long and complex treaty Jay negotiated in 1794 failed to achieve these goals. But it settled the conflict with Britain, avoiding a likely war. It provided for undisputed American sovereignty over the entire Northwest and produced a reasonably satisfactory commercial relationship with a nation whose trade was important to the United States. Nevertheless, when the terms became known in America, criticism was intense. Opponents of the treaty went to great lengths to defeat it in the Senate, but in the end the Senate ratified what was by then known as Jay's Treaty.

Jay's Treaty paved the way for a settlement of important American disputes with Spain. Under Pinckney's Treaty (negotiated by Thomas Pinckney and signed in 1795), *Pinckney's Treaty* Spain recognized the right of Americans to navigate the Mississippi to its mouth and to deposit goods at New Orleans for reloading on oceangoing ships; agreed to fix the northern boundary of Florida along the 31st parallel; and commanded its authorities to prevent the Indians in Florida from launching raids north across the border.

THE DOWNFALL OF THE FEDERALISTS

Since almost everyone in the 1790s agreed that there was no place in a stable republic for organized parties, the emergence of the Republicans as a powerful and apparently permanent opposition seemed to the Federalists a grave threat to national stability. And so when major international perils confronted the government in the 1790s, the temptation to move forcefully against this "illegitimate" opposition was strong.

The Election of 1796

George Washington refused to run for a third term as president in 1796. Jefferson was the obvious presidential candidate of the Republicans that year, but the Federalists faced a more difficult choice. Hamilton had created too many enemies to be a credible candidate. Vice President John Adams, who was directly associated with none of the controversial Federalist achievements, received the party's nomination for president at a caucus of the Federalists in Congress.

The Federalists were still clearly the dominant party. But without Washington to mediate, they fell victim to fierce factional rivalries. Adams defeated Jefferson by *John Adams Elected* only three electoral votes and assumed the presidency as head of a divided party facing a powerful opposition. Jefferson became vice president as a result of finishing second. (Not until the adoption of the Twelfth Amendment in 1804 did electors vote separately for president and vice president.)

The Quasi War with France

American relations with Great Britain and Spain improved as a result of Jay's and Pinckney's Treaties. But the nation's relations with revolutionary France quickly deteriorated. French vessels captured American ships on the high seas. The French government refused to receive Charles Cotesworth Pinckney when he arrived in Paris as the new American minister. In an effort to stabilize relations, Adams appointed a bipartisan commission to negotiate with France. When the Americans arrived in Paris in 1797, three agents of the French foreign minister, Prince Talleyrand, demanded a loan for France and a bribe for French officials before any negotiations could begin. Pinckney, a member of the commission, responded, "No! No! Not a sixpence!"

When Adams heard of the incident, he sent a message to Congress urging preparations for war. Before giving the commissioners' report to Congress, he deleted the names of the three French agents and designated them only as Messrs. X, Y, and Z. When the report was *The "XYZ Affair"* published, the "XYZ Affair," as it quickly became known, provoked widespread popular outrage at France's actions and strong popular support for the Federalists' response. For nearly two years, 1798 and 1799, the United States found itself engaged in an undeclared war with France.

Adams persuaded Congress to cut off all trade with France, to abrogate the treaties of 1778, and to authorize American vessels to capture French armed ships on the high seas. In 1798, Congress created the De-

The "Quasi War"

partment of the Navy. The navy soon won a number of duels and captured a total of eighty-five French ships. The United States also began cooperating closely with the British. In response, the French began trying to conciliate the United States. Adams sent another commission to Paris in 1800, and the new French government (headed now by "First Consul" Napoleon Bonaparte) agreed to a treaty with the United States that canceled the old agreements of 1778 and established new commercial arrangements. As a result, the "quasi war" came to a reasonably peaceful end.

Repression and Protest

The conflict with France helped the Federalists increase their majorities in Congress in 1798. They now began to consider ways to silence the Republican opposition. The result was some of the most controversial legislation in American history: the Alien and Sedition Acts.

The Alien and Sedition Acts

The Alien Act placed new obstacles in the way of foreigners who wished to become American citizens, and it strengthened the president's hand in dealing with aliens. The Sedition Act allowed the government to prosecute those who engaged in "sedition" against the government. In theory, only libelous or treasonous activities were subject to prosecution; but since such activities had no clear definition, the law, in effect, gave the government authority to stifle virtually any opposition. The Republicans interpreted the new laws as part of a Federalist campaign to destroy them.

President Adams signed the new laws but was cautious in implementing them. He did not deport any aliens, and he prevented the government from launching a broad crusade against the Republicans. But the Alien Act discouraged immigration and encouraged some foreigners already in the country to leave. And the administration used the Sedition Act to arrest and convict ten men, most of them Republican newspaper editors whose only crime had been criticism of the Federalists in government.

Republican leaders began to look for ways to reverse the Alien and Sedition Acts. Some looked to the state legislatures for help. They developed a theory to justify action by the states against the federal government in two sets of resolutions of 1798–1799, one written (anonymously) by Jefferson and

Virginia and Kentucky Resolutions

adopted by the Kentucky legislature and the other drafted by Madison and approved by the Virginia legislature. The Virginia and Kentucky Resolutions, as

CONGRESSIONAL BRAWLERS, 1798 This savage cartoon was inspired by the celebrated fight on the floor of the House of Representatives between Matthew Lyon, a Republican representative from Vermont, and Roger Griswold, a Federalist from Connecticut. Griswold (at right) attacks Lyon with his cane, and Lyon retaliates with fire tongs. Other members of Congress are portrayed enjoying the battle. *(New York Public Library)*

they were known, used the ideas of John Locke and the Tenth Amendment to the Constitution to argue that the federal government had been formed by a "compact" or contract among the states and possessed only certain delegated powers. Whenever a party to the contract, a state, decided that the central government had exceeded those powers, it had the right to "nullify" the appropriate laws.

The Republicans did not win wide support for the nullification idea; they did, however, succeed in elevating their dispute with the Federalists to the level of a national crisis. By the late 1790s, the entire nation was deeply and bitterly politicized. State legislatures at times resembled battlegrounds. Even the United States Congress was plagued with violent disagreements. In one celebrated incident in the chamber of the House of Representatives, Matthew Lyon, a Republican from Vermont, responded to an insult from Roger Griswold, a Federalist from Connecticut, by spitting in Griswold's eye. Griswold attacked Lyon with his cane, Lyon fought back with a pair of fire tongs, and soon the two men were wrestling on the floor.

The "Revolution" of 1800

These bitter controversies shaped the presidential election of 1800. The presidential candidates were the same as four years earlier: Adams for the Federalists, Jefferson for the

Election of 1800

Republicans. But the campaign of 1800 was very different from the one preceding it. Adams and Jefferson themselves displayed reasonable dignity, but their supporters showed no such restraint. The Federalists accused Jefferson of being a dangerous radical and his followers of being wild men who, if they should come to power, would bring on a reign of terror comparable to that of the French Revolution. The Republicans portrayed Adams as a tyrant conspiring to become king, and they accused the Federalists of plotting to impose slavery on the people. The election was close, and the crucial contest was in New York. There, Aaron Burr mobilized an organization of Revolutionary War veterans, the Tammany Society, to serve as a Republican political machine. Through Tammany's efforts, the party carried the city by a large majority, and with it the state. Jefferson was, apparently, elected.

But an unexpected complication soon jeopardized the Republican victory. The Constitution called for each elector to "vote by ballot for two persons." The expectation was that an elector would cast one vote for his party's presidential candidate and the other for his party's vice presidential candidate. To avoid a tie, the Republicans had intended that one elector would refrain from voting for the party's vice-presidential candidate, Aaron Burr. But when the votes were counted, Jefferson and Burr each had 73. No candidate had a majority, and the House of Representatives had to choose between the two top candidates, Jefferson and Burr. Each state delegation would cast a single vote.

The new Congress, elected in 1800 with a Republican majority, was not to convene until after the inauguration of the president, so it was the Federalist Congress that had to decide the question. After a long deadlock, several leading Federalists concluded that Burr was too unreliable to trust with the presidency. On the thirty-sixth ballot, Jefferson was elected.

After the election of 1800, the only branch of the federal government left in Federalist hands was the judiciary. The Adams administration spent its last months in office taking steps to make the party's hold on the courts secure. With the Judiciary Act of 1801, the Federalists reduced the number of Supreme Court justiceships by one but greatly increased the number of federal judgeships as a whole. Adams quickly appointed Federalists to the newly created positions. He also appointed a leading Federalist, John Marshall, to be chief justice of the Supreme Court, a position Marshall held for 34 years. Indeed, there were charges that he stayed up until midnight on his last day in office to finish signing the new judges' commissions. These officeholders became known as the "midnight appointments."

The Judiciary Act of 1801

Even so, the Republicans viewed their victory as almost complete. The nation had, they believed, been saved from tyranny. The exuberance with which the victors viewed the future—and the importance they ascribed to the defeat of the Federalists—was evident in the phrase Jefferson himself later used to describe his election. He called it the "Revolution of 1800."

CONCLUSION

The writing of the Constitution of 1787 was the single most important political event in the history of the United States. In creating a "federal" system of dispersed authority—authority divided among national and state governments, authority divided among an executive, a legislature, and a judiciary—the young nation sought to balance its need for an effective central government against its fear of concentrated and despotic power. The ability of the delegates to the Constitutional Convention to compromise gave evidence of the deep yearning among them for a stable political system. The same willingness to compromise allowed the greatest challenge to the ideals of the new democracy—slavery—to survive intact.

The writing and ratifying of the Constitution settled some questions about the shape of the new nation. The first twelve years under the government created by the Constitution solved others. And yet by the year 1800, a basic disagreement about the future of the nation remained unresolved and was creating bitter divisions and conflicts within the political world. The election of Thomas Jefferson to the presidency that year opened a new chapter in the nation's public history. It also brought to a close, at least temporarily, savage political conflicts that had seemed to threaten the nation's future.

FOR FURTHER REFERENCE

Charles Beard, *An Economic Interpretation of the Constitution of the United States* (1913) is one of the seminal works of modern American historical inquiry, although its interpretation is no longer widely accepted. Gordon Wood, *The Creation of the American Republic* (1969) is the leading analysis of the intellectual path from the Declaration of Independence to the American Constitution. Jack Rakove, *Original Meanings: Politics and Ideas in the Making of the Constitution* (1996) connects the politics of the 1780s with the political ideas embedded in the Constitution. Stanley Elkins and Eric McKitrick, *The Age of Federalism* (1993) provides a detailed overview of political and economic development in the 1790s. Joyce Appleby, *Capitalism and a New Social Order: The Republican Vision of the 1790s* (1984) highlights liberal and capitalist impulses unleashed after the ratification of the Constitution. Joseph Ellis is the author of several highly regarded books on the founders: *After the Revolution: Profiles of Early American Culture* (1979), which examines some of the framers of the new nation; *American Sphinx: The Character of Thomas Jefferson* (1997); *Founding Brothers: The Revolutionary Generation* (2000); and *Passionate Sage: The Character and Legacy of John Adams* (1993). David McCullough, *John Adams* (2001) is a vivid, sympathetic, and outstandingly popular biography.

For quizzes, Internet resources, references to additional books and films, and more, consult this book's Online Learning Center site at www.mhhe.com/unfinishednation4.

THE JOURNAL OF LEWIS AND CLARK This page is from the journal the explorers Meriwether Lewis and William Clark kept on their famous journey through the United States had acquired in the Louisiana Purchase—and beyond. Shown here is one of the rough maps they drew to describe the lands they had seen. *(© British Museum)*

TIME LINE

1793	1800	1801	1803	1804-1806	1804	1807	
Eli Whitney invents cotton gin	U.S. capital moves to Washington	Second Great Awakening begins	Louisiana Purchase	Lewis and Clark expedition	Jefferson reelected	Embargo	
		Marshall chief justice of Supreme Court	*Marbury* v. *Madison*				

❧

THE JEFFERSONIAN ERA

The Rise of Cultural Nationalism
Stirrings of Industrialism
Jefferson the President
Doubling the National Domain
Expansion and War
The War of 1812

homas Jefferson and his followers assumed control of the national government in 1801 as the champions of a distinctive vision of America. They favored a society of sturdy, independent farmers, happily free from the workshops, the industrial towns, and the city mobs of Europe. They celebrated localism and republican simplicity. Above all, they proposed a federal government of sharply limited power.

Almost nothing worked out as they had planned, for during their years in power the young republic was developing in ways that made much of their vision obsolete. The American economy became steadily more diversified and complex, making the ideal of a simple, agrarian society impossible to maintain. American cultural life was dominated by a vigorous and ambitious nationalism. And Jefferson himself contributed to the changes by exercising strong national authority at times, and by arranging the greatest single increase in the size of the United States in its history.

1808	1809	1810	1811	1812	1814	1815	
Madison elected president	Non-Intercourse Act	Macon's Bill No. 2	Battle of Tippecanoe	U.S. declares war on Great Britain	Hartford Convention	Battle of New Orleans	
	Tecumseh Confederacy formed			Madison reelected	Treaty of Ghent		

THE RISE OF CULTURAL NATIONALISM

In many respects, American cultural life in the early nineteenth century reflected the Republican vision of the nation's future. Opportunities for education increased, the nation's literary and artistic life began to free itself from European influences, and American religion began to adjust to the spread of Enlightenment rationalism. In other respects, however, the new culture was posing a serious challenge to Republican ideals.

Educational and Literary Nationalism

Importance of a Virtuous Citizenry

Central to the Republican vision of America was the concept of a virtuous and enlightened citizenry. Republicans believed, therefore, in the creation of a nationwide system of public schools in which all male citizens would receive free education. Such hopes were not fulfilled. Schooling remained primarily the responsibility of private institutions, most of which were open only to those who could afford to pay for them. In the South and in the mid-Atlantic states, most schools were run by religious groups. In New England, private academies were often more secular, many of them modeled on those founded by the Phillips family at Andover, Massachusetts, in 1778, and at Exeter, New Hampshire, three years later. Many were frankly aristocratic in outlook. There were a few educational institutions open to the poor, but not nearly enough to accommodate everyone, and the education they offered was usually clearly inferior to that provided for more prosperous students.

Private secondary schools such as those in New England generally accepted only male students; even many public schools excluded females from the classroom. Yet the late eighteenth and early nineteenth centuries did see some important advances in education for women. As Americans began to place a higher value on the importance of the "republican mother" who would help train the new generation, they began to ask how mothers could raise their children to be enlightened if the mothers themselves were uneducated. Such concerns helped speed the creation of female academies throughout the nation (usually for the daughters of affluent families). In 1789, Massachusetts required that its public schools serve females as well as males. Other states, although not all, soon followed.

Judith Sargent Murray

Some women aspired to more. In 1784, Judith Sargent Murray published an essay defending the right of women to education. Men and women were equal in intellect and equal in potential, Murray argued. Women, therefore, should have precisely the same educational opportunities as men. What was more, they should have opportunities to earn their own livings and to establish roles

THE PENNSYLVANIA HOSPITAL As the ideas of the Enlightenment spread through American culture in the eighteenth and nineteenth centuries, encouraging the belief that every individual was a divine being and could be redeemed from even the most miserable condition, hospitals and asylums—such as this institution in Pennsylvania—began to emerge to provide settings for the redemption of the poor, the ill, and the deviant. *(The Library Company of Philadelphia)*

for themselves in society apart from their husbands and families. Murray's ideas attracted relatively little support.

Because Jefferson and his followers liked to think of Native Americans as "noble savages" (uncivilized but not necessarily uncivilizable) they hoped that schooling the Indians in white culture would "uplift" the tribes. Missionaries and mission schools proliferated among the tribes. There were no comparable efforts to educate enslaved African Americans.

Higher education similarly diverged from Republican ideals. The number of colleges and universities in America grew substantially, from nine at the time of the Revolution to twenty-two in 1800. None of the new schools, however, was truly public. Even universities established by state legislatures relied on private contributions and tuition fees to survive. Scarcely more than one white man in a thousand (and virtually no women, blacks, or Indians) had access to any college education, and those few who did attend universities were, almost without exception, members of prosperous, propertied families.

Higher Education

Medicine and Science

Medicine and science were not always closely connected to one another in the early nineteenth century, but many physicians were working hard to strengthen the link. The University of Pennsylvania created the first American medical school early in the nineteenth century. Most doctors, however, studied medicine by working with an established practitioner. Some American physicians believed in applying new scientific methods to medicine, but they had to struggle against age-old prejudices and superstitions. Efforts to teach anatomy, for example, encountered strong public hostility because of the dissection of cadavers that the study required. Municipal authorities had virtually no understanding of medical science and almost no idea of what to do in the face of the severe epidemics that so often swept their populations; only slowly did they respond to warnings that lack of adequate sanitation programs was to blame for much disease.

Individual patients often had more to fear from their doctors than from their illnesses. Even the leading advocates of scientific medicine often embraced useless and dangerous treatments. George Washington's death in 1799 was probably less a result of the minor throat infection that had afflicted him than of his physicians' efforts to cure him by bleeding and purging.

The medical profession also used its newfound commitment to the "scientific" method to justify expanding its control over kinds of care that had traditionally been outside its domain. Most *Decline of Midwifery* childbirths, for example, had been attended by female midwives. In the early nineteenth century, physicians began to handle deliveries themselves. Among the results of that change was a narrowing of opportunities for women and a restriction of access to childbirth care for poor mothers (who could have afforded midwives, but who could not pay the higher physicians' fees).

Cultural Aspirations of the New Nation

Establishing a National Culture Many Americans dreamed of an American literary and artistic life that would rival the greatest achievements of Europe. The 1772 "Poem on the Rising Glory of America" predicted that America was destined to become the "seat of empire" and the "final stage" of civilization. The Connecticut schoolmaster and lawyer Noah Webster (author of widely used American spellers and dictionaries) echoed such sentiments, arguing that the American schoolboy should be educated as a nationalist. "As soon as he opens his lips," Webster wrote, "he should rehearse the history of his own country; he should lisp the praise of liberty, and of those illustrious heroes and statesmen who have wrought a revolution in her favor."

A growing number of native authors began working to create a strong American literature. Among the most ambitious was the Philadelphia writer Charles Brockden Brown. But his fascination with horror and deviance kept him from developing a popular audience. More successful was Washington Irving of New York, whose popular folk tales, recounting the adventures of such American rustics as Ichabod Crane and Rip Van Winkle, made him the widely acknowledged leader of American literary life in the early eighteenth century.

Religion and Revivalism

The American Revolution had weakened traditional forms of religious practice. It had elevated ideas of individual liberty and reason that challenged many ecclesiastical traditions. By the 1790s, only a small proportion of white Americans were members of formal churches, and ministers were complaining about the "decay of vital piety."

Religious traditionalists were particularly alarmed about the emergence of new, "rational" religious doctrines—theologies that reflected modern, scientific attitudes. "Deism," which had originated among Enlightenment philosophers in *"Deism"* France, attracted such educated Americans as Jefferson and Franklin and by 1800 was reaching a moderately broad popular audience. Deists accepted the existence of God, but they considered Him a remote being who, after having created the universe, had withdrawn from direct involvement with the human race and its sins. Religious skepticism also produced the philosophies of "universalism" and "unitarianism." Disciples of these new ideas rejected the traditional Calvinist belief in predestination and the idea of the Trinity. Jesus was only a great religious teacher, they claimed, not the son of God. But religious skepticism appeared more powerful than it actually was, in part because those who clung to more traditional faiths were for a time confused and disorganized. Beginning in 1801, however, traditional religion staged a dramatic comeback in the form of a wave of revivalism known as the Second Great Awakening.

The origins of the Awakening lay in the efforts of conservative theologians to fight the spread of religious rationalism and in the efforts of church establishments to revitalize their organizations. Presbyterians expanded their efforts on the western fringes of white settlement. The Methodists sent itinerant preachers throughout the nation to win recruits for the new church, which soon became the fastest-growing denomination in America. Almost as successful were the Baptists, who found an especially fervent following in the South.

By 1800, the revivalist energies of all these denominations were combining to create the greatest surge of evangelical fervor since the first Great Awakening sixty years before. In only a few years, the revivalists mobilized a large proportion of the American people, and membership in those churches embracing revivalism was mushrooming. At Cane Ridge, Kentucky, in the summer *Cane Ridge*

THE CAMP MEETING Camp meetings became a popular feature of evangelical religion in America beginning around 1800. By the 1820s, there were about 1,000 such meetings a year, most of them in the South and the West. This lithograph, which dates from the 1830s, illustrates the central role of women in the religious revivals of the time. *(Lithograph by Kennedy and Lucas, after A. Rider, © The New-York Historical Society)*

of 1801, a group of evangelical ministers presided over the nation's first "camp meeting"—an extraordinary revival that lasted several days and impressed all who saw it with its size (some estimated that 25,000 people attended) and its fervor. Such events became common in subsequent years.

Message of the Second Great Awakening   The basic message of the Second Great Awakening was that individuals must readmit God and Christ into their daily lives; must embrace a fervent, active piety; and must reject the skeptical rationalism that threatened traditional beliefs. Yet the wave of revivalism did not restore the religion of the past. Few denominations any longer accepted the idea of predestination, and the belief that a person could affect his or her own chances for salvation added intensity to the individual's search for salvation. The Awakening, in short, combined a more active piety with a belief in a God whose grace could be attained through faith and good works.

One of the striking features of the Awakening was the preponderance of women within it. Female converts far outnumbered males. That may have been in part because of the movement of industrial work out of the home and into the factory. That process, which was making rapid strides *New Roles for Women* in the early nineteenth century, robbed women of one of their most important social roles. Religious enthusiasm provided, among other things, access to a new range of activities associated with the churches—charitable societies ministering to orphans and the poor, missionary organizations, and others—in which women came to play important roles.

In some areas of the country, revival meetings were open to people of all races. From these revivals emerged a group of black preachers who became important figures within the slave community. Some of them translated the apparently egalitarian religious message of the Awakening—that salvation was available to all—into a similarly egalitarian message for blacks in the present world. Out of black revival meetings in Virginia, for example, arose an elaborate plan in 1800 (devised by Gabriel Prosser, the brother of a black preacher) for a slave rebellion and an attack on Richmond. The plan was discovered and foiled in advance by whites, but revivalism continued in subsequent years to create occasional racial unrest in the South.

The spirit of revivalism was particularly strong among Native Americans. Presbyterian and Baptist missionaries were active among the southern tribes and sparked a wave of conversions. But the most important revivalism came from the efforts of Handsome Lake, a Seneca whose seemingly miraculous "rebirth" *Handsome Lake* after years of alcoholism helped give him a special stature within his tribe. Handsome Lake called for a revival of traditional Indian ways. That meant repudiating the individualism of white society and restoring the communal quality of the Indian world. Handsome Lake's message spread through the scattered Iroquois communities that had survived the military and political setbacks of previous decades and inspired many Indians to give up whiskey, gambling, and other destructive customs derived from white society. But Handsome Lake also encouraged Christian missionaries to become active within the tribes, and he urged Iroquois men to abandon their roles as hunters and become sedentary farmers instead. Iroquois women, who had traditionally done the farming, were to move into more domestic roles.

STIRRINGS OF INDUSTRIALISM

While Americans were engaged in a revolution to win their independence, an even more important revolution was in progress in England: the emergence of modern industrialism. Power-driven machines were permitting manufacturing to become more rapid and extensive—with profound social and economic consequences. Not since the agrarian revolution thousands of years earlier, when humans had turned from hunting to farming for sustenance, had there been an economic change of a *The Industrial Revolution* magnitude comparable to the industrial revolution.

PAWTUCKET BRIDGE AND FALLS One reason for the growth of the textile industry in New England in the early nineteenth century was that there were many sources of water power in the region to run the machinery in the factories. That was certainly the case with Slater's Mill, one of the first American textile factories, which was located in Pawtucket, Rhode Island, alongside a powerful waterfall. This view was painted by an anonymous artist in the 1810s. *(Courtesy The Rhode Island Historical Society)*

Technology in America

Nothing even remotely comparable to the English industrial revolution occurred in America in the first two decades of the nineteenth century. Yet even while Jeffersonians warned of the dangers of rapid economic change, they were witnessing a series of technological advances that would ultimately help ensure that the United States too would be transformed. Some of these technological advances were imported from England. Despite efforts by the British government to prevent the export of textile machinery or the emigration of skilled mechanics, a number of immigrants with advanced knowledge of English technology arrived in the United States eager to introduce the new machines to America. Samuel Slater, for example, used the knowledge he had acquired before leaving England to build a spinning mill in Pawtucket, Rhode Island, for the Quaker merchant Moses Brown in 1790.

America in the early nineteenth century also produced notable inventors of its own. In 1793, Eli Whitney invented a machine that performed the arduous task of removing the seeds from short-staple cotton quickly

The Cotton Gin and the Spread of Slavery

and efficiently. It was dubbed the cotton gin ("gin" was a derivative of "engine"). With the device a single operator could clean as much cotton in a few hours as a group of workers had once needed a whole day to do. The results were profound. Soon cotton growing spread throughout the South. (Previously it had been restricted largely to the coast and the Sea Islands, the only places where long-staple cotton—easily cleaned without the cotton gin—could be grown.) Within a decade, the total cotton crop increased eightfold. African-American slavery, which with the decline of tobacco production had seemed for a time to be a dwindling institution, expanded and firmly fixed itself upon the South. The large supply of domestically produced fiber also served as a strong incentive to entrepreneurs in New England and elsewhere to develop a native textile industry.

Whitney was an important figure in the history of American technology for another reason as well—as a major figure in introducing the concept of interchangeable parts to the United States. As machines such as the cotton gin began to be widely used, it became increasingly important that owners of such machines have access to spare parts—and that the parts be made so that they would fit the machines properly. Whitney not only designed the cotton gin, therefore, but designed machine tools that could manufacture its component parts to exact specifications. The U.S. government later commissioned Whitney to manufacture 1,000 muskets for the army. Each part of the gun had to be interchangeable with the equivalent part in every other gun.

Interchangeability was of great importance in the United States because of the great distances many people had to travel to reach towns or cities and the relatively limited transportation systems available to them. *Importance of Interchangeable Parts* Interchangeable parts meant that a farmer could repair a machine himself rather than transport it over great distances to a machine shop or armory. But the interchangeability that Whitney championed was not easy to achieve. In theory, many parts were designed to be interchangeable. In reality, the actual manufacturing of such parts was for many years not nearly as precise as it was supposed to be. Farmers and others often had to do considerable fitting before the parts would work in their equipment. Not until later in the nineteenth century would machine tools be developed to the point that parts could be made truly interchangeable.

Transportation Innovations

One of the prerequisites for industrialization is a transportation system that allows the efficient movement of raw materials to factories and of finished goods to markets. The United States had no such system in the early years of the republic, and thus it had no domestic market extensive enough to justify large-scale production. But projects were under way that would ultimately remove the transportation obstacle.

One such project was the development of the steamboat. England had pioneered steam power, and even steam navigation, in the eighteenth century, and there had been experiments in America in the 1780s and 1790s in various forms of steam-powered transportation. A major advance emerged out of the efforts of the inventor Robert *Robert Fulton's Steamboat* Fulton and the promoter Robert R. Livingston,

THE GLOBAL INDUSTRIAL REVOLUTION

While Americans were engaged in a revolution to win their independence, they were also taking the first steps toward an at least equally important revolution—one that was already in progress in England and Europe. It was the emergence of modern industrialism. Historians differ over precisely when the industrial revolution began, but it is clear that by the end of the eighteenth century it was well under way in many parts of the world. A hundred years later, the global process of industrialization had transformed the societies of Britain, most of continental Europe, Japan, and the United States. Its social and economic consequences were complex and profound and continue today to shape the nature of global society.

For Americans, the industrial revolution was largely a product of rapid changes in Great Britain, the nation with which they had the closest relations. Britain was the first nation to develop significant industrial capacity. The factory system took root in England in the late eighteenth century, revolutionizing the manufacture of cotton thread and cloth. One invention followed another in quick succession. Improvements in weaving drove improvements in spinning, and these changes created a demand for new devices for carding (combing and straightening the fibers for the spinner). Water, wind, and animal power continued to be important in the textile industry; but more important was the emergence of steam power—which began to proliferate after the appearance of James Watt's advanced steam engine (patented in 1769). Cumbersome and inefficient by modern standards, Watt's engine was nevertheless a major improvement over the earlier "atmospheric" engine of Thomas Newcomen. England's textile industry quickly became the most profitable in the world, and it helped encourage comparable advances in other fields of manufacturing as well. Despite the efforts of the British government to prevent the export of English industrial technology, knowledge of the new machines reached other nations quickly, usually through the emigration of people who had learned the technology in British factories.

America benefited the most from English technology, because it received more immigrants from Great Britain than from any other country. But English technology spread quickly to the nations of continental Europe as well. Belgium was the first, developing a significant coal, iron, and armaments industry in the early nineteenth century. France—profiting from the immigration of approximately fifteen thousand British workers with advanced technological skills—had created a substantial industrial capacity in textiles and metals by the end of the 1820s, which in turn contributed to a great boom in railroad construction later in the century. German industrialization progressed rapidly after 1840, beginning with coal and iron production and then, in the 1850s, moving into large-scale railroad construction. By the late nineteenth century, Germany had created some of the world's largest industrial corporations. In Japan, the sudden intrusion of American and European traders helped cause the so-called Meiji reforms of the 1880s and 1890s, which launched a period of rapid industrialization there as well.

Industrialization changed not just the world's economies, but also its societies. First in England, and then in Europe, America, and Japan, social systems underwent wrenching changes. Hundreds of thousands of men and women moved from rural areas into cities to work in factories, where they experienced both the benefits and the costs of industrialization. The standard of living of the new working class, when objectively quantified, was usually significantly higher than that of the rural poor. Most of those who moved from farm to factory, in other words, experienced some improvement in nutrition and other material circumstances, and even in their health. But the psychological costs of being suddenly uprooted from one way of life and thrust into another, fundamentally different, one could outweigh the economic gains. There was little in most workers' prior experience to prepare them for the nature of industrial labor. It was disciplined, routinized work with a fixed and rigid schedule, a sharp contrast to the varying, seasonal work pattern of the rural economy. Nor were many factory workers prepared for life in the new industrial towns and expanding cities. Industrial workers experienced, too, a fundamental change in their relationship with their employers. Unlike rural landlords and local aristocrats, factory owners and managers—the new class of industrial capitalists, many of them accumulating unprecedented wealth—were usually remote and inaccessible figures. They dealt with their workers impersonally, and the result was a growing schism between the two classes—each lacking access to or understanding of the other. Working men and women throughout the globe began thinking of themselves as a distinct class, with common goals and interests. And their efforts simultaneously to adjust to their new way of life and to resist its most damaging aspects sometimes created great social turbulence. Battles between workers and employers became a characteristic feature of industrial life throughout the world.

Life in industrial nations changed at every level. Populations in industrial nations grew rapidly, and people began to live longer. At the same time, industrial cities began to produce great increases in pollution, crime, and—until modern sanitation systems emerged—infectious disease. Around the industrial world, middle classes expanded and came, in varying degrees, to dominate the economy (although not always the culture or the politics) of their nations.

Not since the agrarian revolution thousands of years earlier, when many humans had turned from hunting to farming for sustenance, had there been an economic change of a magnitude comparable to the industrial revolution. Centuries of traditions, of social patterns, of cultural and religious assumptions were challenged and, often, shattered. The tentative stirrings of industrial activity in the United States in the early nineteenth century, therefore, were part of a vast movement that over the course of the next century was to transform much of the globe.

(text continued from page 175)

who made significant advances in steam-powered navigation that made possible the launching of a steamboat large enough to carry passengers. Their *Clermont*, equipped with paddle wheels and an English-built engine, sailed up the Hudson in the summer of 1807.

Meanwhile, what was to become known as the "turnpike era" had begun. In 1794, a corporation   *The "Turnpike Era"* constructed a toll road running the sixty miles from Philadelphia to Lancaster, Pennsylvania, with a hard-packed surface of crushed stone, which provided a good year-round surface with effective drainage (but was very

THE COTTON GIN Eli Whitney's cotton gin revolutionized the cotton economy of the South by making the processing of short-staple cotton simple and economical. These 1794 drawings are part of Whitney's application for a federal patent on his device. *(The National Archives and Records Administration)*

expensive to use). The Pennsylvania venture proved so successful that similar turnpikes (so named from the kind of tollgate frequently used) were laid out from other cities to neighboring towns.

The process of building the turnpikes was a difficult one. Companies had to survey their routes with many things in mind, particularly elevation. Horse-drawn vehicles had great difficulty traveling along roads with more than a five-degree incline, which required many roads to take very circuitous routes to avoid climbing straight up steep hills. Building roads over mountains was an almost insurmountable task, and no company was successful in doing so until governments began to participate in the financing of the projects.

Country and City

Despite all the changes, America remained an overwhelmingly rural and agrarian nation. Only 3 percent of the population lived in towns of more than 8,000 in 1800. Even the nation's largest cities could not begin to compare with such European capitals as London and Paris (although Philadelphia, with 70,000 residents, New York, with 60,000, and others were becoming centers of commerce, learning, and urban culture comparable to many of the secondary cities of Europe).

People who lived in cities and towns lived dif-   *City Life*
ferently from the vast majority of Americans who
continued to work as farmers. Among other things, urban life produced affluence, and affluent people sought increasing elegance and refinement in their homes, their grounds, and their dress. They also looked for diversions—music, theater, dancing, and, for many people, horse racing. It was natural that horse racing would appeal to Americans in this era, when horses were virtually the only means of transportation other than walking for most people. Informal horse racing had begun as early as the 1620s, and the first formal race course opened near New York City in 1665. By the early nineteenth century, horse racing was a popular activity in most areas of the country. The crowds that gathered at horse races were an early sign of the vast appetite for popular, public entertainments that would be an enduring part of American culture.

It was still possible for some to believe that this small, half-formed nation might not become a complex modern society. But the forces already at work would soon lastingly transform the United States. And Thomas Jefferson, for all his commitment to the agrarian ideal, found himself, as president, obliged to confront and accommodate them.

JEFFERSON THE PRESIDENT

Privately, Thomas Jefferson may well have considered his victory over John Adams in 1800 to be what he later termed it: a revolution "as real . . . as that of 1776." Publicly, however, he was restrained and conciliatory, attempting to minimize the differences between the two parties and calm the passions that the bitter campaign had aroused. There was no complete repudiation of Federalist policies, no true "revolution." Indeed, at times Jefferson seemed to outdo the Federalists at their own work.

The Federal City and the "People's President"

The relative unimportance of the federal government during the Jeffersonian era was symbolized by the character of the newly founded national capital, the city of Washington. There were many who envisioned that the raw, uncompleted town would soon emerge as a great and majestic city. The French architect Pierre L'Enfant had de-   *L'Enfant's Vision*
signed the capital on a grand scale. Many Americans believed Washington would become the Paris of the United States.

THOMAS JEFFERSON This 1805 portrait by the noted American painter Rembrandt Peale shows Jefferson at the beginning of his second term as president. It also conveys (through the simplicity of dress and the slightly unkempt hair) the image of democratic simplicity that Jefferson liked to project as the champion of the "common man." *(© The New-York Historical Society)*

Reality of Washington, D.C. In reality, throughout most of the nineteenth century Washington remained little more than a straggling, provincial village. Although the population increased steadily from the 3,200 counted in the 1800 census, it never rivaled that of New York, Philadelphia, or the other major cities of the nation. The city remained a raw, inhospitable community. Members of Congress viewed Washington not as a home but as a place to visit briefly during sessions of the legislature. Most lived in a cluster of simple boardinghouses in the vicinity of the Capitol. It was not unusual for a member of Congress to resign his seat in the midst of a session to return home if he had an opportunity to accept the more prestigious post of member of his state legislature.

Jefferson was a wealthy planter by background, but as president he conveyed to the public an image of plain, almost crude disdain for pretension. He walked like an ordinary citizen to and from his inauguration at the Capitol. In the presidential mansion, which had not yet acquired the name "White House," he disregarded the courtly etiquette of his predecessors. He did not always bother to dress up, prompting the British ambassador to complain of being received by the president in clothes that were "indicative of utter slovenliness and indifference to appearances."

Yet Jefferson managed nevertheless to impress most of those who knew him. He was one of the nation's most intelligent and creative men, with a wider range of interests and accomplishments than any major public figure in American history with the possible exception of Benjamin Franklin. In addition to politics and diplomacy, he was an active architect, educator, inventor, scientific farmer, and philosopher-scientist.

Jefferson was, above all, a shrewd and practical politician. He worked hard to exert influence as the *Jefferson the Politician* leader of his party, giving direction to Republicans in Congress by quiet and sometimes even devious means. Although the Republicans had objected strenuously to the efforts of their Federalist predecessors to build a network of influence through patronage, Jefferson used his powers of appointment as an effective political weapon. Like Washington before him, he believed that federal offices should be filled with men loyal to the principles and policies of the administration. By the end of his second term practically all federal jobs were held by loyal Republicans. Jefferson was a popular president during his first term and had little difficulty winning reelection against the Federalist Charles C. Pinckney in 1804. Jefferson won by the overwhelming electoral majority of 162 to 14, and Republican membership of both houses of Congress increased.

Dollars and Ships

Under Washington and Adams, the Republicans believed, the government had been needlessly extravagant. Yearly federal expenditures had nearly tripled between 1793 and 1800. The public debt had also risen, and an extensive system of internal taxation had been erected.

The Jefferson administration moved deliberately to reverse these trends. In 1802, the president *Limiting the Federal Government* persuaded Congress to abolish all internal taxes, leaving customs duties and the sale of western lands as the only sources of revenue for the government. Meanwhile, Secretary of the Treasury Albert Gallatin drastically reduced government spending. Although Jefferson was unable entirely to retire the national debt as he had hoped, he did cut it almost in half (from $83 million to $45 million).

Jefferson also scaled down the armed forces. He reduced the already tiny army of 4,000 men to 2,500. He pared down the navy from twenty-five ships in commission to seven. Anything but the smallest of standing armies, he argued, might menace civil liberties and civilian control of government. Yet Jefferson was not a pacifist. At the same time that he was reducing the size of the army and navy, he helped establish the United States Military Academy at West Point, founded in 1802. And when trouble started brewing overseas, he began again to build up the fleet. Such trouble appeared first in the Mediterranean, off the coast of northern Africa.

For years the Barbary states of North Africa—Morocco, Algiers, Tunis, and Tripoli—had been demanding protection money, paid to avoid piracy, from all nations whose ships sailed the Mediterranean. During the 1780s and 1790s the United States, too, had agreed to treaties providing for annual tribute to the Barbary states, but Jefferson showed reluctance to continue this policy of appeasement.

Challenging the Barbary Pirates   In 1801, the pasha of Tripoli forced Jefferson's hand. Unhappy with American responses to his demands, he ordered the flagpole of the American consulate chopped down—a symbolic declaration of war. Jefferson responded cautiously and built up American naval forces in the area over the next several years. Finally, in 1805, he agreed to terms by which the United States ended the payment of tribute to Tripoli but paid a substantial (and humiliating) ransom for the release of American prisoners.

Conflict with the Courts

Having won control of the executive and legislative branches of government, the Republicans looked with suspicion on the judiciary, which remained largely in the hands of Federalist judges. Soon after Jefferson's first inauguration, his followers in Congress launched an attack on this last preserve of the opposition. Their first step was the repeal of the Judiciary Act of 1801, thus eliminating the judgeships to which Adams had made his "midnight appointments."

The debate over the courts led to one of the most important judicial decisions in the history of the nation. Federalists had long maintained that the Supreme Court had the authority to nullify acts of Congress, and the Court itself had actually exercised the power of judicial review in 1796 when it upheld the validity of a law passed by Congress. But the Court's authority in this area would not be secure, it was clear, until it actually declared a congressional act unconstitutional. In 1803, in the case *Marbury v. Madison*   of *Marbury* v. *Madison*, it did so. William Marbury, one of Adams's "midnight appointments," had been named a justice of the peace in the District of Columbia. But his commission, although signed and sealed, had not been delivered to him before Adams left office. When Jefferson took office, his secretary of state, James Madison, refused to hand over the commission. Marbury asked the Supreme Court to direct Madison to perform his official duty. But the Court ruled that while Marbury had a right to his commission, the Court had no authority to order Madison to deliver it. On the surface, therefore, the decision was a victory for the administration. But of much greater importance than the relatively insignificant matter of Marbury's commission was the Court's reasoning in the decision.

The original Judiciary Act of 1789 had given the Court the power to compel executive officials to act in such matters as the delivery of commissions, and it was on that basis that Marbury had filed his suit. But the Court ruled that Congress had exceeded its authority, that the Constitution defined the powers of the judiciary, and that the legislature had no right to expand them. The relevant section of the 1789 act was, therefore, void. In seeming to deny its own authority, the Court was in fact radically enlarging it. The justices had repudiated a relatively minor power (the power to force the delivery of a commission) by asserting a vastly greater one (the power to nullify an act of Congress).

The chief justice of the United States at the time of the ruling (and until 1835) was John Marshall. A *John Marshall* leading Federalist and prominent Virginia lawyer, he had served John Adams as secretary of state. In 1801, just before leaving office, Adams had appointed him chief justice, and almost immediately Marshall established himself as the dominant figure of the Court, shaping virtually all its most important rulings—including, of course, *Marbury* v. *Madison.* Through a succession of Republican presidents, he battled to give the federal government unity and strength. And in so doing, he established the judiciary as a coequal branch of government with the executive and the legislature.

DOUBLING THE NATIONAL DOMAIN

In the same year Jefferson was elected president of the United States, Napoleon Bonaparte made himself ruler of France with the title of first consul. In the year Jefferson was reelected, Napoleon named himself emperor. The two men had little in common, yet for a time they were of great assistance to each other in international politics.

Jefferson and Napoleon

Having failed in a grandiose plan to seize India from the British Empire, Napoleon began to *Napoleon's North* dream of restoring French power in the New *American Dream* World. The territory east of the Mississippi, which France had ceded to Great Britain in 1763, was now part of the United States, but Napoleon hoped to regain the lands west of the Mississippi, which belonged to Spain. In 1800, under the secret Treaty of San Ildefonso, France regained title to Louisiana, which included almost the whole of the Mississippi Valley to the west of the river. The Louisiana Territory would, Napoleon hoped, become the heart of a great French empire in America.

Jefferson was unaware at first of Napoleon's imperial ambitions in America, and for a time he pursued a foreign policy that reflected his well-known admiration for France. But he began to reassess American relations with the French when he heard rumors of the secret transfer of Louisiana. Particu-

Importance of New Orleans

larly troubling to Jefferson was French control of New Orleans, the outlet through which the produce of the fast-growing western regions of the United States was shipped to the markets of the world.

Jefferson was even more alarmed when, in the fall of 1802, he learned that the Spanish intendant at New Orleans (who still governed the city, since the French had not yet taken formal possession of the region) had announced a disturbing new regulation. American ships sailing the Mississippi River had for many years been accustomed to depositing their cargoes in New Orleans for transfer to oceangoing vessels. The intendant now forbade the practice, even though Spain had guaranteed Americans that right in the Pinckney Treaty of 1795.

Westerners demanded that the federal government do something to reopen the river, and the president faced a dilemma. If he yielded to the frontier clamor and tried to change the policy by force, he would run the risk of a major war with France. If he ignored the westerners' demands, he might lose political support. But Jefferson saw another solution. He instructed Robert Livingston, the American ambassador in Paris, to negotiate for the purchase of New Orleans. Livingston, on his own authority, proposed that the French sell the United States the rest of Louisiana as well.

In the meantime, Jefferson persuaded Congress to appropriate funds for an expansion of the army and the construction of a river fleet, and he hinted that American forces might soon descend on New Orleans and that the United States might form an alliance with Great Britain if the prob

Napoleon's Offer

lems with France were not resolved. Perhaps in response, Napoleon suddenly decided to offer the United States the entire Louisiana Territory.

Napoleon had good reasons for the decision. His plans for an empire in America had already gone seriously awry, partly because a yellow fever epidemic had wiped out much of the French army in the New World and partly because the expeditionary force he wished to send to reinforce the troops had been icebound in a Dutch harbor through the winter of 1802–1803. By the time the harbor thawed in the spring of 1803, Napoleon was preparing for a renewed war in Europe. He would not, he realized, have the resources to secure an empire in America.

The Louisiana Purchase

Faced with Napoleon's sudden proposal, Livingston and James Monroe, whom Jefferson had sent to Paris to assist in the negotiations, had to decide whether they should accept it even if they had no authorization to do so. But fearful that Napoleon might withdraw the offer, they decided to proceed. After some haggling over the price, Livingston and Monroe signed an agreement with Napoleon on April 30, 1803.

By the terms of the treaty, the United States was to pay a total of 80 million francs ($15 million) to the French government. The United States was also to grant certain exclusive commercial privileges to France in the port of New Orleans and was to incorporate the residents of Louisiana into the Union with the same rights and privileges as other citizens. The boundaries of the purchase were not clearly defined.

In Washington, the president was both pleased and embarrassed when he received the treaty. He was pleased with the terms of the bargain; but he was uncertain about his authority to accept it, since the Constitution said nothing about the acquisition of new territory. But Jefferson's advisers persuaded him that his *Jefferson's Ideological Dilemma* treaty-making power under the Constitution would justify the purchase of Louisiana, and Congress promptly approved the treaty. Finally, late in 1803, General James Wilkinson, commissioner of the United States, took formal control of the territory on behalf of the United States. Before long, the Louisiana Territory was organized on the general pattern of the Northwest Territory, with the assumption that it would be divided eventually into states. The first of these was admitted to the Union as the state of Louisiana in 1812.

Exploring the West

Meanwhile, a series of explorations was revealing the geography of the far-flung new territory to white Americans. In 1803, Jefferson helped plan an expedition that was to cross the continent to the Pacific Ocean, gather geographical facts, and investigate prospects for trade with the Indians. He named as its leader the thirty-two-year-old *Lewis and Clark* Meriwether Lewis, a veteran of Indian wars who was skilled in the ways of the wilderness. Lewis chose as a colleague the twenty-eight-year-old William Clark, an experienced frontiersman and Indian fighter. In the spring of 1804, Lewis and Clark, with a company of four dozen men, started up the Missouri River from St. Louis. With the Shoshone woman Sacajawea as their interpreter, they eventually crossed the Rocky Mountains, descended along the Snake and Columbia Rivers, and in the late autumn of 1805 camped on the Pacific coast. In September 1806, they were back in St. Louis with elaborate records of the geography and the Indian civilizations they had observed along the way.

While Lewis and Clark were on their journey, Jefferson dispatched other explorers to other parts of the Louisiana Territory. Lieutenant Zebulon Montgomery Pike, twenty-six years old, led an expedition in the fall of 1805 from St. Louis into the upper Mississippi Valley. In the summer of 1806, he set out again, proceeding up the valley of the Arkansas River and into what later became Colorado. His account of his western travels helped create an enduring (and inaccurate) impression among most Americans that the land between the Missouri and the Rockies was a desert that farmers could never cultivate.

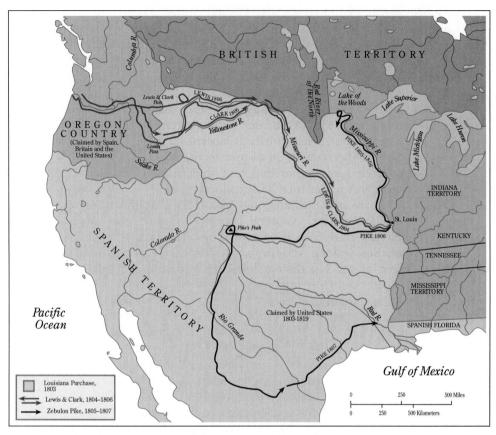

EXPLORING THE LOUISIANA PURCHASE, 1804–1807 When Jefferson purchased the Louisiana territory from France in 1803, he doubled the size of the nation. But few Americans knew what they had bought. The Lewis and Clark Expedition set out in 1804 to investigate the new territories, and this map shows their route, along with that of another inveterate explorer Zebulon Pike. Note the vast distances the two parties covered (including, in both cases, a great deal of land outside the Louisiana Purchase). Note, too, how much of this enormous territory lay outside the orbit of even these ambitious explorations. ◆ *How did the American public react to the addition of these new territories?*

 For an interactive version of this map go to www.mhhe.com/unfinishednation4ch7maps

The Burr Conspiracy

Jefferson's triumphant reelection in 1804 suggested that most of the nation approved the new territorial acquisition. But some New England Federalists raged against it. They realized that the more new states joined the Union, the less power the Federalists and their region would retain. In Massachusetts, a group of the most extreme Federalists, known as the Essex Junto, concluded that the only recourse for New England was to se-

Essex Junto

cede from the Union and form a separate "northern confederacy." If a northern confederacy was to have any hope for lasting success as a separate nation, the Federalists believed, it would have to include New York and New Jersey as well as New England. But the leading Federalist in New York, Alexander Hamilton, refused to support the secessionist scheme.

Federalists in New York then turned to Hamilton's greatest political rival, Vice President Aaron Burr. Burr accepted a Federalist proposal that he become their candidate for governor of New York in 1804, and there were rumors that he had also agreed to support the Federalist plans for secession. Hamilton accused Burr of plotting treason and made numerous private remarks, widely reported in the press, about Burr's "despicable" character. When Burr lost the election, he blamed his defeat on Hamilton's malevolence and challenged him to a duel. Hamilton feared that refusing Burr's challenge would brand him a coward. And so, on a July morning in 1804, the two men met at Weehawken, New Jersey. Hamilton was mortally wounded; he died the next day.

Hamilton and Burr

Burr now had to flee New York to avoid an indictment for murder. He found new outlets for his ambitions in the West. Even before the duel, he had begun corresponding with General James Wilkinson, now governor of the Louisiana Territory. Burr and Wilkinson, it seems clear, hoped to lead an expedition that would capture Mexico from the Spanish. But there were also rumors that they wanted to separate the Southwest from the Union and create a western empire that Burr would rule. There is little evidence that these rumors were true.

Whether true or not, many of Burr's opponents chose to believe the rumors—including, ultimately, Jefferson himself. When Burr led a group of armed followers down the Ohio River by boat in 1806, disturbing reports flowed into Washington (the most alarming from Wilkinson, who had suddenly turned against Burr) that an attack on New Orleans was imminent. Jefferson ordered the arrest of Burr and his men as traitors. Burr was brought to Richmond for trial. But Chief Justice Marshall limited the evidence the government could present and defined the charge in such a way that the jury had little choice but to acquit Burr.

The Burr conspiracy was in part the story of a single man's soaring ambitions and flamboyant personality. But it was also a symbol of the larger perils still facing the new nation. With a central government that remained deliberately weak, with ambitious political leaders willing, if necessary, to circumvent normal channels in their search for power, the legitimacy of the federal government—and indeed the existence of the United States as a stable and united nation—remained to be fully established.

EXPANSION AND WAR

Conflicts in Europe and North America

Two very different conflicts were taking shape in the last years of Jefferson's presidency. One was the continuing tension in Europe, which in 1803 escalated once again into a full-scale conflict (the Napoleonic Wars). As fighting between the British and the French increased, each side took steps to prevent the United States from trading with the other. The other conflict occurred in North America itself, a result of the ceaseless westward expansion of white settlement, which was colliding with a native population committed to protecting its lands from intruders. In both the North and the South, the threatened tribes mobilized to resist white encroachments. They began as well to forge connections with British forces in Canada and Spanish forces in Florida. The Indian conflict on land, therefore, became intertwined with the European conflict on the seas, and ultimately helped cause the War of 1812.

Conflict on the Seas

In 1805, at the Battle of Trafalgar, a British fleet virtually destroyed what was left of the French navy. Because France could no longer challenge the British at sea, Napoleon now chose to pressure England in other ways. The result was what he called the Continental System, designed to close the European continent to British trade. Napoleon issued a series of decrees barring British ships and neutral ships touching at British ports from

Embargo and Blockade

landing their cargoes at any European port controlled by France or its allies. The British government replied to Napoleon's decrees by establishing a blockade of the European coast. The blockade required that any goods being shipped to Napoleon's Europe be carried either in British vessels or in neutral vessels stopping at British ports—precisely what Napoleon's policies forbade.

America's Predicament

In the early nineteenth century, the United States had developed one of the most important merchant marines in the world, one that soon controlled a large proportion of the trade between Europe and the West Indies. But the events in Europe now challenged that control, because American ships were caught between Napoleon's decrees and Britain's blockade. If they sailed directly for the European continent, they risked being captured by the British navy. If they sailed by way of a British port, they ran the risk of seizure by the French. Both of the warring powers were violating America's rights as a neutral nation. But most Americans considered the British, with their greater sea power, the worse offender—especially since British vessels frequently stopped American ships on the high seas and seized sailors off the decks, making them victims of "impressment."

Impressment

Many British sailors called their navy—with its floggings, its low pay, and its terrible shipboard conditions—a "floating hell." Few volunteered. Most had had to be "impressed" (forced) into the service. At every opportunity they deserted. By 1807, many of these deserters had emigrated to the United States and joined the American merchant marine or the American navy. To check this loss of manpower, the British claimed the right to stop and search American merchantmen and reimpress deserters. They did not claim the right to take native-born Americans, but they did insist on the right to seize naturalized Americans born on British soil. In practice, the British navy often made no careful distinctions, impressing British deserters and native-born Americans alike into their service.

In the summer of 1807, the British went to more provocative extremes. Sailing from Norfolk, with several alleged deserters from the British navy among the crew, the American naval frigate *Chesapeake* was hailed by the British ship *Chesapeake-Leopard Incident* *Leopard*. When the American commander, James Barron, refused to allow the British to search the *Chesapeake*, the *Leopard* opened fire. Barron had no choice but to surrender, and a boarding party from the *Leopard* dragged four men off the American frigate.

When news of the *Chesapeake-Leopard* incident reached the United States, there was a great popular clamor for revenge. But Jefferson and Madison tried to maintain the peace. Jefferson expelled all British warships from American waters to lessen the likelihood of future incidents. Then he sent instructions to his minister in England, James Monroe, to demand from the British government an end to impressment. The British government disavowed the actions of the *Leopard's* commanding officer and recalled him; it offered compensation for those killed and wounded in the incident; and it promised to return three of the captured sailors (one of the original four had been hanged). But the British cabinet refused to renounce impressment and instead reasserted its right to recover deserting seamen.

"Peaceable Coercion"

In an effort to prevent future incidents that might bring the nation again to the brink of war, Jefferson persuaded Congress to pass a drastic measure late in 1807. It was known as the Embargo, *Jefferson's Embargo* and it prohibited American ships from leaving the United States for any foreign port anywhere in the world. The law was widely evaded, but it was effective enough to create a serious depression throughout most of the nation. Hardest hit were the merchants and shipowners of the Northeast, most of them Federalists.

The presidential election of 1808 came in the midst of this Embargo-induced depression. James Madison was elected president, but the Federalist candidate, Charles Pinckney again, ran much more strongly than he had in 1804. The Embargo was clearly a growing political liability, and Jefferson decided to back down. A few days before leaving office, he approved a bill ending his experiment with what he called "peaceable coercion."

Madison's Non-Intercourse Act
To replace the Embargo, Congress passed the Non-Intercourse Act just before Madison took office. It reopened trade with all nations but Great Britain and France. A year later, in 1810, the Non-Intercourse Act expired and was replaced by Macon's Bill No. 2, which reopened free commercial relations with Britain and France but authorized the president to prohibit commerce with either belligerent if it should continue violating neutral shipping after the other had stopped. Napoleon, in an effort to induce the United States to reimpose the Embargo against Britain, announced that France would no longer interfere with American shipping. Madison announced that an embargo against Great Britain alone would automatically go into effect early in 1811 unless Britain renounced its restrictions on American shipping.

In time, this new, limited embargo persuaded England to repeal its blockade of Europe. But the repeal came too late to prevent war. In any case, naval policies were only part of the reason for tensions between Britain and the United States.

The "Indian Problem" and the British

Given the ruthlessness with which white settlers in North America had dislodged Indian tribes to make room for expanding settlement, it was hardly surprising that ever since the Revolution most Indians had continued to look to England for protection. The British in Canada, for their part, had relied on the Indians as partners in the lucrative fur trade. There had been relative peace in the Northwest for over a decade after Jay's Treaty and Anthony Wayne's victory over the tribes at Fallen Timbers in 1794. But the

Conflict between Settlers and Indians
1807 war crisis following the *Chesapeake-Leopard* incident revived the conflict between Indians and white settlers. Two important (and very different) men emerged to lead it: William Henry Harrison and Tecumseh.

The Virginia-born Harrison, already a veteran Indian fighter at age twenty-six, went to Washington as the congressional delegate from the Northwest Territory in 1799. An advocate of development in the western lands, he was largely responsible for the passage in 1800 of the so-called Harrison Land Law, which

William Henry Harrison
enabled white settlers to acquire farms from the public domain on much easier terms than before.

In 1801, Jefferson appointed Harrison governor of Indiana Territory to administer the president's proposed solution to the "Indian problem." Jefferson offered the Indians a choice: they could convert themselves into settled farmers and become a part of white society, or they could migrate west of the Mississippi. In either case, they would have to give up their claims to their tribal lands in the Northwest.

Jefferson considered the assimilation policy a benign alternative to the continuing conflict between Indians and white settlers. But to the tribes, the new policy seemed far from benign, especially given the bludgeonlike efficiency with which Harrison set out to implement it. He used threats, bribes, trickery, and whatever other tactics he felt would help him. By 1807, the United States had extracted treaty rights to eastern Michigan, southern Indiana, and most of Illinois from reluctant tribal leaders.

Jefferson's Assimilation Proposal

Meanwhile, in the Southwest, white Americans were taking millions of acres from other tribes in Georgia, Tennessee, and Mississippi. The Indians wanted desperately to resist, but the separate tribes were helpless by themselves against the power of the United States. They might have accepted their fate passively but for the emergence of two new factors.

One factor was the policy of British authorities in Canada. After the *Chesapeake* incident, they began to expect an American invasion of Canada and took desperate measures for their own defense. Among those measures were efforts to renew friendship with the Indians.

Tecumseh and the Prophet

The second, and more important, factor intensifying the border conflict was the rise of two remarkable native leaders. One was Tenskwatawa, a charismatic religious leader and orator known as "the Prophet." He had experienced a mystical awakening in the process of recovering from alcoholism. Having freed himself from what he considered the evil effects of white culture, he began to speak to his people of the superior virtues of Indian civilization and the sinfulness and corruption of the white world. In the process, he inspired a religious revival that spread through numerous tribes and helped unite them. The Prophet's headquarters at the meeting of Tippecanoe Creek and the Wabash River (known as Prophetstown) became a sacred place for people of many tribes. Out of their common religious experiences, they began to consider joint military efforts as well.

The Prophet's brother Tecumseh—"the Shooting Star," chief of the Shawnees—emerged as the leader of these efforts. Tecumseh understood, as few other Indian leaders had, that only through united action could the tribes hope to resist the steady advance of white civilization. Beginning in 1809, he set out to unite all the tribes of the Mississippi Valley into what became known as the Tecumseh Confederacy. Together, he promised, they would *The Tecumseh Confederacy* halt white expansion, recover the whole Northwest, and make the Ohio River the boundary between the United States and Indian country. He maintained that Harrison and others, by negotiating treaties with individual tribes, had obtained no real title to land. The land belonged to all the tribes; none of them could rightfully cede any of it without the consent of the others. In 1811, Tecumseh left Prophetstown and traveled down the Mississippi to visit the tribes of the South and persuade them to join the alliance.

During Tecumseh's absence, Governor Harrison saw a chance to destroy the growing influence of the two Indian leaders. With 1,000 soldiers he camped near Prophetstown, and on November 7, 1811, he provoked an armed conflict. Although the white forces suffered losses as heavy as those of the natives, Harrison drove off the Indians and burned the town.

Battle of Tippecanoe The Battle of Tippecanoe (named for the creek near which it was fought) disillusioned many of the Prophet's followers, and Tecumseh returned to find the confederacy in disarray. But there were still warriors eager for combat, and by spring of 1812 they were active along the frontier, raiding white settlements and terrifying settlers.

The bloodshed along the western borders was largely a result of the Indians' own initiative, but Britain's agents in Canada had encouraged and helped to supply the uprising. To Harrison and most white residents of the regions, there seemed only one way to make the West safe for Americans: to drive the British out of Canada and annex that province to the United States.

Florida and War Fever

While white "frontiersmen" in the North demanded the conquest of Canada, those in the South looked to the acquisition of Spanish Florida. The territory was a continuing threat to whites in the southern United States. Slaves escaped across the Florida border; Indians in Florida

Coveted Florida launched frequent raids north. But white southerners also coveted Florida because through it ran rivers that could provide residents of the Southwest with access to valuable ports on the Gulf of Mexico.

In 1810, American settlers in West Florida (the area presently part of Mississippi and Louisiana) seized the Spanish fort at Baton Rouge and asked the federal government to annex the territory to the United States. President Madison happily agreed and then began planning to get the rest of Florida, too. The desire for Florida became yet another motivation for war with Britain. Spain was Britain's ally, and a war with England might provide an excuse for taking Spanish as well as British territory.

By 1812, therefore, war fever was raging on both the northern and southern borders of the United States. The demands of the residents of these areas found substantial support in Washington among a group of de-

"War Hawks" termined young congressmen who soon earned the name "War Hawks."

In the congressional elections of 1810, voters elected a large number of representatives of both parties eager for war with Britain. The most influential of them came from the new states in the West or from the backcountry of the old states in the South. Two of their leaders, both recently elected to the House of Representatives, were Henry Clay of Kentucky and John C. Calhoun of South Carolina, men of great intellect, magnetism, and ambition. Both were supporters of war with Great Britain.

Clay was elected Speaker of the House in 1811, and he appointed Calhoun to the crucial *Clay and Calhoun Call for War* Committee on Foreign Affairs. Both men began agitating for the conquest of Canada. Madison still preferred peace but was losing control of Congress. On June 18, 1812, he approved a declaration of war against Britain.

THE WAR OF 1812

The British were not eager for an open conflict with the United States. Even after the Americans declared war, Britain largely ignored them for a time. But in the fall of 1812, Napoleon launched a catastrophic campaign against Russia that left his army in disarray. By late 1813, with the French empire on its way to final defeat, Britain was able to turn its military attention to America.

Battles with the Tribes

In the summer of 1812, American forces invaded Canada through Detroit. They soon had to retreat back to Detroit and in August surrendered the fort there. Other invasion efforts also failed. In the meantime, Fort Dearborn (later Chicago) fell before an Indian attack.

Things went only slightly better for the United States on the seas. At first, American frigates won some spectacular victories over British warships. But by 1813, the British navy was counterattacking effectively, driving the American frigates to cover and imposing a blockade on the United States.

The United States did, however, achieve significant early military successes on the Great Lakes. First, the Americans took command of Lake Ontario; this permitted them to raid and burn York (now Toronto), the capital of Canada. American forces then seized control of Lake Erie, mainly through the work of the young Oliver Hazard Perry, who engaged and dispersed a British fleet at Put-in Bay on September 10, 1813. This made possible, at last, a *Put-in Bay* more successful invasion of Canada by way of Detroit. William Henry Harrison pushed up the river Thames into upper Canada and on October 5, 1813, won a victory notable for the death of Tecumseh, who was serving as a brigadier general in the British army. The Battle of the Thames resulted in no lasting occupation of Canada, but it weakened and disheartened the Indians of the Northwest.

In the meantime, another white military leader was striking an even harder blow at the Indians of the Southwest. The Creeks, supplied by the

Spaniards in Florida, had been attacking white settlers near the Florida border. Andrew Jackson, a wealthy Tennessee planter and a general in the state militia, set off in pursuit of the Creeks. On March 27, 1814, in the Battle of Horseshoe Bend, Jackson's men took terrible revenge on the Indians, slaughtering women and children along with warriors. The tribe agreed to cede most of its lands to the United States and retreated westward. The battle also won Jackson a commission as major general in the United States Army, and in that capacity he led his men farther south into Florida. On November 7, 1814, he seized the Spanish fort at Pensacola.

Battles with the British

But the victories over the tribes were not enough to win the war. After the surrender of Napoleon in 1814, England prepared to invade the United States. A British armada sailed up the Patuxent River from Chesapeake Bay and landed an army that marched to nearby Bladensburg, on the outskirts of Washington, where it dispersed a poorly trained force of American militiamen. On August 24, 1814, the British troops entered Washington and put the government to flight. Then they set fire to several public buildings, including the White House, in retaliation for the earlier American burning of the Canadian capital at York.

The British Invasion

Leaving Washington in partial ruins, the invading army proceeded up the bay toward Baltimore. But Baltimore, guarded by Fort McHenry, was prepared. To block the approaching fleet, the American garrison had sunk several ships in the Patapsco River (the entry to Baltimore's harbor), thus forcing the British to bombard the fort from a distance. Through the night of September 13, Francis Scott Key (a Washington lawyer on board one of the British ships) watched the bombardment. The next morning, "by the dawn's early light," he could see the flag on the fort still flying; he recorded his pride in the moment by writing a poem—"The Star-Spangled Banner." The British withdrew from Baltimore, and Key's words were soon set to the tune of an old English drinking song. (In 1931 "The Star-Spangled Banner" became the official national anthem.)

Meanwhile, American forces repelled another British invasion in northern New York; at the Battle of Plattsburgh, on September 11, 1814, they turned back a much more numerous British naval and land force. In the South, a formidable array of battle-hardened British veterans landed below New Orleans and prepared to advance north up the Mississippi. Awaiting the British was Andrew Jackson with a motley collection of Tennesseans, Kentuckians, Creoles, blacks, pirates, and regular army troops drawn up behind earthen breastworks. On January 8, 1815, the redcoats advanced on the American fortifications, but the exposed British forces were no match for Jackson's well-protected men. After the Americans had repulsed several waves of attackers, the British finally retreated, leaving behind 700 dead, 1,400 wounded,

Battle of New Orleans

THE BURNING OF WASHINGTON This dramatic engraving somewhat exaggerates the extent of the blazes in Washington when the British occupied the city in August 1814. But the invaders did set fire to the Capitol, the White House, and other public buildings in retaliation for the American burning of the Canadian capital at York. *(Bettmann/Corbis)*

and 500 prisoners. Jackson's losses: 8 killed, 13 wounded. Only later did news reach North America that the United States and Britain had signed a peace treaty several weeks before the Battle of New Orleans.

The Revolt of New England

With a few notable exceptions, the military efforts of the United States between 1812 and 1815 consisted of a series of failures. As a result, the American government faced increasing opposition as the contest dragged on. In New England, opposition both to the war and to the Republican government that was waging it was so extreme that some Federalists celebrated British victories. In Congress, in the meantime, the Republicans had continual trouble with the Federalist opposition, led by a young con- *Federalist Opposition to War* gressman from New Hampshire, Daniel Webster.

By now the Federalists were very much in the minority in the country as a whole, but they were still the majority party in New England. Some of them began to dream of creating a separate nation in that region. Talk of secession reached a climax in the winter of 1814–1815.

THE WAR OF 1812 These three maps illustrate the military maneuvers of the British and the Americans during the War of 1812. The large map at top shows all the theaters of the war, from New Orleans to southern Canada. The large detail at bottom shows the extended land and water battle along the Canadian border and in the Great Lakes. The small detail in the bottom right corner of the upper map shows the fighting around Washington and Baltimore. Note how in all these theaters, there are about the same number of British and American victories. ◆ *What brought this inconclusive war finally to an end?*

 For an interactive version of this map go to www.mhhe.com/unfinishednation4ch7maps

On December 15, 1814, delegates from the New England states met in Hartford, Connecticut, to discuss their grievances against the Madison administration. The would-be seceders at the Hartford Convention were outnumbered by a comparatively moderate majority. But while the convention's report only hinted at secession, it reasserted the right of nullification and proposed seven amendments to the Constitution—amendments designed to protect New England from the growing influence of the South and the West.

The Hartford Convention

Because the war was going so badly, the New Englanders assumed that the Republicans would have to agree to their demands. Soon after the convention adjourned, however, the news of Jackson's victory at New Orleans reached the cities of the Northeast. A day or two later, reports of a peace treaty arrived from abroad. In the changed atmosphere these apparent triumphs produced, the Hartford Convention and the Federalist party came to seem futile, irrelevant, even treasonable.

The Peace Settlement

Serious negotiations between the United States and Britain began in August 1814, when American and British diplomats met in Ghent, Belgium. John Quincy Adams, Henry Clay, and Albert Gallatin led the American delegation. Although both sides began with extravagant demands, the final treaty did very little except end the fighting itself. The Americans gave up their demand for a British renunciation of impressment and for the cession of Canada to the United States. The British abandoned their call for creation of an Indian buffer state in the Northwest and made other, minor territorial concessions. The treaty was signed on Christmas Eve 1814.

Treaty of Ghent

Both sides had reason to accept this skimpy agreement. The British, exhausted and in debt from their prolonged conflict with Napoleon, were eager to settle the lesser dispute in North America. The Americans realized that with the defeat of Napoleon in Europe, the British would no longer have much incentive to interfere with American commerce.

Other settlements followed the Treaty of Ghent. A commercial treaty in 1815 gave Americans the right to trade freely with England and much of the British Empire. The Rush-Bagot agreement of 1817 provided for mutual disarmament on the Great Lakes; eventually (although not until 1872) the Canadian-American boundary became the longest "unguarded frontier" in the world.

For the other parties to the War of 1812—the Indian tribes east of the Mississippi—the conflict proved another disastrous blow to the capacity of Indians to resist white expansion. Tecumseh was dead. The British were gone from the Northwest. The intertribal alliance that Tecumseh and the Prophet had forged was in disarray. The end of the war served to spur white movement westward, into land the Indians were less than ever able to defend.

Disastrous Consequences for the Indians

CONCLUSION

Thomas Jefferson called his election to the presidency the "Revolution of 1800," and his supporters believed that his victory would bring a dramatic change in the character of the nation—a retreat from Hamilton's dreams of a powerful, developing nation and a return to an ideal of a simple agrarian republic.

But American society was changing rapidly, making it virtually impossible for the Jeffersonian dream to prevail. The nation's population was expanding and diversifying. Its cities were growing, and its commercial life was becoming ever more important. In 1803, Jefferson himself made one of the most important contributions to the growth of the United States: the Louisiana Purchase, which dramatically expanded the physical boundaries of the nation—and which began extending white settlement deeper into the continent. In the process, it greatly widened the battles between Europeans and Native Americans.

The growing national pride and commercial ambitions of the United States gradually created another serious conflict with Great Britain: the War of 1812, a war that was settled finally in 1814 on terms at least mildly favorable to the United States. By then, the bitter party rivalries that had characterized the first years of the republic had to some degree subsided, and the nation was poised to enter what became known, quite inaccurately, as the "Era of Good Feelings."

FOR FURTHER REFERENCE

Joseph J. Ellis, *American Sphinx: The Character of Thomas Jefferson* (1997) is a perceptive study of the man. Henry Adams, *History of the United States During the Administration of Jefferson and Adams*, 9 vols. (1889–1891) is one of the great literary achievements of early American historiography. Frank Bergon, ed., *The Journals of Lewis and Clark* (1989) is a concise abridgement of these fascinating accounts of their explorations. James Ronda, *Lewis and Clark Among the Indians* (1984) examines the exploration from a Native American perspective. Thomas C. Cochran, *Frontiers of Change: Early Industrialization in America* (1981) summarizes economic development in the early republic. Jeanne Boydston, *Home and Work: Housework, Wages, and the Ideology of Labor in the Early Republic* (1990) argues that the cultural status of women declined as the market revolution began to transform the American economy. Peter S. Onuf, *The Language of American Nationhood* (2000) examines nationalist rhetoric and ideas in the Jeffersonian era. Joyce Appleby, *Inheriting the Revolution: The First Generation of Americans* (2000) examines the adjustment of the revolutionary generation to the burdens of nationhood. Drew McCoy, *The Elusive Republic: Political Economy in Jeffersonian America* (1980) traces the Jeffersonian struggle to keep the United States free from European-style corruption and decay. Paul Finkleman, *Slavery and the Founders: Race and Liberty*

in the Age of Jefferson (1996) considers the problem of slavery in the early Republic. Donald Hickey, *The War of 1812: A Forgotten Conflict* (1989) is an account of the war. Anthony F. C. Wallace, *Jefferson and the Indians: The Tragic Fate of the First Americans* (1999) is a critical study of the impact of Jefferson's policies on the tribes. J. C. A. Stagg, *Mr. Madison's War: Politics, Diplomacy, and Warfare in the Early American Republic, 1783–1830* (1983) argues that James Madison led the United States to war against Great Britain in order to preserve vital American commercial interests, but that he underestimated New England opposition to the war.

For quizzes, Internet resources, references to additional books and films, and more, consult this book's Online Learning Center site at www.mhhe.com/unfinishednation4.

***FOURTH OF JULY PICNIC AT WEYMOUTH LANDING (C. 1845), BY
SUSAN MERRETT*** Celebrations of Independence Day, like this one in
eastern Massachusetts, became major festive events throughout the United
States in the early nineteenth century, a sign of rising American nationalism.
*(Susan Torrey Merritt, American, 1826–1879, Anti-Slavery Picnic at Weymouth
Landing, Massachusetts, c. 1845, watercolor, gouache, and collage on paper, 74.9 × 100 cm,
Gift of Elizabeth R. Vaughan, 1950.1846 image © The Art Institute of Chicago)*

TIME LINE

1815	1816	1818	1819	
U.S. takes western lands from Indians	Second Bank of U.S.	Seminole War ends	Panic and depression	
	Monroe elected president		*Dartmouth College v. Woodward; McCulloch v. Maryland*	

VARIETIES OF AMERICAN NATIONALISM

Stabilizing Economic Growth
Expanding Westward
The "Era of Good Feelings"
Sectionalism and Nationalism
The Revival of Opposition

L ike a "fire bell in the night," as Thomas Jefferson put it, the issue of slavery arose after the War of 1812 to threaten the unity of the nation. The debate began when the territory of Missouri applied for admission to the Union, raising the question of whether it would be a free or a slaveholding state. But the larger issue was whether the vast new western regions of the United States would ultimately move into the orbit of the North or the South.

The Missouri crisis was significant because it was a sign of the sectional crises to come. But at the time, it was also significant because it stood in such sharp contrast to the rising American nationalism of the years following the war. Whatever forces might be working to pull the nation apart, stronger ones were acting for the moment to draw it together.

STABILIZING ECONOMIC GROWTH

The end of the War of 1812 allowed the United States to resume its economic growth and territorial expansion. A vigorous postwar boom led to a disastrous bust in 1819. Brief though it was, the collapse was evidence that the United States continued to lack some of the basic institutions necessary to sustain long-term growth.

1820	1823	1824	1828
Missouri Compromise	Monroe Doctrine	John Quincy Adams elected	Tariff of abominations
Monroe reelected			Jackson elected president

The Government and Economic Growth

Postwar Economic Problems The War of 1812 produced chaos in shipping and banking, and it exposed dramatically the inadequacy of the existing transportation and financial systems. The aftermath of the war, therefore, saw the emergence of a series of political issues connected with national economic development.

The wartime experience underlined the need for another national bank. After the expiration of the first Bank's charter, a large number of state banks had issued vast quantities of bank notes, creating a confusing variety of currency of widely differing value. It was difficult to tell what any bank note was really worth, and counterfeiting was easy. In response *Second Bank of the United States* to these problems, Congress chartered a second Bank of the United States in 1816, much like its predecessor of 1791 but with more capital. The national bank could not forbid state banks from issuing notes, but its size and power enabled it to compel the state banks to issue only sound notes or risk being forced out of business.

Congress also acted to promote manufacturing, which the war (by cutting off imports) had already greatly stimulated. The American textile industry had experienced a particularly dramatic growth. Between 1807 and 1815, the total number of cotton spindles in the country increased more than fifteenfold, from 8,000 to 130,000. Until 1814, the textile factories—most of them in New England—produced only yarn and thread; families operating hand looms at home did the actual weaving of cloth. Then the Boston merchant Francis Cabot Lowell, after examining textile machinery in England, developed a power loom better than its English counterpart. In 1813, in Waltham, Massachusetts, Lowell founded the first mill in America to carry on the processes of spinning and weaving under a single roof.

But the end of the war suddenly dimmed the prospects for American industry. British ships swarmed into American ports and unloaded cargoes of manufactured goods, many priced below cost. In *The Protective Tariff* 1816, protectionists in Congress passed a tariff law that effectively limited competition from abroad on a wide range of items, including cotton cloth, despite objections from agricultural interests, who stood to pay higher prices for manufactured goods.

Transportation

Inadequate Transportation System The nation's most pressing economic need was for improvements in its transportation system. An old debate resumed: Should the federal government help to finance roads and other "internal improvements"? The idea of using government funds to finance road building was not a new one. When Ohio entered the Union in 1803, the federal government agreed that part of the proceeds from the sale of public lands there should finance

AN EARLY MILL IN NEW ENGLAND This early folk painting of about 1814 shows the small town of East Chelmford, Massachusetts—still primarily agrarian, with its rural houses, open fields, and grazing livestock, but with a small textile mill already operating along the stream, at right. A little more than a decade later, the town had been transformed into a major manufacturing center and renamed for the family that owned the mills: Lowell. (*Part of the Town of Chelmsford by Miss Warren. Abby Aldrich Rockefeller Folk Art Center, Williamsburg, Virginia*)

road construction. And in 1807, Congress enacted a law proposed by the Jefferson administration that permitted using revenues from Ohio land sales to finance a National Road from the Potomac River to the Ohio. By 1818, the highway ran as far as Wheeling, Virginia, on the Ohio River; and the Lancaster Pike, financed in part by the state of Pennsylvania, extended westward to Pittsburgh.

At the same time, steam-powered shipping was expanding rapidly. By 1816, river steamers were beginning to journey up and down the Mississippi to the Ohio River, and up the Ohio as far as Pittsburgh. Steamboats were soon carrying more cargo on the Mississippi than all the earlier forms of river transport—flatboats, barges, and others—combined. They stimulated the agricultural economy of the West and the South by providing access to markets at greatly reduced cost, and they enabled eastern manufacturers to send their finished goods west much more readily.

Nevertheless, serious gaps in the nation's transportation network remained, as experience during the War of 1812 had shown. Once the British blockade had cut off Atlantic shipping, the coastal roads had become choked by the unaccustomed volume of north-south traffic. Congress passed a bill introduced by Representative John C. Calhoun that allowed the

Federally Funded Improvements Debated

THE *CLERMONT'S* ENGINE Robert Fulton's *Clermont* became the first steamboat to travel from New York to Albany (in 32 hours) in 1809. Its great paddle was driven by a powerful piston, which was driven in turn by power generated by a steam boiler. This is Fulton's own drawing of the engine system. *(© The New-York Historical Society)*

use of government funds to finance internal improvements, but Madison, on his last day in office, vetoed it. He supported the purpose of the bill, he explained, but he believed that Congress lacked authority to fund the improvements without a constitutional amendment. For a time, state governments and private enterprise were left on their own to build the transportation network necessary for the growing American economy.

EXPANDING WESTWARD

One reason for the growing interest in internal improvements was the dramatic surge in westward expansion in the years following the War of 1812. By the time of the census of 1820, white settlers had pushed well beyond the Mississippi River, and the population of the western regions was increasing more rapidly than that of the nation as a whole.

The Great Migration

The westward movement of the white American population was one of the most important developments of the century. There were several major reasons for this expansion.

One reason was population growth, which drove many white Americans out of the East. Between 1800 and 1820, the population nearly doubled—from 5.3 million to 9.6 million. Most Americans were still farmers, and the agricultural lands of the East were by now largely occupied or exhausted. In the South, the spread of the plantation system limited opportunities for new settlers. Another reason was that the West itself was becoming increasingly attractive to white settlers. Land there was much more plentiful than it was in the East. And in the aftermath of the War of 1812, the federal government continued its policy of pushing the Indian tribes farther and farther west. Migrants from throughout the East flocked in increasing numbers to what was then known as the Old Northwest (now part of the Midwest), most of them via the Ohio and Monongahela Rivers. Once on the Ohio, most floated downstream on flatboats, then left the river (often at Cincinnati) and traveled overland with wagons, handcarts, packhorses, cattle, and hogs.

Reasons for Westward Expansion

White Settlers in the Old Northwest

Having arrived at their destination, most settlers built lean-tos or cabins and then hewed clearings out of the forest and planted crops of corn to supplement the wild game they caught and the domestic animals they had brought with them. It was a rough and lonely existence. Men, women, and children worked side by side in the fields—and at times had virtually no contact for weeks or months with anyone outside their own families.

Life in the western territories was not, however, entirely solitary or individualistic. Migrants often journeyed westward in groups and built new communities with schools, churches, and stores. The labor shortage in the interior led neighbors to develop systems of mutual aid. They gathered periodically to raise a barn, clear land, or harvest crops.

Another common feature of life in the Northwest was mobility. Individuals and families were constantly on the move, settling for a few years in one place and then selling their land (often at a significant profit) and resettling somewhere else. When new areas for settlement opened farther to the west, it was often the people already on the western edges of white settlement—rather than those who remained in the East—who flocked to them first.

A Mobile Society

The Plantation System in the Old Southwest

In the Old Southwest (now generally known as the Deep South), the new agricultural economy emerged along different lines. The market for cot-

Cotton and the Expansion of Slavery

ton continued to grow, and the Southwest contained a broad zone where cotton could thrive. That zone included what was to become known as the Black Belt of central Alabama and Mississippi, a vast prairie with a dark, productive soil.

The first arrivals in the uncultivated regions of the Old Southwest were usually small farmers who made rough clearings in the forest. But wealthier planters soon followed. They bought up the cleared or partially cleared land, and the original settlers moved farther west and started over again. Success in the wilderness was by no means assured, even for the wealthiest settlers. Many settlers managed to do little more than subsist in their new environment, and others experienced utter ruin. But some planters soon expanded small clearings into vast cotton fields. They replaced the cabins of the early pioneers with more sumptuous log dwellings and ultimately with imposing mansions. They also built up large slave work forces.

New States in the West

The rapid growth of the Old Northwest and Southwest resulted in the admission of four new states to the Union: Indiana in 1816, Mississippi in 1817, Illinois in 1818, and Alabama in 1819.

Trade and Trapping in the Far West

Not many Anglo-Americans yet knew much about or were much interested in the far western areas of the continent. But a significant trade nevertheless began to develop between these western regions and the United States early in the nineteenth century, and it grew steadily for decades.

Mexico, which continued to control Texas, California, and much of the rest of the far Southwest, won its independence from Spain in 1821. Almost immediately, it opened its northern territories to trade with the United States. American traders poured into the region. Merchants from the United States quickly displaced Indian and Mexican traders. In New Mexico, for example, the Missouri trader William Becknell began in 1821 to offer American manufactured goods for sale, priced considerably below the inferior Mexican goods that had dominated the market in the past. Mexico effectively lost its markets in its own colony as a steady traffic of commercial wagon trains began moving back and forth along the Santa Fe Trail between Missouri and New Mexico.

Astor's American Fur Company

Fur traders created a wholly new kind of commerce. After the War of 1812, John Jacob Astor's American Fur Company and others extended their operations from the Great Lakes area westward to the Rockies. At first, fur traders did most of their business by purchasing pelts from the Indi-

THE RENDEZVOUS The annual rendezvous of fur trappers and traders was a major event in the lives of the lonely men who made their livelihoods gathering furs. It was also a gathering of representatives of the many cultures that mingled in the Far West, among them Anglo-Americans, French Canadians, Indians, and Hispanics. *(Denver Public Library)*

ans. But increasingly, white trappers entered the region and joined the Iroquois and other Indians in pursuit of beaver and other furs.

The trappers, or "mountain men," who began trading in the Far West were small in number. But they developed important relationships with the existing residents of the West—Indian and Mexican—and altered the character of society there. White trappers were mostly young, single men. Perhaps unsurprisingly, many of them entered into sexual relationships with Indian and Mexican women. They also recruited the women as helpers in the difficult work of preparing furs and skins for trading. Perhaps two-thirds of the white trappers married Indian or Hispanic women.

In 1822, Andrew and William Ashley founded the Rocky Mountain Fur Company and recruited white trappers to move permanently into the *Rocky Mountain Fur Company* Rockies. The Ashleys dispatched supplies annually to their trappers in exchange for furs and skins. The arrival of the supply train became the occasion for a gathering of scores of mountain men, some of whom lived much of the year in considerable isolation.

But however isolated their daily lives, these mountain men were closely bound up with the expanding market economy. Some were employees of the Rocky Mountain Fur Company, earning a salary in return for providing a steady supply of furs. Others trapped on their own and simply sold their furs for cash, but they too depended on merchants from the East for their livelihoods. Whatever the character of the transactions, the bulk of the profits from the trade flowed to the merchants, not the trappers.

Eastern Images of the West

Americans in the East were only dimly aware of the world of the trappers, and the trappers themselves did little to enlighten others. More important *Exploring the West* in increasing eastern awareness of the West were explorers, many of them dispatched by the United States government. In 1819 and 1820, with instructions from the War Department to find the source of the Red River, Stephen H. Long led nineteen soldiers on a journey up the Platte and South Platte Rivers through what is now Nebraska and eastern Colorado (where he discovered the peak that would be named for him), and then returned eastward along the Arkansas River through what is now Kansas. He failed to find the headwaters of the Red River. But he wrote an influential report on his trip, which echoed the dismissive conclusions of Zebulon Pike fifteen years before. The region "between the Missouri River and the Rocky Mountains," Long wrote, "is almost wholly unfit for cultivation, and of course uninhabitable by a people depending upon agriculture for their subsistence." On the published map of his expedition, he labeled the Great Plains the "Great American Desert."

THE "ERA OF GOOD FEELINGS"

The expansion of the economy, the growth of white settlement and trade in the West, the creation of new states—all reflected the rising spirit of nationalism that was permeating the United States in the years following the War of 1812. That spirit found reflection for a time as well in the character of national politics.

The End of the First Party System

Ever since 1800, the presidency seemed to have been the special possession of Virginians. After two terms in office Jefferson chose his secretary of state, James Madison of Virginia, to succeed him, and after two more terms, Madison secured the presidential nomination for his secretary of state, James Monroe, also of Virginia. Many in the North were expressing *The Virginia Dynasty* impatience with the so-called Virginia Dynasty, but the Republicans had no difficulty electing their candidate in 1816. Monroe received 183 ballots in the electoral college; his Federalist opponent, Rufus King of New York, received only 34.

Monroe was sixty-one years old when he became president. He entered office under what seemed to be remarkably favorable circumstances. With the decline of the Federalists, his party faced no serious opposition. With the conclusion of the War of 1812, the nation faced no important international threats. Some American politicians had dreamed since the first days of the republic of a time in which partisan divisions and factional

THE INAUGURATION OF JAMES MONROE, 1816 The ruins of part of the United States Capitol, burned by the British two years earlier late in the War of 1812, provided a bleak backdrop for James Monroe's first inauguration in 1816. *(Bettmann/Corbis)*

disputes might come to an end. In the prosperous postwar years, Monroe attempted to use his office to realize that dream.

He made that clear, above all, in the selection of his cabinet. For secretary of state, he chose the New Englander and former Federalist John Quincy Adams. Jefferson, Madison, and Monroe had all served as secretary of state before becoming president; Adams, therefore, immediately became the heir apparent, suggesting that the "Virginia Dynasty" would soon come to an end. Speaker of the House Henry Clay declined an offer to be secretary of war, so Monroe named John C. Calhoun instead.

Soon after his inauguration, Monroe made a good-will tour through the country. In New England, so recently the scene of rabid Federalist discontent, he was greeted *Monroe's Good-will Tour* everywhere with enthusiastic demonstrations. The *Columbian Centinel*, a Federalist newspaper in Boston, observed that an "era of good feelings" had arrived. And on the surface, at least, the years of Monroe's presidency did appear to be an "era of good feelings." In 1820, Monroe was reelected without opposition. For all practical purposes, the Federalist Party had now ceased to exist.

John Quincy Adams and Florida

Like his father, the second president of the United States, John Quincy Adams had spent much of his life in diplomatic service. And even before becoming secretary of state, he had become one of the great diplomats in American history. He was also a committed nationalist, and he considered his most important task to be the promotion of American expansion.

SEMINOLE DANCE This 1838 drawing by a U.S. military officer portrays a dance by Seminole Indians near Fort Butler in Florida. It was made in the midst of the prolonged Second Seminole War, which ended in 1842 with the removal of most of the tribe from Florida to reservations west of the Mississippi. *(The Huntington Library, San Marino, California)*

His first challenge was Florida. The United States had already annexed West Florida, but that claim was in dispute. Most Americans, moreover, still believed the nation should gain possession of the entire peninsula. In 1817, Adams began negotiations with the Spanish minister, Luis de Onís, in hopes of resolving the dispute and gaining the entire territory for the United States.

In the meantime, however, events were taking their own course in Florida itself. Andrew Jackson, now in command of American troops along the Florida frontier, had orders from Secretary of War Calhoun to "adopt the necessary measures" to stop continuing raids on American territory by Seminole Indians south of the border. *The Seminole War* Jackson used those orders as an excuse to invade Florida and seize the Spanish forts at St. Marks and Pensacola. The operation became known as the Seminole War.

Instead of condemning Jackson's raid, Adams urged the government to assume responsibility for it. The United States, he told the Spanish, had the right under international law to defend itself against threats from across its borders. Since Spain was unwilling or unable to curb those threats, America had simply done what was necessary. Jackson's raid demonstrated to the Spanish that the United States could easily take Florida by force. Adams implied that the nation might consider doing so.

Onís realized, therefore, that he had little choice but to come to terms with the Americans. Under the provisions of the Adams-Onís Treaty of 1819, Spain ceded all of Florida to the United States and gave up its claim to territory north of the 42nd parallel in the Pacific Northwest. In return, the American government gave up its claims to Texas.

Adams-Onís Treaty

The Panic of 1819

But the Monroe administration had little time to revel in its diplomatic successes, for the nation was falling victim to a serious economic crisis: the Panic of 1819. It followed a period of high foreign demand for American farm goods and thus of exceptionally high prices for American farmers. The rising prices for farm goods had stimulated a land boom in the western United States. Fueled by speculative investments, land prices soared.

The availability of easy credit to settlers and speculators—from the government (under the land acts of 1800 and 1804), from state banks and wildcat banks, even for a time from the rechartered Bank of the United States—fueled the land boom. Beginning in 1819, however, new management at the national bank began tightening credit, calling in loans, and foreclosing mortgages. This precipitated a series of failures by state banks, and the result was a financial panic. Six years of depression followed.

Tight Credit

Some Americans saw the Panic of 1819 and the widespread distress that followed as a warning that rapid economic growth and territorial expansion would destabilize the nation. But by 1820 most Americans were irrevocably committed to the idea of growth and expansion.

SECTIONALISM AND NATIONALISM

For a brief but alarming moment in 1819–1820, the increasing differences between the North and the South threatened the unity of the United States—until the Missouri Compromise averted a sectional crisis for a time. The forces of nationalism continued to assert themselves, and the federal government began to assume the role of promoter of economic growth.

The Missouri Compromise

When Missouri applied for admission to the Union as a state in 1819, slavery was already well established there. Even so, Representative James Tallmadge, Jr. of New York proposed an amendment to the Missouri statehood bill that would prohibit the further introduction of slaves into Missouri and provide for

Tallmadge Amendment

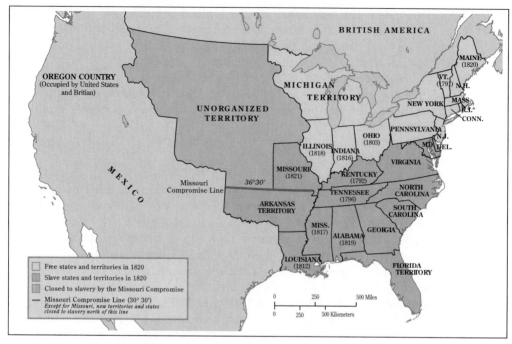

THE MISSOURI COMPROMISE, 1820 This map illustrates the way in which the Missouri Compromise proposed to settle the controversy over slavery in the new western territories of the United States. The compromise rested on the virtually simultaneous admission of Missouri and Maine to the Union, one a free state and the other a slave one. Note the red line extending beyond the southern border of Missouri, which in theory established a permanent boundary between areas in which slavery could be established and areas where it could not be. ◆ *What precipitated the Missouri Compromise?*

 For an interactive version of this map go to www.mhhe.com/unfinishednation4ch8maps

the gradual emancipation of those already there. The Tallmadge Amendment provoked a controversy that was to rage for the next two years.

Since the beginning of the republic, new states had come into the Union more or less in pairs, one from the North, another from the South. In 1819, there were eleven free states and eleven slave states; the admission of Missouri would upset that balance. Hence the controversy over slavery and freedom in Missouri.

Crisis Averted   Complicating the Missouri question was the application of Maine (previously the northern part of Massachusetts) for admission as a new (and free) state. Speaker of the House Henry Clay informed northern members that if they blocked Missouri from entering the Union as a slave state, southerners would block the admission of Maine. But Maine ultimately offered a way out of the impasse, as the Senate agreed to combine the Maine and Missouri proposals into a single bill. Maine would be admitted as a free state, Missouri as a slave state. Then Senator Jesse B. Thomas of Illinois proposed an amendment prohibiting slavery in the rest of the Louisiana Purchase territory north of the southern boundary of Missouri (the 36°30′ parallel). The Senate adopted the Thomas Amendment, and Speaker Clay, with great difficulty, guided the amended Maine-Missouri bill through the House.

Nationalists in both North and South hailed this settlement—which became known as the Missouri Compromise—as a happy resolution of a danger to the Union. But the debate over it had revealed a strong undercurrent of sectionalism.

Marshall and the Court

John Marshall served as chief justice of the United States from 1801 to 1835. More than anyone but the framers themselves, he molded the development of the Constitution: strengthening the judicial branch at the expense of the executive and legislative branches, increasing the power of the federal government at the expense of the states, and advancing the interests of the propertied and commercial classes.

Committed to promoting commerce, the Marshall Court staunchly defended the inviolability of contracts. In *Fletcher* v. *Peck* (1810), which arose out of a series of notorious land frauds in Georgia, the Court had to decide whether the Georgia legislature of 1796 could repeal the act of the previous legislature granting lands under shady circumstances to the Yazoo Land Companies. In a unanimous decision, Marshall held that a land grant was a valid contract and could not be repealed even if corruption was involved.

Dartmouth College v. *Woodward* (1819) further expanded the meaning of the contract clause of the Constitution. Having gained control of the New *Dartmouth College v. Woodward* Hampshire state government, Republicans tried to revise Dartmouth College's charter to convert the private college into a state university. Daniel Webster argued the college's case. The Dartmouth charter, he insisted, was a contract, protected by the same doctrine that the Court had already upheld in *Fletcher* v. *Peck*. The Court ruled for Dartmouth, proclaiming that corporation charters such as the one the colonial legislature had granted the college were contracts and thus inviolable. The decision placed important restrictions on the ability of state governments to control corporations.

In overturning the act of the legislature and the decisions of the New Hampshire courts, the justices also implicitly claimed for themselves the right to override the decisions of state courts. But advocates of states' rights, especially in the South, continued to challenge its right to do so. In *Cohens* v. *Virginia* (1821), Marshall explicitly affirmed the constitutionality of federal review of state court decisions. The states had given up part of their sovereignty in ratifying the Constitution, he explained, and their courts must submit to federal jurisdiction.

JOHN MARSHALL The imposing figure in this early photograph is John Marshall, the most important chief justice of the Supreme Court in American history. A former secretary of state, Marshall served as chief justice from 1801 until his death in 1835 at the age of 80. Such was the power of his intellect and personality that he dominated his fellow justices throughout that period, regardless of their previous party affiliations or legal ideologies. Marshall established the independence of the Court, gave it a reputation for nonpartisan integrity, and established its powers, which were only vaguely described by the Constitution. *(The National Archives and Records Administration)*

"Implied Powers" Confirmed   Meanwhile, in *McCulloch* v. *Maryland* (1819), Marshall confirmed the "implied powers" of Congress by upholding the constitutionality of the Bank of the United States. The Bank had become so unpopular in the South and the West that several of the states tried to drive branches out of business. This case presented two constitutional questions to the Supreme Court: Could Congress charter a bank? And if so, could individual states ban it or tax it? Daniel Webster, one of the Bank's attorneys, argued that establishing such an institution came within the "necessary and proper" clause of the Constitution and that the power

to tax involved a "power to destroy." If the states could tax the Bank at all, they could tax it to death. Marshall adopted Webster's words in deciding for the Bank.

In the case of *Gibbons* v. *Ogden* (1824), the Court strengthened Congress's power to regulate interstate commerce. The state of New York had granted the steamboat company of Robert Fulton and Robert Livingston the exclusive right to carry passengers on the Hudson River to New York City. Fulton and Livingston then gave Aaron Ogden the business of carrying passengers across the river between New York and New Jersey. But Thomas Gibbons, with a license granted under an act of Congress, began competing with Ogden for the ferry traffic. Ogden brought suit against him and won in the New York courts. Gibbons appealed to the Supreme Court. The most important question facing the justices was whether Congress's power to give Gibbons a license to operate his ferry superseded the state of New York's power to grant Ogden a monopoly. Marshall claimed that the power of Congress to regulate interstate commerce (which, he said, included navigation) was "complete in itself" and might be "exercised to its utmost extent." Ogden's state-granted monopoly, therefore, was void.

The decisions of the Marshall Court estab- *Federal Primacy Established*
lished the primacy of the federal government over the states in regulating the economy and opened the way for an increased federal role in promoting economic growth. They protected corporations and other private economic institutions from local government interference. They were, in short, highly nationalistic decisions.

The Court and the Tribes

The nationalist inclinations of the Marshall Court were visible as well in a series of decisions concerning the legal status of Indian tribes within the United States. But these decisions did not simply affirm the supremacy of the United States; they also carved out a distinctive position for Native Americans within the constitutional structure.

The first of the crucial Indian decisions was in the case of *Johnson* v. *McIntosh* (1823). Leaders of the Illinois and Pinakeshaw tribes had sold parcels of their land to a group of white settlers (including Johnson) but had later signed a treaty with the federal government ceding territory that included those same parcels to the United States. The government proceeded to grant homestead rights to new white settlers (among them McIntosh) on the land claimed by Johnson. The Court was asked to decide which claim had precedence. Marshall's ruling, not surprisingly, favored the United States. But in explaining it, he offered a preliminary definition of the place of Indians within the nation. The tribes had a basic right to their tribal lands, he said, that preceded all other American law. Individual American citizens could not buy or take land from the tribes; only the federal government—the supreme authority—could do that.

Worcester v. Georgia   Even more important was the Court's 1832 decision in *Worcester* v. *Georgia*, in which the Court invalidated a Georgia law that attempted to regulate access by U.S. citizens to Cherokee country. Only the federal government could do that, Marshall claimed. The tribes, he explained, were sovereign entities in much the same way Georgia was a sovereign entity—"distinct political communities, having territorial boundaries within which their authority is exclusive." In defending the power of the federal government, he was also affirming, indeed expanding, the rights of the tribes to remain free from the authority of state governments.

The Marshall decisions, therefore, did what the Constitution itself had not done: they defined a place for Indian tribes within the American political system. The tribes had basic property

Tribal Rights Affirmed   rights. They were sovereign entities not subject to the authority of state governments. But the federal government, like a "guardian" governing its "ward," had ultimate authority over tribal affairs.

The Latin American Revolution and the Monroe Doctrine

Just as the Supreme Court was asserting American nationalism in the shaping of the country's economic life, so the Monroe administration was asserting nationalism in foreign policy. As always, American diplomacy was principally concerned with Europe. But in the 1820s, dealing with Europe forced the United States to develop a policy toward Latin America.

Americans looking southward in the years following the War of 1812 beheld a gigantic spectacle: the Spanish Empire in its death throes and a whole continent in revolt. Already the United States had developed a profitable trade with Latin America. Many believed the success of the anti-Spanish revolutions would further strengthen America's position in the region.

In 1815, the United States proclaimed neutrality in the wars between Spain and its rebellious colonies. But the United States sold ships and supplies to the revolutionaries, a clear indication that it was not genuinely neutral but was trying to help the insurgents. Finally, in 1822, President Monroe established diplomatic relations with five new nations—La Plata (later Argentina), Chile, Peru, Colombia, and Mexico—making the United States the first country to recognize them.

In 1823, Monroe went further and announced a policy that would ultimately be known (beginning some thirty years

The "Monroe Doctrine"   later) as the "Monroe Doctrine," even though it was primarily the work of John Quincy Adams. "The American continents," Monroe declared, ". . . are henceforth not to be considered as subjects for future colonization by any European powers." The United States would consider any foreign challenge to the sovereignty of existing American nations an unfriendly act. At the same time, he proclaimed,

"Our policy in regard to Europe . . . is not to interfere in the internal concerns of any of its powers."

The Monroe Doctrine emerged directly out of America's relations with Europe in the 1820s. Many Americans feared that Spain's European allies (notably France) would assist Spain in an effort to retake its lost empire. Even more troubling was the fear that Great Britain had designs on Cuba. Monroe and Adams wanted to keep Cuba in Spanish hands until it fell to the Americans.

The Monroe Doctrine had few immediate effects, but it was important as an expression of the growing spirit of nationalism in the United States in the 1820s. And it established the idea of the United States as the dominant power in the Western Hemisphere.

THE REVIVAL OF OPPOSITION

After 1816, the Federalist Party offered no presidential candidate and soon ceased to exist as a national political force. The Republican Party was the only organized force in national politics. By the late 1820s, however, partisan divisions were emerging once again. *Renewed Partisan Divisions* In some respects, the division mirrored the schism that had produced the first party system in the 1790s. The Republicans had in many ways come to resemble the early Federalist regimes in their promotion of economic growth and centralization. And the opposition objected to the federal government's expanding role in the economy. There was, however, a crucial difference. At the beginning of the century, the opponents of centralization had also often been opponents of economic growth. Now, in the 1820s, the controversy involved not *whether* but *how* the nation should continue to expand.

The "Corrupt Bargain"

Until 1820, presidential candidates were nominated by caucuses of the two parties in Congress. But in 1824, "King Caucus" was overthrown. The Republican caucus nominated *"King Caucus" Overthrown* William H. Crawford of Georgia, the favorite of the extreme states' rights faction of the party. But other candidates received nominations from state legislatures and won endorsements from irregular mass meetings throughout the country.

One of them was Secretary of State John Quincy Adams. But he was a man of cold and forbidding manners, with little popular appeal. Another contender was Henry Clay, the Speaker of the House. He had a devoted personal following and a definite and coherent program: the "American System," which proposed creating a great home market for factory and farm producers by raising the protective tariff, strengthening the national bank, and financing internal improvements. Andrew Jackson, the fourth major candidate, had no significant political record—even though he was a new member of the United States Senate. But he was a military hero and had the help of shrewd political allies from his home state of Tennessee.

Jackson received more popular and electoral votes than any other candidate, but not a majority. The Twelfth Amendment to the Constitution (passed in the aftermath of the contested 1800

Disputed Election   election) required the House of Representatives to choose among the three candidates with the largest numbers of electoral votes. Crawford was seriously ill. Clay was out of the running, but he was in a strong position to influence the result. Jackson was Clay's most dangerous political rival in the West, so Clay supported Adams, in part because Adams was an ardent nationalist and a likely supporter of the American System. With Clay's endorsement, Adams won election in the House.

The Second President Adams

The Jacksonians believed their large popular and electoral pluralities entitled their candidate to the presidency, and they were enraged when he lost. But they grew angrier still when Adams named Clay his secretary of state. The State Department was the well-established route to the presidency, and Adams thus appeared to be naming Clay as his own successor. The outrage the Jacksonians expressed at what they called a "corrupt bargain" haunted Adams throughout his presidency.

Adams proposed an ambitiously nationalist program reminiscent of Clay's American System, but Jacksonians in Congress blocked most of it.

Diplomatic Frustrations   Adams also experienced diplomatic frustrations. He appointed delegates to an international conference that the Venezuelan liberator, Simón Bolívar, had called in Panama in 1826. But Haiti was one of the participating nations, and southerners in Congress opposed the idea of white Americans mingling with the black delegates. Congress delayed approving the Panama mission so long that the American delegation did not arrive until after the conference was over.

Even more damaging to the administration was its support for a new tariff on imported goods in 1828. This measure originated with the demands of Massachusetts and Rhode Island woolen manufacturers. But to win support from middle and western states, the administration had to accept duties on other items. In the process, it antagonized the original New England supporters of the bill; the benefits of protecting their manufactured goods from foreign competition now had to be weighed against the prospects of having to pay more for raw materials. Adams signed the

The "Tariff of Abominations"   bill, earning the animosity of southerners, who cursed it as the "tariff of abominations."

Jackson Triumphant

By the time of the 1828 presidential election, a new two-party system had begun to emerge. On one side stood the supporters of John Quincy Adams, who called themselves the National Republicans and who supported the economic nationalism of the preceding years. Opposing them were the followers of Andrew Jackson, who took the name Democratic Republicans. Adams attracted the support of most of the remaining Federalists; Jackson appealed to a broad coalition that opposed the "economic aristocracy."

But issues seemed to count for little in the end, as the campaign degenerated into a war of personal invective. The Jacksonians charged that Adams as president had been guilty of gross waste and extravagance. Adams's supporters hurled even worse accusations at Jackson. They called him a murderer and distributed a "coffin handbill," which listed, within coffin-shaped outlines, the names of militiamen whom Jackson was said to have shot in cold blood during the War of 1812. (The men had been deserters who were legally executed after sentence by a court-martial.) And they called his wife a bigamist. Jackson had married his beloved Rachel at a time when the pair incorrectly believed her first husband had divorced her. (When Jackson's wife first read of the accusations against her shortly after the election, she collapsed, and a few weeks later, died.)

Jackson's victory was decisive, but sectional. *Jackson Victorious* Adams swept virtually all of New England and showed significant strength in the mid-Atlantic region. Nevertheless, the Jacksonians considered their victory as complete and as important as Jefferson's in 1800. Once again, the forces of privilege had been driven from Washington. Once again, a champion of democracy would occupy the White House. America had entered, some Jacksonians claimed, a new era of democracy, the "era of the common man."

CONCLUSION

In the aftermath of the War of 1812, a vigorous nationalism came increasingly to characterize the political and popular culture of the United States. In all regions of the country, white men and women celebrated the achievements of the early leaders of the republic, the genius of the Constitution, and the success of the nation in withstanding serious challenges both from without and within. Party divisions faded.

But the broad nationalism of the so-called era of good feelings disguised some deep divisions. Indeed, the character of American nationalism differed substantially from one region, and one group, to another.

Battles continued between those who favored a strong central government committed to advancing the economic development of the nation and those who wanted a decentralization of power to open opportunity to more people. Battles continued as well over the role of slavery in American life—and in particular over the place of slavery in the new western territories. The Missouri Compromise of 1820 postponed the day of reckoning on that issue—but only for a time.

FOR FURTHER REFERENCE

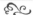

Frederick Jackson Turner, *The Frontier in American History* (1920) is the classic statement of American exceptionalism; Turner argued that the western frontier endowed the United States with a distinctive, individualist, and democratic national character. John Mack Faragher, *Women and Men on the Overland Trail* (1979) was an early and influential book in the "new western history" that challenged Turner; his *Sugar Creek* (1987) portrays the society of the Old Northwest in the early nineteenth century. Robert V. Remini, *Andrew Jackson and the Course of American Empire: 1767–1821* (1977) emphasizes Andrew Jackson's importance in American territorial expansion in the South prior to 1821 and in the development of American nationalism. Morton J. Horwitz, *The Transformation of American Law, 1780–1865* (1977), an important work in American legal history, connects changes in the law to changes in the American economy. R. Kent Newmyer, *John Marshall and the Heroic Age of the Supreme Court* (2002) is a more sympathetic study of the early Court. Ernest R. May, *The Making of the Monroe Doctrine* (1975) presents the history of a leading principle of American foreign policy.

For quizzes, Internet resources, references to additional books and films, and more, consult this book's Online Learning Center site at www.mhhe.com/unfinishednation4.

DETAIL FROM *THE VERDICT OF THE PEOPLE* (1855), BY GEORGE CALEB BINGHAM This scene of an election-day gathering is peopled almost entirely by white men. Women and blacks were barred from voting, but among white males political rights expanded substantially in the 1830s and 1840s. *(© The Saint Louis Art Museum. Gift of Bank of America)*

TIME LINE

1830	1830–1838	1831	1832	1832–1833	1833	
Webster and Hayne debate	Indians expelled from Southeast	Anti-Mason Party holds first convention	Jackson vetoes recharter of Bank of U.S.	Nullification crisis	Jackson removes deposits from Bank of U.S.	
			Jackson reelected		Commercial panic	

CHAPTER NINE

JACKSONIAN AMERICA

The Rise of Mass Politics
"Our Federal Union"
The Removal of the Indians
Jackson and the Bank War
The Emergence of the Second Party System
Politics After Jackson

M any Americans were growing apprehensive about the future of their republic as the nation expanded. Some feared that the rapid growth of the United States would produce social chaos; they insisted that the country's first priority must be to establish order and a clear system of authority. Others argued that the greatest danger facing the nation was the growth of inequality and privilege; they believed that society's goal should be to eliminate the favored status of powerful elites and make opportunity more widely available. Advocates of this latter vision seized control of the federal government in 1829 with the inauguration of Andrew Jackson.

THE RISE OF MASS POLITICS

On March 4, 1829, thousands of Americans from all regions of the country crowded before the United States Capitol to watch the inauguration of Andrew Jackson. After *Jackson Inaugurated* the ceremonies, the crowd poured into a public reception at the White House, where, in their eagerness to shake the new president's hand, they filled the state rooms to overflowing, trampled one another, soiled the

1835	1835–1842	1836	1837–1844	1840	1841	
Taney named chief justice of Supreme Court	Seminole War	Specie Circular Van Buren elected president	Panic and depression	William Henry Harrison elected president Independent Treasury Act	Harrison dies; Tyler becomes president	

carpets, and damaged the upholstery. "It was a proud day for the people," wrote Amos Kendall, one of Jackson's closest political associates. Supreme Court justice Joseph Story, a friend and colleague of John Marshall, remarked with disgust: "The reign of King 'Mob' seems triumphant."

In fact, the "age of Jackson" was much less a triumph of the common people than Kendall hoped and Story feared. But it did mark a transformation of American politics. Once restricted to a relatively small elite of property owners, politics now became open to virtually all the nation's white male citizens. In a political sense at least, the era had some claim to the title the Jacksonians gave it: the "era of the common man."

The Expanding Electorate

The Franchise Expanded

Until the 1820s, relatively few Americans had been permitted to vote; most states restricted the franchise to white male property owners or taxpayers or both. But even before Jackson's election, the franchise began to expand. Change came first in Ohio and other new states of the West, which, on joining the Union, adopted constitutions that guaranteed all adult white males—not just property owners or taxpayers—the right to vote and permitted all voters the right to hold public office. Older states, concerned about the loss of their population to the West, began to drop or reduce their own property ownership or taxpaying requirements.

The wave of state reforms was generally peaceful, but in Rhode Island democratization efforts created considerable instability. The Rhode Island constitution barred more than half the adult males in the state from voting in the 1830s. In 1840, the lawyer and activist Thomas L. Dorr and a group of his followers formed a "People's party," held a convention, drafted a new constitution, and submitted it to a popular vote. It was overwhelmingly approved, and the Dorrites began to set up a new government, with Dorr as governor. The existing legislature, however, rejected the legitimacy of Dorr's constitution. And so, in 1842, two governments were claiming to be the real power in Rhode Island. The old state government proclaimed that Dorr and his followers were rebels and began to imprison them. The Dorrites, meanwhile, made an ineffectual effort to capture the state arsenal.

The Dorr Rebellion

The Dorr Rebellion, as it was known, quickly failed, but the episode helped spur the old guard to draft a new constitution that greatly expanded the suffrage.

The democratization process was far from complete. In much of the South, of course, no slaves could vote. In addition, southern election laws continued to favor the planters and politicians of the older counties. Free blacks could not vote anywhere in the South and hardly anywhere in the North. In no state could women vote. Nowhere was the ballot secret, and often it was cast as a spoken vote, which meant that voters could be easily bribed or intimidated. Despite the persisting limitations, however, the number of voters increased much more rapidly than did the population as a whole.

PEOPLE'S
Constitutional and State Rights'
TICKET.
[*Election Monday, April 18th, 1842.*]

FOR GOVERNOR,
THOMAS W. DORR,
OF PROVIDENCE.

FOR LIEUTENANT GOVERNOR,
AMASA EDDY, JR.
OF GLOCESTER.

WILLIAM H. SMITH, *Secretary of State.*
JOSEPH JOSLIN, *General Treasurer.*
JONAH TITUS, *Attorney General.*

For Sheriff of the County of Providence,
BURRINGTON ANTHONY.

THE DORR REBELLION The democratic sentiments that swept much of the nation in the 1830s and 1840s produced, among many other things, the Dorr Rebellion (as its opponents termed it) in Rhode Island. Thomas Dorr was one of many Rhode Islanders who denounced the state's constitution, which limited voting rights to a small group of property owners known as "freeholders." The dissidents crafted a new constitution and submitted it to a vote; a majority of the state's citizens approved it. But the legislature refused to acknowledge its legitimacy, and the result was two separate elections in 1842 for the same state offices. Dorr ran for governor under the new constitution, and was elected by a majority of the people. This "ticket" was what his supporters placed in ballot boxes as they cast their votes. Another candidate, Samuel King, ran under the old constitution, and was elected by the freeholders. Both men were inaugurated, and not until President Tyler threatened federal intervention on behalf of King did the Dorr movement crumble. A year later, however, the state ratified a new constitution extending the franchise. (*Courtesy The Rhode Island Historical Society, RHi X5 304*)

One of the most striking political trends of the early nineteenth century was the change in the *Politics Reformed* method of choosing presidential electors. In 1800, the legislatures had chosen the presidential electors in ten states, and the people in only six. By 1828, electors were chosen by popular vote in every state but South Carolina. In the presidential election of 1824, fewer than 27 percent of adult white males had voted. In the election of 1828, the figure was 58 percent; and in 1840, 80 percent.

The Legitimization of Party

Although factional competition was part of American politics almost from the beginning of the republic, acceptance of the idea of party was not. But in the 1820s and 1830s, most Americans gradually came to consider permanent, institutionalized parties to be a desirable part of the political process.

The elevation of the idea of party occurred first at the state level, most prominently in New York. There, Martin Van Buren led a dissident political faction (known as the "Bucktails" or the "Albany Regency"). In the years after the War of 1812 this group began to challenge the established political elite led by the aristocratic governor, De Witt Clinton. They argued that only an institutionalized party, based in the populace, could ensure genuine democracy. The alternative was the sort of closed elite that Clinton had created. For a party to survive, moreover, it must have a permanent opposition. Competing parties would force politicians to remain continually sensitive to the will of the people; they would check and balance each other in much the same way that the different branches of government checked and balanced one another.

By the late 1820s, this new idea of party had spread beyond New York. The election of Jackson in 1828, the result of a popular movement that stood apart from the usual political elites, seemed further to legitimize it.

The Two-Party System In the 1830s, finally, a fully formed two-party system began to operate at the national level. The anti-Jackson forces began to call themselves the Whigs. Jackson's followers called themselves Democrats, thus giving a permanent name to what is now the nation's oldest political party.

President of the Common Man

Andrew Jackson embraced a distinct and simple theory of democracy. Government, he said, should offer "equal protection and equal benefits" to all its white male citizens and favor no one region or class over another. In practice, that meant launching an assault on what Jackson considered the citadels of the eastern aristocracy and making an effort to extend opportunities to the rising classes of the West and the South.

Jackson's first target was the entrenched officeholders in the federal government. Jackson bitterly denounced what he considered a class of permanent officeholders. Offices, he said, belonged to the people, not to a self-serving bureaucracy. Equally important, a large turnover in the bureaucracy would allow him to reward his own supporters with offices. One of Jackson's allies, William L. Marcy of New York, once explained, "To the

The "Spoils System" victors belong the spoils"; and patronage, the process of giving out jobs as political rewards, became known as the "spoils system." Although Jackson removed no more

ANDREW JACKSON EN ROUTE TO WASHINGTON, 1829 Only a few weeks after Andrew Jackson's wife died (a result, he believed, of vicious attacks on her by his political enemies), the president-elect began a slow, triumphal procession from Tennessee to Washington, greeted by throngs of admirers in every town through which he passed. *(The Library of Congress)*

than one-fifth of the existing federal officeholders, his embrace of the spoils system helped cement its place in party politics.

Jackson's supporters also worked to transform the process by which presidential candidates were selected. In 1832, the president's followers staged a national convention to renominate him. Through the convention, its founders believed, power in the party would arise directly from the people in a great democratic conclave rather than from such elite political institutions as the congressional caucus.

"OUR FEDERAL UNION"

Jackson's commitment to extending power beyond entrenched elites led him to want to reduce the functions of the federal government. A concentration of power in Washington would, he believed, restrict opportunity to people with political connections. But Jackson was also strongly committed to the preservation of the Union. Thus at the same time that he was promoting an economic program to reduce the power of the national government, he was asserting the supremacy of the Union in the face of a

JACKSONIAN DEMOCRACY

To many Americans in the 1820s and 1830s, Andrew Jackson was a champion of democracy, a symbol of the spirit of antielitism and egalitarianism that was sweeping American life. Historians, however, have disagreed sharply not only in their assessments of Jackson himself but in their portrayal of American society in his era.

The "progressive" historians of the early twentieth century tended to see Jacksonian politics as a forebear of their own battles against economic privilege and political corruption. Frederick Jackson Turner encouraged scholars to see Jacksonianism as a protest by the people of the frontier against the conservative aristocracy of the East, which they believed restricted their own freedom and opportunity. Jackson represented those who wanted to make government responsive to the will of the people rather than to the power of special interests. The culmination of this progressive interpretation of Jacksonianism was the publication in 1945 of Arthur M. Schlesinger, Jr.'s *The Age of Jackson*. Schlesinger was less interested in the regional basis of Jacksonianism than the disciples of Turner had been. Jacksonian Democracy, he argued, was the effort "to control the power of the capitalist groups, mainly Eastern, for the benefit of non-capitalist groups, farmers and laboring men, East, West, and South." He portrayed Jacksonianism as an early version of modern reform efforts to "restrain the power of the business community."

Richard Hofstadter, in an influential 1948 essay, sharply disagreed. Jackson, he argued, was the spokesman of rising entrepreneurs—aspiring businessmen who saw the road to opportunity blocked by the monopolistic power of Eastern aristocrats. The Jacksonians opposed special privileges only to the extent that those privileges blocked their own road to success. They were less sympathetic to the aspirations of those below them. Bray Hammond, writing in 1957, argued similarly that the Jacksonian cause was "one of enterpriser against capitalist." Other historians saw Jacksonianism less as a democratic reform movement than as a nostalgic effort to restore a lost past. Marvin Meyers's *The Jacksonian Persuasion* (1957) argued that Jackson and his followers looked with misgivings on the new industrial society emerging around them and yearned instead for a restoration of the agrarian, republican virtues of an earlier time.

In the 1960s, historians began taking less interest in Jackson and his supporters and more in the social and cultural bases of American politics in the time of Jackson. Lee Benson's *The Concept of Jacksonian Democracy* (1961) used quantitative techniques to demonstrate the role of religion and ethnicity in shaping party divisions. Edward Pessen's *Jacksonian America* (1969) portrayed America in the Jacksonian era as an increasingly stratified society. This inclination to look more closely at society than at formal "Jacksonianism" has continued into the 1980s and 1990s. Sean Wilentz, in *Chants Democratic* (1984), examined the rise of a powerful class identification among workers in New York, who were attracted less to Jackson than to an artisanal notion of democracy.

Gradually, this attention to the nature of society has led to reassessments of Jackson himself and the nature of his regime. In *Fathers and Children* (1975), Michael Rogin portrays Jackson as a leader determined to secure the supremacy of white men in the United States. Alexander Saxton, in *The Rise and Fall of the White Republic* (1990) makes the related argument that "Jacksonian Democracy" was explicitly a white man's democracy that rested on the subjugation of slaves, women, and Native Americans. But the portrayal of Jackson as a champion of the common man has not vanished from scholarship entirely. The most renowned postwar biographer of Jackson, Robert V. Remini, argues that, despite the flaws in his democratic vision, he was a genuine "man of the people."

(text continued from page 227)

potent challenge. For no sooner had he entered office than his own vice president—John C. Calhoun—began to champion a controversial constitutional theory: nullification.

Calhoun and Nullification

Calhoun had once been an outspoken protectionist and had strongly supported the tariff of 1816. But by the late 1820s, many South Carolinians had come to believe that the "tariff of abominations" was responsible for the stagnation of their state's economy—even though the stagnation was largely a result of the exhaustion of South Carolina's farmland, which could no longer compete effectively with the newly opened and fertile lands of the Southwest. Some exasperated Carolinians were ready to consider a drastic remedy—secession.

Calhoun's future political hopes rested on how he met this challenge in his home state. He did so by developing the theory of nullification. Drawing from the ideas of Madison and Jefferson and citing the Tenth Amendment to the Constitution, Calhoun argued that since the federal government was a creation of the states, the states—not the courts or Congress—were the final arbiters of the constitutionality of federal laws. If a state concluded that Congress had passed an unconstitutional law, then it could hold a special convention and declare the federal law null and void within the state. The nullification doctrine—and the idea of using it to nullify the 1828 tariff— *Calhoun's Theory of Nullification* quickly attracted broad support in South Carolina. But it did nothing to help Calhoun's standing within the new administration, in part because he had a powerful rival in Martin Van Buren.

The Rise of Van Buren

Van Buren had won election to the governorship of New York in 1828 and then resigned in 1829 when Jackson appointed him secretary of state. He soon established himself as a member both of the *Martin Van Buren* official cabinet and of the president's unofficial circle of political allies, known as the "Kitchen Cabinet." Van Buren's influence with the president was unmatched and grew stronger still as a result of a quarrel over etiquette that drove a wedge between the president and Calhoun.

Peggy O'Neale was the attractive daughter of a Washington tavern keeper with whom both Andrew Jackson and his friend John H. Eaton had taken lodgings while serving as senators from Tennessee. O'Neale was married, but rumors circulated in Washington in the mid-1820s that she and Senator Eaton were having an affair. O'Neale's husband died in 1828, and she and Eaton were soon married. A few weeks later, Jackson named Eaton secretary of war and thus made the new Mrs. Eaton a cabinet wife. The rest of the administration wives, led by Mrs. Calhoun, refused to receive her. Jackson was furious and demanded that the members of the cabinet accept her into their social world. Calhoun, under pressure from his wife, refused. Van Buren, a widower, befriended the Eatons and thus ingratiated himself with Jackson. By 1831, Jackson had chosen Van Buren to succeed him in the White House, apparently ending Calhoun's dreams of the presidency.

The Webster-Hayne Debate

In January 1830, in the midst of a routine debate over federal policy toward western lands, a senator from Connecticut suggested that all land sales and surveys be temporarily discontinued. Robert Y. Hayne, a young senator from South Carolina, responded, charging that slowing down the growth of the West was a way for the East to retain its political and economic power. He hoped his stance would attract support from westerners in Congress for South Carolina's drive to lower the tariff. Both the South and the West, he argued, were victims of the tyranny of the Northeast. He hinted that the two regions might combine to defend themselves against that tyranny.

Daniel Webster, now a senator from Massachusetts, attacked Hayne, and through him Calhoun, for what he considered

States' Rights versus National Power

their challenge to the integrity of the Union—in effect, challenging Hayne to a debate not on public lands and the tariff but on the issue of states' rights versus national power. Hayne responded with a defense of the theory of nullification. Webster then spent two full afternoons delivering what became known as his "Second Reply to Hayne." He concluded with the ringing appeal: "Liberty and Union, now and for ever, one and inseparable!"

Both sides now waited to hear what President Jackson thought of the argument. The answer became clear at the annual Democratic Party banquet in honor of Thomas Jefferson. After dinner, guests delivered a series of toasts. The president arrived with a written text in which he had underscored certain words: "Our Federal Union—It must be preserved." While he spoke, he looked directly at Calhoun. The diminutive Van Buren, who stood on his chair to see better, thought he saw Calhoun's hand shake and a trickle of wine run down his glass as he responded to the president's toast with his own: "The Union, next to our liberty most dear."

The Nullification Crisis

In 1832, finally, the controversy over nullification produced a crisis when South Carolinians responded angrily to a congressional tariff bill that offered them no relief from the 1828 "tariff of abominations." Almost immediately, the legislature summoned a state convention, which voted to nullify the tariffs of 1828 and 1832 and to forbid the collection of duties within the state. At the same time, South Carolina elected Hayne to serve as governor and Calhoun to replace Hayne as senator.

Jackson insisted that nullification was treason. He strengthened the federal forts in South Carolina and ordered a warship to Charleston. When Congress convened early in 1833, Jackson proposed a force bill authorizing the president to use the military to see that acts of Congress were obeyed. Violence seemed a real possibility.

Force Bill Proposed

Calhoun faced a predicament as he took his place in the Senate. Not a single state had come to South Carolina's support. But the timely intervention of Henry Clay, newly elected to the Senate, averted a crisis. Clay devised a compromise by which the tariff would be lowered gradually so that, by 1842, it would reach approximately the same level as in 1816. The compromise and the force bill were passed on the same day, March 1, 1833. Jackson signed them both. In South Carolina, the convention reassembled and repealed its nullification of the tariffs. But unwilling to allow Congress to have the last word, the convention nullified the force act—a purely symbolic act, since the tariff had already been repealed. Calhoun and his followers claimed a victory for nullification, which had, they insisted, forced the revision of the tariff. But the episode taught Calhoun and his allies that no state could defy the federal government alone.

Clay's Compromise

THE REMOVAL OF THE INDIANS

Andrew Jackson's attitude toward the Indian tribes that remained in the eastern United States was simple and clear: He wanted them to move west. Jackson harbored a deep hostility toward the Indians drawn from his earlier experiences leading military campaigns against the tribes. In this he was little different from most white Americans.

White Attitudes toward the Tribes

In the eighteenth century, many whites had shared Thomas Jefferson's view of the Indians as "noble savages," with an inherent dignity that made civilization possible among them. By the first decades of the nineteenth century, however, this attitude was fading, particularly among the whites in the West. They were coming to view Native Americans simply as "savages." That was one reason for the growing white commitment to removing the Indians from all the lands east of the Mississippi. But white westerners also favored removal to put an end to violence and conflict in the western areas of white settlement. Most of all, however, they wanted valuable land that the tribes still possessed.

Events in the Northwest added urgency to the issue of removal. In Illinois, an alliance of Sauk (or Sac) and Fox Indians under Black Hawk fought white settlers in 1831–1832 in an effort to overturn what Black Hawk considered an illegal treaty ceding tribal lands in that state to the

The Black Hawk War   United States. The Black Hawk War was notable for the viciousness of the white military efforts. White forces attacked the Indians even when they attempted to surrender, pursued them as they retreated, and slaughtered many of them. But its real impact was to reinforce the determination of whites to remove all the tribes to the West.

The "Five Civilized Tribes"

Even more troubling to the government in the 1830s were the remaining Indian tribes of the South. In western Georgia, Alabama, Mississippi, and Florida lived what were known as the "Five Civilized Tribes"—the Cherokee, Creek, Seminole, Chickasaw, and Choctaw. In 1830, both the federal government and several southern states were accelerating efforts to remove the tribes to the West. Most were too weak to resist, but some fought back.

The Cherokees tried to stop the state of Georgia from taking their

Cherokee Legal Resistance   lands through an appeal in the Supreme Court, and the Court's rulings in *Cherokee Nation* v. *Georgia* and *Worcester* v. *Georgia* supported the tribe's contention that the state had no authority to negotiate with tribal representatives. But Jackson repudiated the decisions, reportedly responding to news of the rulings with the contemptuous statement: "John Marshall has made his decision. Now let him enforce it." Then, in 1835, the United States government extracted a treaty from a minority faction of the Cherokees that ceded to Georgia the tribe's land in that state in return for $5 million and a reservation west of the Mississippi. The great majority of the 17,000 Cherokees did not recognize the treaty as legitimate. But Jackson sent an army of 7,000 under General Winfield Scott to round them up and drive them westward.

BLACK HAWK AND WHIRLING THUNDER After his defeat by white settlers in Illinois in 1832, the famed Sauk warrior Black Hawk and his son, Whirling Thunder, were captured and sent on a tour by Andrew Jackson, displayed to the public as trophies of war. They showed such dignity through the ordeal that much of the white public quickly began to sympathize with them. This portrait, by John Wesley Jarvis, was painted on the tour's final stop, in New York City. Black Hawk wears the European-style suit, while Whirling Thunder wears native costume to emphasize his commitment to his tribal roots. Soon thereafter, Black Hawk returned to his tribe, wrote a celebrated autobiography, and died in 1838. *(Bettmann/Corbis)*

Trails of Tears

About 1,000 Cherokee fled to North Carolina, where eventually the federal government provided *Removal* them with a small reservation in the Smoky Mountains that survives today. But most of the rest made a long, forced trek to "Indian Territory," what later became Oklahoma, beginning in the winter of 1838. Thousands, perhaps a quarter or more of the émigrés, perished before reaching their unwanted destination. In the harsh new reservations, the survivors remembered the terrible journey as "The Trail Where They Cried," the Trail of Tears.

Between 1830 and 1838, virtually all the Five Civilized Tribes were forced to travel to Indian Territory. The Choctaws of Mississippi and western Alabama were the first to make the trek, beginning in 1830. The army moved out the Creeks of eastern Alabama and western Georgia in 1836. The Chickasaws in northern Mississippi began the long march westward a year later, and the Cherokees, finally, a year after that.

Only the Seminoles in Florida were able to resist the pressures, and even their success was limited. Like other tribes, the Seminoles had agreed under pressure to a settlement by which they ceded their lands to the United States and agreed to move to Indian Territory within three years. Most did move west, but a substantial minority, under the leadership of the chieftain Osceola, balked and staged an uprising be- *Osceola Defiant* ginning in 1835 to defend their lands. (Joining the

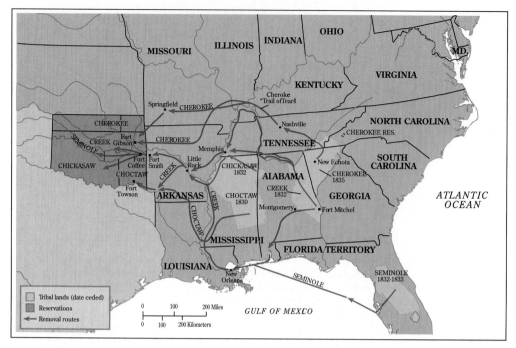

THE EXPULSION OF THE TRIBES, 1830–1835 Andrew Jackson was famous well before he became president for his military exploits against the tribes. Once in the White House, he ensured that few Indians would remain in the southern states of the nation, now that white settlement was increasing there. The result was a series of dramatic "removals" of Indian tribes out of their traditional lands and into new territories west of the Mississippi—mostly in Oklahoma. Note the very long distance many of these tribes had to travel. ◆ *Why was the route of the Cherokees, shown in the upper portion of the map, known as the "Trail of Tears"?*

 For an interactive version of this map go to www.mhhe.com/unfinishednation4ch9maps

Indians in their struggle was a group of runaway black slaves, who had been living with the tribe.) Jackson sent troops to Florida, but the Seminoles and their black allies were masters of guerrilla warfare in the jungle-like Everglades. Finally, in 1842, the government abandoned the war. By then, many of the Seminoles had been either killed or forced westward.

The Meaning of Removal

By the end of the 1830s, virtually all the important Indian societies east of the Mississippi had been removed to the West. The tribes had ceded over 100 million acres of eastern land to the federal government; they had received in return about $68 million and 32 million acres in the far less hospitable lands west of the Mississippi. There they lived, divided by tribe into a series of separate reservations, in a territory surrounded by a string of United States forts, in a region whose climate and topography bore little relation to anything they had known before.

What were the alternatives to the removal of the eastern Indians? There was probably never any realistic possibility that the government could stop white expansion westward. But there were, in theory at least, alternatives to the brutal removal policy. The West was filled with examples of white settlers and native tribes living side by side. In the pueblos of New Mexico, in the fur trading posts of the Pacific Northwest, in parts of Texas and California, settlers from Mexico, Canada, and the United States had created societies in which Indians and whites were in intimate contact with each other. Sometimes these close contacts between whites and Indians were beneficial to both sides; often they were cruel and exploitive. But the early multiracial societies of the West did not separate whites and Indians. They demonstrated ways in which the two cultures could interact, each shaping the other.

Alternatives to Removal

By the mid-nineteenth century, however, white Americans had adopted a different model. Much as the early British settlers along the Atlantic coast had established "plantations," from which natives were, in theory, to be excluded, so the western whites of later years believed that Indians could not be partners in the creation of new societies in the West. They were obstacles to be removed and, as far as possible, isolated.

JACKSON AND THE BANK WAR

Jackson was quite willing to use federal power against the Indian tribes. Where white Americans were concerned, however, he was more reluctant. An early example of that was his 1830 veto of a congressional measure providing a subsidy to the proposed Maysville Road in Kentucky. The bill was unconstitutional, Jackson argued, because the road in question lay entirely within Kentucky and was not, therefore, a part of "interstate commerce." But the bill was also unwise because it committed the government to what Jackson considered extravagant expenditures. A similar resistance to federal power lay behind Jackson's war against the Bank of the United States.

Biddle's Institution

The Bank of the United States had a monopoly on the deposits of the federal government, which owned one-fifth of the Bank's stock; it also provided credit to growing enterprises; issued bank notes that served as a dependable medium of exchange throughout the country; and exercised a restraining effect on the less well-managed state banks. Nicholas Biddle, who ran the Bank from 1823 on, had done much to put the institution on a sound and prosperous basis. Nevertheless, many Americans—among them Andrew Jackson— were determined to destroy it.

Nicholas Biddle

"Soft-money" versus "Hard-money"

Opposition to the Bank came from two very different groups: the "soft-money" faction and the "hard-money" faction. Advocates of soft money consisted largely of state bankers and their allies. They objected to the Bank of the United States because it restrained the state banks from issuing notes freely. The hard-money supporters believed that coin was the only safe currency, and they condemned all banks that issued bank notes, including the Bank of the United States. The soft-money advocates were believers in rapid economic growth and speculation; the hard-money forces embraced older ideas of "public virtue" and looked with suspicion on expansion and speculation. Jackson himself supported the hard-money position. He made it clear that he would not favor renewing the charter of the Bank of the United States, which was due to expire in 1836.

Recharter Bill Vetoed

Biddle was a Philadelphia aristocrat, unaccustomed to politics. But in his efforts to save the Bank, he began granting banking favors to influential men. In particular, he relied on Daniel Webster, whom he named the Bank's legal counsel and director of the Boston branch. Webster helped Biddle enlist the support of Henry Clay as well. Clay, Webster, and other advisers persuaded Biddle to apply to Congress for a recharter bill in 1832, four years ahead of the expiration date. Congress passed the recharter bill; Jackson vetoed it; and the Bank's supporters in Congress failed to override the veto. The Bank question then emerged as the paramount issue of the 1832 election, just as Clay had hoped.

In 1832, Clay ran for president as the unanimous choice of the National Republicans. But the "Bank War" failed to provide Clay with the winning issue for which he had hoped. Jackson, with Van Buren as his running mate, won an overwhelming victory with 55 percent of the popular vote and 219 electoral votes.

The "Monster" Destroyed

Jackson was now more determined than ever to destroy the "monster." He could not legally abolish the Bank before the expiration of its charter. But he weakened it by removing the government's deposits from it. His secretary of the treasury believed that such an action would destabilize the financial system and refused to give the order. Jackson fired him and appointed a replacement. When the new secretary similarly procrastinated, Jackson fired him, too, and named a third: Roger B. Taney, the attorney general, a close friend and loyal ally of the president.

Government Deposits Removed

Taney soon began taking the government's deposits out of the Bank of the United States and putting them in a number of state banks. In response, Biddle called in loans and raised interest rates, explaining that without the government deposits the Bank's resources were stretched too thin. His actions precipitated a short recession.

As financial conditions worsened in the winter of 1833–1834, supporters of the Bank sent petitions to Washington urging a rechartering of the Bank. But the Jacksonians blamed the recession on Biddle and refused. The banker finally carried his contraction of credit too far and had to reverse himself to appease the business community. His hopes of winning a recharter of the Bank died in the process. Jackson *Jackson's Political Victory* had won a considerable political victory. But when the Bank of the United States died in 1836, the country was left with a fragmented and chronically unstable banking system that would plague the economy for many years.

The Taney Court

In the aftermath of the Bank War, Jackson moved against the most powerful remaining institution of economic nationalism: the Supreme Court. In 1835, when John Marshall died, the president appointed as the new chief justice his trusted ally Roger B. Taney. Taney did not bring a sharp break in constitutional interpretation, but he did help modify Marshall's vigorous nationalism.

Perhaps the clearest indication of the new judicial climate was the celebrated case of *Charles* *Charles River Bridge v. Warren Bridge* *River Bridge* v. *Warren Bridge* of 1837. The case involved a dispute between two Massachusetts companies over the right to build a bridge across the Charles River between Boston and Cambridge. One company had a longstanding charter from the state to operate a toll bridge, a charter that the firm claimed guaranteed it a monopoly of the bridge traffic. Another company had applied to the legislature for authorization to construct a second, competing bridge that would—since it would be toll-free—greatly reduce the value of the first company's charter. The first company contended that in granting the second charter, the legislature was engaging in a breach of contract; and it noted that the Marshall Court, in the *Dartmouth College* case and other decisions, had ruled that states had no right to abrogate contracts. But now Taney supported the right of Massachusetts to award the second charter. The object of government, Taney maintained, was to promote the general happiness, an object that took precedence over the rights of property. A state, therefore, had the right to amend or abrogate a contract if such action was necessary to advance the well-being of the community. The decision reflected one of the cornerstones of the Jacksonian idea: that the key to democracy was an expansion of economic opportunity, which would not occur if older corporations could maintain monopolies.

THE EMERGENCE OF THE
SECOND PARTY SYSTEM

Jackson's tactics in crushing first the nullification movement and then the Bank of the United States helped galvanize a growing opposition coalition. It began as a gathering of national political leaders opposed to Jackson's use of power. Denouncing the president as "King Andrew I," they began to refer to themselves as Whigs, after the party in England that traditionally worked to limit the power of the king. With the emergence of the Whigs, the nation once again had two competing political parties. What scholars now call the "second party system" had begun its relatively brief life.

The Two Parties

The philosophy of the Democratic Party in the 1830s bore the stamp of Andrew Jackson. The federal government, the Democrats believed, should be limited in power, except to the degree that it worked to eliminate social and economic arrangements that en-

Democrats' Emphasis on Opportunity

trenched privilege and stifled opportunity. The rights of states should be protected except to the extent that state governments interfered with social and economic mobility. Jacksonian Democrats celebrated "honest workers," "simple farmers," and "forthright businessmen" and contrasted them to the corrupt, monopolistic, aristocratic forces of established wealth. Democrats were more likely than Whigs to support territorial expansion, which would, they believed, widen opportunities for aspiring Americans. Among the most radical members of the party—the so-called Locofocos, mainly workingmen and small businessmen and professionals in the Northeast—sentiment was strong for a vigorous, perhaps even violent, assault on monopoly and privilege.

The political philosophy that became known as Whiggery favored expanding the power of the federal government and encouraging industrial and commercial development. Whigs were cau-

Whig Calls for Industrial Development

tious about westward expansion, fearful that rapid territorial growth would produce instability. Their vision of America was of a nation rising to greatness as a commercial and manufacturing power. And although Whigs insisted that their vision would result in increasing opportunities for all Americans, they tended to attribute particular value to the entrepreneurs and institutions that most effectively promoted economic growth.

The Whigs were strongest among the more substantial merchants and manufacturers of the Northeast, the wealthier planters of the South, and the ambitious farmers and rising commercial class of the West. The Democrats drew more support from smaller merchants and the workingmen of the Northeast; from Southern planters suspicious of industrial growth; and from westerners who favored a predominantly agrarian economy. Whigs tended to be wealthier than Democrats, tended to have more aristocratic backgrounds, and tended to be more commercially ambitious. But Whigs and Democrats alike were more interested in winning elections than in maintaining philosophical purity. And both parties made adjustments from region to region in order to attract the largest possible number of voters.

In New York, for example, the Whigs developed a popular following through a movement known as Anti-Masonry. The Anti-Mason Party had emerged in the 1820s in response to widespread resentment against the secret and exclusive, hence supposedly undemocratic, Society of Freemasons. Such resentment increased in 1826 when a former Mason, William Morgan, mysteriously disappeared from his home in Batavia, New York, shortly before he was scheduled to publish a book that would allegedly expose the secrets of Freemasonry. The assumption was widespread that Morgan had been abducted and murdered by the vengeful Masons. Whigs seized on the Anti-Mason frenzy to launch spirited attacks on Jackson and Van Buren (both Freemasons), implying that the Democrats were connected with the antidemocratic conspiracy.

Religious and ethnic divisions also played an important role in determining the constituencies of *Religious and Ethnic Divisions* the two parties. Irish and German Catholics tended to support the Democrats, who appeared to share their own vague aversion to commercial development and who seemed to respect their cultural values. Evangelical Protestants gravitated toward the Whigs because they associated the party with constant development and improvement. They envisioned a society progressing steadily toward unity and order, and they looked on the new immigrant communities as groups that needed to be disciplined and taught "American" ways.

The Whig Party was more successful at defining its positions and attracting a constituency than it was in uniting behind a national leader. No one person was ever able to command the loyalties of the party in the way Jackson commanded the loyalties of the Democrats. Instead, Whigs tended to divide their allegiance among three major figures: Henry Clay, Daniel Webster, and John C. Calhoun.

Clay won support from many of those who favored internal improvements and economic development, what he called the American System; such improvements were es- *The American System* pecially important to people living in the western states. But Clay's image as a devious political operator and his identification with the West was a liability. He ran for president three times and never won. Daniel Webster won broad support among the Whigs with his passionate speeches in defense of the Constitution and the Union; but his close connection with the Bank of the United States and the protective tariff, his reliance on rich men for financial support, and his excessive fondness for brandy prevented him from developing enough of a national constituency to win him the office he so desperately wanted. John C. Calhoun never considered himself a true Whig, and his identification with the nullification controversy in effect disqualified him from national leadership in any case. Yet he sided with Clay and Webster on the issue of the national bank, and he shared with them a strong animosity toward Andrew Jackson.

Van Buren Elected   The Whigs competed relatively evenly with the Democrats in congressional, state, and local races, but they managed to win only two presidential elections in the more than twenty years of their history. Their problems became particularly clear in 1836. The Democrats were united behind Andrew Jackson's personal choice for president, Martin Van Buren. The Whigs could not even agree on a single candidate. Instead, they ran several candidates: in different regions, hoping they might separately draw enough votes from Van Buren to prevent his getting a majority and throw the election to the House of Representatives, where the Whigs might be better able to elect one of their candidates. In the end, however, Van Buren won easily, with 170 electoral votes to 124 for all his opponents.

POLITICS AFTER JACKSON

Andrew Jackson retired from public life in 1837, the most beloved political figure of his age. Martin Van Buren was less fortunate. He could not match Jackson's personal magnetism, and his administration suffered from economic difficulties that hurt both him and his party.

The Panic of 1837

Van Buren's success in the 1836 election was a result in part of a nationwide economic boom. Canal and railroad builders were at a peak of activity. Prices were rising, and credit was plentiful. The land business, in particular, was booming. Between 1835 and 1837, the *Boom* government sold nearly 40 million acres of public land, nearly three-fourths of it to speculators. These land sales, along with revenues the government received from the tariff of 1833, created a series of substantial federal budget surpluses and made possible a steady reduction of the national debt. From 1835 to 1837, the government for the first and only time in its history was out of debt, with a substantial surplus in the Treasury.

Congress and the administration now faced the question of what to do with the Treasury surplus. Support soon grew for returning the federal surplus to the states. An 1836 "distribution" act required the federal government to pay its surplus funds to the states each year in four quarterly installments as interest-free, unsecured loans. No one expected the "loans" to be repaid. The states spent the money quickly, mainly to promote the construction of highways, railroads, and canals. The distribution of the surplus thus gave further stimulus to the economic boom. At the same time, the withdrawal of federal funds strained the state banks in which they had been deposited by the government; the banks had to call in their own loans to make the transfer of funds to the state governments.

Congress did nothing to check the speculative fever. But Jackson feared that the government was selling land for state bank notes of questionable value. In 1836 he issued an executive order, the "specie circular." It provided that in payment for public lands, the government would accept only gold or silver coins or currency backed by gold or silver. The specie circular produced a financial panic that began in the first months of Van Buren's presidency. Banks and businesses failed; unemployment grew; there were bread riots in some of the larger cities; and prices fell, especially the price of land. Many railroad and canal projects failed; several of the debt-burdened state governments ceased to pay interest on their bonds, and a few repudiated their debts, at least temporarily. It was the worst depression in American history to that point, and it lasted for five years. It was a political catastrophe for Van Buren and the Democrats.

Bust

The Van Buren Program

The Van Buren administration did little to fight the depression. Some of the steps it took—borrowing money to pay government debts and accepting only specie for payment of taxes—may have made things worse. Other efforts failed in Congress: a "preemption" bill that would have given settlers the right to buy government land near them before it was opened for public sale, and another bill that would have lowered the price of land. Van Buren did succeed in establishing a ten-hour workday on all federal projects by issuing a presidential order, but he had few legislative achievements.

The most important and controversial measure in the president's program was a proposal for a new financial system. Under Van Buren's plan, known as the "independent treasury" or "subtreasury" system, government funds would be placed in an independent treasury in Washington and in subtreasuries in other cities. No private banks would have the government's money or name to use as a basis for speculation. Van Buren called a special session of Congress in 1837 to consider the proposal, which failed in the House. In 1840, the administration finally succeeded in driving the measure through both houses of Congress.

"Independent Treasury" System

The Log Cabin Campaign

As the campaign of 1840 approached, the Whigs realized that they would have to settle on one candidate for president. In December 1839, they

THE NEW YORK SUN This 1834 front page of the *Sun*, which had begun publication a year earlier, contains advertisements, light stories, a description of a slave auction in Charleston, South Carolina, and homespun advice: "Life is short. The poor pittance of several years is not worth being a villain for." (© *The New-York Historical Society*)

William Henry Harrison held their first nominating convention. Passing over Henry Clay, they chose William Henry Harrison, a renowned soldier and a popular national figure. The Democrats again nominated Van Buren.

The 1840 campaign was the first in which the new and popular "penny press" carried news of the candidates to large audiences. Newspapers of the "penny press" were deliberately livelier and even more sensationalistic than the newspapers of the past, which had been almost entirely directed at the upper classes. The New York *Sun*, the first of the new breed, began publishing in 1833 and was from the beginning self-consciously egalitarian. It soon had the largest circulation in New York. Other, similar papers soon began appearing in other cities—reinforcing the increasingly democratic character of political culture and encouraging the inclination of both parties to try to appeal to ordinary voters as they planned their campaigns.

The campaign of 1840 also illustrated how fully the spirit of party competition had established itself in America. The Whigs—who had emerged as a party largely because of their opposition to Andrew Jackson's common-man democracy—presented themselves in 1840 as the party of the common people. So, of course, did the Democrats. Both parties used the same tech-

WHIG HEADQUARTERS The Whig Party managed in 1840 to disguise its relatively elitist roots by portraying its presidential candidate, the patrician General William Henry Harrison, as a product of a log cabin who enjoyed drinking hard cider from a jug. Pictures of log cabins abounded in Whig campaign posters, as seen in this drawing of a Harrison rally in Philadelphia. *(Bettmann/Corbis)*

niques of mass voter appeal; what mattered was not *Mass Voter Appeal* the philosophical purity of the party but its ability to win votes. The Whig campaign was particularly effective in portraying William Henry Harrison, a wealthy member of the frontier elite with a considerable estate, as a simple man of the people who loved log cabins and hard cider. The Democrats, already weakened by the depression, had no effective defense against such tactics. Harrison won the election with 234 electoral votes to 60 for Van Buren and with a popular majority of 53 percent.

The Frustration of the Whigs

But the Whigs found the four years after their resounding victory frustrating and divisive. In large part, that was because their appealing new president died of pneumonia one month after taking office. Vice President John Tyler of Virginia succeeded him.

Tyler was a former Democrat who had left the party in reaction to what he considered Jackson's excessively egalitarian program. But his approach to public policy still showed signs of his Democratic past. The president did agree to bills abolishing Van Buren's independent-treasury system and raising tariff rates. But he refused to support Clay's attempt to recharter the Bank of the United States. And he vetoed several internal improvement bills sponsored by Clay and other congressional Whigs. Finally, a conference of congressional Whigs read Tyler out of the party. Every cabinet member but Webster, who was serving as secretary of state, resigned; five former Democrats took their places. When Webster, too, left the cabinet, Tyler appointed Calhoun, who had rejoined the Democratic Party, to replace him.

A New Political Alignment   A new political alignment was taking shape. Tyler and a small band of conservative southern Whigs were preparing to rejoin the Democrats. Into the common man's party of Jackson and Van Buren was arriving a faction with decidedly aristocratic political ideas, men who thought that government had an obligation to protect and even expand the institution of slavery and who believed in states' rights with almost fanatical devotion.

Whig Diplomacy

In the midst of these domestic controversies, anti-British factions in Canada launched an unsuccessful rebellion against the colonial government there in 1837. When the insurrection failed, some of the rebels took refuge near the United States border and chartered an American steamship, the *Caroline*, to ship them supplies across the Niagara River *Tensions with Britain* from New York. British authorities in Canada seized the *Caroline* and burned it, killing one American in the process. Resentment in the United States grew rapidly. At the same time, tensions flared over the boundary between Canada and Maine, which had been in dispute since the treaty of 1783. In 1838, rival groups of Americans and Canadians, mostly lumberjacks, began moving into the Aroostook River region in the disputed area, precipitating a violent brawl between them that became known as the "Aroostook War."

Several years later, in 1841, an American ship, the *Creole*, sailed from Virginia for New Orleans with more than 100 slaves aboard. En route the slaves mutinied, seized possession of the ship, and took it to the Bahamas. British officials there declared the slaves free, and the English government refused to overrule them. Many Americans, especially southerners, were furious.

At this critical juncture a new government eager to reduce tensions with the United States came to power in Great Britain. It sent Lord Ashburton, an admirer of America, to negotiate an agreement on the Maine *Webster-Ashburton Treaty* boundary and other matters. The result was the Webster-Ashburton Treaty of 1842, under which the United States received slightly more than half the disputed area and agreed to a revised northern boundary as far west as the Rocky Mountains. Ashburton also eased the memory of the *Caroline* and *Creole* affairs by expressing regret and promising no future "officious interference" with American ships. Anglo-American relations improved significantly.

During the Tyler administration, the United States established its first diplomatic relations with China. In the Treaty of Wang Hya, concluded in 1844, American diplomats secured the same trading privileges as the English. In the next ten years, American trade with China steadily increased. *Treaty of Wang Hya*

In their diplomatic efforts, at least, the Whigs were able to secure some important successes. But by the end of the Tyler administration, the party could look back on few other victories. In the election of 1844, the Whigs lost the White House.

CONCLUSION

The election of Andrew Jackson to the presidency in 1828 represented the emergence of a new political world. Throughout the American nation, the laws governing political participation were loosening and the number of people permitted to vote (which eventually included most white males, but almost no one else) was increasing. Along with this expansion of the electorate was emerging a new spirit of party politics.

Jackson set out as president to entrench his party, the Democrats, in power. He was also a fierce defender of the West and a sharp critic of what he considered the stranglehold of the aristocratic East on the nation's economic life. He sought to limit the role of the federal government in economic affairs and worked to destroy the Bank of the United States, which he considered a corrupt vehicle of aristocratic influence. And he confronted the greatest challenge to American unity yet to have emerged in the young nation—the nullification crisis of 1832–1833—with a strong assertion of the power and importance of the Union. These positions won him broad popularity and ensured his reelection in 1832 and the election of his designated successor, Martin Van Buren, in 1836.

But a new coalition of anti-Jacksonians, who called themselves the Whigs, launched a powerful new party that used much of the same anti-elitist rhetoric the Democrats had used to win support for their own much more nationalist program. Their emergence culminated in the campaign of 1840 with the election of the first Whig president.

FOR FURTHER REFERENCE

Arthur M. Schlesinger, J., *The Age of Jackson* (1945) represents Jacksonian politics as an eastern, urban democratic movement of working men and upper-class intellectuals. Bray Hammond, *Banks and Politics in America from the Revolution to the Civil War* (1957) challenges Schlesinger by arguing that the Bank War was essentially a struggle between different groups of capitalist elites. Howard Bodenhorn, *A History of Banking in Antebellum America: Financial Markets and Economic Development in the Era of Nation-Building* (2000) is a more recent examination of the American banking system in the early republic. Harry L. Watson, *Liberty and Power: The Politics of Jacksonian America* (1990) provides an important newer synthesis of Jacksonian politics. Donald B. Cole, *Martin Van Buren and the American Political System* (1984) examines the emergence of modern notions of party through the career of Van Buren. Richard Hofstadter, *The Idea of a Party System: The Rise of Legitimate Opposition in the United States, 1740–1840* (1969) traces the growing acceptance of the idea of partisan competition. Daniel Walker Howe, *The Political Culture of the American Whigs* (1979) analyzes the careers of several leading Whig politicians including the Whig triumvirate of Calhoun, Clay, and Webster. William V. Freehling, *Prelude to Civil War: The Nullification Controversy in South Carolina* (1966) argues that South Carolina planters' anxiety over the fate of slavery was at the heart of the nullification crisis. Francis P. Prucha, *American Indian Policy in the Formative Years* (1962) is an overview of early Indian policy by the leading scholar of the subject. Michael Rogin, *Fathers and Children: Andrew Jackson and the Destruction of American Indians* (1975) offers a more radical and idiosyncratic perspective on Jackson's career as an Indian fighter using the methods of psychoanalysis. Sean Wilentz, *Chants Democratic: New York City and the Rise of the American Working Class, 1788–1850* (1984) is an important study of working-class ideology during the Jacksonian period.

For quizzes, Internet resources, references to additional books and films, and more, consult this book's Online Learning Center site at www.mhhe.com/unfinishednation4.

THE LOWELL MILLS Fifteen years earlier, Lowell, Massachusetts, had been a small farming village known as East Chelmsford. By the 1840s, when Fitzhugh Lane painted *The Middlesex Company Woolen Mills*, the town had become one of the most famous manufacturing centers in America and a magnet for visitors from around the world. Lane's painting shows female workers, who dominated the labor force in Lowell, entering the factory. (Middlesex Company Woolen Mill, Lowell, MA, *c. 1848. Artist unknown. American Textile History Museum, Lowell, Massachusetts*)

TIME LINE

1817-1825	1830	1830s	1834	1837	
Erie Canal constructed	Baltimore and Ohio Railroad begins operation	Immigration from southern Ireland begins	Lowell mills women strike	Native American Association fights immigration	
			McCormick patents mechanical reaper		

AMERICA'S ECONOMIC REVOLUTION

The Changing American Population
Transportation and Communications Revolutions
Commerce and Industry
Men and Women at Work
Patterns of Society
The Agricultural North

When the United States entered the War of 1812, it was still an essentially agrarian nation. There were, to be sure, some substantial cities in America. There was also modest but growing manufacturing, mainly in the Northeast. But the overwhelming majority of Americans were farmers and tradespeople.

By the time the Civil War began in 1861, the United States had transformed itself. Most Americans were still rural people. But even most farmers were now part of a national, and even international, market economy. Equally important, the United States was beginning to challenge the industrial nations of Europe for supremacy in manufacturing. The nation had experienced the beginning of its industrial revolution.

THE CHANGING AMERICAN POPULATION

The American industrial revolution was a result of many factors: advances in transportation and communications, the growth of manufacturing technology, and the development of new systems of business organization, and perhaps above all, population growth.

	1844	1845	1846	1847	1852	
	Morse sends first telegraph message	Native American Party formed	Rotary press invented	John Deere manufactures steel plows	American Party (Know Nothings) formed	

Three trends characterized the American population between 1820 and 1840. The population was increasing rapidly. Much of it was moving westward. And much of it was becoming concentrated in towns and cities, where the new residents provided a work force for industry.

Rapid Population Growth   The American population had stood at only 4 million in 1790. By 1820, it had reached 10 million; and by 1840, 17 million. One reason for the growth was improvements in public health; the number and ferocity of epidemics slowly declined, as did the mortality rate as a whole. But the population increase was also a result of a high birth rate. In 1840, white women bore an average of 6.14 children each.

The African-American population increased more slowly than the white population. After 1808, when the importation of slaves became illegal, the proportion of blacks to whites in the nation as a whole steadily declined. The slower increase of the black population was a result of its comparatively high death rate. Slave mothers had large families, but life was shorter for both slaves and free blacks than for whites—a result of the enforced poverty in which virtually all African Americans lived.

Burgeoning Immigration   Immigration, choked off by wars in Europe and economic crises in America, contributed little to the American population in the first three decades of the nineteenth century. Of the total 1830 population of nearly 13 million, the foreign-born numbered fewer than 500,000. Soon, however, immigration began to grow once again. Reduced transportation costs and increasing economic opportunities in America helped stimulate the immigration boom, as did deteriorating economic conditions in some areas of Europe. The migrations introduced new groups to the United States. In particular, the number of immigrants arriving from the southern (Catholic) counties of Ireland began to grow.

Much of this new European immigration flowed into the rapidly growing cities of the Northeast. But urban growth was a result of substantial internal migration as well. As the agricultural regions of New England and other areas grew less profitable, more and more people picked up stakes and moved—some to promising agricultural regions in the West, but many to eastern cities.

Immigration and Urban Growth, 1840–1860

Rapid Urbanization   The growth of cities accelerated dramatically between 1840 and 1860. The population of New York, for example, rose from 312,000 to 805,000 making it the nation's largest and most commercially important city. Philadelphia's population grew over the same twenty-year period from 220,000 to 565,000; Boston's, from 93,000 to 177,000. By 1860, 26 percent of the population of the free states was living in towns (places of 2,500 people or more) or cities, up from 14 percent in 1840. In the South, by contrast, the increase of urban residents was only from 6 percent in 1840 to 10 percent in 1860.

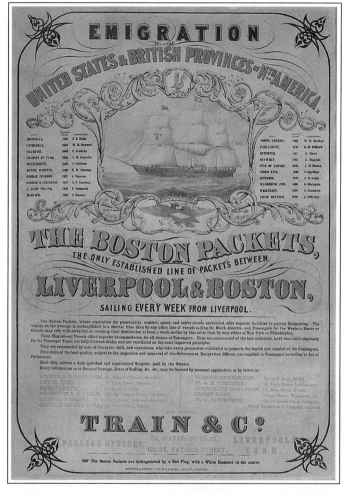

AN APPEAL TO EMIGRANTS This widely distributed advertising card was one of many appeals to potential English and Irish travelers to America in the 1830s and 1840s. Like many such companies, it tried to attract both affluent passengers (by boasting of "superior accommodations") and working-class people of modest means. *(Courtesy of The Bostonian Society/Old State House)*

The booming agricultural economy of the western regions of the nation produced significant urban growth as well. Between 1820 and 1840, communities that had once been small villages or trading posts became major cities: St. Louis, Pittsburgh, Cincinnati, Louisville. All of them became centers of the growing carrying trade that connected the farmers of the Midwest with New Orleans and, through it, the cities of the Northeast. After 1830, however, an increasing proportion of this trade moved from the Mississippi River to the Great Lakes and created major new urban centers that gradually superseded the river ports. Among them were Buffalo, Detroit, Milwaukee, Cleveland, and Chicago.

The enlarged urban population was to a large degree a result of the flow of two major groups of people into cities: the native farmers of the Northeast, who were being forced off the land by competition from the West; and immigrants from Europe. Between 1840 and 1850, more than 1.5 million Europeans moved to America. In the 1850s, the number rose to 2.5 million. Almost half the residents of New York City in the 1850s were recent immigrants. In St. Louis, Chicago, and Milwaukee, the foreign-born outnumbered those of native birth. Few immigrants settled in the South.

Irish and German Immigrants The newcomers came from many different countries, but the overwhelming majority came from Ireland and Germany. By 1860, there were more than 1.5 million Irish-born and approximately 1 million German-born people in the United States. Most of the Irish stayed in the eastern cities where they landed and became part of the unskilled labor force. The largest single group of Irish immigrants were young, single women, who worked in factories or in domestic service. Germans, who—unlike the Irish—usually arrived with at least some money and often came in family groups, generally moved on to the Northwest, where they became farmers or went into business in the western towns.

The Rise of Nativism

Many politicians eagerly courted the support of the new arrivals. Others, however, viewed the growing foreign population with alarm. Some argued that the immigrants were racially inferior or that they corrupted politics by selling their votes. Others complained that they were stealing jobs from the native work force. Protestants worried that the growing Irish population would increase the power of the Catholic Church in America. Older-stock Americans feared that immigrants would become a radical force in politics. Out of these fears and prejudices emerged a number of secret societies to combat the "alien menace."

Native American Party The first was the Native American Association, founded in 1837, which in 1845 became the Native American Party. In 1850, it joined with other nativist groups to form the Supreme Order of the Star-Spangled Banner, whose demands included banning Catholics or aliens from holding public office, enacting more restrictive naturalization laws, and establishing literacy tests for voting. The order adopted a strict code of secrecy, which included a secret password: "I know nothing." Ultimately, members of the movement came to be known as the "Know-Nothings."

The Know-Nothings After the 1852 elections, the Know-Nothings created a new political organization that they called the American Party. It scored an immediate and astonishing success in the elections of 1854. The Know-Nothings did well in Pennsylvania and New York and actually won control of the state government in Massachusetts. Outside the Northeast, however, their progress was more modest. After

1854, the strength of the Know-Nothings declined and the party soon disappeared.

TRANSPORTATION AND COMMUNICATIONS REVOLUTIONS

Just as the industrial revolution required an expanding population, it also required an efficient system of transportation and communications. The first half of the nineteenth century saw dramatic changes in both.

The Canal Age

From 1790 until the 1820s, the so-called turnpike era, the United States had relied largely on roads for internal transportation. But roads alone were not adequate for the nation's expanding needs. And so, in the 1820s and 1830s, Americans began to turn to other means of transportation as well.

The larger rivers became increasingly important as steamboats replaced the slow barges that had previously dominated water traffic. The new riverboats carried the corn and wheat of northwestern farmers and the cotton and tobacco of southwestern planters to New Orleans. From New Orleans, oceangoing ships took the cargoes on to eastern ports or abroad.

But this roundabout river-sea route satisfied neither western farmers nor eastern merchants, who wanted a way to ship goods directly to the urban markets and ports of *Advantages of Canals* the Atlantic coast. New highways across the mountains provided a partial solution to the problem. But the costs of hauling goods overland, although lower than before, were still too high for anything except the most compact and valuable merchandise. And so interest grew in building canals.

The job of financing canals fell largely to the states. New York was the first to act. It had the natural advantage of a good land route between the Hudson River and Lake Erie through the only break in the Appalachian chain. But the engineering tasks were still imposing. The distance was more than 350 miles, and the route was interrupted by high ridges and thick woods. After a long public debate, canal advocates prevailed. Digging began on July 4, 1817.

The building of the Erie Canal was the greatest construction project Americans had ever undertaken. *Impact of the Erie Canal* The canal itself was basically a simple ditch forty feet wide and four feet deep, with towpaths along the banks for the horses or mules that were to draw the canal boats. But its construction involved hundreds of difficult cuts and fills to enable the canal to pass through hills and over valleys, stone aqueducts to carry it across streams, and eighty-eight locks, of heavy masonry with great wooden gates, to permit ascents and descents. The

CANALS IN THE NORTHEAST, 1823–1860 The great success of the Erie Canal, which opened in 1825, inspired decades of energetic canal building in many areas of the United States, as this map illustrates. But none of the new canals had anything like the impact of the original Erie Canal, and thus none of New York's competitors—among them Baltimore, Philadelphia, and Boston—were able to displace it as the nation's leading commercial center. ◆ *What form of transportation ultimately displaced the canals?*

For an interactive version of this map go to www.mhhe.com/unfinishednation4ch10maps.

Erie Canal opened in October 1825, amid elaborate ceremonies and celebrations, and traffic was soon so heavy that within about seven years tolls had repaid the entire cost of construction. By providing a route to the Great Lakes, the canal gave New York access to Chicago and the growing markets of the West. The Erie Canal also contributed to the decline of agriculture in New England. Now that it was so much cheaper for western farmers to ship their crops east, people farming marginal land in the Northeast found themselves unable to compete.

The system of water transportation extended farther when the states of Ohio and Indiana, inspired by the success of the Erie Canal, provided water connections between Lake Erie and the Ohio River. These canals made it possible to ship goods by inland waterways all the way from New York to New Orleans.

One of the immediate results of these new transportation routes was

Increased Settlement in the Northwest

increased white settlement in the Northwest, because it was now easier for migrants to make the westward journey and to ship their goods back to

RACING ON THE RAILROAD Peter Cooper designed and built the first steam-powered locomotives in America in 1830 for the Baltimore and Ohio railroad. On August 28 of that year, he raced his locomotive (the "Tom Thumb") against a horse-drawn railroad car. This sketch depicts the moment when Cooper's engine overtook the horse-car. *(Museum of the City of New York)*

eastern markets. Much of the western produce continued to go downriver to New Orleans, but an increasing proportion went east to New York. And manufactured goods from throughout the East now moved in growing volume through New York and then to the West via the new water routes.

Rival cities along the Atlantic seaboard took alarm at the prospect of New York's acquiring access to (and control over) so vast a market, largely at their expense. But they had limited success in catching up. Boston, its way to the Hudson River blocked by the Berkshire Mountains, did not even try to connect itself to the West by canal. Philadelphia, Baltimore, Richmond, and Charleston all aspired to build water routes to the Ohio Valley, but never completed them. Some cities, however, saw opportunities in a different and newer means of transportation. Even before the canal age had reached its height, the era of the railroad was beginning.

The Early Railroads

Railroads played a relatively small role in the nation's transportation system in the 1820s and 1830s, but railroad pioneers laid the groundwork *Organizational and Technological Significance* in those years for the great surge of railroad building in midcentury. Eventually, railroads became the primary transportation system for the United States. They also eventually became critical sites of development for innovations in technology and corporate organization.

Railroads emerged from a combination of technological and entrepreneurial innovations: the invention of tracks, the creation of steam-powered locomotives, and the development of trains as public carriers of passengers and freight. By 1804, both English and American inventors had experimented with steam engines for propelling land vehicles. In 1820, John Stevens ran a locomotive and cars around a circular track on his New Jersey estate. And in 1825, the Stockton and Darlington Railroad in England became the first line to carry general traffic.

The Baltimore and Ohio   American entrepreneurs quickly grew interested in the English experiment. The first company to begin actual operations was the Baltimore and Ohio, which opened a thirteen-mile stretch of track in 1830. In New York, the Mohawk and Hudson began running trains along the sixteen miles between Schenectady and Albany in 1831. By 1836, more than a thousand miles of track had been laid in eleven states.

The Triumph of the Rails

After 1840, railroads gradually supplanted canals and all other forms of transport. In 1840, the total railroad trackage of the country was under 3,000 miles. By 1860, it was over 27,000 miles. The Northeast developed the most comprehensive and efficient system, with twice as much trackage per square mile as the Northwest and four times as much as the South. Railroads even crossed the Mississippi at several points by great iron bridges. Chicago eventually became the rail center of the West.

The emergence of the great train lines diverted traffic from the main water routes—the Erie Canal and the Mississippi River. By lessening the dependence of the West on the Mississippi, the railroads also helped weaken further the connection between the Northwest and the South.

Importance of Government Funding   Railroad construction required massive amounts of capital. Some of it came from private sources, but much of it came from government funding. State and local governments invested in railroads, but even greater assistance came from the federal government in the form of public land grants. By 1860, Congress had allotted over 30 million acres to eleven states to assist railroad construction.

It would be difficult to exaggerate the impact of the rails on the American economy, on American society, even on American culture. It was, according to one writer, "the resistless chariot of civilization with scythed axles mowing down ignorance and prejudice as it whirls along . . . [driving] the shadows of the past . . . into the dim woods." Where railroads went, towns, ranches, and farms grew up rapidly along their routes. Areas once cut off from markets during winter and other spells of bad weather found that the railroad could transport goods to and from them at any time of year.

Economic Effects of the Railroad   Most of all, the railroads cut the time of shipment and travel. In the 1830s, traveling from New York to Chicago by lake and canal took roughly three weeks. By railroad in the 1850s, the same trip took less than two days.

The railroads were much more than a fast and economically attractive form of transportation. They were also a breeding ground for technological advances; a key to the nation's economic growth; and the birthplace of the modern corporate form of organization. They also became a symbol of the nation's technological prowess. To many people, railroads were the most visible sign of the country's progress and greatness.

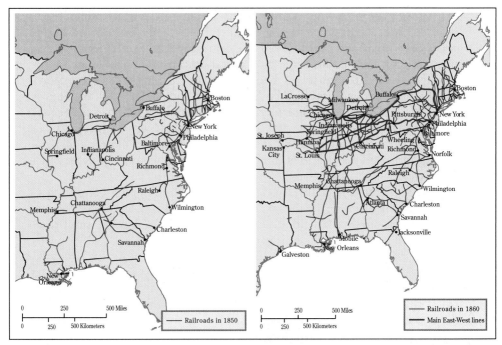

RAILROAD GROWTH, 1850–1860 These two maps illustrate the dramatic growth in the extent of American railroads in the 1850s. Note the particularly extensive increase in mileage in the upper Midwest (known at the time as the Northwest). Note too the relatively smaller increase in railroad mileage in the South. Railroads forged a close economic relationship between the upper Midwest and the Northeast, and weakened the Midwest's relationship to the South. ◆ *How did this contribute to the South's growing sense of insecurity within the Union?*

 For an interactive version of this map go to www.mhhe.com/unfinishednation4ch10maps

The Telegraph

What the railroad was to transportation the telegraph was to communication—a dramatic advance over traditional methods and a symbol of national progress and technological expertise.

Before the invention of the telegraph, communication over great distances on land could be achieved only by direct, physical contact. That meant that virtually all long-distance communication relied on the mail, which traveled first on horseback and coach, and later by railroad. There were obvious disadvantages to this system, not the least of which was the difficulty in coordinating the railroad schedules. By the 1830s, experiments with many methods of improving long-distance communication had been conducted, among them using the sun and reflective devices to send light signals as far as 187 miles.

In 1832, Samuel F. B. Morse—a professor of art with an interest in science—began experimenting with a different system. Fascinated with the possibilities of electricity,

Samuel Morse

Morse set out to find a way to send signals along an electrical cable. Technology did not yet permit the use of electrical wiring to send reproductions of the human voice or any complex information. But Morse realized that electricity itself could serve as a communication device—that pulses of electricity could themselves become a kind of language. He experimented at first with a numerical code, in which each number would represent a word on a list available to recipients. Gradually, however, he became convinced of the need to find a more universal telegraphic "language," and he developed what became the Morse Code, in which alternating long and short bursts of electrical current would represent individual letters.

By 1835, Morse had developed his idea for telegraphic communication to the point that he was ready to promote it. Eight years later, Congress appropriated $30,000 for the construction of an experimental telegraph line between Baltimore and Washington; in May 1844, it was complete, and Morse succeeded in transmitting the news of James K. Polk's nomination for the presidency over the wires from Baltimore to Washington. By 1860, more than 50,000 miles of wire connected most parts of the country; a year later, the Pacific Telegraph, with 3,595 miles of wire, opened between New York and San Francisco. By then, nearly all the independent lines had joined in one organization, the Western Union Telegraph Company. The telegraph spread rapidly across Europe as well, and in 1866, the first transatlantic cable was laid across the Atlantic.

Western Union Telegraph Company

One of the first beneficiaries of the telegraph was the growing system of rails. Telegraph wires often ran alongside railroad tracks, and telegraph offices were often located in railroad stations. The telegraph allowed railroad operators to communicate directly with stations in cities, small towns, and even rural hamlets—to alert them to schedule changes, warn them about delays and breakdowns, and convey other information about the movement of the trains. Among other things, this new form of communication helped prevent accidents by alerting stations to problems that in the past engineers had to discover for themselves.

New Forms of Journalism

Another beneficiary of the telegraph was American journalism, which used the wires to get news from around the country—and eventually, the world—that had once taken days, weeks, and even months to reach them, in the space of a few hours. Where once the exchange of national and international news relied on the cumbersome exchange of newspapers by mail, now it was possible for papers to share their reporting. In 1846, newspaper publishers from around the nation formed the Associated Press to promote cooperative news gathering by wire.

Other technological advances spurred the development of the American press. In 1846, Richard Hoe invented the steam cylinder rotary press, making it possible to print newspapers much more rapidly and cheaply than had been possible in the past. Among other things, the rotary press spurred the dramatic growth of mass-circulation newspapers. The New York *Sun*, the most widely circulated paper in the nation, had 8,000 readers in 1834. By 1860, its successful rival the *New*   *New York Herald* *York Herald*—benefiting from the speed and economies of production the rotary press made possible, had a circulation of 77,000.

COMMERCE AND INDUSTRY

By the middle years of the nineteenth century, the United States had developed the beginnings of a modern capitalist economy and an advanced industrial capacity. But the economy had developed along highly unequal lines—benefiting some classes and some regions far more than others.

The Expansion of Business, 1820–1840

American business grew rapidly in the 1820s and 1830s in part because of important innovations in business management. Individuals or limited partnerships continued to operate most businesses, and the dominating figures were still the great merchant capitalists, who generally had sole ownership of their enterprises. In some larger businesses, however, the individual merchant capitalist was giving way to the corporation. Corporations had the advantage of combining the resources of a large number   *Advantages of Corporations* ber of shareholders, and they began to develop particularly rapidly in the 1830s, when some legal obstacles to their formation were removed. Previously, a corporation could obtain a charter only by a special act of a state legislature; by the 1830s, states were beginning to pass general incorporation laws, under which a group could secure a charter merely by paying a fee. The laws also permitted a system of limited liability, in which individual stockholders risked losing only the value of their own investment if a corporation should fail; they were not liable (as they had been in the past) for the corporation's larger losses. These changes made possible much larger manufacturing and business enterprises.

The Emergence of the Factory

The most profound economic development in mid-nineteenth-century America was the rise of the factory. Before the War of 1812, most manufacturing took place within households or in small workshops. Early in the nineteenth century, however, New England textile manufacturers began using new machines driven by water power that allowed them to bring their operations together under a single roof. This "factory system," as it came to be known, soon penetrated the shoe industry and other industries as well.

Dramatic Industrial Growth   Between 1840 and 1860, American industry experienced particularly dramatic growth. For the first time, the value of manufactured goods was roughly equal to that of agricultural products. More than half of the approximately 140,000 manufacturing establishments in the country in 1860 were located in the Northeast, and they included most of the larger enterprises. The Northeast thus produced more than two-thirds of the manufactured goods and employed nearly three-quarters of the men and women working in manufacturing.

Advances in Technology

Even the most highly developed industries were still relatively immature. American cotton manufacturers, for example, produced goods of coarse grade; fine items continued to come from England. But by the 1840s, significant advances were occurring.

Machine Tools   Among the most important was in the manufacturing of machine tools—the tools used to make machinery parts. The government supported much of the research and development of machine tools, often in connection with supplying the military. For example, a government armory in Springfield, Massachusetts, developed two important tools—the turret lathe (used for cutting screws and other metal parts) and the universal milling machine (which replaced the hand chiseling of complicated parts and dies)—early in the nineteenth century. The precision grinding machine (which became critical to, among other things, the construction of sewing machines) was designed in the 1850s to help the United States Army produce standardized rifle parts. The federal armories such as those at Springfield and Harpers Ferry, Virginia, where these and other tools were developed, became the breeding ground for many technological discoveries. By the 1840s, the machine tools used in the factories of the Northeast were already better than those in most European factories.

One important result of the creation of better machine tools was that the principle of interchangeable parts now found its way into many industries. Eventually, interchangeability would revolutionize watch and clock making, the manufacturing of locomotives, the creation of steam engines, and the making of many farm tools. It would also help make possible bicycles, sewing machines, typewriters, cash registers, and eventually the automobile.

New Sources of Energy   Industrialization was also profiting from the introduction of new sources of energy. Coal was replacing wood and water power. The production of coal, most of it mined around Pittsburgh in western Pennsylvania, leaped from 50,000 tons in 1820 to 14 million tons in 1860. The new power source made it possible to locate mills away from running streams and thus permitted industry to expand still more widely.

THE EARLY SEWING MACHINE *Scientific American*, which reported American scientific and technological achievements, was a popular journal in the mid-nineteenth century. Here it gives front-page attention to the design and construction of Isaac Singer's sewing machine, alongside articles trumpeting news of the progress of the railroads and urging the invention of a ballpoint pen. (*Scientific American, 1851*)

The great technological advances in American industry owed much to American inventors. In 1830, the number of inventions patented was 544; in 1860, it stood at 4,778. Several industries provide particularly vivid examples of how a technological innovation could produce a major economic change. In 1839, Charles Goodyear, a New England hardware merchant, discovered a method of vulcanizing rubber (treating it to give it greater strength and elasticity); by 1860, his process had found over 500 uses and had helped create a major American rubber industry. In 1846, Elias Howe of Massachusetts constructed a sewing machine; Isaac Singer made improvements on it, and the Howe-Singer machine was soon being used in the manufacture of ready-to-wear clothing.

Innovations in Corporate Organization

The merchant capitalists remained figures of importance in the 1840s. In such cities as New York, Philadelphia, and Boston, influential mercantile groups operated shipping lines to southern ports or dispatched fleets of trading vessels to the ports of Europe and Asia. But *Rise of the Industrial Ruling Class* merchant capitalism was declining by the middle of the century. This was partly because British competitors were stealing much of America's export trade, but mostly because there were greater opportunities for profit in manufacturing than in trade. That was one reason why industries developed first in the Northeast: an affluent merchant class already existed there and had the money and the will to finance them. The emerging industrial capitalists soon became the new ruling class, the aristocrats of the Northeast, with far-reaching economic and political influence.

MEN AND WOMEN AT WORK

In the 1820s and 1830s, factory labor came primarily from the native-born population. After 1840, the growing immigrant population became the most important new source of workers.

Recruiting a Native Work Force

Recruiting a labor force was not an easy task in the early years of the factory system. Ninety percent of the American people in the 1820s still lived and worked on farms. Many of the relatively small number of urban residents were skilled artisans who owned and managed their own shops. The available unskilled workers were not numerous enough to form a reservoir from which the new industries could draw. But dramatic improvements in agricultural production, particularly in the Midwest, meant that each region no longer had to feed itself; it could import the food it needed. As a result, some of the relatively unprofitable farming areas of the East began to decline, and rural people began leaving the land to work in the factories.

Two systems of recruitment emerged to bring this new labor supply to the expanding textile mills. One, common in the mid-Atlantic states, brought whole families from the farm to work together in the mill. The second system, common in Massachusetts, enlisted young women, mostly *Lowell System* farmers' daughters in their late teens and early twenties. It was known as the Lowell or Waltham

WOMEN AT WORK This early photograph of female millworkers standing before their machines suggests something of the primitive quality of early factories—dimly lit, cramped, with conditions that offered little protection against accidents. All the women in this picture are wearing hair tightly pulled back, to prevent it from being caught in one of the machines. *(Courtesy George Eastman House)*

system, after the towns in which it first emerged. Many of these women worked for several years in the factories, saved their wages, and then returned home to marry and raise children. Others married men they met in the factories or in town. Most eventually stopped working in the mills and took up domestic roles instead.

Labor conditions in these early years of the factory system, hard as they often were, remained significantly better than they would later become. The Lowell workers, for example, lived in clean boardinghouses and dormitories, which the factory owners maintained for them. They were well fed and carefully supervised. Wages for the Lowell workers were relatively generous by the standards of the time. The women even published a monthly magazine, the *Lowell Offering*.

Yet even these relatively well-treated workers found the transition from farm life to factory work difficult. Forced to live among strangers in a regimented environment, many women had difficulty adjusting to the nature of factory work. However uncomfortable women may have found factory work, they had few other options. Work in the mills was in many cases virtually the only alternative to returning to farms that could no longer support them.

The paternalistic factory system of Lowell did not, in any case, survive for long. In the competitive textile market as it developed in the 1830s and 1840s, manufacturers found it difficult to maintain the high living standards and reasonably attractive working conditions with which they had begun. Wages declined; the hours of work lengthened; the conditions of the boardinghouses deteriorated. In 1834, mill workers in Lowell organized a union—the Factory Girls Association— which staged a strike to protest a 25 percent wage cut. Two years later, the association struck again—against a rent increase in the boardinghouses. Both strikes failed, and a recession in 1837 virtually destroyed the organization. Eight years later the Lowell women, led by the militant Sarah Bagley, created the Female Labor Reform Association and began agitating for a ten-hour day and for improvements in conditions in the mills. The new association also turned to state government and asked for legislative investigation of conditions in the mills. By then, however, the character of the factory work force was changing again. Many mill girls were gradually moving into other occupations: teaching, domestic service, or marriage. And textile manufacturers were turning to a less demanding labor supply: immigrants.

Factory Girls Association

The Immigrant Work Force

The increasing supply of immigrant workers after 1840 was a boon to manufacturers and other entrepreneurs. These new workers, because of their growing numbers and their unfamiliarity with their new country, had even less leverage than the women they at times displaced, and thus they often encountered far worse working conditions. Poorly paid construction gangs, made up increasingly of Irish immigrants, performed the heavy, unskilled work on turnpikes, canals, and railroads. Many of them lived in flimsy shanties, in grim conditions that endangered the health of their families (and reinforced native prejudices toward the "shanty Irish"). Irish workers began to predominate in the New England textile mills as well in the 1840s. Employers began paying piece rates rather than a daily wage and used other devices to speed up production and exploit the labor force more efficiently. The factories themselves were becoming large, noisy, unsanitary, and often dangerous places to work; the average workday was extending to twelve, often fourteen hours; and wages were declining. Women and children, whatever their skills, earned less than most men.

Cheap Immigrant Labor

The Factory System and the Artisan Tradition

Factories were also displacing the trades of skilled artisans. The artisan tradition was as much a part of the older, republican vision of America as the tradition of sturdy yeoman farmers. Independent craftsmen clung to a vision of economic life that was in some ways very different from the one the new capitalist class was promoting. It was a vision based not just on

A TOLEWARE MAKER, C. 1850 By the middle of the nineteenth century, skilled artisans—such as this maker of handcrafted kitchenware—were rapidly being replaced by semiskilled workers producing similar goods in factories. The craftsman pictured here conveys some of the important elements of the vanishing artisanal world: formal dress in the workplace, to suggest his status as a highly skilled craftsman; pride in his workmanship; and a middle-class sensibility that, in the end, made it difficult for artisans to fight the forces driving them toward obsolescence. *(Collection of Zelda P. Mackay, San Francisco, CA)*

the idea of individual, acquisitive success but also on a sense of a "moral community." Skilled artisans valued their independence; they also valued the stability and relative equality within their economic world.

Some artisans made successful transitions into small-scale industry. But others found themselves unable to compete with the new factory-made goods. In the face of this competition from indus- *Deskilling* trial capitalists, skilled workers in cities such as Philadelphia, Baltimore, Boston, and New York formed societies for mutual aid. During the 1820s and 1830s, these craft societies began to combine on a citywide basis and set up central organizations known as trade unions. In 1834, delegates from six cities founded the National Trades' Union, and in 1836, printers and cordwainers (makers of high-quality shoes and boots) set up their own national craft unions.

Hostile laws and hostile courts handicapped the unions. The Panic of 1837 and the depression that followed weakened the movement further. But the failure of these first organizations did not end the efforts by workers to gain control over their productive lives.

Fighting for Control

Workers made continuous efforts to improve their lots. They tried, with little success, to persuade state legislatures to pass laws setting a maximum workday and regulating child labor. The greatest legal victory of industrial workers came in Massachusetts in 1842, when the state supreme court, in *Commonwealth* v. *Hunt*, declared that unions were lawful organizations and that the strike was a lawful weapon. Other state courts gradually accepted the principles of the Massachusetts decision, but employers continued to resist.

Commonwealth v. Hunt

Virtually all the early craft unions excluded women. As a result, women began establishing their own protective unions by the 1850s. Like the male craft unions, the female protective unions had little power in dealing with employers. They did, however, serve an important role as mutual aid societies for women workers.

Many factors combined to inhibit the growth of effective labor resistance. Among the most important was the flood of immigrant laborers into the country. The newcomers were usually willing to work for lower wages than native workers; and because they were so numerous, manufacturers had little difficulty replacing disgruntled or striking workers with eager immigrants. Ethnic divisions and tensions often led workers to channel their resentments into internal bickering rather than into their shared grievances against employers. Another obstacle was the sheer strength of the industrial capitalists, who had not only economic but political and social power.

PATTERNS OF SOCIETY

The industrial revolution was making the United States dramatically wealthier by the year. It was also making society more unequal, and it was transforming social relationships at almost every level.

The Rich and the Poor

The commercial and industrial growth of the United States greatly elevated the average income of the American people. But this increasing wealth was being distributed highly unequally. Substantial groups of the population shared hardly at all in the economic growth: slaves, Indians, landless

Highly Unequal Distribution of Wealth

CENTRAL PARK To affluent New Yorkers, the construction of the city's great Central Park was important because it provided them with an elegant setting for their daily carriage rides—an activity ostensibly designed to expose the riders to fresh air but that was really an occasion for them to display their finery to their neighbors. (WCTU Parade, Great Riot, & Fashionable "Turn-outs" in Central Park. *The Museum of the City of New York*)

farmers, and many of the unskilled workers on the fringes of the manufacturing system. But even among the rest of the population, disparities of income were increasingly marked. Merchants and industrialists were accumulating enormous fortunes; and because there was now a significant number of rich people living in cities, a distinctive culture of wealth began to emerge.

In large cities, people of great wealth gathered together in neighborhoods of astonishing opulence. They founded clubs and developed elaborate social rituals. They looked increasingly for ways to display their wealth—in the great mansions they built, the showy carriages in which they rode, the lavish household goods they accumulated, the elegant social establishments they patronized. New York developed a particularly elaborate high society. The construction of the city's great Central Park, which began in the 1850s, was in part a result of pressure from the members of high society, who wanted an elegant setting for their daily carriage rides.

There was also a significant population of genuinely destitute people emerging in the growing urban centers of the nation. These were people who were not merely poor, in the sense of having to struggle to sustain themselves. They were al- *The Urban Poor* most entirely without resources, often homeless, dependent on charity or crime or both for survival. Substantial numbers of people actually starved to death or died of exposure. Some of these "paupers," as contemporaries called them, were recent immigrants. Some were widows and orphans, stripped of the family structures that allowed most working-class Americans to survive. Some were people suffering from alcoholism or mental illness, unable to work. Others were victims of native prejudice—barred from all but the most menial employment because of race or ethnicity. The Irish were particular victims of such prejudice.

Harsh Life for Free Blacks Among the worst victims were free blacks. Most major urban areas had significant black populations. Some of these African Americans were descendants of families that had lived in the North for generations. Others were former slaves who had escaped or been released by their masters. In material terms, at least, life was not always much better for them in the North than it had been in slavery. Most had access to very menial jobs at best. In most parts of the North, blacks could not vote, could not attend public schools, indeed could not use any of the public services available to white residents. Even so, most blacks preferred life in the North, however arduous, to life in the South.

Social Mobility

Despite the contrasts between conspicuous wealth and conspicuous poverty in antebellum America, there was relatively little overt class conflict. For one thing, life, in material terms at least, was better for most factory workers than it had been on the farms or in the European societies from which they had migrated. There was also a significant amount of mobility within the working class, which helped limit discontent. A few workers managed to move from poverty to riches by dint of work, ingenuity, and luck—a very small number, but enough to support the dreams of those who watched them. And a much larger number of workers managed to move at least one notch up the ladder—for example, becoming in the course of a lifetime a skilled, rather than an unskilled, laborer.

Geographical Mobility More important than social mobility was geographical mobility. Some workers saved money, bought land, and moved west to farm it. But few urban workers, and even fewer poor ones, could afford to make such a move. Much more common was the movement of laborers from one industrial town to another. These migratory workers were often the victims of layoffs, looking for better opportunities elsewhere. Their search may seldom have led to a marked improvement in their circumstances, but the rootlessness of this large segment of the work force—one of the most distressed segments—made effective organization and protest more difficult.

Middle-Class Life

For all the visibility of the very rich and the very poor in antebellum society, the fastest-growing group in America was the middle class. Economic development opened many more opportunities for people to own or work in businesses, to own shops, to engage in trade, to enter professions, and to administer organizations. In earlier times, when ownership of land had been the only real basis of wealth, society had been divided between people with little or no land (people Europeans generally called peasants) and a landed gentry (which in Europe usually became an inherited aristocracy). Once commerce and industry became a source of wealth, these rigid distinctions broke down; many people could become prosperous without owning land, but by providing valuable services.

Middle-class life in the years before the Civil War rapidly established itself as the most influential cultural form of urban America. Middle-class families lived in solid and often substantial homes. Their houses lined city streets, larger in size and more elaborate in design than the cramped, functional rowhouses in working-class neighborhoods—but also far less lavish than the great houses of the very rich. Like the wealthy, middle-class people tended to own their homes. Workers and artisans were increasingly becoming renters.

Rapidly Expanding Middle Class

Middle-class women usually remained in the home and cared for the household, although increasingly they were also able to hire servants—usually young, unmarried immigrant women. One of the aspirations of middle-class women in an age when doing the family's laundry could take an entire day was to escape from some of the drudgery of housework.

New household inventions altered, and greatly improved, the character of life in middle-class homes. Perhaps the most important was the invention of the cast-iron stove, which began to replace fireplaces as the principal vehicle for cooking in the 1840s. These wood- or coal-burning devices were hot, clumsy, and dirty by the standards of the twentieth century; but compared to the inconvenience and danger of cooking on an open hearth, they seemed a great luxury. Stoves gave cooks more control over the preparation of food and allowed them to cook several things at once.

New Household Inventions

Middle-class diets were changing rapidly, and not just because of the wider range of cooking the stove made possible. The expansion and diversification of American agriculture and the ability of farmers to ship goods to urban markets by rail from distant regions greatly increased the variety of food available in cities. Fruits and vegetables were difficult to ship over long distances in an age with little refrigeration, but families had access to a greater variety of meats, grains, and dairy products than they had had in the past. A few households acquired iceboxes, which allowed them to keep fresh meat and dairy products for as long as several days without spoilage. Most families, however, did not yet have any kind of refrigeration. For them, preserving food meant curing meat with salt and preserving fruits in sugar. Diets were generally much heavier and starchier than they are today, and middle-class people tended to be considerably stouter than would be considered healthy or fashionable now.

Middle-class homes came to differentiate themselves from those of workers and artisans in other ways as well. They were more elaborately decorated and furnished. Houses that had once had bare walls and floors now had carpeting, wallpaper, and curtains. The spare, simple styles of eighteenth-century homes gave way to the much more elaborate, even baroque household styles of the Victorian era—styles increasingly characterized by crowded, even cluttered rooms, dark colors, lush fabrics, and heavy furniture and draperies. Middle-class homes also became larger. It became less common for children to share beds and for all members of families to sleep in the same room. Parlors and dining rooms separate from the kitchen—once a luxury reserved largely for the wealthy—became the norm now for the middle class as well. Some urban middle-class homes had indoor plumbing and indoor toilets by the 1850s—a significant advance over the outdoor wells and privies that had been virtually universal only a few years earlier.

The Changing Family

The new industrializing society produced profound changes in the nature and function of the family. At the heart of the transformation was the movement of families from farms to urban areas. The family patterns of

Declining Patriarchy

the countryside, where powerful fathers controlled their children's futures by controlling the distribution of land to them, could not survive the move to a city or town. Sons and daughters in urban households were much more likely to leave the family in search of work than they had been in the rural world.

Another important change was the shift of income-earning work out of the home and into the shop, mill, or factory. In the early decades of the nineteenth century, the family itself had been the principal unit of economic activity. Now most income earners left home each day to work

Emergence of Public and Private Spheres

elsewhere. A sharp distinction began to emerge between the public world of the workplace and the private world of the family. The world of the family was now dominated not by production but by housekeeping, child rearing, and other primarily domestic concerns.

Accompanying the changing economic function of the family was a decline in the birth rate. In 1800, the average American woman could be expected to give birth to approximately seven children. By 1860, the average woman bore five children. The birth rate fell most quickly in urban areas and among middle-class women.

The "Cult of Domesticity"

The growing separation between the workplace and the home helped cause increasingly sharp distinctions between the social roles of men and women. Those distinctions affected not only factory workers and farmers but members of the growing middle class as well.

Traditional inequalities remained. Women had many fewer legal and political rights than did men, and within the family they remained under the virtually absolute authority of their husbands. Women were seldom encouraged in pursuing education above the primary level. Not until 1837 did any college or university accept women students: Oberlin in Ohio, which educated both women and men; and Mt. Holyoke in Massachusetts, founded by Mary Lyon as an academy for women. *Establishment of Women's Colleges*

However unequal the positions of men and women in the preindustrial era, those positions had generally been defined within the context of a household in which all members played important economic roles. In the middle-class family of the new industrial society, by contrast, the husband was assumed to be the principal, usually the only, income producer. The wife was now expected to remain in the home and to engage in largely domestic activities. The image of women changed from one of contributors to the family economy to one of guardians of the "domestic virtues." Middle-class women learned to place a higher value on keeping a clean, comfortable, and well-appointed home; on entertaining; on dressing elegantly and stylishly.

Within their own separate sphere, middle-class women began to develop a distinctive female culture. A "lady's" literature began to emerge. There were romantic novels, which focused on the private sphere that middle-class women now inhabited. There were women's magazines, which focused on fashions, shopping, homemaking, and other purely domestic concerns. *Women's Separate Sphere*

This "cult of domesticity," as some scholars have called it, gave many women greater material comfort than they had enjoyed in the past and placed a higher value on their "female virtues." At the same time, it left women increasingly detached from the public world, with few outlets for their interests and energies. Except for teaching and nursing, work by women outside the household gradually came to be seen as a lower-class preserve. *Advantages and Drawbacks*

Working-class women continued to work in factories and mills, but under conditions far worse than those that the original, more "respectable" women workers of Lowell and Waltham had experienced. Domestic service became another frequent source of female employment. Now that production had moved outside the household, women who needed to earn money had to move outside their own homes to do so.

Leisure Activities

Leisure time was scarce for all but the wealthiest Americans. Most people worked long hours. Vacations—paid or unpaid—were rare. For most people, Sunday was the only respite from work; and Sundays were generally reserved for religion and rest. For many working-class and middle-class people, therefore, holidays took on *Importance of Holidays* a special importance. That was one reason for the strikingly elaborate celebrations of the Fourth of July in the nineteenth century. The celebrations were not just expressions of patriotism. They were a way of enjoying one of the few nonreligious holidays from work available to most Americans.

In rural America, the erratic pattern of farmwork gave many people some relief from the relentless working schedules of city residents. For urban people, however, leisure was something to be seized in what few free moments they had. Men gravitated to taverns for drinking, talking, and game-playing after work. Women gathered in one another's homes for conversation and card games. For educated people, reading became one of the principal leisure activities. Newspapers and magazines proliferated rapidly, and books became staples of affluent homes. Women were particularly avid readers, and women writers created a new genre of fiction specifically for females—the "sentimental novel," which often offered idealized visions of women's lives and romances.

Vibrant Culture of Public Leisure   There was also a vigorous culture of public leisure. In larger cities, theaters were becoming increasingly popular; and while some of them catered to particular social groups, others attracted audiences that crossed class lines. Wealthy people, middle-class people, workers and their families—all could sometimes be found together watching a performance. Much of the popular theater of the time consisted of melodrama based on popular novels or American myths. But much of it reflected the great love of Shakespeare that extended through all levels of the theater-going population.

By the 1830s, Shakespeare was the most popular playwright in America. American performances of his work tended to be lively, irreverent, and highly inaccurate. Plays were abbreviated and sandwiched into programs containing other popular works. So familiar were many Shakespearean plots that parodies of them were staples of regional theater, through productions of such comedies as *Hamlet and Egglet* or *Julius Sneezer*. American audiences were noisy and rambunctious, and at times crowded onto the stage to participate in battle or crowd scenes. Their loyalties to their favorite actors were so strong that in 1849 there was a major riot at New York's Astor Place Opera House when supporters of a popular American Shakespearean actor, Edwin Forrest, gathered to protest a visit from an eminent English Shakespearean, Charles Macready.

Minstrel shows—in which white actors wearing blackface mimicked (and ridiculed) African-American culture—became increasingly popular. Public sporting events—boxing, horse racing, cockfighting (already becoming controversial), and others—often attracted considerable audiences. Baseball—not yet organized into professional leagues—was beginning to attract large crowds when played in city parks or fields on the edges of towns. A particularly exciting event in many communities was the arrival of the circus.

Popular tastes in public spectacle tended toward the bizarre and the fantastic. Relatively few people traveled; and in the absence of film, radio, television, or even much photography, they hungered for visions of unusual phenomena that contrasted with their normal experiences. People going to the theater or the circus or the museum wanted to see things that amazed and even frightened them. Perhaps the most celebrated provider of such experiences was the famous and unscrupu- *P. T. Barnum* lous showman P. T. Barnum, who opened the American Museum in New York in 1842—not a showcase for art or nature, but a great freak show populated by midgets (the most famous named Tom Thumb), Siamese twins, magicians, and ventriloquists. Barnum was a genius in publicizing his ventures with garish posters and elaborate newspaper announcements. Later, in the 1870s, he launched the famous circus for which he is still best remembered.

One of the ways Barnum tried to draw visitors to his museum was by engaging lecturers. He did so because he understood that the lecture was one of the most popular forms of entertainment in nineteenth-century America. Men and women flocked in enormous numbers to lyceums, churches, schools, and auditoriums to hear lecturers explain the latest advances in science, describe their visits to exotic places, provide vivid historical narratives, or rail against the evils of alcohol or slavery. Messages of social uplift and reform attracted rapt audiences, particularly among women.

THE AGRICULTURAL NORTH

Even in the rapidly urbanizing and industrializ- *Growth of Commercial Farming* ing Northeast, and more so in what nineteenth-century Americans called the Northwest (what Americans today call the Midwest), most people remained tied to the agricultural world. But agriculture, like industry and commerce, was becoming increasingly a part of the new capitalist economy.

Northeastern Agriculture

The story of agriculture in the Northeast after 1840 is one of decline and transformation. The reason for the decline was simple: the farmers of the section could no longer compete with the new and richer soil of the Northwest. In 1840, the leading wheat-growing states were New York, Pennsylvania, Ohio, and Virginia; in 1860 they were Illinois, Indiana, Wisconsin, Ohio, and Michigan. In raising corn, Illinois, Ohio, and Missouri supplanted New York, Pennsylvania, and Virginia. In 1840 the most important cattle-raising areas in the country were New York, Pennsylvania, and New England; but by the 1850s the leading cattle states were Illinois, Indiana, Ohio, and Iowa in the West and Texas in the South.

Some eastern farmers responded to these changes by moving west themselves and establishing new farms. Still others moved to mill towns and became laborers. Some farmers, however, remained on the land and turned to the task of supplying food to the growing cities of the East; they raised vegetables (truck farming) or fruit and sold their produce in nearby towns. Supplying milk, butter, and cheese to local urban markets also attracted many farmers in central New York, southeastern Pennsylvania, and various parts of New England.

The Old Northwest

Industrial Growth in the Northwest

Life was different in the states of the Northwest. There was some industry in this region, and in the two decades before the Civil War the section experienced steady industrial growth. There were flourishing industrial and commercial areas in and around Cleveland (on Lake Erie) and Cincinnati, the center of meatpacking in the Ohio Valley. Farther west, Chicago was emerging as the national center of the agricultural machinery and meatpacking industries. Most of the major industrial activities of the West either served agriculture (as in the case of farm machinery) or relied on agricultural products (as in flour milling, meatpacking, whiskey distilling, and the making of leather goods).

Some areas of the Northwest were not yet dominated by whites. Indians remained the most numerous inhabitants of large portions of the upper third of the Great Lakes states until after the Civil War. In those areas, hunting and fishing, along with some sedentary agriculture, remained the principal economic activities.

Rapid Expansion of Farming

For the settlers who populated the lands farther south, the Northwest was primarily an agricultural region. Its rich and plentiful lands made farming a lucrative and expanding activity there. Thus the typical citizen of the Northwest was not the industrial worker or poor, marginal farmer but the owner of a reasonably prosperous family farm.

Industrialization, in both the United States and Europe, provided the greatest boost to agriculture. With the growth of factories and cities in the Northeast, the domestic market for farm goods increased dramatically. The growing national and worldwide demand for farm products resulted in steadily rising farm prices. For most farmers, the 1840s and early 1850s were years of increasing prosperity.

The expansion of agricultural markets had profound effects on sectional alignments in the United States. The North-

Growing Ties between Northeast and Northwest

west sold most of its products to the Northeast and became an important market for the products of eastern industry. A strong economic relationship was emerging between the two sections that was profitable to both—and that was increasing the isolation of the South within the Union.

By 1850, the growing western white population was moving into the prairie regions on both sides of the Mississippi. These farmers cleared for-

MCCORMICK'S REAPER This 1850 advertisement for the automatic reaper created by Cyrus McCormick was aimed at farmers in Ohio and Illinois. But the reaper's greatest impact was to be in the vast grain-growing regions farther west, which were already attracting large numbers of white settlers and would attract many more in the decades to come. *(International Harvester)*

est lands or made use of fields the Indians had cleared many years earlier. And they began to develop a timber industry to make use of the forests that remained. Wheat was the staple crop of the region, but other crops—corn, potatoes, and oats—and livestock were also important.

The Northwest also increased production by adopting new agricultural techniques. Farmers *New Agricultural Techniques* began to cultivate new varieties of seed, notably Mediterranean wheat, which was hardier than the native type; and they imported better breeds of animals, such as hogs and sheep from England and Spain. Most important were improved tools and farm machines. The cast-iron plow remained popular because its parts could be replaced when broken. An even better tool appeared in 1847, when John Deere established at Moline, Illinois, a factory to manufacture steel plows, which were more durable than those made of iron.

Two new machines heralded a coming revolution in grain production. The most important was *McCormick Reaper* the automatic reaper, the invention of Cyrus H. McCormick of Virginia. The reaper took the place of sickle, cradle, and hand labor. Pulled by a team of horses, it had a row of horizontal knives on one side for cutting wheat; the wheels drove a paddle that bent the stalks over the knives, which then fell onto a moving belt that carried it into the back of the vehicle. The reaper enabled a crew of six or seven men to harvest in a day as much wheat as fifteen men could harvest using the older methods. McCormick, who had patented his device in 1834, established a factory at Chicago in 1847. By 1860, more than 100,000 reapers were in use on western farms. Almost as important to the grain grower was the thresher—a machine that separated the grain from the wheat stalks. Threshers appeared in large numbers after 1840. Before that, farmers generally flailed grain by hand or used farm animals to tread it. The Jerome I. Case factory in Racine, Wisconsin, manufactured most of the threshers. (Modern "harvesters" later combined the functions of the reaper and the thresher.)

The Northwest was the most self-consciously democratic section of the country. But its democracy was of a relatively conservative type—capitalistic, property-conscious, middle-class. Abraham Lincoln, an Illinois Whig, voiced the economic opinions of many of the people of his section. "I take it that it is best for all to leave each man free to acquire property as fast as he can," said Lincoln. "Some will get wealthy. I don't believe in a law to prevent a man from getting rich; it would do more harm than good. . . . When one starts poor, as most do in the race of life, free society is such that he knows he can better his condition; he knows that there is no fixed condition of labor for his whole life."

Rural Life

Life for farming people varied greatly from one region to another. In the more densely populated areas east of the Appalachians and in the easternmost areas of the Northwest, farmers were usually part of relatively vibrant communities and made extensive use of the institutions of those communities— the churches, schools, stores, and taverns. As white settlement moved further west, farmers became more isolated and had to struggle to find any occasions for contact with people outside their own families.

Although the extent of social interaction differed from one area to another, the forms of interaction were usually very similar. Religion drew farm communities together perhaps more than any other force. Town or village churches were popular meeting places, both for services and for social events—most of them dominated by women. Even in areas with no organized churches, farm families—and, again, women in particular— gathered in one another's homes for prayer meetings, Bible readings, and other religious activities. Weddings, baptisms, and funerals also brought communities together.

Rural Social Interaction   But religion was only one of many reasons for interaction. Farm people joined together frequently to share tasks such as barn raising. On those occasions, families would gather and create a festive atmosphere of celebration. Women prepared large suppers while the men worked on the barn and the children played. Large numbers of families gathered together at harvest time to help bring in crops, husk corn, or thresh wheat. Women came together to share domestic tasks, holding "bees" in which groups of women joined together to make quilts, baked goods, preserves, and other products.

Despite the many social gatherings farm families managed to create, they had much less contact with popular culture and public social life than people who lived in towns and cities. Rural people treasured their links to the outside world—letters from relatives and friends in distant places, newspapers and magazines from cities they had never seen, catalogs advertising merchandise that their local stores never had. Yet many also valued the relative autonomy that a farm life gave them. One reason many rural Americans looked back nostalgically on country life once they moved to the city was that they sensed that in the urban world they did not have as much control over the patterns of their daily lives as they had once known.

CONCLUSION

Between the 1820s and the 1850s, the American economy experienced the beginnings of an industrial revolution—a change that transformed almost every area of life in fundamental ways.

The American industrial revolution was a result of many things: population growth, advances in transportation and communication, new technologies that spurred the development of factories capable of mass producing goods, the recruiting of a large industrial labor force, and the creation of corporate bodies capable of managing large enterprises. The new economy expanded the ranks of the wealthy and helped create a large new middle class. It also created high levels of inequality.

Sources of the Industrial Revolution

Culture in the industrializing areas of the North changed, too, and there were important changes in the structure and behavior of the family, in the role of women, and in the way people used their leisure time and encountered popular culture. The changes helped widen the gap in experience and understanding between the generation of the Revolution and the generation of the mid-nineteenth century. They also helped widen the gap between North and South.

FOR FURTHER REFERENCE

John Bodnar, *The Transplanted: A History of Immigrants in America* (1985) is a useful survey. Matthew Frye Jacobson, *Whiteness of a Different Color: European Immigrants and the Alchemy of Race* (1999) is a wide-ranging cultural history of immigration. Charles G. Sellers, *The Market Revolution: Jacksonian America, 1815–1846* (1991) demonstrates the overwhelming impact of the market revolution on American social and political development. George R. Taylor, *The Transportation Revolution* (1951) is a classic account of economic development in the antebellum period. Christopher Clark, *The*

Roots of Rural Capitalism: Western Massachusetts, 1780–1860 (1990) is an examination of the impact of emerging capitalism on a rural area. Paul Johnson, *A Shopkeeper's Millennium: Society and Revivals in Rochester, New York, 1815–1837* (1978) explores the changing character of class relations in upstate New York in an age of rapid economic development. Alice Kessler-Harris, *Out to Work: A History of Wage-Earning Women in the United States* (1982) is a broad history of women in the wage labor force. Thomas Dublin, *Transforming Women's Work: New England Lives in the Industrial Revolution* (1994) looks in particular at the mill towns of the northeast. Mary Ryan, *Cradle of the Middle Class: The Family in Oneida County, New York, 1790–1865* (1981) demonstrates the relationship between the market revolution and the changing character of middle-class family structure. Christine Stansell, *City of Women: Sex and Class in New York, 1789–1860* (1983) explores the female world of antebellum New York City. Paul W. Gates, *The Farmer's Age: Agriculture, 1815–1860* (1966) is an important overview. Alan Taylor, *William Cooper's Town: Power and Persuasion on the Frontier in the Early American Republic* (1995) examines the early years of Cooperstown, New York, and the impact on it of the rise of the market and of democratic politics. Witold Rybczynski, *A Clearing in the Distance: Frederick Law Olmsted and America in the Nineteenth Century* (1999) is a perceptive and engaging study of the man who, along with Calvert Vaux, designed New York City's Central Park and other important American landscapes.

For quizzes, Internet resources, references to additional books and films, and more, consult this book's Online Learning Center site at www.mhhe.com/unfinishednation4.

THE NEW ORLEANS COTTON EXCHANGE   Edgar Degas, the great French impressionist, painted this scene of cotton traders examining samples in the New Orleans cotton exchange in 1873. By this time the cotton trade was producing less impressive profits than those that had made it the driving force of the booming southern economy of the 1850s. Degas's mother came from a Creole family of cotton brokers in New Orleans, and two of the artist's brothers (depicted here reading a newspaper and leaning against a window) joined the business in America.
(Giraudon/Art Resource, NY)

TIME LINE

1800	1808	1820s	1822	1831	
Gabriel Prosser's unsuccessful slave revolt	Slave importation banned	Depression in tobacco prices begins	Denmark Vesey's conspiracy	Nat Turner slave rebellion	
		High cotton production in Southwest			

CHAPTER ELEVEN

COTTON, SLAVERY, AND THE OLD SOUTH

The Cotton Economy
Southern White Society
Slavery: The "Peculiar Institution"
The Culture of Slavery

The South, like the North, experienced dramatic growth in the middle years of the nineteenth century. Southerners fanned out into the Southwest. The southern agricultural economy grew increasingly productive and increasingly prosperous. Trade in such staples as sugar, rice, tobacco, and above all cotton made the South a major force in international commerce. It also tied the South securely to the emerging capitalist world of the United States and its European trading partners.

Yet despite all these changes, the South experienced a much less fundamental transformation in these years than did the North. It had begun the nineteenth century a primarily agricultural region; it remained overwhelmingly agrarian in 1860. It had begun the century with few important cities and little industry; and so it remained sixty years later. In 1800, a plantation system dependent on slave labor had dominated the southern economy; by 1860, that system had only strengthened its grip on the region. As one historian has written, "The South grew, but it did not develop."

	1833	1837	1846	1849	
	John Randolph frees 400 slaves	Cotton prices plummet	*De Bow's Review* founded	Cotton production boom	

THE COTTON ECONOMY

The most important economic development in the mid-nineteenth-century South was the shift of economic power from the "upper South," the original southern states along the Atlantic coast, to the "lower South," the expanding agricultural regions in the new states of the Southwest. That shift reflected above all the growing dominance of cotton in the southern economy.

The Rise of King Cotton

Declining Tobacco Economy Much of the upper South continued to rely on the cultivation of tobacco. But the market for that crop was notoriously unstable, and tobacco rapidly exhausted the land on which it grew. By the 1830s, therefore, many farmers in the old tobacco-growing regions of Virginia, Maryland, and North Carolina were shifting to other crops, while the center of tobacco cultivation was moving westward, into the Piedmont area.

The southern regions of the coastal South—South Carolina, Georgia, and parts of Florida—continued to rely on the cultivation of rice, a more stable and lucrative crop. But rice demanded substantial irrigation and needed an exceptionally long growing season (nine months), so cultivation of that staple remained restricted to a relatively small area. Sugar growers along the Gulf Coast, similarly, enjoyed a reasonably profitable market for their crop. But sugar cultivation required intensive (and debilitating) labor and a long growing time; only relatively wealthy planters could afford to engage in it. In addition, producers faced major competition from the great sugar plantations of the Caribbean. Sugar cultivation, therefore, did not spread much beyond a small area in southern Louisiana and eastern Texas. Long-staple (Sea Island) cotton was another lucrative crop, but like rice and sugar, it could grow only in a limited area—the coastal regions of the Southeast.

SLAVERY AND COTTON IN THE SOUTH, 1820 AND 1860 The two maps on the opposite page show the remarkable spread of cotton cultivation in the South in the decades before the Civil War. Both maps show the areas of cotton cultivation (the light-orange colored areas) as well as areas with large slave populations (the darker rust dotted or solid areas). Note how in the top map, which represents 1820, cotton production is concentrated largely in the East, with a few areas scattered among Alabama, Mississippi, Louisiana, and Tennessee. Slavery is concentrated along the Georgia and South Carolina coast, areas in which long-staple cotton was grown, with only a few other areas of highly dense slave populations. By 1860, the South had changed dramatically. Cotton production had spread throughout the lower South, from Texas to northern Florida, and slavery had moved with it. Slavery was also much denser in the tobacco-growing regions of Virginia and North Carolina, which had also grown. ◆ *How did this economic shift affect the white South's commitment to slavery?*

 For an interactive version of this map go to www.mhhe.com/unfinishednation4ch11maps

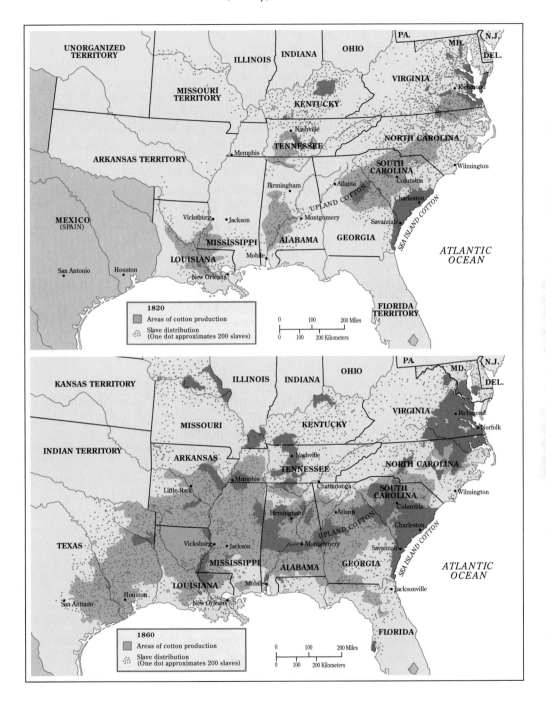

The decline of the tobacco economy in the upper South, and the inherent limits of the sugar, rice, and long-staple cotton economies farther south, might have forced the region to shift its attention to other, nonagricultural pursuits had it not been for the growing importance of a new product that soon overshadowed all else: short-staple cotton. This was a hardier and coarser strain of cotton that could grow successfully in a variety of climates and in a variety of soils. It was harder to process than the long-staple variety because its seeds were difficult to remove from the fiber. But the invention of the cotton gin had largely solved that problem.

Short-Staple Cotton

Demand for cotton increased rapidly in the nineteenth century with the growth of the textile industry in Britain in the 1820s and 1830s and in New England in the 1840s and 1850s. In response to that demand, beginning in the 1820s, cotton production spread rapidly. From the western areas of South Carolina and Georgia, production moved into Alabama and Mississippi and then into northern Louisiana, Texas, and Arkansas. By the 1850s, cotton had become the linchpin of the southern economy. There were periodic booms and busts, but the cotton economy continued to grow. By the time of the Civil War, cotton constituted nearly two-thirds of the total export trade of the United States. It was little wonder that southern politicians now proclaimed: "Cotton is king!"

Increasing Cotton Cultivation

Cotton production boomed in the newly settled areas of what came to be known as the "lower South" (or, in a later era, the "Deep South"). Some began to call it the "Cotton Kingdom." The prospect of tremendous profits drew settlers to the lower South by the thousands. Some were wealthy planters from the older states, but most were small slaveholders or slaveless farmers who hoped to move into the planter class.

Rapid Expansion of Slavery

A similar shift, if an involuntary one, occurred in the slave population. Between 1840 and 1860, according to some estimates, 410,000 slaves moved from the upper South to the cotton states—either accompanying masters who were themselves migrating to the Southwest or (more often) sold to planters already there. The sale of slaves to the Southwest became an important economic activity in the upper South.

Southern Trade and Industry

In the face of this booming agricultural expansion, other forms of economic activity developed slowly in the South. There was growing activity in flour milling and in textile and iron manufacturing, particularly in the upper South, but industry remained an insignificant force in comparison with the agricultural economy. The total value of southern textile manufactures in 1860 was $4.5 million—a threefold increase over the value of

HAULING THE WHOLE WEEK'S PICKING

HAULING THE WHOLE WEEK'S PICKING This watercolor by William Henry Brown, painted in approximately 1842, portrays a slave family loading cotton onto a wagon, presumably after a hard day of picking. Even young children participate in the chores. Brown was an artist known for his silhouettes, a form popular in the nineteenth century. (One of his later subjects was Abraham Lincoln.) This picture is part of a five-foot cutout he made as a gift to a family he was visiting. *(William Henry Brown,* Hauling the Whole Weeks Picking, *1842. The Historic New Orleans Collection, 1975.93.1 & 1975.93.2)*

those goods twenty years before, but only about 2 percent of the value of the cotton exported that year.

The limited nonfarm commercial sector that did develop in the South was largely intended to serve the needs of the plantation economy. Particu- *Obstacles to Economic Development*

larly important were the brokers, or "factors," who marketed the planters' crops. The South had only a very rudimentary financial system, and the factors often also served the planters as bankers, providing them with credit. Other obstacles to economic development included the South's inadequate transportation system. Canals were almost nonexistent; most roads were crude and unsuitable for heavy transport; and railroads, although they expanded substantially in the 1840s and 1850s, failed to tie the region together effectively. The principal means of transportation was water. Planters generally shipped their crops to market along rivers or by sea; most manufacturing was in or near port towns.

The South was, therefore, becoming more and more dependent on the manufacturers, merchants, and professionals of the North. Some southerners began to advocate economic independence for the region, among them James D. B. De Bow of New Orleans, whose maga- *De Bow's Commercial Review*

zine, *De Bow's Commercial Review*, called for southern commercial and agricultural expansion and economic independence from the North. Yet even *De Bow's Commercial Review* was filled with advertisements from northern manufacturing firms; and its circulation was far smaller in the South than such northern magazines as *Harper's Weekly*.

DE BOW'S COMMERCIAL REVIEW J. D. B. De Bow, owner and editor of the South's leading magazine, presented his *Review* as a commercial publication—designed for those committed to commerce. But it also contained essays and articles promoting the South's way of life and what many white southerners considered the region's distinctive (and superior) culture. *(Courtesy of Archives and History, Jackson, MI.)*

Sources of Southern Difference

An important question about antebellum southern history is why the region did so little to develop a larger industrial and commercial economy of its own. Why did it remain so different from the North?

Part of the reason was the great profitability of the region's agricultural system. In the Northeast, many people had turned to manufacturing as the agricultural economy of the region declined. In the *Sources of Uneven Development* South, the agricultural economy was booming, and ambitious people eager to profit from the emerging capitalist economy had little incentive to look elsewhere. Another reason was that wealthy southerners had so much capital invested in their land and their slaves that they had little left for other investments. Some historians have suggested that the southern climate—with its long, hot, steamy summers—was less suitable for industrial development than the climate of the North.

But the southern failure to create a flourishing commercial or industrial economy was also in part the result of a set of values distinctive to the South. Many white southerners liked to think of themselves as representatives of a special way of life. Southerners were, they *Distinct Southern Values* argued, more concerned with a refined and gracious way of life than with rapid growth and development. But appealing as this image was to southern whites, it conformed to the reality of southern society in very limited ways.

SOUTHERN WHITE SOCIETY

Only a small minority of southern whites owned slaves. In 1860, when the white population was just above 8 million, the number of slaveholders was only 383,637. Even with all members of slaveowning families included in the figures, those living in slaveowning households still amounted to perhaps no more than one-quarter of the white population. And only a small proportion of this relatively small number of slaveowners owned slaves in substantial numbers.

The Planter Class

How, then, did the South come to be seen as a society dominated by wealthy landowning planters? In large part, it was because the planter aristocracy exercised power and influence far in excess of their numbers.

Planter Aristocracy's Dominance

White southerners liked to compare their planter class to the old upper classes of England and Europe. In fact, most of the southern upper class was not at all similar to the landed aristocracies of the Old World. In some areas of the upper South, the great aristocrats were indeed people whose families had occupied positions of wealth and power for generations. In most of the South, however, there was no longstanding landed aristocracy. As late as the 1850s, many of the great landowners in the lower South were still first-generation settlers, who had only relatively recently started to live in the comfort and luxury for which they became famous. Large areas of the South had been settled and cultivated for less than two decades at the time of the Civil War.

Nor was the world of the planter nearly as leisured and genteel as the aristocratic myth would suggest. Growing staple crops was a business. Planters were, in many respects, just as much competitive capitalists as the industrialists of the North. Even many affluent planters lived rather modestly, their wealth so heavily invested in land and slaves that there was little left for personal comfort. And white planters, including some substantial ones, tended to move frequently as new and presumably more productive areas opened up to cultivation.

Wealthy southern whites sustained their image of themselves as aristocrats in many ways. They adopted an elaborate code of "chivalry," which obligated white men to defend their "honor," often through dueling. They avoided such "coarse" occupations as trade and commerce; those who did not become planters often gravitated toward the military. The aristocratic ideal also found reflection in the definition of a special role for southern white women.

The Aristocratic Ideal

A GEORGIA PLANTATION This map of the Hopeton Plantation in South Carolina shows both how much plantations were connected to the national and world markets, and how much they tried to be self-sufficient. Note the large areas of land devoted to the growing of cotton, rice, and sugar cane, all of them crops for the market. ◆ *Why would a plantation in this part of the South be so much more diversified in the market crops it raised than the cotton plantations in the Mississippi Delta?* Note also the many crops grown for the local market or for consumption by residents of the plantation—potatoes, vegetables, corn, and others. The top left of the map shows the distribution of living quarters, with slaves' quarters grouped together very near the owner's residence. ◆ *Why would planters want their slaves living nearby? Why might slaves be unhappy about being so close to their owners?*

The "Southern Lady"

In some respects, affluent white women in the South occupied roles very similar to those of middle-class white women in the North. Their lives generally centered in the home, where (according to the South's social ideal) they served as companions to and hostesses for their husbands and as nurturing mothers for their children. "Genteel" southern white women seldom engaged in public activities or found income-producing employment.

But the life of the "southern lady" was also in many ways very different from that of her northern counterpart. For one thing, the cult of honor in the region meant that southern white men gave particular importance to the defense of women. In practice, this generally meant

Female Subordinance Reinforced

that white men were even more dominant and white women even more subordinate in southern culture than they were in the North. Social theorist George Fitzhugh wrote in the 1850s: "Women, like children, have but one right, and that is the right to protection. The right to protection involves the obligation to obey."

More important in determining the role of southern white women, however, was that the vast majority of them lived on farms, with little access to the "public world" and thus few opportunities to look beyond their roles as wives and mothers. For many white women, living on farms of modest size meant a fuller engagement in the economic life of the family than was becoming typical for middle-class women in the North. These women engaged in spinning, weaving, and other production; they participated in agricultural tasks; they helped supervise the slave work force. On the larger plantations, however, even these limited roles were often considered unsuitable for white women, and the "plantation mistress" became, in some cases, more an ornament for her husband than an active part of the economy or the society. Southern white women also had less access to education than their northern counterparts. The few female "academies" in the South trained women primarily to be suitable wives.

Southern white women had other special bur- *Special Burdens* dens as well. The southern white birth rate remained nearly 20 percent higher than that of the nation as a whole, and infant mortality in the region remained higher than elsewhere. The slave labor system also had a mixed impact on white women. It helped spare many of them from certain kinds of arduous labor, but it also damaged their relationships with their husbands. Male slaveowners had frequent sexual relationships with the female slaves on their plantations; the children of those unions served as a constant reminder to white women of their husbands' infidelities. Black women (and men) were obviously the most important victims of such practices, but white women suffered, too.

The Plain Folk

The typical white southerner was a yeoman farmer. Some of these "plain folk," as they became known, owned a few slaves, with whom they worked and lived more closely than did the larger planters. Some plain folk, most of whom owned their own land, devoted themselves largely to subsistence farming; others grew cotton or other crops for the market, but usually could not produce enough to allow them to expand their operations or even get out of debt.

One reason was the southern educational system. For the sons of wealthy planters, the region provided ample opportunities to gain an education. In 1860 there were 260 southern colleges and universities, public and private, with 25,000 students enrolled in them. But as in the rest of the United States, universities *Inadequate Educational Opportunities* were only within the reach of the upper class. The elementary and secondary schools of the South were not only fewer than but also inferior to those of the Northeast. The South had more than 500,000 illiterate whites, over half the nation's total.

The subordination of the plain folk to the planter class raises an important question: Why did lower-class whites not oppose the aristocratic social system from which they benefited so little?

Some nonslaveowning whites did oppose the planter elite, but for the most part in limited ways and in isolated areas. These were mainly the *"Hill People"* "hill people," who lived in the Appalachian ranges east of the Mississippi, in the Ozarks to the west of the river, and in other "hill country" or "backcountry" areas. Of all southern whites, they were the most isolated from the mainstream of the region's life. They practiced a simple form of subsistence agriculture and owned practically no slaves. They were, in most respects, unconnected to the new commercial economy that dominated the great cotton-planting region of the South.

Such whites frequently expressed animosity toward the planter aristocracy. The mountain region was the only part of the South to resist the movement toward secession when it finally developed. Even during the Civil War itself, many refused to support the Confederacy.

Far greater in number, however, were the nonslaveowning whites who lived in the midst of the plantation system. Many, *Dependence on the Plantation* perhaps most of them, accepted that system because they were tied to it in important ways. Small farmers depended on the local plantation aristocracy for many things: access to cotton gins, markets for their modest crops and their livestock, credit or other financial assistance in time of need. In many areas, moreover, the poorest resident of a county might easily be a cousin of the richest aristocrat. In the 1850s, the boom in the cotton economy allowed many small farmers to improve their economic fortunes. Some bought more land, became slaveowners, and moved into at least the fringes of plantation society. Others simply felt more secure in their positions as independent yeomen and hence more likely to embrace the fierce regional loyalty that was spreading throughout the white South in these years.

There were other white southerners, however, who shared almost not at all in the plantation economy and yet continued to accept its premises. These were known variously as "crackers," "sand hillers," or "poor white trash." Occupying the infertile lands of the pine barrens, the red hills, and the swamps, they lived in genuine squalor. Many owned no land and supported themselves by foraging or hunting. Others worked at times as common laborers for their neighbors. Their degradation resulted partly from dietary deficiencies and disease. They resorted at times to eating clay (hence the tendency of more affluent whites to refer to them disparagingly as "clay eaters"), and they suffered from pellagra, hookworm, and malaria. Planters and small farmers alike held them in contempt.

Even among these southerners—the true outcasts of white society in the region—there was no real opposition to the plantation system or slavery. In part, undoubtedly, this was because these men and women were so benumbed by poverty that they had little strength to protest. But it re-

sulted also from perhaps the single greatest unifying factor among the southern white population:
their perception of race. However poor and miserable white southerners
might be, they could still look down on the black population of the region
and feel a bond with their fellow whites born of a determination to maintain their racial supremacy.

SLAVERY: THE "PECULIAR INSTITUTION"

White southerners often referred to slavery as the "peculiar institution."
By that they meant not that the institution was odd but that it was distinctive, special. American slavery was indeed distinctive. The South in the
mid-nineteenth century was the only area in the Western world—except
for Brazil, Cuba, and Puerto Rico—where slavery still existed. Slavery,
more than any other single factor, isolated the South from the rest of
American society.

Within the South itself, the institution of slavery had paradoxical results. On the one hand, it isolated blacks from whites. As a result, African
Americans under slavery began to develop a society and culture of their
own. On the other hand, slavery created a unique bond between blacks and
whites—masters and slaves—in the South. The two groups may have maintained separate spheres, but each sphere was deeply influenced by the other.

Varieties of Slavery

The slave codes of the southern states forbade
slaves to hold property, to leave their masters'
premises without permission, to be out after dark, to congregate with
other slaves except at church, to carry firearms, or to strike a white person
even in self-defense. The codes prohibited whites from teaching slaves to
read or write and denied slaves the right to testify in court against white
people. The laws contained no provisions to legalize slave marriages or divorces. If an owner killed a slave while punishing him, the act was generally not considered a crime. Slaves, however, faced the death penalty for
killing or even resisting a white person and for inciting revolt. The codes
also contained extraordinarily rigid provisions for defining a person's race.
Anyone with a trace (or often even a rumor) of African ancestry was defined as black.

Enforcement of the laws, however, was spotty and uneven. Some
slaves did acquire property, did learn to read and write, and did assemble
with other slaves. White owners themselves handled most transgressions
by their slaves and inflicted widely varying punishments. In other words,
despite the rigid provisions of law, there was in reality considerable variety
within the slave system. Some slaves lived in almost prisonlike conditions,

THE CHARACTER OF SLAVERY

No issue in American history has produced a more spirited debate than the nature of plantation slavery. The debate began even before the Civil War, when abolitionists strove to expose slavery to the world as a brutal, dehumanizing institution, while Southern defenders of slavery tried to depict it as a benevolent, paternalistic system. But by the late nineteenth century, with white Americans eager for sectional conciliation, most Northern and Southern chroniclers of slavery began to accept a romanticized and unthreatening picture of the Old South and its peculiar institution.

The first major scholarly examination of slavery was Ulrich B. Phillips's *American Negro Slavery* (1918), which portrayed slavery as an essentially benign institution in which kindly masters looked after submissive and generally contented African Americans. Phillips's apologia for slavery remained the authoritative work on the subject for nearly thirty years.

In the 1940s, challenges to Phillips began to emerge. In 1941, for example, Melville J. Herskovits challenged Phillips's contention that black Americans retained little of their African cultural inheritance. In 1943, Herbert Aptheker published a chronicle of slave revolts as a way of challenging Phillips's claim that blacks were submissive and content.

A somewhat different challenge to Phillips emerged in the 1950s from historians who emphasized the brutality of the institution. Kenneth Stampp's *The Peculiar Institution* (1956) and Stanley Elkins's *Slavery* (1959) described a labor system that did serious physical and psychological damage to its victims. They portrayed slavery as something like a prison, in which men and women had virtually no space to develop their own social and cultural lives. Elkins compared the system to Nazi concentration camps and likened the childlike "Sambo" personality of slavery to the tragic distortions of character produced by the Holocaust.

In the early 1970s, an explosion of new scholarship on slavery shifted the emphasis away from the damage the system inflicted on African Americans and toward the striking success of the slaves themselves in building a culture of their own. John Blassingame in 1973 argued that "the most remarkable aspect of the whole process of enslavement is the extent to which the American-born slaves were able to retain their ancestors' culture." Herbert Gutman, in *The Black Family in Slavery and Freedom* (1976), challenged the prevailing belief that slavery had weakened and even destroyed the African-American family. On the contrary, he argued, the black family survived slavery with impressive strength, although with some significant differences from the prevailing form of the white family. Eugene Genovese's *Roll, Jordan, Roll* (1974) revealed how African Americans manipulated the paternalist assumptions that lay at the heart of slavery to build a large cultural space of their own where they could develop their own family life, social traditions, and religious patterns. That same year, Robert Fogel and Stanley Engerman published their controversial *Time on the Cross*, a highly quantitative study that supported some of the claims of Gutman and Genovese about black achievement but that went much further in portraying slavery as a successful and reasonably humane (if ultimately immoral) system. Slave workers, they argued, were better treated and lived in greater comfort than most Northern industrial workers of the same era. Their conclusions produced a storm of criticism.

Some of the most important recent scholarship on slavery extends the notion of slave autonomy to discussions of African-American women. Elizabeth Fox-Genovese's *Within the Plantation Household* (1988) examined the lives of both white and black women on the plantation. She portrayed slave women as defined by their dual roles as members of the plantation work force and anchors of the black family. Slave women, she argued, professed loyalty to their mistresses when forced to serve them as domestics; but their real loyalty remained to their own communities and families.

(text continued from page 291)

rigidly and harshly controlled by their masters. Many (probably most) others enjoyed considerable flexibility and autonomy.

The nature of the relationship between masters and slaves depended in part on the size of the plantation. White farmers with few slaves generally supervised their workers directly and often worked closely alongside them. The paternal relationship *Paternal Relationship* between such masters and their slaves could be warm and benevolent. It could also be tyrannical and cruel. In general, African Americans themselves preferred to live on larger plantations, where they had a chance for a social world of their own.

Although the majority of slaveowners were small farmers, the majority of slaves lived on plantations of medium or large size, with substantial slave work forces. Thus the relationship between master and slave was much less intimate for the typical slave than for the typical slaveowner. Substantial planters often hired overseers and even assistant overseers to represent them. "Head drivers," trusted and responsible slaves often assisted by several subdrivers, acted under the overseer as foremen.

Life under Slavery

Slaves generally received an adequate yet simple diet, consisting mainly of cornmeal, salt pork, molasses, and on special occasions fresh meat or poultry. Many slaves cultivated gardens for their own use. Their masters provided them with cheap clothing and shoes. They lived in rough cabins, called slave quarters. The plantation mistress or a doctor retained by the owner provided some medical care, but slave women themselves—as "healers" and midwives, or simply as mothers—were the more important source.

Slaves worked hard, beginning with light tasks as children. Their workdays were longest at harvest time. Slave women worked particularly hard. They generally labored in *Work Conditions* the fields with the men, and they also handled cooking, cleaning, and child rearing. Many slave families were divided. Husbands and fathers often lived

RETURNING FROM THE COTTON FIELD In this photograph, South Carolina field workers return after a day of picking cotton, some of their harvest carried in bundles on their heads. A black slave driver leads the way. *(©The New-York Historical Society)*

on neighboring plantations; at times, one spouse (usually the male) would be sold to a plantation owner far away. As a result, black women often found themselves acting in effect as single parents.

Slaves were, as a group, much less healthy than southern whites. After 1808, when the importation of slaves became illegal, the proportion of blacks to whites in the nation as a whole steadily declined. The slower increase of the black population was a result of its comparatively high death rate. Slave mothers had large families, but the enforced poverty in which *High Mortality Rates* virtually all African Americans lived ensured that fewer of their children would survive to adulthood than the children of white parents. Even those who did survive typically died at a younger age than the average white person.

Household servants had a somewhat easier life—physically at least— than did field hands. On a small plantation, the same slaves might do both field work and housework. But on a large estate, there would generally be a separate domestic staff: nursemaids, housemaids, cooks, butlers, coachmen. These people lived close to the master and his family, eating the leftovers from the family table. Between the blacks and whites of such households affectionate, almost familial relationships might develop. More often, however, house servants resented their isolation from their fellow slaves and the lack of privacy that came with living in such close proximity to the master's family. Among other things, that proximity meant that their transgressions were more visible than those of field hands. When emancipation came after the Civil War, it was often the house servants who were the first to leave the plantations of their former owners.

Female household servants were especially vulnerable to sexual abuse by their masters and white overseers. In addition to being subjected to unwanted sexual attention from white men, female slaves often received vindictive treatment from white women. Plantation mistresses naturally resented the sexual liaisons between their husbands and female slaves. Punishing their husbands was not usually possible, so they often punished the slaves instead—with arbitrary beatings, increased workloads, and various forms of psychological torment.

Sexual Abuse

Slavery in the Cities

The conditions of slavery in the cities differed significantly from those in the countryside. On the relatively isolated plantations, slaves had little contact with free blacks and lower-class whites, and masters maintained a fairly direct and effective control. In the city, however, a master often could not supervise his slaves closely and at the same time use them profitably. Even if they slept at night in carefully watched backyard barracks, they moved about during the day alone, performing errands of various kinds.

There was a considerable market in the South for common laborers, particularly since, unlike in the North, there were few European immigrants to perform menial chores. As a result, masters often hired out slaves for such tasks. Slaves on contract worked in mining and lumbering (often far from cities), but others worked on the docks and on construction sites, drove wagons, and performed other unskilled jobs in cities and towns. Slave women and children worked in the region's few textile mills. Particularly skilled workers such as blacksmiths or carpenters were also often hired out. After regular working hours, many of them fended for themselves; thus urban slaves gained numerous opportunities to mingle with free blacks and with whites. In the cities, the line between slavery and freedom was less distinct than on the plantation.

Relative Autonomy of Urban Slaves

Free Blacks

There were about 250,000 free blacks in the slaveholding states by the start of the Civil War, more than half of them in Virginia and Maryland. In some cases, they were slaves who had somehow earned money with which they managed to buy their own and their families' freedom. It was most often urban blacks, with their greater freedom of movement and activity, who could take that route. One example was Elizabeth Keckley, a slave woman who bought freedom for herself and her son with proceeds from sewing. She later became a seamstress, personal servant, and companion to Mary Todd Lincoln in the White House. But few masters had any incentive, or inclination, to give up their slaves, so this route was open to relatively few people.

New Restrictions on Manumission

Some slaves were set free by a master who had moral qualms about slavery, or by a master's will after his death—for example, the more than 400 slaves belonging to John Randolph of Roanoke, freed in 1833. From the 1830s on, however, state laws governing slavery became more rigid, in part in response to the fears Nat Turner's revolt (see p. 297) created among white southerners. The new laws made it more and more difficult, and in some cases practically impossible, for owners to set free (or "manumit") their slaves.

A few free blacks attained wealth and prominence. Some owned slaves themselves, usually relatives whom they had bought in order to ensure their ultimate emancipation. In a few cities—New Orleans, Natchez, and Charleston—free black communities managed to flourish relatively unmolested by whites and with some economic stability. Most southern free blacks, however, lived in abject poverty. Yet, great as were the hardships of freedom, blacks usually preferred them to slavery.

Slave Resistance

Slaveowners, and many other white Americans after emancipation, liked to argue that the slaves were generally content, "happy with their lot." That may have been true in some cases. But it is clear that the vast majority of southern blacks yearned for freedom. Evidence for that can be found, if nowhere else, in the reaction of slaves when emancipation finally came. Virtually all reacted to freedom with great joy; relatively few chose to remain in the service of the whites who had owned them before the Civil War.

Adaptation and Resistance

Rather than contented acceptance, the dominant response of blacks to slavery was a complex one: a combination of adaptation and resistance. At the extremes, slavery could produce two very different reactions, each of which served as the basis for a powerful stereotype in white society. One extreme was what became known as the "Sambo"—the shuffling, grinning, head-scratching, deferential slave who acted out the role that he recognized the white world expected of him. More often than not, the "Sambo" pattern of behavior was a charade, a facade assumed in the presence of whites. The other extreme was the slave rebel—the African American who could not bring himself or herself to either acceptance or accommodation but remained forever rebellious.

Slave Revolts

Actual slave revolts were extremely rare, but the knowledge that they were possible struck terror into the hearts of white southerners everywhere. In 1800, Gabriel Prosser gathered 1,000 rebellious slaves outside Richmond; but two Africans gave the

HARRIET TUBMAN WITH ESCAPED SLAVES Harriet Tubman (c. 1820–1913) was born into slavery in Maryland. In 1849, when her master died, she escaped to Philadelphia to avoid being sold out of state. Over the next ten years, she assisted first members of her own family and then up to 300 other slaves to escape from Maryland to freedom. During the Civil War, she served alternately as a nurse and as a spy for Union forces in South Carolina. She is shown here, on the left, with some of the slaves she had helped to free. *(Smith College Museum of Art)*

plot away, and the Virginia militia stymied the uprising before it could begin. Prosser and thirty-five others were executed. In 1822, the Charleston free black Denmark Vesey and his followers—rumored to total 9,000—made preparations for revolt; but again word leaked out, and suppression and retribution followed. On a summer night in 1831, Nat Turner, a slave preacher, led a band of African Americans armed with guns and axes from house to house in Southampton County, Virginia. They killed sixty white men, women, and children before being overpowered by state and federal troops. More than a hundred blacks were executed in the aftermath.

For the most part, however, resistance to slavery took other, less violent forms. Some blacks attempted to resist by running away. A small number managed to escape to the North or to Canada, especially after sympathetic whites and free blacks began organizing secret escape routes, known as the "underground railroad," to assist them in flight. But the odds against a successful escape were very high. The hazards of distance and the slaves' ignorance of geography were serious obstacles. So were the white "slave patrols," which stopped wandering blacks on sight throughout the South demanding to see travel permits. Despite all the obstacles to success, however, blacks continued to run away from their masters in large numbers.

Day-to-day Slave Resistance   But perhaps the most important method of resistance was simply a pattern of everyday behavior by which blacks defied their masters. That whites so often considered blacks to be lazy and shiftless suggests one means of resistance: refusal to work hard. Some slaves stole from their masters or from neighboring whites. Some performed isolated acts of sabotage: losing or breaking tools or performing tasks improperly. In extreme cases, blacks might make themselves useless by cutting off their fingers or even committing suicide. A few turned on their masters and killed them. The extremes, however, were rare. For the most part, blacks resisted by building subtle methods of rebellion into their normal patterns of behavior.

THE CULTURE OF SLAVERY

Resistance was only part of the slave response to slavery. Another was an elaborate process of adaptation. One of the ways blacks adapted was by developing their own, separate culture, one that enabled them to sustain a sense of racial pride and unity.

Slave Religion

A separate slave religion was not supposed to exist. Almost all African Americans were Christians by the early nineteenth century. Some had converted voluntarily and some in response to persuasion or coercion from their masters and Protestant missionaries who evangelized among them. Masters expected their slaves to worship under the supervision of white ministers. Indeed, autonomous black churches were banned by law, and many slaves became members of the same denominations as their owners.

Black Christianity   Nevertheless, blacks throughout the South developed their own version of Christianity, at times incorporating into it such practices as voodoo or other polytheistic religious traditions of Africa. Or they simply bent religion to the special circumstances of bondage.

African-American religion was more emotional than its white counterpart and reflected the influence of African customs and practices. Slave prayer meetings routinely involved fervent chanting, spontaneous exclamations from the congregation, and ecstatic conversion experiences. Black religion was also more joyful and affirming than that of many white denominations. And above all, African-American religion emphasized the dream of freedom and deliverance. In their prayers and songs and sermons, black Christians talked and sang of the day when the Lord would "call us home," "deliver us to freedom," "take us to the Promised Land."

And while their white masters generally chose to interpret such language merely as the expression of hopes for life after death, many blacks themselves used the images of Christian salvation to express their own dream of freedom in the present world.

In cities and towns in the South, some African Americans had their own churches, where free blacks occasionally worshiped alongside slaves. In the countryside, however, slaves usually attended the same churches as their masters. Seating in such churches was usually segregated. Blacks sat in the rear or in balconies. They held their own services later, often in secret, usually at night.

Language and Music

In many areas, slaves retained a language of their own. Having arrived in America speaking many different African languages, the first generations of slaves had as much difficulty communicating with one another as they did with white people. To overcome these barriers, they learned a simple, common language (known to linguists as "pidgin"). It retained some African words, but it drew primar- *"Pidgin"* ily, if selectively, from English. And while slave language grew more sophisticated as blacks spent more time in America, some features of this early pidgin survived in black speech for many generations.

Music was especially important in slave society. Again, the African heritage was an important influence. African music relied heavily on rhythm, and so did black music in America. Africans thought of music as an accompaniment to dance, and so did blacks in America. The banjo became important to slave music. But most important were voices and song.

Field workers often used songs to pass the time; since they sang them in the presence of the whites, they usually attached relatively innocuous words to them. But African Americans also created more politically challenging music in the relative privacy of their own religious services. It was there that the tradition of the spiritual emerged. *Importance of Slave Spirituals* Through the spiritual, Africans in America not only expressed their religious faith, but also lamented their bondage and expressed continuing hope for freedom.

Slave songs were rarely written down and often seemed entirely spontaneous; but much slave music was really derived from African and Caribbean traditions passed on through generations. Performers also improvised variations on other songs they had heard. Slaves often created instruments for themselves out of whatever materials were at hand. When the setting permitted it, African Americans danced to their music—dances very different from and much more spontaneous than the formal steps that nineteenth-century whites generally learned. They also used music to accompany another of their important cultural traditions: storytelling.

THE OLD PLANTATION This painting, by an unidentified folk artist of the early nineteenth century, suggests the importance of music in the lives of plantation slaves in America. Banjos, such as the one the black musician at right is playing, were originally African instruments. *(The Old Plantantion, c. 1790–1800. Abby Aldrich Rockefeller Folk Art Museum. Colonial Williamsburg Foundation, Williamsburg, VA)*

The Slave Family

The slave family was the other crucial institution of black culture in the South. Like religion, it suffered from legal restrictions. Nevertheless, what we now call the "nuclear family" consistently emerged as the dominant kinship model among African Americans.

Black women generally began bearing children at younger ages than most whites, often as early as age fourteen or fifteen (sometimes as a result of unwanted sexual relations with their masters). Slave communities did not condemn premarital pregnancy in the way white society did, and black couples would often begin living together before marrying. It was custom-

Slave Marriages

ary, however, for couples to marry—in a ceremony involving formal vows—soon after conceiving a child. Many marriages occurred between slaves living on neighboring plantations. Husbands and wives sometimes visited each other with the permission of their masters, but often such visits had to be in secret, at night. Family ties were generally no less strong than those of whites.

When marriages did not survive, it was often because of circumstances over which blacks had no control. Up to a third of all black families were broken apart by the slave trade. That produced some of the other distinctive characteristics of the black family. Extended kinship networks were strong and important, and often helped compensate for the breakup of nuclear families. A slave forced suddenly to move to a new area, far from his or her family, might create fictional kinship ties and become "adopted" by a family in the new community. Even so, the impulse to maintain contact with a spouse and children remained strong long after the breakup of a family. One of the most frequent causes of flight from the plantation was a slave's desire to find a husband, wife, or child who had been sent elsewhere.

However much blacks resented their lack of freedom, they often found it difficult to maintain *Paternalism* an entirely hostile attitude toward their owners. They depended on whites for the material means of existence—food, clothing, and shelter—and they relied on them as well for security and protection. There was, in short, a paternal relationship between slave and master—sometimes harsh, sometimes kindly, but always important. That paternalism, in fact, became a vital instrument of white control. By creating a sense of mutual dependence, whites helped reduce resistance to an institution that, in essence, served only the interests of the ruling race.

CONCLUSION

While the North was creating a complex and rapidly developing commercial-industrial economy, the South was expanding its agrarian economy without making many fundamental changes in its character. Great migrations took many southern whites, and even more African-American slaves, into new agricultural areas in the Deep South, where they created a booming "cotton kingdom." The cotton economy created many great fortunes, and some modest ones. It also entrenched the planter class as the dominant force within southern society—both as owners of vast numbers of slaves and as patrons, creditors, landlords, and marketers for the large number of poor whites who lived on the edge of the planter world.

The differences between the North and the South were a result of differences in natural resources, social structure, climate, and culture. Above all, they were the result of the existence within the South of an unfree labor system that prevented the kind of social fluidity that an industrializing society usually requires.

FOR FURTHER REFERENCE

Peter Kolchin, *American Slavery, 1619–1877* (1993) is an excellent recent synthesis of the history of slavery in the United States from the settlement of Virginia through Reconstruction. James Oakes, *Slavery and Freedom* (1990) provides an overview of southern politics and society in the antebellum period. Eugene Genovese's classic study *Roll, Jordan, Roll: The World the Slaves Made* (1974) argues that masters and slaves forged a system of mutual obligations within a fundamentally coercive social system. Genovese's *The Political Economy of Slavery* (1965) argues that slavery blocked southern economic development. James Oakes, *The Ruling Race: A History of American Slaveholders* (1982) argues that slaveowners were hardheaded businessmen and capitalists. Frederick Douglass's *Narrative of the Life of Frederick Douglass*, first published in 1845, is a classic autobiography. Elizabeth Fox-Genovese, *Within the Plantation Household* (1988) argues against the idea that black and white women shared a community of interests on southern plantations. Charles Joyner, *Down by the Riverside: A South Carolina Slave Community* (1984) is a fine study of slavery in a single community. Charles C. Bolton, *Poor Whites of the Antebellum South: Tenants and Laborers in Central North and Northeast Mississippi* (1994) is a good study of a neglected group in the southern population. Bertram Wyatt-Brown, *Southern Honor: Ethics and Behavior in the Old South* (1982) argues that concepts of honor lay at the core of southern white identity in the antebellum period. Steven Hahn, *The Roots of Southern Populism: Yeomen Farmers and the Transformation of the Georgia Upcountry, 1850–1890* (1983) argues that white farmers in upcountry regions of the antebellum South maintained economically self-sufficient communities on the periphery of the market.

For quizzes, Internet resources, references to additional books and films, and more, consult this book's Online Learning Center at www.mhhe.com/unfinishednation4.

GIRL'S EVENING SCHOOL (C. 1840), ANONYMOUS Schooling for women, which expanded significantly in the mid-nineteenth century, included training in domestic arts (as indicated by the sewing table at right), as well as in reading, writing, and other basic skills.   *(Unidentified artist, American, c. 1840. Girls' Evening School. Graphite pencil and watercolor, 34.3 x 46.0 cm. © 2003 Museum of Fine Arts, Boston. Gift of Maxim Karolik, 53.2431)*

TIME LINE

1821	1826	1830	1831	1833	1837	1840	1841	
New York constructs first penitentiary	Cooper's *The Last of the Mohicans*	Joseph Smith publishes the Book of Mormon	The *Liberator* begins publication	American Antislavery Society founded	Horace Mann secretary of Massachusetts Board of Education	Liberty Party formed	Brook Farm founded	

ANTEBELLUM CULTURE AND REFORM

The Romantic Impulse

Remaking Society

The Crusade against Slavery

T he United States in the mid-nineteenth century was growing rapidly in geographical extent, in population, and in the size and complexity of its economy. Most Americans were excited by the new possibilities that economic growth was providing. But they were also painfully aware of the dislocations that it was creating.

One result of these conflicting attitudes was the emergence of movements to "reform" the nation. Some rested on an optimistic faith in human nature, a belief that within every individual resided a spirit that was basically good and that society should attempt to unleash. A second impulse was a desire for order and control. With their traditional values and institutions being challenged and eroded, many Americans yearned above all for a restoration of stability and discipline. Often, this impulse embodied a conservative nostalgia for better, simpler times. But it also inspired efforts to create new institutions of social control, suited to the realities of the new age.

By the end of the 1840s, however, one issue—slavery—had come to overshadow all others. And one group of reformers—the abolitionists—had become the most influential of all.

1845	1848	1850	1851	1852	1854	1855
Frederick Douglass's autobiography	Women's rights convention at Seneca Falls, N.Y.	Hawthorne's *The Scarlet Letter*	Melville's *Moby Dick*	Beecher Stowe's *Uncle Tom's Cabin*	Thoreau's *Walden*	Whitman's *Leaves of Grass*
	Oneida Community founded					

THE ROMANTIC IMPULSE

"In the four quarters of the globe," wrote the English wit Sydney Smith in 1820, "who reads an American book? or goes to an American play? or looks at an American picture or statue?" The answer, he assumed, was obvious: no one.

American intellectuals were painfully aware of the low regard in which Europeans held their culture, and they tried to create an artistic life that would express their own nation's special virtues. At the same time, many of the nation's cultural leaders were striving for another kind of liberation, *The Spirit of Romanticism* which was—ironically—largely an import from Europe: the spirit of romanticism. In literature, in philosophy, in art, even in politics and economics, American intellectuals were committing themselves to the liberation of the human spirit.

Nationalism and Romanticism in American Painting

When Sydney Smith asked in 1820 who looked at an American painting, he was expressing the almost universal belief among European artists that they—and they alone—stood at the center of the world of art. But in the United States, a great many people were, in fact, looking at American paintings—and they were doing so not because the paintings introduced them to the great traditions of Europe, but because they believed Americans were creating important new artistic traditions of their own.

American painters sought to capture the undiluted power of nature by portraying some of the nation's most spectacular and undeveloped areas. The first great school of American painters emerged in New York. Frederic Church, Thomas Cole, Thomas Doughty, and Asher *Hudson River School* Durand—who were, along with others, known as the Hudson River School—painted the spectacular vistas of the rugged and still largely untamed Hudson Valley. Like Ralph Waldo Emerson and Henry David Thoreau, whom many of the painters read and admired (see pp. 309–310), they considered nature—far more than civilization—the best source of wisdom and fulfillment. In portraying the Hudson Valley, they seemed to announce that in America, unlike in Europe, "wild nature" still existed; and that America, therefore, was a nation of greater promise than the played-out lands of the Old World.

In later years, some of the Hudson River painters traveled further west. Their enormous canvases of great natural wonders—the Yosemite Valley, Yellowstone, the Rocky Mountains—touched a passionate chord among the public. Some of the most famous of their paintings—particularly the works of Albert Bierstadt and Thomas Moran—traveled around the country attracting enormous crowds.

KINDRED SPIRITS Thomas Cole was one of the early leaders of the Hudson River School of artists in New York, and he is shown here, in a painting by Asher Durand, standing in the wilderness of the Hudson Valley with the great New York poet and editor William Cullen Bryant, a hero of mid-nineteenth-century intellectual life. Durand, who succeeded Cole as a leader of the Hudson Valley School, painted this scene not long after Cole's death. It was inspired by a moving eulogy Bryant had given at Cole's funeral, and Durand concluded that the two men were "kindred spirits" in their reverence for nature. Durand himself once wrote that "art must be a vision of God through nature." (Thomas Cole and William Cullen Bryant *by Asher Durand, New York Public Library, Special Collections*)

An American Literature

The effort to create a distinctively American literature made considerable progress in the 1820s through the work of the first great American novelist: James Fenimore Cooper. What most distinguished his work was its evocation of the American West. Cooper had a lifelong fascination with the human relationship to nature and with the challenges (and dangers) of America's expansion westward. His most important novels—among them *The Last of the Mohicans* (1826) and *The Deerslayer* (1841)—explored the experience of rugged white frontiersmen with Indians, pioneers, violence, and the law. Cooper evoked the ideal of the independent individual with a natural inner goodness—an ideal that many Americans feared was in jeopardy.

Another later group of American writers displayed more clearly the appeal of romanticism to the nation's artists and intellectuals. In 1855,

Walt Whitman Walt Whitman published his first book of poems, *Leaves of Grass*. His poems celebrated democracy, the liberation of the individual spirit, and the pleasures of the flesh. Whitman helped liberate verse from traditional, restrictive conventions; he also expressed a yearning for emotional and physical release and personal fulfillment—a yearning perhaps rooted in part in his own experience as a homosexual living in a society profoundly intolerant of unconventional sexuality.

Less exuberant was Herman Melville, perhaps the greatest American writer of his era. The most important of his novels was *Moby Dick*, published in 1851—the story of Ahab, the powerful, driven captain of a whaling vessel, who was obsessed with his search for Moby Dick, the great white whale that had once maimed him. It was a story of courage and of the strength of human will. But it was also a tragedy of pride and revenge, and an uncomfortable metaphor for the harsh, individualistic, achievement-driven culture of nineteenth-century America.

Literature in the Antebellum South

Edgar Allan Poe Similarly bleak were the works of the southern writer Edgar Allan Poe, who produced stories and poems that were primarily sad and macabre. His first book, *Tamerlane and Other Poems* (1827), received little recognition. But later works, including his most famous poem, "The Raven" (1845), established him as a major, if controversial, literary figure. Poe evoked images of individuals rising above the narrow confines of intellect and exploring the deeper world of the spirit and the emotions. Yet that world, he seemed to say, contained much pain and horror. Other American writers were contemptuous of Poe's work and his message, but he was ultimately to have a profound effect on European poets.

Poe, however, was something of an exception in the world of southern literature. The South experienced a literary flowering of its own in the mid-nineteenth century, and it produced writers and artists who were, like their northern counterparts, concerned with defining the nature of American society and of the American nation. But white southerners tended to produce very different images of what that society was and should be.

Southern novelists of the 1830s (among them Beverly Tucker, William Alexander Caruthers, and John Pendleton Kennedy) produced historical romances or romantic eulogies of the plantation system of the

William Gilmore Simms upper South. The most distinguished of the region's men of letters was William Gilmore Simms. For a time, his work expressed a broad nationalism that transcended his regional background; but by the 1840s he too had become a strong defender of southern institutions—especially slavery—against the encroachments of the North. There was, he believed, a unique quality to southern life that it was the duty of intellectuals to defend.

One group of southern writers, however, produced works that were more broadly American. These were writers from the fringes of plantation society, who depicted the world of the backwoods rural areas. Augustus B. Longstreet, Joseph G. Baldwin, Johnson J. Hooper, and others focused on ordinary people and poor whites. Instead of romanticizing their subjects, they were deliberately and sometimes painfully realistic. And they seasoned their sketches with a robust, vulgar humor that was new to American literature. These southern realists established a tradition of American regional humor that was ultimately to find its most powerful voice in Mark Twain.

The Transcendentalists

One of the outstanding expressions of the romantic impulse in America came from a group of New England writers and philosophers known as the transcendentalists. Borrowing heavily from German and English writers and philosophers, the transcendentalists embraced a theory of the individual that rested on a distinction between what they called "reason" and "understanding." Reason, as they defined it, had little to do with rationality. It was, rather, the individual's innate capacity to grasp beauty and truth by giving full expression to the instincts and emotions. Understanding, by contrast, was the use of intellect in the narrow, artificial ways imposed by society; it involved the repression of instinct and the victory of externally imposed learning. Every person's goal, therefore, should be liberation from "understanding" and, instead, the cultivation of "reason." Each individual should strive to "transcend" the limits of the intellect and allow the emotions, the "soul," to create an "original relation to the Universe."

Transcendentalist philosophy emerged first in America among a small group of intellectuals centered in Concord, Massachusetts, and led by Ralph Waldo Emerson. A Unitarian minister in his youth, Emerson left the clergy in 1832 to devote himself to writing, teaching, and lecturing. In "Nature" (1836), Emerson wrote that in the quest for self-fulfillment, individuals should work for a communion with the natural world: "in the woods, we return to reason and faith. . . . Standing on the bare ground,—my head bathed by the blithe air, and uplifted into infinite space,—all mean egotism vanishes. . . . I am part and particle of God." In other essays, he was even more explicit in advocating a commitment of the individual to the full exploration of inner capacities.

Ralph Waldo Emerson

Almost as influential as Emerson was Henry David Thoreau. Thoreau went even further in repudiating the repressive forces of society, which produced, he said, "lives of quiet desperation." Each individual should work for self-realization by resisting pressures to conform to society's expectations and responding instead to his or her own instincts. Thoreau's own effort to free himself— immortalized in *Walden* (1854)—led him to build a small cabin in the Concord woods on the edge of Walden Pond, where he lived alone for

Thoreau's Walden

two years as simply as he could, attempting to liberate himself from what he considered society's excessive interest in material comforts. Thoreau's rejection of what he considered the artificial constraints of society extended to his relationship with government. In his 1849 essay "Resistance to Civil Government," he argued that a government that required an individual to violate his or her own morality had no legitimate authority. The proper response was "civil disobedience," or "passive resistance"—a public refusal to obey unjust laws.

The Defense of Nature

As the tributes of Emerson and Thoreau to the power of nature suggest, a small but influential group of Americans in the mid- and late nineteenth century feared the impact of the new capitalist enthusiasms on the integrity of the natural world. "The mountains and cataracts, which were to have made poets and painters," wrote the essayist Oliver Wendell Holmes, "have been mined for anthracite and dammed for water power."

New Understanding of Nature   To the transcendentalists, as well as to others, nature was not just a setting for economic activity, as many farmers, miners, and others believed. It was the source of deep, personal human inspiration—the vehicle through which individuals could best realize the truth within their own souls. Genuine spirituality, they argued, did not come from formal religion, but through communion with the natural world. "In wildness is the preservation of the world," Thoreau once wrote. Humans separated from nature, he believed, would lose a substantial part of their humanity.

In making such claims, the transcendentalists were among the first Americans to anticipate the environmental movement of the twentieth century. They had no scientific basis for their defense of the wilderness, little sense of the twentieth-century notion of the interconnectedness of species. But they did believe in, and articulate, an essential unity between humanity and nature—a spiritual unity, they believed, without which civilization would be impoverished. They looked at nature, they said, "with new eyes," and with those eyes they saw that "behind nature, throughout nature, spirit is present."

Visions of Utopia

Although transcendentalism was at its heart an individualistic philosophy, it helped spawn one of the most famous of all nineteenth-century experiments in communal living: Brook Farm. The dream of the Boston transcendentalist George Ripley, Brook Farm was established in 1841 as an experimental community in West Roxbury, Massachusetts. There, according to Ripley, individuals would gather to create a new society that would

Failure of Brook Farm   permit every member to have full opportunity for self-realization. All residents would share equally in

PLAN FOR THE COLONY AT NEW HARMONY The English reformer Robert Owen came to America in the 1820s to create an experimental community in which to test his own theories of cooperative living. This architect's drawing reveals the grandiose plans Owen and his followers had for the colony, which was in Indiana on the banks of the Wabash River on the site of an earlier social experiment by German idealists. In this plan, which was never constructed, the architecture reflects the sense of order and rationality Owen hoped to bring to the community. The plan was designed "to form a new combination of circumstances, capable of producing permanently greater physical, moral, and intellectual advantages . . . than have ever yet been realized in any age or country." *(The Library of Congress)*

the labor of the community so that all could share as well in the leisure, which was essential for cultivation of the self. The tension between the ideal of individual freedom and the demands of a communal society took their toll on Brook Farm. Many residents became disenchanted and left. When a fire destroyed the central building of the community in 1847, the experiment dissolved.

Among the original residents of Brook Farm was the writer Nathaniel Hawthorne, who expressed his disillusionment with the experiment and, to some extent, with transcendentalism in a series of novels. In *The Blithedale Romance* (1852), he wrote scathingly of Brook Farm itself. In other novels—most notably *The Scarlet Letter* (1850) and *The House of the Seven Gables* (1851)—he wrote equally passionately about the price individuals pay for cutting themselves off from society. Egotism, he claimed (in an indirect challenge to the transcendentalist faith in the self), was the "serpent" that lay at the heart of human misery.

Brook Farm was one of many experimental communities in the years before the Civil War. The Scottish industrialist and philanthropist Robert Owen founded an experimental community in Indiana in 1825, which he named New Harmony. It *New Harmony* was to be a "Village of Cooperation," in which every resident worked and lived in total equality. The community was an economic failure, but the vision that had inspired it continued to enchant some Americans. Dozens of other "Owenite" experiments began in other locations in the ensuing years.

Redefining Gender Roles

Many of the new utopian communities were centrally concerned with the relationship between men and women. Some experimented with a radical redefinition of gender roles.

Redefined Gender Roles   Such a redefinition was central to one of the most enduring of the utopian colonies of the nineteenth century: the Oneida Community, established in 1848 in upstate New York by John Humphrey Noyes. The Oneida "Perfectionists," as residents of the community called themselves, rejected traditional notions of family and marriage. All residents, Noyes declared, were "married" to all other residents; there were to be no permanent conjugal ties. But Oneida was not, as horrified critics often claimed, an experiment in unrestrained "free love." It was a place where the community carefully monitored sexual behavior; where women were protected from unwanted childbearing; and where children were raised communally, often seeing little of their own parents. The Oneidans took pride in what they considered their liberation of women from the demands of male "lust" and from the traditional bonds of family.

The Shakers, too, made a redefinition of traditional gender roles central to their society. Founded by "Mother" Ann Lee in the 1770s, the society of the Shakers survived into the twentieth century. (A tiny remnant is left today.) But the Shakers attracted a particularly large following in the mid-nineteenth century and established more than twenty communities throughout the Northeast and Northwest in the 1840s. They derived their name from a unique religious ritual—in which members of a congregation would "shake" themselves free of sin while performing a loud chant and an ecstatic dance.

The most distinctive feature of Shakerism, however, was its commitment to complete celibacy—which meant, of *Commitment to Celibacy* course, that no one could be born into Shakerism; all Shakers had to choose the faith voluntarily. Shakerism attracted about 6,000 members in the 1840s, more women than men. They lived in communities where contacts between men and women were strictly limited, and they endorsed the idea of sexual equality. Within Shaker society, women exercised the greatest power.

The Shakers were not, however, motivated only by a desire to escape the burdens of traditional gender roles. They were trying as well to create a society separated and protected from the chaos and disorder that they believed had come to characterize American life as a whole. In that, they were much like other dissenting religious sects and other utopian communities of their time.

The Mormons

Among the most important efforts to create a new and more ordered society within the old was that of the Church of Jesus Christ of Latter-day Saints—the Mormons. Mormonism began in upstate New York through

the efforts of Joseph Smith. While still a teenager, *Joseph Smith*
he claimed he was visited by God and in 1830,
when he was just twenty-four, he published a remarkable document—the
Book of Mormon, named for the ancient prophet who he claimed had
written it. It was, he said, a translation of a set of golden tablets he had
found in the hills of New York, revealed to him by an angel of God. The
Book of Mormon told the story of two successful ancient civilizations in
America, whose people had anticipated the coming of Christ and were rewarded when Jesus actually came to America after his resurrection. Ultimately, both civilizations collapsed because of their rejection of Christian
principles. But Smith believed their history as righteous societies could
serve as a model for a new holy community in the United States.

In 1831, gathering a small group of believers around him, Smith began
searching for a sanctuary for his new community of "saints," an effort that
would continue unhappily for more than fifteen years. Time and again the
Latter-day Saints, as they called themselves, attempted to establish peaceful
communities. Time and again they met with persecution from their neighbors, who were suspicious of their radical religious doctrines—their claims
of new prophets, new scripture, and divine authority. Opponents were also
concerned by their rapid growth and their increasing political strength.
Near the end of his life, Joseph Smith introduced the practice of
polygamy (the right of men to take several wives), which became public
knowledge after Smith's death. From then on, polygamy became another
target of anti-Mormon opposition.

Driven from their original settlements in Independence, Missouri,
and Kirtland, Ohio, the Mormons founded a new town in Illinois that
they named Nauvoo. In the early 1840s, it became an imposing and economically successful community. In 1844, however, bitter enemies of
Joseph Smith published an inflammatory attack on him. Smith ordered his
followers to destroy the offending press, and he was subsequently arrested
and imprisoned in Carthage, Illinois. There an angry mob attacked the jail
and shot and killed him. The Mormons soon abandoned Nauvoo and,
under the leadership of Smith's successor, Brigham Young, traveled across
the Great Plains and the Rocky Mountains—a society of 12,000 people, in
one of the largest single group migrations in American history. They established several communities in Utah, including *Utah Founded*
the present Salt Lake City. There, at last, the Mormons were able to create a lasting settlement.

Like other experiments in social organization of the era, Mormonism
reflected a belief in human perfectibility. God had once been a man, the
church taught, and thus every man or woman could aspire to move continu-
ously closer to God. Within a highly developed and centrally directed ecclesiastical structure, Mormons created a haven for people demoralized by the
disorder and uncertainty of the secular world. The original Mormons were,
for the most part, men and women who felt displaced in their rapidly
changing society—economically marginal people left behind by the material

growth and social progress of their era. In the new religion, they found a strong and animating faith. In the society it created, they found security and order.

REMAKING SOCIETY

New Reform Efforts The reform impulse also helped create new movements to remake mainstream society—movements in which, to a striking degree, women formed both the rank and file and the leadership. By the 1830s, such movements had taken the form of organized reform societies.

Revivalism, Morality, and Order

The philosophy of reform arose in part from the optimistic vision of those such as the transcendentalists who preached the divinity of the individual. Another source was Protestant revivalism—the movement that had begun with the Second Great Awakening early in the century and had, by the 1820s, evolved into a powerful force for social reform.

Religious Basis of Reform The New Light evangelicals embraced the optimistic belief that every individual was capable of salvation through his or her own efforts. Partly as a result, revivalism soon became not only a means of personal salvation but an effort to reform the larger society. In particular, revivalism produced a crusade against personal immorality. "The church," said Charles Grandison Finney, the leading revivalist of his time, "must take right ground on the subject of Temperance, the Moral Reform, and all the subjects of practical morality which come up for decision from time to time."

Evangelical Protestantism added major strength to the crusade against drunkenness. No social vice, temperance advocates argued, was more responsible for crime, disorder, and poverty than the excessive use of alcohol. Women complained that men spent money their families needed on alcohol and that drunken husbands often beat and abused their wives. Temperance also appealed to those who were alarmed by immigration; drunkenness, many nativists believed, was responsible for violence and disorder in immigrant communities. By 1840, temperance had become a major national movement, with powerful organizations and more than a million followers who had signed a formal pledge to forgo hard liquor.

Health, Science, and Phrenology

For some Americans, the search for individual and social perfection led to an interest in new theories of health and knowledge. Threats to public health were critical to the sense of insecurity that underlay many reform movements, especially after the terrible cholera epidemics of the 1830s

THE DRUNKARD'S PROGRESS This 1846 lithograph by Nathaniel Currier shows what temperance advocates argued was the inevitable consequence of alcohol consumption. Beginning with an apparently innocent "glass with a friend," the young man rises step by step to the summit of drunken revelry, then declines to desperation and suicide while his abandoned wife and child grieve. *(The Library of Congress)*

and 1840s. Cholera is a severe bacterial infection of *Cholera Epidemics* the intestines, usually a result of consuming contaminated food or water. In the nineteenth century, fewer than half of those who contracted the disease normally survived. Thousands of people died of cholera during its occasional outbreaks, and in certain cities the effects were truly catastrophic. Nearly a quarter of the population of New Orleans died in an 1833 epidemic. Many municipalities established city health boards to try to find solutions to the problems of epidemics. But the medical profession of the time, unaware of the nature of bacterial infections, had no answers.

Instead, many Americans turned to nonscientific theories for improving health. Affluent men and, especially, women flocked to health spas for the celebrated "water cure" (known to modern scientists as hydrotherapy), which purported to improve health through immersing people in hot or cold baths or wrapping them in wet sheets. Although the water cure in fact delivered few of the benefits its promoters promised, it did have some therapeutic value; some forms of hydrotherapy are still in use today. Other people adopted new dietary theories. Sylvester Graham, a Connecticut-born Presbyterian minister and committed reformer, won many followers with his prescriptions for eating fruits, vegetables, and bread made from coarsely ground flour—a prescription not unlike some dietary theories today—instead of meat. (The "Graham cracker" is made from a kind of flour named for him.)

PHRENOLOGY This lithograph illustrates some of the ideas of the popular "science" of phrenology in the 1830s. Drawing from the concepts of the German writer Johann Gaspar Spurzheim, American phrenologists promoted the belief that a person's character and talents could be understood by the formation of his or her skull; that the brain was, in fact, a cluster of autonomous organs, each controlling some aspect of human thought or behavior. In this diagram, the areas of the brain that supposedly control "identity," "acquisitiveness," "secretiveness," "marvelousness," and "hope" are clearly identified. The theory has no scientific basis. *(The Library of Congress)*

Perhaps strangest of all to modern sensibilities was the widespread be-

Phrenology

lief in the new "science" of phrenology, which appeared first in Germany and became popular in the United States beginning in the 1830s through the efforts of Orson and Lorenzo Fowler, publishers of the *Phrenology Almanac*. Phrenologists argued that the shape of an individual's skull was an important indicator of his or her character and intelligence. They made elaborate measurements of bumps and indentations to calculate the size (and, they claimed, the strength) of different areas of the brain. Phrenology seemed to provide a way of measuring an individual's fitness for various positions in life and seemed to promise an end to the arbitrary process by which people matched their talents to occupations and responsibilities. The theory is now universally believed to have no scientific value at all.

Medical Science

In an age of rapid technological and scientific advances, the science of medicine sometimes seemed to lag behind. In part, that was because of the greater difficulty of experimentation in medicine, which required human subjects. In part, it was because of the character of the medical profession, which—in the absence of any significant regulation—attracted many poorly educated people and many quacks. Efforts to regulate the profession were beaten back in the 1830s and 1840s by those who considered the licensing of physicians to be a form of undemocratic monopoly. The prestige of the profession, therefore, remained low.

The biggest problem facing American medicine, however, was the absence of basic knowledge about disease. The great medical achievement of the eighteenth century—the development of a vaccination against smallpox by Edward Jenner—came from no broad theory of infection, but from a brilliant adaptation of folk practices among country people. The development of anesthetics came not from medical doctors at first, but from a New England dentist, William Morton, who was looking for ways to help his patients endure the extraction of teeth. Beginning in 1844, Morton began experimenting with using sulphuric ether. John Warren, a Boston surgeon, soon began using ether to sedate surgical patients. Even these advances met with stiff resistance from some traditional physicians, who mistrusted innovation and experimentation.

Resistance to Scientific Medicine

In the absence of any broad acceptance of scientific methods and experimental practice in medicine, it was very difficult for even the most talented doctors to make progress in treating disease. Even so, halting progress toward the discovery of the germ theory did occur in antebellum America. In 1843, the Boston essayist, poet, and physician Oliver Wendell Holmes published his findings from a study of large numbers of cases of "puerperal fever" (septicemia in children) and concluded that the disease could be transmitted from one person to another. This discovery of contagion met with a storm of criticism, but was later vindicated by the clinical success of the Hungarian physician Ignaz Semmelweis, who noticed that infection seemed to be spread by medical students who had been working with diseased corpses. Once he began requiring students to wash their hands and disinfect their instruments, the infections virtually disappeared.

Education

One of the most important reform movements of the mid-nineteenth century was the effort to produce a system of universal public education. As of 1830, no state had such a system. Soon after that, however, interest in public education began growing rapidly.

Horace Mann's Reforms
The greatest of the educational reformers was Horace Mann, the first secretary of the Massachusetts Board of Education, which was established in 1837. To Mann and his followers, education was the only way to protect democracy, for an educated electorate was essential to the workings of a free political system. Mann reorganized the Massachusetts school system, lengthened the academic year (to six months), doubled teachers' salaries, broadened the curriculum, and introduced new methods of professional training for teachers. Other states followed similar courses: building new schools, creating teachers' colleges, and offering many children access to education for the first time. By the 1850s, the principle (although not yet the reality) of tax-supported elementary schools was established in every state.

Uneven Public Education
Yet the quality of public education continued to vary widely. In some places—Massachusetts, for example—educators were generally capable men and women, often highly trained, who had an emerging sense of themselves as professionals. In other areas, however, teachers were often barely literate, and funding for education was severely limited. In much of the West, where the population was highly dispersed, many children had no access to schools at all. In the South, all African Americans were barred from education, and only about a third of all white children of school age were actually enrolled in schools in 1860. In the North, 72 percent were enrolled, but even there, many students attended classes only briefly and casually.

Among the goals of educational reformers was teaching children a set of social values. These values included thrift, order, discipline, punctuality, and respect for authority. Horace Mann, for example, spoke of the role of public schools in extending democracy and expanding individual opportunity. But he spoke, too, of their role in creating social order: "Train up a child in the way he should go, and when he is old he will not depart from it."

The interest in education also was visible in the growing movement to educate American Indians. Some reformers believed that Indians could be "civilized" if only they could be taught the ways of the white world. Efforts by missionaries and others to educate Indians and encourage them to assimilate were particularly prominent in such areas of the Far West as Oregon, where conflicts with the natives had not yet become acute. Nevertheless, the great majority of Native Americans remained outside the reach of educational reform.

Despite limitations and inequities, the achievements of the school reformers were impressive. By the beginning of the Civil War, the

United States had one of the highest literacy rates of any nation of the world: 94 percent of the pop- *Soaring Literacy Rates* ulation of the North, 83 percent of the white population (and 58 percent of the total population) of the South.

Rehabilitation

The belief in the potential of the individual also sparked the creation of new institutions to help the disabled: institutions that formed part of a great network of charitable activities known as the Benevolent Empire. Among them was the Perkins School for the Blind in Boston. Nothing better exemplified the romantic spirit of the era than the belief of those who founded Perkins that even society's supposedly most disadvantaged members could be helped to discover their own inner strength and wisdom.

Similar impulses produced another powerful movement of reform: the creation of "asylums" for criminals and the mentally ill. In advocating prison and hospital reform, Americans were reacting against one of society's most glaring ills: antiquated jails and mental institutions whose inmates lived in almost inhuman conditions. Beginning in the 1820s, many states built new penitentiaries and mental asylums. New York built the first penitentiary at Auburn in 1821. In Massachusetts, the reformer Dorothea Dix began a national movement for new methods of treating the mentally ill. *Dorothea Dix*

The creation of asylums was an attempt to reform and rehabilitate the inmates. New forms of prison discipline were designed to rid criminals of the "laxness" that had presumably led them astray. Solitary confinement and the imposition of silence on work crews (both instituted in Pennsylvania and New York in the 1820s) were meant to give prisoners opportunities to meditate on their wrongdoings and develop "penitence" (hence the name "penitentiary").

Some of the same impulses that produced asylums underlay the emergence of a new "reform" approach to the problems of Native Americans: the idea of the reservation. For several decades, the dominant thrust of the United States' policy toward the Indians had been relocation. The principal motive behind relocation was simple: getting the tribes out of the way of white civilization. But among some whites there had also been another intent: to move the Indians to a place where they would be allowed to develop to a point at which assimilation might be possible.

It was a small step from the idea of relocation to the idea of the reservation. Just as prisons, asy- *Reservation Concept Born* lums, and orphanages would provide society with an opportunity to train and uplift misfits and unfortunates within white society, so the reservations might provide a way to undertake what one official called "the great work of regenerating the Indian race."

The Rise of Feminism

Many of the women who became involved in reform movements in the 1820s and 1830s came to resent the social and legal restrictions that limited their participation. Out of their concerns emerged the first American feminist movement. Sarah and Angelina Grimké, sisters who had become active and outspoken abolitionists, ignored attacks by men who claimed that their activism was inappropriate to their gender. "Men and women were created equal," they argued. "They are both moral and accountable beings, and whatever is right for man to do, is right for women to do." Other reformers—Catharine Beecher, Harriet Beecher Stowe (her sister), Lucretia Mott, Elizabeth Cady Stanton, Susan B. Anthony, and Dorothea Dix—similarly pressed at the boundaries of "acceptable" female behavior.

In 1840, American female delegates arrived at a world antislavery convention in London, only to be turned away by the men who controlled the proceedings. Angered at the rejection, several of the delegates became convinced that their first duty as reformers should now be to elevate the status of women. Over the next several years, Mott, Stanton, and others began drawing pointed parallels between the plight of women and the plight of slaves; and in 1848, in Seneca Falls, New York, they organized a convention to discuss the question of women's rights. Out of the meeting came the "Declaration of Sentiments and Resolutions," which stated that "all men and women are created equal," that women no less than men are endowed with certain inalienable rights. In demanding the right to vote, they launched a movement for woman suffrage that would survive until the battle was finally won in 1920.

"Declaration of Sentiments and Resolutions"

Many of the women involved in these feminist efforts were Quakers. Quakerism had long embraced the ideal of sexual equality and had tolerated, indeed encouraged, the emergence of women as preachers and community leaders. Of the women who drafted the Declaration of Sentiments, all but Elizabeth Cady Stanton were Quakers.

Feminism's Secondary Status

Feminists benefited greatly from their association with other reform movements, most notably abolitionism, but they also suffered as a result. The demands of women were usually assigned a secondary position to what many considered the far greater issue of the rights of slaves.

THE CRUSADE AGAINST SLAVERY

The antislavery movement was not new to the mid-nineteenth century. But only in 1830 did it begin to gather the force that would ultimately enable it to overshadow virtually all other efforts at social reform.

Early Opposition to Slavery

In the early years of the nineteenth century, those who opposed slavery were, for the most part, a calm and genteel lot, expressing moral disapproval but doing little else. To the extent that there was an organized antislavery movement, it centered on the effort to resettle American blacks in Africa or the Caribbean. In 1817, a group of prominent white Virginians organized the American Colonization Society (ACS), which proposed a gradual freeing of slaves, *American Colonization Society* with masters receiving compensation. The liberated blacks would then be transported out of the country and helped to establish a new society of their own. The ACS received some funding from private donors, some from Congress, some from the legislatures of Virginia and Maryland. And it arranged to have several groups of blacks transported out of the United States, some of them to the west coast of Africa, where in 1830 they established the nation of Liberia. (In 1846, Liberia became an independent black republic, with its capital, Monrovia, named for the American president who had presided over the initial settlement.)

But the ACS was in the end a negligible force. There were far too many blacks in America in the nineteenth century to be transported to Africa by any conceivable program. And the ACS met resistance, in any case, from blacks themselves, many of whom were now three or more generations removed from Africa and, despite their loathing of slavery, had no wish to emigrate.

Garrison and Abolitionism

In 1830, with slavery spreading rapidly in the South and the antislavery movement seemingly on the verge of collapse, a new figure emerged to transform it: William Lloyd Garrison. Born in Massachusetts in 1805, Garrison was in the 1820s *William Lloyd Garrison* an assistant to the New Jersey Quaker Benjamin Lundy, who published the leading antislavery newspaper of the time. Garrison grew impatient with his employer's moderate tone, so in 1831 he returned to Boston to found his own newspaper, the *Liberator.*

Garrison's philosophy was so simple that it was *Garrison's Revolutionary* genuinely revolutionary. Opponents of slavery, he *Philosophy* said, should not talk about the evil influence of slavery on white society; they should talk about the damage the system did to blacks. And they should, therefore, reject "gradualism" and demand the immediate abolition of slavery and the extension to blacks of all the rights of American citizenship. Garrison wrote in a relentless, uncompromising tone. "I am aware," he wrote in the very first issue of the *Liberator,* "that many object to the severity of my language; but is there not cause for severity? I will be as harsh as truth, and as uncompromising as

The United States abolished slavery through the Thirteenth Amendment to the Constitution in 1865, in the aftermath of a great Civil War. But the effort to abolish slavery did not begin nor end in North America. Emancipation in the United States was part of a worldwide antislavery movement that had begun in the late eighteenth century and continued through the end of the nineteenth.

The end of slavery, like the end of monarchies and aristocracies, was one of the ideals of the Enlightenment, which inspired new concepts of individual freedom and political equality. As Enlightenment ideas spread throughout the western world in the seventeenth and eighteenth centuries, introducing the idea of human rights and individual liberty to the concept of civilization, people on both sides of the Atlantic began to examine slavery anew and to ask whether it was compatible with these new ideas. Some Enlightenment thinkers, including some of the founders of the American Republic, believed that freedom was appropriate for white people, but not for people of color. But others came to believe that all human beings had an equal claim to liberty, and their views became the basis for an escalating series of antislavery movements.

Opponents of slavery first targeted the slave trade—the vast commerce in human beings that had grown up in the seventeenth and eighteenth centuries and had come to involve large parts of Europe, Africa, the Caribbean, and North and South America. In the aftermath of the revolutions in America, France, and Haiti in the late eighteenth and early nineteenth centuries, the attack on the slave trade quickly gained momentum. Its central figure was the English reformer William Wilberforce, who spent years attacking Britain's connection with the slave trade. He argued against it on moral and religious grounds, and eventually, after the Haitian revolution, he argued as well that the continuation of slavery would create more slave revolts. In 1807, he persuaded Parliament to pass a law ending the slave trade within the entire British empire. The British example—when combined with heavy political, economic, and even military pressure from London—persuaded many other nations to make the slave trade illegal as well: the United States in 1808, France in 1814, Holland in 1817, Spain in 1845. Trading in slaves continued within countries and colonies where slavery remained legal (including the United States), and some illegal slave trading continued throughout the Atlantic world. But the sale of slaves steadily declined after 1807. The last known shipment of slaves across the Atlantic—from Africa to Cuba—occurred in 1867.

Ending the slave trade was a great deal easier than ending slavery itself, in which many people had major investments and on which much agriculture, commerce, and industry depended. But pressure to abolish slavery grew steadily throughout the nineteenth century, with Wilberforce once more helping to lead the international outcry against the institution. In Haiti, the slave revolts that began in 1791 eventually abolished not only slavery, but also French rule. In some parts of South America, slavery came to an end with the overthrow of Spanish rule in the 1820s. Simón Bolívar, the great leader of Latin American independence, considered abolishing slavery an important part of his mission, freeing those who joined his armies and insisting on constitutional prohibitions of slavery in several of the Constitutions he helped frame. In 1833, the British parliament passed a law abolishing slavery throughout the British empire and compensated slaveowners for freeing their slaves. France abolished slavery in its empire, after years of agitation from abolitionists within France, in 1848. In the Caribbean, Spain followed Britain in slowly eliminating slavery from its colonies. Puerto Rico abolished slavery in 1873; and Cuba became the last colony in the Caribbean to end slavery, in 1886, in the face of increasing slave resistance and the declining profitability of slave-based plantations. Brazil was the last nation in the Americas, ending the system in 1888. The Brazilian military began to turn against slavery after the valiant participation of slaves in Brazil's war with Paraguay in the late 1860s; eventually educated Brazilians began to oppose the system too, arguing that it obstructed economic and social progress.

In the United States, the power of world opinion—and the example of Wilberforce's movement in England—became an important source of the abolitionist movement as it gained strength in the 1820s and 1830s. American abolitionism, in turn, helped reinforce the movements abroad. Frederick Douglass, the former American slave turned abolitionist, became a major figure in the international antislavery movement and was a much-admired and much-sought-after speaker in England and Europe in the 1840s and 1850s. No other nation paid such a terrible price for abolishing slavery as did the United States during its Civil War, but American emancipation was nevertheless a part of a worldwide movement toward emancipation.

(text continued from page 321)

justice. . . . I am in earnest—I will not equivocate—I will not excuse—I will not retreat a single inch—and I will be heard."

Garrison soon attracted a large group of followers throughout the North, enough to enable him to found the New England Antislavery Society in 1832 and a year later, after a convention in Philadelphia, the American Antislavery Society.

Black Abolitionists

Abolitionism had a particular appeal to the free black population of the North. These free blacks lived in conditions of poverty and oppression at times worse than those of their slave counterparts in the South. For all their problems, however, northern blacks were fiercely proud of their freedom and sensitive to the plight of those members of their race who remained in bondage. Many in the 1830s came to support Garrison. But they also rallied to leaders of their own.

The greatest of the black abolitionists was Frederick Douglass. Born a slave in Maryland, *Frederick Douglass* Douglass escaped to Massachusetts in 1838, became an outspoken leader of antislavery sentiment, and spent two years lecturing in England. On his return to the United States in 1847, Douglass purchased his freedom from his Maryland owner and founded an antislavery newspaper, the *North Star,*

FUGITIVE SLAVE LAW CONVENTION Abolitionists gathered in Cazenovia, New York, in August 1850 to consider how to respond to the law recently passed by Congress requiring northern states to return fugitive slaves to their owners. Frederick Douglass is seated just to the left of the table in this photograph of some of the participants. The gathering was unusual among abolitionist gatherings in including substantial numbers of African Americans. *(Madison County Historical Society, Oneida, NY)*

in Rochester, New York. He achieved wide renown as well for his autobiography, *Narrative of the Life of Frederick Douglass* (1845), in which he presented a damning picture of slavery. Douglass demanded not only freedom but full social and economic equality.

Anti-Abolitionism

The rise of abolitionism was a powerful force, but it provoked a powerful opposition as well. Almost all white southerners, of course, were bitterly hostile to the movement. But even in the North, abolitionists were a small, dissenting minority. Some whites feared that abolitionism would produce a destructive war between the sections. Others feared that it would lead to a great influx of free blacks into the North.

Violent Reprisals   The result of such fears was an escalating wave of violence. A mob in Philadelphia attacked the abolitionist headquarters there in 1834, burned it to the ground, and began a bloody race riot. Another mob seized Garrison on the streets of

Boston in 1835 and threatened to hang him. He was saved from death only by being locked in jail. Elijah Lovejoy, the editor of an abolitionist newspaper in Alton, Illinois, was victimized repeatedly and finally killed when he tried to defend his press from attack.

That so many men and women continued to embrace abolitionism in the face of such vicious opposition suggests that abolitionists were not people who made their political commitments lightly or casually. They were strong-willed, passionate crusaders who displayed not only enormous courage and moral strength but at times a fervency that many of their contemporaries found deeply disturbing. The mobs were only the most violent expression of a hostility to abolitionism that many, perhaps most, other white Americans shared.

Abolitionism Divided

By the mid-1830s, the abolitionist crusade had begun to experience serious strains. One reason was the violence of the anti-abolitionists, which persuaded some members of the movement that a more moderate approach was necessary. Another reason was the *Radicals and Moderates* growing radicalism of William Lloyd Garrison, who shocked even many of his own allies (including Frederick Douglass) by attacking not only slavery but the government itself. The Constitution, he said, was "a covenant with death and an agreement with hell." In 1840, Garrison precipitated a formal division within the American Antislavery Society by insisting that women be permitted to participate in the movement on terms of full equality. He continued after 1840 to arouse controversy with new and even more radical stands: an extreme pacifism that rejected even defensive wars; opposition to all forms of coercion—not just slavery, but prisons and asylums; and finally, in 1843, a call for northern disunion from the South.

From 1840 on, therefore, abolitionism moved in many channels and spoke with many different voices. The Garrisonians, with their radical and uncompromising moral stance, remained influential. But others operated in more moderate ways, arguing that abolition could be accomplished only as the result of a long, patient, peaceful struggle. They appealed to the conscience of the slaveholders; and when that produced no results, they turned to political action, seeking to induce the northern states and the federal government to aid the cause. They joined the Garrisonians in helping runaway slaves find refuge in the North or in Canada through what became known as the underground railroad. They helped fund the legal battle over the Spanish slave vessel, *Amistad.* *The Amistad Case* Africans destined for slavery in Cuba had seized the ship from its crew in 1839 and tried to return it to Africa. But the U.S. navy had seized the ship and held the Africans as pirates. But with abolitionist support, legal efforts to declare the Africans free (because the slave trade was by then illegal) finally reached the Supreme Court, where the

UNCLE TOM'S CABIN *Uncle Tom's Cabin* did much to inflame public opinion in both the North and the South in the last years before the Civil War. When Abraham Lincoln was introduced to Stowe once in the White House, he reportedly said to her: "So you are the little lady that has brought this great war." At the time, however, Stowe was equally well known as one of the most successful American writers of sentimental novels. *(Bettmann/Corbis)*

antislavery position was argued by former president John Quincy Adams. The court declared the Africans free in 1841 and antislavery groups funded their passage back to Africa. After the Supreme Court (in *Prigg* v. *Pennsylvania*, 1842) ruled that states need not aid in enforcing the 1793 law requiring the return of fugitive slaves to their owners, abolitionists won passage in several northern states of "personal liberty laws," which forbade state officials to assist in the capture and return of runaways. The antislavery societies also petitioned Congress to abolish slavery in places where the federal government had jurisdiction—in the territories and in the District of Columbia—and to prohibit the interstate slave trade.

Antislavery sentiment underlay the formation in 1840 of the Liberty Party, which ran Kentucky antislavery leader James G. Birney for president. But this party and its successors never campaigned for outright abolition. They stood instead for "free soil," for keeping slavery out of the territories. Some free-soilers were concerned about the welfare of blacks; others were people who cared nothing about slavery but simply wanted to keep the West a country for whites. But the free-soil position would ultimately do what abolitionism never could: attract the support of large numbers of the white population of the North.

The frustrations of political abolitionism drove some critics of slavery to embrace more drastic measures. A few began to advocate violence; it was a group of prominent abolitionists in New England, for example, who funneled money and arms to John Brown for his bloody uprisings in Kansas and Virginia. (See pp. 350 and 355–356.) Others attempted to arouse public anger through propaganda. The most powerful of all abolitionist propaganda was Harriet Beecher Stowe's novel *Uncle Tom's Cabin*, published as a book in 1852. It sold *Uncle Tom's Cabin* more than 300,000 copies within a year of publication and was reissued again and again. It succeeded in bringing the message of abolitionism to an enormous new audience—not only those who read the book but those who watched dramatizations of its story by countless theater companies across the nation. Reviled throughout the South, Stowe became a hero to many in the North. And in both regions, her novel helped inflame sectional tensions to a new level of passion.

Even divided, therefore, abolitionism remained a powerful influence on the life of the nation. Only a relatively small number of people before the Civil War ever accepted the abolitionist position that slavery must be entirely eliminated in a single stroke. But the crusade that Garrison had launched, and that thousands of committed men and women kept alive for three decades, was a constant, visible reminder of how deeply the institution of slavery was dividing America.

CONCLUSION

The rapidly changing society of antebellum America encouraged interest in a wide range of reforms. Writers, artists, intellectuals, and others drew heavily from new European notions of personal liberation and fulfillment—a set of ideas often known as romanticism. But they also strove to create a truly American culture. The literary and artistic life of the nation expressed the rising interest in personal liberation—in giving individuals the freedom to explore their own souls and to find in nature a full expression of their divinity. It also called attention to some of the nation's glaring social problems.

Reformers, too, made use of the romantic belief in the divinity of the individual. They flocked to religious revivals, worked on behalf of such "moral" reforms as temperance, supported education, and articulated some of the first statements of modern feminism. Above all, in the North, they rallied against slavery. Out of this growing antislavery movement emerged a new and powerful phenomenon: abolitionism, which insisted on immediate emancipation of slaves. The abolitionist movement galvanized much of the North. It also contributed greatly to the growing schism between North and South.

FOR FURTHER REFERENCE

Steven Mintz, *Moralists and Moralizers: America's Pre-Civil War Reformers* (1995) and Ronald G. Walters, *American Reformers, 1815–1860* (1978) are good overviews. David Reynolds, *Walt Whitman's America* (1995) is both a cultural biography of Whitman and an evocation of the society Whitman celebrated. Leo Marx, *The Machine in the Garden* (1964) is an influential study of the tension between technological progress and the veneration of nature in the era of early industrialization. Nancy F. Cott, *The Bonds of Womanhood: "Woman's Sphere" in New England, 1780–1835* (1977) argues that nineteenth-century feminism emerged from the separation of home and work in the early nineteenth century. Klaus J. Hansen, *Mormonism and the American Experience* (1981) examines the emergence of the most important new religion in nineteenth-century America. Ellen C. Dubois, *Feminism and Suffrage: The Emergence of an Independent Women's Movement in America, 1848–1869* (1978) examines the origins of the suffrage movement. David Brion Davis, *The Problem of Slavery in the Age of Revolution, 1770–1823* (1975) is an influential study of the rise of antislavery sentiment in the western world. James Brewer Stewart, *Holy Warriors* (1976) is a good summary of the trajectory of abolitionism from the American Revolution through the emancipation. Ronald G. Walters, *The Antislavery Appeal: American Abolitionism After 1830* (1976) emphasizes the religious motivations of antebellum abolitionism. Julie Roy Jeffrey, *The Great Silent Army of Abolitionism: Ordinary Women in the Antislavery Movement* (1988) is a study of the important role women played in fighting slavery.

For quizzes, Internet resources, references to additional books and films, and more, consult this book's Online Learning Center at www.mhhe.com/unfinishednation4.

"BLEEDING KANSAS" The battle over the fate of slavery in Kansas was one of the most turbulent events of the 1850s. This 1855 poster invites antislavery forces to a meeting to protest the actions of the "bogus" pro-slavery territorial legislature, which had passed laws that, among other things, made it illegal to speak or write against slavery. "Squatter sovereignty" was another term for "popular sovereignty," the doctrine that gave residents of the prospective state the power to decide the fate of slavery there. *(Bettmann/Corbis)*

TIME LINE

1836	1844	1846	1848	1850	1852	1853
Texas declares independence from Mexico	Polk elected president	Oregon boundary dispute settled	Treaty of Guadalupe Hidalgo	Compromise of 1850	Pierce elected president	Gadsden Purchase
		U.S. declares war on Mexico	Taylor elected president	Taylor dies; Fillmore becomes president		
		Wilmot Proviso	California gold rush begins			

THE IMPENDING CRISIS

Looking Westward
Expansion and War
The Sectional Debate
The Crisis of the 1850s

Until the 1840s, the tensions between North and South remained relatively contained. Had no new sectional issues arisen, it is possible that the two sections might have resolved their differences peaceably over time. But new issues did arise. From the North came the strident and increasingly powerful abolitionist movement. From the South came a newly militant defense of slavery and the way of life it supported. And from the West, more significantly, came a series of controversies that would ultimately tear the fragile Union apart.

LOOKING WESTWARD

More than a million square miles of new territory came under the control of the United States during the 1840s. By the end of the decade, the nation possessed all the territory of the present-day United States except Alaska, Hawaii, and a few relatively small areas acquired later through border adjustments. Many factors accounted for this great new wave of expansion, but one of the most important was an ideology known as "Manifest Destiny."

1854	1855-1856	1856	1857	1858	1859	1860	
Kansas-Nebraska Act	"Bleeding Kansas"	Buchanan elected president	*Dred Scott* decision	Lecompton constitution defeated	John Brown raids Harper's Ferry	Lincoln elected president	
Republican Party formed							

Manifest Destiny

Territorial Ambitions Manifest Destiny reflected both the growing pride that characterized American nationalism in the mid-nineteenth century and the idealistic vision of social perfection that fueled so much of the reform energy of the time. It rested on the idea that America was destined—by God and by history—to expand its boundaries over a vast area.

By the 1840s, the idea of Manifest Destiny had spread throughout the nation, publicized by the new "penny press," which made newspapers available to a far greater proportion of the population than ever before. Some advocates of Manifest Destiny had relatively limited territorial goals; others envisioned a vast new "empire of liberty" that would include Canada, Mexico, Caribbean and Pacific islands, and ultimately, a few dreamed, much of the rest of the world. Henry Clay and others warned that territorial expansion would reopen the painful controversy over slavery. Their voices, however, could not compete with the enthusiasm over expansion in the 1840s, which began with the issues of Texas and Oregon.

Americans in Texas

Twice in the 1820s, the United States had offered to purchase Texas from the Republic of Mexico, only to meet with indignant Mexican refusals. But in 1824, the Mexican government enacted a colonization law offering *American Immigration to Texas* cheap land and a four-year exemption from taxes to any American willing to move into Texas. Thousands of Americans flocked into the region, the great majority of them white southerners and their slaves, intent on establishing cotton plantations. By 1830, there were about 7,000 Americans living in Texas, more than twice the number of Mexicans there.

Most of the settlers came to Texas through the efforts of American intermediaries, who received sizable land grants from Mexico in return for promising to bring new residents into the region. The most successful of them was Stephen F. Austin, a young immigrant from Missouri who established the first legal American settlement in Texas in 1822. Austin and others recruited many American immigrants to Texas; in the process, they created centers of power in the region that competed with the Mexican government. In 1830, the Mexican government barred any further American immigration into the region. But Americans kept flowing into Texas anyway.

Friction between the American settlers and the Mexican government was already growing in the mid-1830s when instability in Mexico itself drove General Antonio López de Santa Anna to seize power as a dictator. He increased the powers of the national government at the expense of the state governments, a measure that Texans from the United States assumed Santa Anna was aiming specifically at them. Sporadic fighting between Americans and Mexicans in Texas began in 1835, and in 1836, the American settlers defiantly proclaimed their independence from Mexico.

Independence Declared

Santa Anna led a large army into Texas, where the American settlers were divided into several squabbling factions. Mexican forces annihilated an American garrison at the Alamo mission in San Antonio after a famous, if futile, defense by a group of Texas "patriots" that included, among others, the renowned frontiersman and former Tennessee congressman Davy Crockett. Another garrison at Goliad suffered substantially the same fate. By the end of 1836, the rebellion appeared to have collapsed.

But General Sam Houston managed to keep a small force together. And on April 21, 1836, at the Battle of San Jacinto, he defeated the Mexican army and took Santa *Battle of San Jacinto* Anna prisoner. Santa Anna, under pressure from his captors, signed a treaty giving Texas independence.

A number of Mexican residents of Texas *(Tejanos)* had fought with the Americans in the revolution. But soon after Texas won its independence, their positions grew difficult. The Americans did not trust them, feared that they were agents of the Mexican government, and in effect drove many of them out of the new republic. Most of those who stayed had to settle for a politically and economically subordinate status.

One of the first acts of the new president of Texas, Sam Houston, was to send a delegation to Washington with an offer to join the Union. But President Jackson, fearing that adding a large new slave *Annexation Blocked* state to the Union would increase sectional tensions, blocked annexation and even delayed recognizing the new republic until 1837.

Spurned by the United States, Texas cast out on its own. England and France, concerned about the growing power of the United States, saw Texas as a possible check on its growth and began forging ties with the new republic. At that point, President Tyler persuaded Texas to apply for statehood again in 1844. But northern senators, fearing the admission of a new slave state, defeated it.

Oregon

Control of what was known as Oregon country, in the Pacific Northwest, was, along with Texas, a major political issue in the 1840s. Both Britain and the United States claimed sovereignty in the region. Unable to resolve their conflicting claims diplomatically, they agreed in an 1818 treaty to allow citizens of each country equal access to the territory. This arrangement, known as "joint occupation," contin- *"Joint Occupation"* ued for twenty years.

In fact, at the time of the treaty neither Britain nor the United States had established much of a presence in Oregon country. White settlement in the region consisted largely of American and Canadian fur traders, and the most significant white settlements were scattered fur trading posts. But American interest in Oregon grew substantially in the 1820s and 1830s.

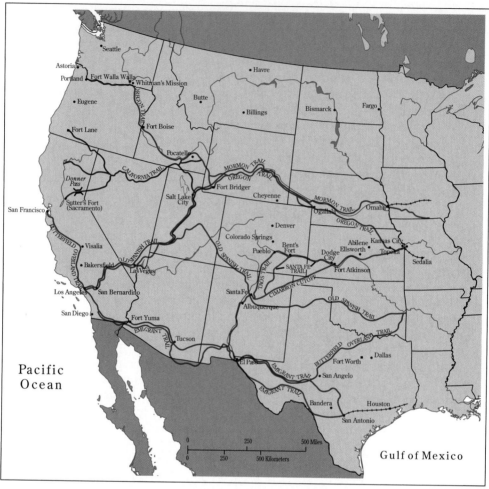

WESTERN TRAILS IN 1860 This map shows how much of western North America had little or no non-Indian population in 1800. As settlers began the long process of exploring and establishing farms and businesses in the West, major trails began to develop to facilitate travel and trade between the region and the more thickly settled areas to the East. Note how many of the trails lead to California and how few of them lead into any of the far northern regions of United States territory. Note too the important towns and cities that grew up along these trails. ◆ *What other, later forms of transportation performed the functions that these trails performed prior to the Civil War?*

By the mid-1840s, white Americans substantially outnumbered the *Growing American Settlements* British in Oregon. They had also devastated much of the Indian population, in part through a measles epidemic that spread through the Cayuse. American settlements had spread up and down the Pacific coast, and the new settlers were urging the United States government to take possession of the disputed Oregon Territory.

CROSSING THE PLAINS A long wagon train carries migrants across the Plains toward Montana in 1866. This photograph gives some indication of the rugged condition of even some of the most well-traveled trails. (© *The New-York Historical Society*)

The Westward Migration

The migrations into Texas and Oregon were part of a larger movement that took hundreds of thousands of white and black Americans into the far western regions of the continent between 1840 and 1860. The largest number of migrants were from the Old Northwest (today's Midwest). Most traveled in family groups, until the early 1850s, when the great California gold rush attracted many single men (see pp. 343–344). Most were relatively young people. Few were wealthy, but many were relatively prosperous. Poor people who could not afford the trip on their own usually had to join other families or groups as laborers—men as farm or ranch hands, women as domestic servants, teachers, or, in some cases, prostitutes. Groups heading for areas where mining or lumbering was the principal economic activity consisted mostly of men. Those heading for farming regions traveled mainly as families.

Migrants generally gathered in one of several major depots in Iowa and Missouri (Independence, St. Joseph, or Council Bluffs), joined a wagon train led by hired guides, and set off with their belongings piled in covered wagons, livestock trailing behind. The major route west was the 2,000-mile Oregon Trail, which stretched from In- *The Oregon Trail* dependence across the Great Plains and through the South Pass of the Rocky Mountains. From there, migrants moved north into Oregon or south (along the California trail) to the northern

California coast. Other migrations moved along the Santa Fe Trail, southwest from Independence into New Mexico.

However they traveled, overland migrants faced an arduous journey. Most passages lasted five or six months (from May to November), and there was always pressure to get through the Rockies before the snows began, often not an easy task given the very slow pace of most wagon trains. There was also the danger of disease; many groups were decimated by cholera. Almost everyone walked the great majority of the time, to lighten the load for the horses drawing the wagons. The women, who did the cooking and washing at the end of the day, generally worked harder than the men, who usually rested when the caravan halted.

Only a few expeditions experienced Indian attacks. In the twenty years before the Civil War, fewer than 400 migrants (slightly more than one-tenth of 1 percent) died in conflicts with the tribes. In fact, Indians were usually more helpful than dangerous to the white migrants. They often served as guides, and they traded horses, clothing, and fresh food with the travelers.

Indian Assistance

Despite the traditional image of westward migrants as rugged individualists, most travelers found the journey a very communal experience. That was partly because many expeditions consisted of groups of friends, neighbors, or relatives who had decided to pull up stakes and move west together. And it was partly because of the intensity of the journey. It was a rare expedition in which there were not some internal conflicts before the trip was over; but those who made the journey successfully generally learned the value of cooperation.

EXPANSION AND WAR

The growing number of white Americans in the lands west of the Mississippi put great pressure on the government in Washington to annex Texas, Oregon, and other territory. And in the 1840s, these expansionist pressures helped push the United States into war.

The Democrats and Expansion

In preparing for the election of 1844, the two leading candidates—Henry Clay and Martin Van Buren—both tried to avoid taking a stand on the controversial issue of the annexation of Texas. Sentiment for expansion was mild within the Whig Party, and Clay had no difficulty securing the nomination despite his noncommittal position. But many southern Democrats supported annexation, and the party passed over Van Buren to nominate James K. Polk.

Polk had represented Tennessee in the House of Representatives for fourteen years, four of them as Speaker, and had subsequently served as governor. But by 1844, he had been out of public office for three years.

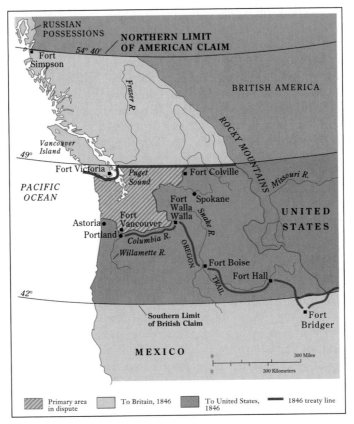

THE OREGON BOUNDARY, 1846 One of the last major boundary disputes between the United States and Great Britain involved the territory known as Oregon—the large region on the Pacific Coast north of California (which in 1846 was still part of Mexico). For years, America and Britain had overlapping claims on the territory. The British claimed land as far south as the present state of Oregon, while the Americans claimed land extending well into what is now Canada. Tensions over the Oregon border at times rose to the point that many Americans were demanding war, some using the slogan "54-40 or fight," referring to the latitude of the northernmost point of the American claim. ◆ *How did President James K. Polk defuse the crisis?*

What made his victory possible was his support for the position, expressed in the Democratic platform, "that the re-occupation of Oregon and the re-annexation of Texas at the earliest practicable period are great American measures." By combining the Oregon and Texas questions, the Democrats hoped to appeal to both northern and southern expansionists. Polk carried the election by 170 electoral votes to 105.

Polk Elected

Polk entered office with a clear set of goals and with plans for attaining them. John Tyler accomplished the first of Polk's goals for him in the last days of his own presidency. Interpreting the election returns as a mandate for the annexation of Texas, the outgoing president won congressional approval for it in February 1845. That December, Texas became a state.

Polk himself resolved the Oregon question. The British minister in
Compromise over Oregon Washington brusquely rejected a compromise Polk
offered that would establish the United States–
Canadian border at the 49th parallel. Incensed, Polk again asserted the
American claim to all of Oregon. There was loose talk of war on both sides
of the Atlantic—talk that in the United States often took the form of the bel-
licose slogan "Fifty-four forty or fight!" (a reference to where the Americans
hoped to draw the northern boundary of their part of Oregon). But neither
country really wanted war. Finally, the British government accepted Polk's
original proposal to divide the territory at the 49th parallel. On June 15,
1846, the Senate approved a treaty that fixed the boundary there.

The Southwest and California

One of the reasons the Senate and the president had agreed so readily to
the British offer to settle the Oregon question was that new tensions were
emerging in the Southwest. As soon as the United States admitted Texas
to statehood in 1845, the Mexican government broke diplomatic relations
with Washington. Mexican-American relations grew still worse when a
Texas Boundary Disputed dispute developed over the boundary between
Texas and Mexico. Texans claimed the Rio Grande
as their western and southern border. Mexico, although still not conced-
ing the loss of Texas, argued nevertheless that the border had always been
the Nueces River, to the north of the Rio Grande. Polk accepted the
Texas claim, and in the summer of 1845 he sent a small army under General Zachary Taylor to Texas to protect the new state against a possible
Mexican invasion.

Part of the area in dispute was New Mexico, whose Spanish and Indian residents lived in a multiracial society that had by the 1840s endured
for nearly a century and a half. In the 1820s, the Mexican government had
invited American traders into the region, hoping to speed development of
the province. And New Mexico, like Texas, soon began to become more
American than Mexican. A flourishing commerce soon developed between
Santa Fe and Independence, Missouri.

California Americans were also increasing their interest in
California. In this vast region lived members of
several western Indian tribes and perhaps 7,000 Mexicans. Gradually,
however, white Americans began to arrive: first maritime traders and cap-
tains of Pacific whaling ships, who stopped to barter goods or buy supplies; then merchants, who established stores, imported merchandise, and
developed a profitable trade with the Mexicans and Indians; and finally pi-
oneering farmers, who entered California from the east, by land, and settled in the Sacramento Valley. Some of these new settlers began to dream
of bringing California into the United States.

President Polk soon came to share their dream and committed himself
to acquiring both New Mexico and California for the United States. At the

same time that he dispatched the troops under Taylor to Texas, he sent secret instructions to the commander of the Pacific naval squadron to seize the California ports if Mexico declared war. Representatives of the president quietly informed Americans in California that the United States would respond sympathetically to a revolt against Mexican authority there.

The Mexican War

Having appeared to prepare for war, Polk turned to diplomacy and dispatched a special minister to try to buy off the Mexicans. But Mexican leaders rejected the American offer to purchase the disputed territories. On January 13, 1846, as soon as he heard the news, Polk ordered Taylor's army in Texas to move across the Nueces River, where it had been stationed, to the Rio Grande. For months, the Mexicans refused to fight. But finally, according to disputed American accounts, some Mexican troops crossed the Rio Grande and attacked a unit of American soldiers. On May 13, 1846, Congress declared war by votes of 40 to 2 in the Senate and 174 to 14 in the House. *War Declared*

Whig critics charged that Polk had deliberately maneuvered the country into the conflict and had staged the border incident that had precipitated the declaration. Many argued that the hostilities with Mexico were draining resources and attention away from the more important issue of the Pacific Northwest; and when the United States finally reached its agreement with Britain on the Oregon question, opponents claimed that Polk had settled for less than he should have because he was preoccupied with Mexico. Opposition intensified as the war continued and as the public became aware of the casualties and expense.

Victory did not come as quickly as Polk had hoped. The president ordered Taylor to cross the Rio Grande, seize parts of northeastern Mexico, beginning with the city of Monterrey, and then march on to Mexico City itself. Taylor captured Monterrey in September 1846, but he let the Mexican garrison evacuate without pursuit. Polk now began to fear that Taylor lacked the tactical skill for the planned advance against Mexico City. He also feared that, if successful, Taylor would become a powerful political rival (as, in fact, he did).

In the meantime, Polk ordered other offensives against New Mexico and California. In the summer of 1846, a small army under Colonel Stephen W. Kearny captured Santa Fe with no opposition. Then Kearny proceeded to California, where he joined a conflict already in progress that was being staged jointly by American settlers, a well-armed exploring party led by John C. Frémont, and the American navy: the so-called Bear Flag Revolt. Kearny brought the *Bear Flag Revolt* disparate American forces together under his command, and by the autumn of 1846 he had completed the conquest of California.

But Mexico still refused to concede defeat. At this point, Polk and General Winfield Scott, the commanding general of the army and its

THE MEXICAN WAR, 1846–1848 Shortly after the settlement of the Oregon border dispute with Britain, the United States entered a war with Mexico over another contested border. This map shows the movement of Mexican and American troops during the fighting, which extended from the area around Santa Fe south to Mexico City and west to the coast of California. Note the American use of its naval forces to facilitate a successful assault on Mexico City, and other assaults on the coast of California. Note, too, how unsuccessful the Mexican forces were in their battles with the United States. Mexico won only one battle—a relatively minor one at San Pasqual near San Diego—in the war. ◆ *How did President Polk deal with the popular clamor for the United States to annex much of present-day Mexico?*

 For an interactive version of this map go to www.mhhe.com/unfinishednation4ch13maps

STEPHEN KEARNY IN SANTA FE Colonel Stephen Kearny led a small U.S. military party to Santa Fe in 1846 and seized the town without opposition. In this 1909 drawing (which the artist Kenneth Chapman acknowledged was not entirely accurate), Kearny raises the American flag over the "old palace" in Santa Fe. The image appeared on a U.S. postage stamp in 1946. *(Kenneth Chapman,* Drawing of Steven Kearny in Santa Fe, *1909. Courtesy of the Museum of New Mexico)*

finest soldier, launched a bold new campaign. Scott assembled an army at Tampico, which the navy transported down the Mexican coast to Veracruz. With an army that never numbered more than 14,000, Scott advanced 260 miles along the Mexican National Highway toward Mexico City, kept American casualties low, and never lost a battle before finally seizing the Mexican capital. A new Mexican government took power and announced its willingness to negotiate a peace treaty.

President Polk continued to encourage those who demanded that the United States annex much of Mexico itself. At the same time, he was growing anxious to get the war finished quickly. Polk had sent a special presidential envoy, Nicholas Trist, to negotiate a settlement. On February 2, 1848, he reached agreement with the new Mexican *Treaty of Guadalupe Hidalgo* government on the Treaty of Guadalupe Hidalgo, by which Mexico agreed to cede California and New Mexico to the United States and acknowledge the Rio Grande as the boundary of Texas. In return, the United States promised to assume any financial claims its new citizens had against Mexico and to pay the Mexicans $15 million. Trist had obtained most of Polk's original demands, but he had not satisfied the new, more expansive dreams of acquiring additional territory in Mexico itself. Polk angrily claimed that Trist had violated his instructions, but he soon realized that he had no choice but to accept the treaty to silence a bitter battle growing between ardent expansionists demanding the annexation of "All Mexico!" and antislavery leaders charging that the expansionists were conspiring to extend slavery to new realms. The president submitted the Trist treaty to the Senate, which approved it by a vote of 38 to 14.

THE SECTIONAL DEBATE

James Polk tried to be a president whose policies transcended sectional divisions. But conciliating the sections was becoming an ever more difficult task, and Polk gradually earned the enmity of northerners and westerners alike, who believed his policies favored the South at their expense.

Slavery and the Territories

In August 1846, while the Mexican War was still in progress, Polk asked Congress to appropriate $2 million for purchasing *Wilmot Proviso* peace with Mexico. Representative David Wilmot of Pennsylvania, an antislavery Democrat, introduced an amendment to the appropriation bill prohibiting slavery in any territory acquired from Mexico. The so-called Wilmot Proviso passed the House but failed in the Senate. Southern militants contended that all Americans had equal rights in the new territories, including the right to move their slaves (which they considered property) into them.

As the sectional debate intensified, President *Growing Sectional Debate* Polk supported a proposal to extend the Missouri Compromise line through the new territories to the Pacific coast, banning slavery north of the line and permitting it south of the line. Others supported a plan, originally known as "squatter sovereignty" and later by the more dignified phrase "popular sovereignty," which would allow the people of each territory to decide the status of slavery there. The debate over these various proposals dragged on for many months.

The presidential campaign of 1848 dampened the controversy for a time as both Democrats and Whigs tried to avoid the slavery question. When Polk, in poor health, declined to run again, the Democrats nominated Lewis Cass of Michigan, a dull, aging party regular. The Whigs nominated General Zachary Taylor of Louisiana, hero of the Mexican War but a man with no political experience whatsoever. Opponents of slavery found the choice of candidates unsatisfying, and out of their discontent emerged the new Free-Soil Party, whose candidate was former president Martin Van Buren.

Taylor won a narrow victory. But while Van Buren failed to carry a single state, he polled an impressive 291,000 votes (10 percent of the *Free-Soil Party* total), and the Free-Soilers elected ten members to Congress. The emergence of the Free-Soil Party as

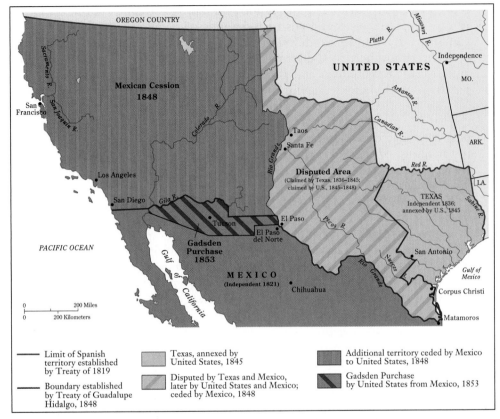

SOUTHWESTERN EXPANSION, 1845–1853 The annexation of much of what is now Texas in 1845, the much larger territorial gains won in the Mexican War in 1848, and the purchase of additional land from Mexico in 1853 completed the present continental border of the United States.◆ *What great event shortly after the Mexican War contributed to a rapid settlement of California by migrants from the eastern United States?*

 For an interactive version of this map go to www.mhhe.com/unfinishednation4ch13maps

an important political force signaled the inability of the existing parties to contain the political passions slavery was creating. It was an important part of a process that would lead to the collapse of the second party system in the 1850s.

The California Gold Rush

By the time Taylor took office, the pressure to resolve the question of slavery in the far western territories had become more urgent as a result of dramatic events in California. In January 1848, a foreman working in a sawmill owned by John Sutter (one of California's leading ranchers) found traces of gold in the foothills of the Sierra Nevada. Within months, news of the discovery had spread throughout the nation and much of the world. Almost immediately, hundreds of thousands of people began flocking to California in a frantic search for gold.

The atmosphere in California at the peak of the gold rush was one of almost crazed excitement and greed. Most migrants to the Far West prepared carefully before making the journey. But the California migrants (known as "Forty-niners") threw caution to the *"Forty-niners"* winds. They abandoned farms, jobs, homes, families; they piled onto ships and flooded the overland trails. The overwhelming majority of the Forty-niners (perhaps 95 percent) were men, and the society they created on their arrival in California was unusually fluid and volatile because of the almost total absence of women, children, or families.

The gold rush also attracted some of the first Chinese migrants to the western United States. News of the discoveries created great excitement in China, particularly in impoverished areas. It was, of course, extremely difficult for a poor Chinese peasant to get to America; but many young, adventurous people (mostly men) decided to go anyway—in the belief that they could quickly become rich and then return to China. Emigration brokers loaned many migrants money for passage to California, which the migrants were to pay off out of their earnings there.

The gold rush was producing a serious labor shortage in California, as many male workers left their jobs and flocked to the gold fields. That created opportunities for many people who needed work (including Chinese immigrants). It also led to a frenzied exploitation of Indians that resembled slavery in all but name. A new state law per- *Indians Exploited* mitted the arrest of "loitering" or orphaned Indians and their assignment to a term of "indentured" labor.

The gold rush was of critical importance to the growth of California, but not for the reasons most of the migrants hoped. There was substantial gold in the hills of the Sierra Nevada, and many people got rich from it. But only a tiny fraction of the Forty-niners ever found gold. Some disappointed migrants returned home after a while. But many stayed in California and swelled both the agricultural and urban populations of the territory. By 1856, for example, San Francisco—whose population had been 1,000 before the gold rush—was the home of over 50,000 people. By the early 1850s, California, which had always had a diverse population, had become even more heterogeneous. The gold rush had attracted not just white Americans but Europeans, Chinese, South Americans, Mexicans, free blacks, and slaves who accompanied southern migrants. Conflicts over gold intersected with racial and ethnic tensions to make the territory an unusually turbulent place.

Rising Sectional Tensions

Zachary Taylor believed statehood could become the solution to the issue of slavery in the territories. As long as the new lands remained territories, the federal government was responsible for deciding the fate of slavery within them. But once they became states, he thought, their own governments would be able to settle the slavery question. At Taylor's urging, California quickly adopted a constitution that prohibited slavery, and in December 1849 Taylor asked Congress to admit California as a free state.

Congress balked, in part because of several *Sectional Conflict over Slavery* other controversies concerning slavery that were complicating the debate. One was the effort of antislavery forces to abolish slavery in the District of Columbia. Another was the emergence of personal liberty laws in northern states, which barred courts and police officers from helping to return runaway slaves to their owners. But the biggest obstacle to the president's program was the white South's fear that new free states would be added to the northern majority. The number of free and slave states was equal in 1849—fifteen each. But the admission of California would upset the balance; and New Mexico, Oregon, and Utah—all candidates for statehood—might upset it further.

Even many otherwise moderate southern leaders now began to talk about secession from the Union. In the North, every state legislature but one adopted a resolution demanding the prohibition of slavery in the territories.

The Compromise of 1850

Faced with this mounting crisis, moderates and unionists spent the winter of 1849–1850 trying to frame a great compromise. *Clay's Compromise Debated* The aging Henry Clay, who was spearheading the effort, believed that no compromise could last unless it settled all the issues in dispute between the sections. As a result, he took several measures that had been proposed separately, combined them into a single piece of legislation, and presented it to the Senate on January 29, 1850. Among the bill's provisions were the admission of California as a free state; the formation of territorial governments in the rest of the lands acquired from Mexico, without restrictions on slavery; the abolition of the slave trade, but not slavery itself, in the District of Columbia; and a new and more effective fugitive slave law. These resolutions launched a debate that raged for seven months.

But in July, after six months of impassioned wrangling, a new, younger group of leaders emerged and took control of the debate from the old "triumvirate" of Webster, Clay, and Calhoun. The new leaders of the Senate were able, as the old leaders had not been, to produce a compromise. One spur to the compromise was the disappearance of the most powerful obstacle to it: the president. On July 9, 1850, Taylor suddenly died—the victim of a violent stomach disorder. He was succeeded by Millard Fillmore of New York—a dull, handsome, dignified man who understood the political importance of flexibility. He supported compromise and used his powers of persuasion to swing northern Whigs into line.

The new leaders also benefited from their own pragmatic tactics. Stephen A. Douglas, a senator from Illinois, proposed breaking up the

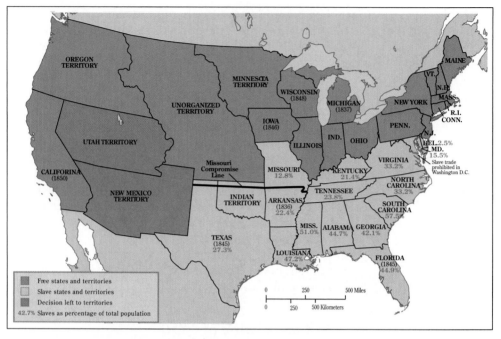

SLAVE AND FREE TERRITORIES UNDER THE COMPROMISE OF 1850 The acquisition of vast new western lands raised the question of the status of slavery in new territories organized for statehood by the United States. Tension between the North and South on this question led in 1850 to a great compromise, forged in Congress, to settle this dispute. The compromise allowed California to join the Union as a free state and introduced the concept of "popular sovereignty" for other new territories.◆ *How well did the compromise of 1850 work?*

 For an interactive version of this map go to www.mhhe.com/unfinishednation4ch13maps

"omnibus bill" that Clay had envisioned as a great, comprehensive solution to the sectional crisis and to introduce instead a series of separate measures to be voted on one by one. Thus representatives of different sections could support those elements of the compromise they liked and oppose those they did not. Douglas also gained support with complicated backroom deals linking the compromise to such nonideological matters as the sale of government bonds and the construction of railroads. As a result of his efforts, by mid-September Congress had enacted and the president had signed all the components of the compromise.

Compromise Achieved   The Compromise of 1850 was a victory of self-interest. Still, members of Congress hailed the measure as a triumph of statesmanship; and Millard Fillmore, signing it, called it a just settlement of the sectional problem, "in its character final and irrevocable."

THE CRISES OF THE 1850s

For a few years after the Compromise of 1850, the sectional conflict seemed briefly to be forgotten amid booming prosperity and growth. But the tensions between North and South remained.

The Uneasy Truce

Both major parties endorsed the Compromise of 1850 in 1852, and both nominated presidential candidates unidentified with sectional passions. The Democrats chose the obscure New Hampshire politician Franklin Pierce and the Whigs the military hero General Winfield Scott. But the sectional question was a divisive influence in the election anyway, and the Whigs were the principal victims. They suffered massive defections from antislavery members angered by the party's evasiveness on the issue. Many of them flocked to the Free-Soil Party, whose antislavery presidential candidate, John P. Hale, repudiated the Compromise of 1850. The divisions among the Whigs helped produce a victory for the Democrats in 1852.

Franklin Pierce attempted to maintain harmony by avoiding divisive issues, particularly slavery. But it was an impossible task. Northern opposition to the Fugitive Slave Act intensified quickly after 1850, when southerners began appearing oc- *Fugitive Slave Act Opposed* casionally in northern states to pursue people they claimed were fugitives. Mobs formed in some northern cities to prevent enforcement of the law, and several northern states also passed their own laws barring the deportation of fugitive slaves. White southerners watched with growing anger and alarm as the one element of the Compromise of 1850 that they had considered a victory seemed to become meaningless as a result of northern defiance.

"Young America"

One of the ways Franklin Pierce hoped to dampen sectional controversy was through his support of a movement in the Democratic Party known as "Young America." Its adherents saw the expansion of American democracy throughout the world as a way to divert attention from the controversies over slavery. The great liberal and nationalist revolutions of 1848 in Europe stirred them to dream of a republican Europe with governments based on the model of the United States. They dreamed as well of acquiring new territories in the Western Hemisphere.

But efforts to extend the nation's domain could not avoid becoming entangled with the sectional crisis. Pierce had been pursuing unsuccessful diplomatic attempts to buy Cuba from Spain (efforts begun in 1848 by Polk). In 1854, however, a group of his envoys sent him a private document

Ostend Manifesto from Ostend, Belgium, making the case for seizing Cuba by force. When the Ostend Manifesto, as it became known, was leaked to the public, antislavery northerners charged the administration with conspiring to bring a new slave state into the Union.

The South, for its part, opposed all efforts to acquire new territory that would not support a slave system. The kingdom of Hawaii agreed to join the United States in 1854, but the treaty died in the Senate because it contained a clause prohibiting slavery in the islands. A powerful movement to annex Canada to the United States similarly foundered, at least in part because of slavery.

Slavery, Railroads, and the West

What fully revived the sectional crisis, however, was the same issue that had produced it in the first place: slavery in the territories. By the 1850s, the line of substantial white settlement had moved beyond the boundaries of Missouri, Iowa, and what is now Minnesota into a great expanse of plains, which many white Americans had once believed was unfit for cultivation. Now it was becoming apparent that large sections of this region were, in fact, suitable for farming. In the states of the Old Northwest, therefore, prospective settlers urged the government to open the area to them, provide territorial governments, and dislodge the Indians located there so as to make room for white settlers. There was relatively little opposition from any segment of white society to this proposed violation of Indian rights. But the interest in further settlement raised two issues that did prove highly divisive and that gradually became entwined with each other: railroads and slavery.

As the nation expanded westward, the problem of communication between the older states and the areas west of the Mississippi River became more and more critical. As a result, broad support began to emerge for *Transcontinental Railroad and Slavery* building a transcontinental railroad. The problem was where to place it—and in particular, where to locate the railroad's eastern terminus, where the line could connect with the existing rail network east of the Mississippi. Northerners favored Chicago, while southerners supported St. Louis, Memphis, or New Orleans. The transcontinental railroad had become part of the struggle between the North and the South.

Pierce's secretary of war, Jefferson Davis of Mississippi, removed one obstacle to a southern route. Surveys indicated that a railroad with a southern terminus would have to pass through an area in Mexican territory. But in 1853 Davis sent James Gadsden, a southern railroad builder, to Mexico, where he persuaded the Mexican government to accept $10 million in exchange for a strip of land that today comprises part of Arizona and New Mexico. The so-called Gadsden *Gadsden Purchase* Purchase only accentuated the sectional rivalry.

The Kansas-Nebraska Controversy

As a senator from Illinois and the acknowledged leader of northwestern Democrats, Stephen A. Douglas naturally wanted the transcontinental railroad for his own section. He also realized the strength of the principal argument against the northern route: that it would run mostly through country with a substantial Indian population. As a result, he introduced a bill in January 1854 to organize (and thus open to white settlement) a huge new territory, known as Nebraska, west of Iowa and Missouri.

Douglas knew the South would oppose his bill because it would prepare the way for a new free state; the proposed territory was north of the Missouri Compromise line (36°3′) and hence closed to slavery. In an effort to make the measure acceptable to southerners, Douglas inserted a provision that the status of slavery in the territory would be determined by the territorial legislature. In theory, the region could choose to open itself to slavery. When southern Democrats demanded more, Douglas agreed to an additional clause explicitly repealing the Missouri Compromise. He also agreed to divide the area into two territories— *Kansas-Nebraska Act* Nebraska and Kansas—instead of one. The new, second territory (Kansas) was somewhat more likely to become a slave state. In its final form the measure was known as the Kansas-Nebraska Act. President Pierce supported the bill, and after a strenuous debate, it became law in May 1854 with the unanimous support of the South and the partial support of northern Democrats.

No piece of legislation in American history produced so many immediate, sweeping, and ominous consequences. It divided and destroyed the Whig Party. It divided the northern Democrats (many of whom were appalled at the repeal of the Missouri Compromise) and drove many of them from the party. Most important of all, it spurred the creation of a new party that was frankly sectional in composition and creed. People in both major parties who opposed Douglas's bill began to call themselves Anti-Nebraska Democrats and Anti-Nebraska Whigs. In 1854, they formed a new organization and named it the Republican *Republican Party Established* Party. It instantly became a major force in American politics. In the elections of that year, the Republicans won enough seats in Congress to permit them, in combination with allies among the Know-Nothings, to organize the House of Representatives.

"Bleeding Kansas"

White settlers began moving into Kansas almost immediately after the passage of the Kansas-Nebraska Act. In the spring of 1855, elections were held for a territorial legislature. There were only about 1,500 legal voters in Kansas by then, but thousands of Missourians, some traveling in armed bands into Kansas, swelled the vote to over 6,000. The result was that pro-slavery forces elected a majority to the legislature, which immediately legalized slavery. Outraged free-staters elected their own delegates to a constitutional convention, which met at Topeka and adopted a constitution excluding slavery. They then chose their own governor and legislature and petitioned Congress for statehood. President Pierce denounced them as traitors and threw the full support of the federal government behind the pro-slavery territorial legislature. A few months later a pro-slavery federal marshal assembled a large posse, consisting mostly of Missourians, to arrest the free-state leaders, who had set up their headquarters in Lawrence. The posse sacked the town, burned the "governor's" house, and destroyed several printing presses. Retribution came quickly.

Among the most fervent abolitionists in Kansas was John Brown, a grim, fiercely committed zealot who had moved to Kansas with his sons so that they could fight to make it a free state. After the events in Lawrence, he gathered six followers (including four of his sons) and in one night murdered five pro-slavery settlers. This terrible episode, known as the

Pottawatomie Massacre

Pottawatomie Massacre, led to more civil strife in Kansas—irregular, guerrilla warfare conducted by armed bands, some of them more interested in land claims or loot than in ideologies. Northerners and southerners alike came to believe that the events in Kansas illustrated (and were caused by) the aggressive designs of the other section. "Bleeding Kansas" became a symbol of the sectional controversy.

Another symbol soon appeared, in the United States Senate. In May 1856, Charles Sumner of Massachusetts rose to give a speech entitled "The Crime Against Kansas." In it, he gave particular attention to Senator Andrew P. Butler of South Carolina, an outspoken defender of slavery. The South Carolinian was, Sumner claimed, the "Don Quixote" of slavery, having "chosen a mistress . . . who, though ugly to others, is always lovely to him, though polluted in the sight of the world, is chaste in his sight . . . the harlot slavery."

The pointedly sexual references and the general viciousness of the speech enraged Butler's nephew, Preston Brooks, a member of the House of Representatives from South Carolina. Several days after the speech,

Sumner Caned

Brooks approached Sumner at his desk in the Senate chamber during a recess, raised a heavy cane, and began beating him repeatedly on the head and shoulders. Sumner, trapped in his chair, rose in agony with such strength that he tore the desk from the bolts holding it to the floor. Then he collapsed, bleeding and unconscious. So severe were his injuries that he was unable to return to the Senate for four years. Throughout the North, he became a hero—a martyr to the barbarism of the South. In the South, Preston Brooks became a hero, too. Censured by the House, he resigned his seat, returned to South Carolina, and stood successfully for reelection.

The Free-Soil Ideology

What had happened to produce such deep hostility between the two sections? In part, the tensions were reflections of the two sections' differing economic and territorial interests. But they were also reflections of a hardening of ideas in both North and South.

In the North, assumptions about the proper structure of society came to center on the belief in "free soil" and "free labor." Most white northerners came to believe *"Free Soil" and "Free Labor"* that the existence of slavery was dangerous not because of what it did to blacks but because of what it threatened to do to whites. At the heart of American democracy, they argued, was the right of all citizens to own property, to control their own labor, and to have access to opportunities for advancement.

According to this vision, the South was the antithesis of democracy—a closed, static society, in which slavery preserved an entrenched aristocracy. While the North was growing and prospering, the South was stagnating, rejecting the values of individualism and progress. The South was, northern free-laborites further maintained, engaged in a *"Slave Power Conspiracy"* conspiracy to extend slavery throughout the nation and thus to destroy the openness of northern capitalism and replace it with the closed, aristocratic system of the South. The only solution to this "slave power conspiracy" was to fight the spread of slavery and extend the nation's democratic (i.e., free-labor) ideals to all sections of the country.

This ideology, which lay at the heart of the new Republican Party, also strengthened the commitment of Republicans to the Union. Since the idea of continued growth and progress was central to the free-labor vision, the prospect of dismemberment of the nation was unthinkable.

The Pro-Slavery Argument

In the South, in the meantime, a very different ideology was emerging out of a rapid hardening of position among southern whites on the issue of slavery. It was a result of many things: the Nat Turner uprising in 1831, which terrified southern whites; the expansion of the cotton economy into the Deep South, which made slavery unprecedentedly lucrative; and the growth of the Garrisonian abolitionist movement, with its strident attacks on southern society. The popularity of Harriet Beecher Stowe's *Uncle Tom's Cabin* was perhaps the most glaring evidence of the power of those attacks, but other abolitionist writings had been antagonizing white southerners for years.

In response to these pressures, a number of white southerners produced a new intellectual defense of slavery. Profes- *Intellectual Defense of Slavery* sor Thomas R. Dew of the College of William and

Mary helped begin that effort in 1832. Twenty years later, apologists for slavery summarized their views in an anthology that gave their ideology its name: *The Pro-Slavery Argument.* John C. Calhoun stated the essence of the case in 1837: Slavery was "a good—a positive good." It was good for the slaves because they enjoyed better conditions than industrial workers in the North. Slavery was good for southern society as a whole because it was the only way the two races could live together in peace. It was good for the entire country because the southern economy, based on slavery, was the key to the prosperity of the nation.

Above all, southern apologists argued, slavery was good because it served as the basis for the southern way of life—a way of life superior to any other in the United States, perhaps in the world. White southerners looking at the North saw a spirit of greed, debauchery, and destructiveness. "The masses of the North are venal, corrupt, covetous, mean and selfish," wrote one southerner. Others wrote with horror of the factory system and the crowded, pestilential cities filled with unruly immigrants. But the South, they believed, was a stable, orderly society, free from the feuds between capital and labor plaguing the North. It protected the welfare of its workers. And it allowed the aristocracy to enjoy a refined and accomplished cultural life. It was, in short, an ideal social order in which all elements of the population were secure and content.

The defense of slavery rested, too, on increasingly elaborate arguments about the biological inferiority of African

Black Inferiority Assumed

Americans, who were, white Southerners claimed, inherently unfit to take care of themselves, let alone exercise the rights of citizenship.

Buchanan and Depression

In this unpromising climate, the presidential campaign of 1856 began. Democratic Party leaders wanted a candidate who, unlike President Pierce, was not closely associated with the explosive question of "Bleeding Kansas." They chose James Buchanan of Pennsylvania, who as minister to England had been safely out of the country during the recent controversies. The Republicans, participating in their first presidential contest, endorsed a Whiggish program of internal improvements, thus combining the idealism of antislavery with the economic aspirations of the North. As eager as the Democrats to present a safe candidate, the Republicans nominated John C. Frémont, who had made a national reputation as an explorer of the Far West and who had no political record. The Native American, or Know-Nothing, Party was beginning to break apart, but it nominated former president Millard Fillmore, who also received the endorsement of a sad remnant of the Whig Party.

Election of 1856

After a heated, even frenzied campaign, Buchanan won a narrow victory over Frémont and Fillmore. At the time of his inauguration, Buchanan was, at age sixty-five, the oldest president, except for William Henry Harrison, ever to have taken office. Whether because of age and physical infirmities or because of a more fundamental weakness of character, he became a painfully timid and indecisive president at a critical moment in history.

In the year Buchanan took office, a financial panic struck the country, followed by a depression that lasted several years. In the North, the depression strengthened the Republican Party because distressed manufacturers, workers, and farmers came to believe that the hard times were the result of the unsound policies of southern-controlled Democratic administrations. They expressed their frustrations by moving into an alliance with antislavery elements and thus into the Republican Party.

The Dred Scott *Decision*

On March 6, 1857, the Supreme Court of the United States projected itself into the sectional controversy with one of the most controversial and notorious decisions in its history—its ruling in the case of *Dred Scott* v. *Sandford.* Dred Scott was a Missouri slave, once owned by an army surgeon who had taken Scott with him into Illinois and Wisconsin, where slavery was forbidden. In 1846, after the surgeon died, Scott sued his master's widow for freedom on the grounds that his residence in free territory had liberated him from slavery. The claim was well grounded in Missouri law, and in 1850 the circuit court in which Scott filed the suit declared him free. By now, John Sanford, the brother of the surgeon's widow, was claiming ownership of Scott, and he appealed the circuit court ruling to the state supreme court, which reversed the earlier decision. When Scott appealed to the federal courts, Sanford's attorneys claimed that Scott had no standing to sue because he was not a citizen.

The Supreme Court (which misspelled Sanford's name in its decision) was so divided that it was unable to issue a single ruling on the case. The thrust of the various rulings, however, was a stunning defeat for the antislavery movement. Chief Justice Roger Taney, who wrote one of the majority opinions, declared *Taney's Sweeping Decision* that Scott could not bring a suit in the federal courts because he was not a citizen. Blacks had no claim to citizenship, Taney argued. Slaves were property, and the Fifth Amendment prohibited Congress from taking property without "due process of law." Consequently, Taney concluded, Congress possessed no authority to pass a law depriving persons of their slave property in the territories. The Missouri Compromise, therefore, had always been unconstitutional.

The ruling did nothing to challenge the right of an individual state to prohibit slavery within its borders, but the statement that the federal government was powerless to act on the issue was a drastic and startling one. Southern whites were elated: the highest tribunal in the land had sanctioned parts of the most extreme southern argument. In the North, the decision produced widespread dismay. Republicans threatened that when they won control of the national government, they would reverse the decision—by "packing" the Court with new members.

Deadlock over Kansas

President Buchanan timidly endorsed the *Dred Scott* decision. At the same time, he tried to resolve the controversy over Kansas by supporting its admission to the Union as a slave state. In response, the pro-slavery territorial legislature called an election for delegates to a constitutional convention. The free-state residents refused to participate, claiming that the legislature had discriminated against them in drawing district lines. As a result, the pro-slavery forces won control of the convention, which met in 1857 at Lecompton, framed a constitution legalizing slavery, and refused to give voters a chance to reject it. When an election for a new territorial legislature was called, the antislavery groups turned out to vote and won a majority. The new legislature promptly submitted the Lecompton constitution to the voters, who rejected it by more than 10,000 votes.

Both sides had resorted to fraud and violence, but it was clear nevertheless that a majority of the people of Kansas opposed slavery. Buchanan, however, pressured Congress to admit Kansas under the Lecompton constitution. Stephen A. Douglas and other western Democrats refused to support the president's proposal, which died in the House of Representatives. Finally, in April 1858, Congress approved a compromise: The Lecompton constitution would be submitted to the voters of Kansas again. If it was approved, Kansas would be admitted to the Union; if it was rejected, statehood would be postponed. Again, Kansas voters decisively

Lecompton Constitution Rejected rejected the Lecompton constitution. Not until the closing months of Buchanan's administration in 1861 did Kansas enter the Union—as a free state.

The Emergence of Lincoln

Given the gravity of the sectional crisis, the congressional elections of 1858 took on a special importance. Of particular note was the United States Senate contest in Illinois, which pitted Stephen A. Douglas, the most prominent northern Democrat, against Abraham Lincoln, who was largely unknown outside Illinois.

Lincoln was a successful lawyer who had long been involved in state politics. He had served several terms in the Illinois legislature and one undistinguished term in Congress. But he was not a national figure like Douglas, and so he tried to increase his visibility by engaging Douglas in a series of de-

Lincoln-Douglas Debates bates. The Lincoln-Douglas debates attracted enormous crowds and received wide attention.

At the heart of the debates was a basic difference on the issue of slavery. Douglas appeared to have no moral position on the issue and, Lincoln claimed, did not care whether slavery was "voted up, or voted down." Lincoln's opposition to slavery was more fundamental. If the nation could accept that blacks were not entitled to basic human rights, he argued, then it could accept that other groups—immigrant laborers, for example—could be deprived of rights, too. And if slavery were to extend into the western territories, he argued, opportunities for poor white laborers to better their lots there would be lost.

Lincoln believed slavery was morally wrong, but he was not an abolitionist. That was in part be- *Lincoln's Argument* cause he could not envision an easy alternative to slavery in the areas where it already existed. He shared the prevailing view among northern whites that the black race was not prepared to live on equal terms with whites. He and his party would "arrest the further spread" of slavery. They would not directly challenge it where it already existed, but would trust that the institution would gradually die out there of its own accord.

Douglas's position satisfied his followers sufficiently to produce a Democratic majority in the state legislature, which returned him to the Senate, but it aroused little enthusiasm. Lincoln, by contrast, lost the election but emerged with a growing following both in and beyond the state. And outside Illinois, the elections went heavily against the Democrats. The party retained control of the Senate but lost its majority in the House, with the result that the congressional sessions of 1858 and 1859 were bitterly deadlocked.

John Brown's Raid

The battles in Congress, however, were almost entirely overshadowed by an event that enraged and horrified the entire South. In the fall of 1859, John Brown, the antislavery zealot whose bloody actions in Kansas had inflamed the crisis there, staged an even more dramatic episode, this time in the South itself. With private encouragement and financial aid from some prominent eastern abolitionists, he made elaborate plans to seize a mountain fortress in Virginia from which, he believed, he could foment a slave insurrection in the South. On October 16, he and a group of eighteen followers attacked and seized control of a United States arsenal in Harpers Ferry, Virginia. But the slave uprising Brown hoped to inspire did not occur, and he quickly found himself besieged in the arsenal by citizens, local militia companies, and before long United States troops under the command of Robert E. Lee. After ten of his men were killed, Brown surrendered. He was promptly tried in a Virginia court for treason and sentenced to death. *John Brown Hanged* He and six of his followers were hanged.

No other single event did more than the Harpers Ferry raid to convince white southerners that they could not live safely in the Union. John Brown's raid, many southerners believed (incorrectly) had the support of the Republican Party, and it suggested to them that the North was now committed to producing a slave insurrection.

JOHN BROWN Even in this formal photographic portrait (taken in 1859, the last year of his life), John Brown conveys the fierce sense of righteousness that fueled his extraordinary activities in the fight against slavery. *(The Library of Congress)*

The Election of Lincoln

As the presidential election of 1860 approached, the Democratic Party was torn apart by a battle between southerners, who demanded a strong endorsement of slavery, and westerners, who supported the idea of popular sovereignty. The party convention met in April in Charleston, South Carolina. When the convention endorsed popular sovereignty, delegates from eight states in the lower South walked out. The remaining delegates *Democrats Divided* could not agree on a presidential candidate and finally adjourned after agreeing to meet again in Baltimore in June. The decimated convention at Baltimore nominated Stephen Douglas for president. In the meantime, disenchanted southern Democrats met in Richmond and nominated John C. Breckinridge of Kentucky.

The Republican leaders, in the meantime, were trying to broaden their appeal so as to attract every major interest group in the North that feared the South was blocking its economic aspirations. The platform endorsed such traditional Whig measures as a high tariff, internal improvements, a homestead bill, and a Pacific railroad to be built with federal financial assistance. It supported the right of each state to decide the status of slavery within its borders. But it also insisted that neither Congress nor territorial legislatures could legalize slavery in the territories. The Republican convention chose Abraham Lincoln as the party's presidential nomi-

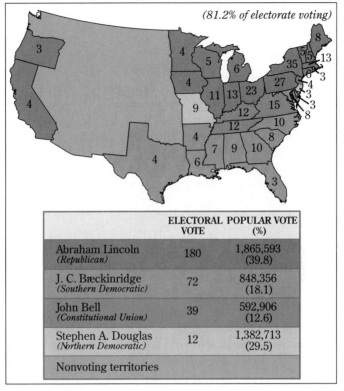

(81.2% of electorate voting)

	ELECTORAL VOTE	POPULAR VOTE (%)
Abraham Lincoln *(Republican)*	180	1,865,593 (39.8)
J. C. Breckinridge *(Southern Democratic)*	72	848,356 (18.1)
John Bell *(Constitutional Union)*	39	592,906 (12.6)
Stephen A. Douglas *(Northern Democratic)*	12	1,382,713 (29.5)
Nonvoting territories		

THE ELECTION OF 1860 The stark sectional divisions that helped produce the Civil War were clearly visible in the results of the 1860 presidential election. Abraham Lincoln, the antislavery Republican candidate, won virtually all the free states. John Breckinridge, a strong pro-slavery southern Democrat, carried most of the South. Lincoln won under 40 percent of the popular vote, but because of the four-way division in the race, managed to win a slim majority of the electoral vote. ◆ *What impact did the election of Lincoln have on the sectional crisis?*

 For an interactive version of this map go to www.mhhe.com/unfinishednation4ch13maps

nee. Lincoln was appealing because of his growing reputation for eloquence, because of his firm but moderate position on slavery, and because his relative obscurity ensured that he would have none of the drawbacks of other, more prominent (and therefore more controversial) Republicans.

In the November election, Lincoln won the presidency with a majority of the electoral votes *Disunion* but only about two-fifths of the fragmented popular vote. The Republicans, moreover, failed to win a majority in Congress. Even so, the election of Lincoln became the final signal to many white southerners that their position in the Union was hopeless. And within a few weeks of Lincoln's victory, the process of disunion began—a process that would quickly lead to a prolonged and bloody war between two groups of Americans, each now convinced that it shared no common ground with the other.

CONCLUSION

In the decades following the War of 1812, a vigorous sense of nationalism pervaded much of American life, helping to smooth over the growing differences among the very different societies emerging in the regions of the United States. During the 1850s, however, the forces that had worked to hold the nation together in the past fell victim to new and much more divisive pressures that were working to split the nation apart.

Driving the sectional tensions of the 1850s was a battle over national policy toward the western territories and over the place of slavery within them. Should slavery be permitted in the new states? And who should decide whether to permit it or not? There were strenuous efforts to craft compromises and solutions to this dilemma: the Compromise of 1850, the Kansas-Nebraska Act of 1854, and others. But despite these efforts, positions on slavery continued to harden in both the North and South. Bitter battles in the territory of Kansas over whether to permit slavery there; growing agitation by abolitionists in the North and pro-slavery advocates in the South; the Supreme Court's controversial *Dred Scott* decision in 1857; the popularity of *Uncle Tom's Cabin* throughout the decade; and the emergence of a new political party—the Republican party—openly and centrally opposed to slavery: all worked to destroy the hopes for compromise and push the South toward secession.

In 1860, all pretense of common sentiment collapsed when no political party presented a presidential candidate capable of attracting national support. The Republicans nominated Abraham Lincoln of Illinois, a little-known politician recognized for his eloquent condemnations of slavery in a Senate race two years earlier. The Democratic party split apart, with its northern and southern wings each nominating different candidates. Lincoln won the election easily, but with less than forty percent of the vote. And almost immediately after his victory, the states of the South began preparing to secede from the Union.

FOR FURTHER REFERENCE

Richard White, *It's Your Misfortune and None of My Own: A History of the American West* (1991) is an excellent presentation of the social and economic history of the region. Anders Stephanson, *Manifest Destiny* (1995) briefly traces the origins of American expansion ideology. Robert M. Johannsen, *To the Halls of Montezuma: The Mexican War in the American Imagination* (1985) examines public attitudes toward the conflict. Paul D. Lack, *The Texas Revolutionary Experience: A Political and Social History, 1835–1836* (1992) chronicles Texas's route to independence from Mexico. Malcolm Rorabaugh, *Days of Gold: The California Gold Rush and the American Nation* (1997) is an account of this seminal event in the history of the West. Susan Lee Johnson, *Roaring Camp: The Social World of the Gold Rush* (2000) examines the experiences of men and women involved in the frenzy. David M. Pletcher, *The Diplomacy of Annexation: Texas, Oregon, and the Mexican War* (1973) is the standard work on war and diplomacy in the 1840s. William W. Freehling, *The Road to Disunion, Vol. 1: Secessionists at Bay, 1776–1854* (1990) explores the successful containment of sectionalism prior to the 1850s. David Potter, *The Impending Crisis, 1848–1861* (1976) is a thorough summary of the decisive decade. Eric Foner, *Free Soil, Free Labor, Free Men* (1970) traces the emergence of the Republican Party. Leonard L. Richards, *The Slave Power: The Free North and Southern Domination, 1780–1860* (2000) examines the long history of sectional tension. Michael Holt, *The Political Crisis of the 1850s* (1978) challenges Foner by emphasizing ethnic and religious alignment in northern politics. Don E. Fehrenbacher, *The Dred Scott Case* (1978) explains the Supreme Court's most infamous decision.

For quizzes, Internet resources, references to additional books and films, and more, consult this book's Online Learning Center site at www.mhhe.com/unfinishednation4.

YOUNG SOLDIER This somber 1864 painting by
Winslow Homer portrays a young Union soldier—
perhaps a drummer boy. When they were not playing
music, drummers and buglers performed other functions
in camp, as barbers, valets, and members of burial teams.
Boys as young as 12 and 13 sometimes joined the army and
grew up quickly in the rough surroundings of the camps.
(*Young Soldier, by Winslow Homer, 1864. Cooper-Hewitt Museum,
Smithsonian Institution. Gift of Charles Savage Homer, 1912-12-
110/Art Resource, NY*)

TIME LINE

1861	1862	1863	
Confederate States of America formed	Battles of Shiloh, Antietam, Second Bull Run	Emancipation Proclamation	
Davis president of Confederacy	Confederacy enacts military draft	Battle of Gettysburg	
Conflict at Fort Sumter		Vicksburg surrenders	
First Battle of Bull Run		Union enacts military draft	
		New York City antidraft riots	

❦

THE CIVIL WAR

The Secession Crisis
The Mobilization of the North
The Mobilization of the South
Strategy and Diplomacy
Campaigns and Battles

By the end of 1860, the cords that had once bound the Union together had snapped. The relatively stable second party system had collapsed, replaced by a new one that accentuated rather than muted regional controversy. The federal government was no longer the remote, unthreatening presence it once had been; the need to resolve the status of the territories had made it necessary for Washington to deal directly with sectional issues. The election of 1860 brought these tensions to a head and precipitated the most terrible war in the nation's history.

THE SECESSION CRISIS

❦

Almost as soon as the news of Abraham Lincoln's election reached the South, militant leaders began to demand an end to the Union.

The Withdrawal of the South

South Carolina, long the hotbed of southern separatism, seceded first, on December 20, 1860. By the time Lincoln took office, six other southern states—Mississippi (January 9, 1861), Florida (January 10), Alabama

	1864	1865	
	Battle of the Wilderness	Lee surrenders to Grant	
	Sherman's March to the Sea	13th Amendment	
	Lincoln reelected		

(January 11), Georgia (January 19), Louisiana (January 26), and Texas (February 1)—had withdrawn from the Union. In February 1861, representatives of the seven seceded states met at Montgomery, Alabama, and formed a new nation—the Confederate States of America. President James Buchanan told Congress in December 1860 that no state had the right to secede from the Union but that the federal government had no authority to stop a state if it did.

The seceding states immediately seized the federal property within their boundaries. But they did not at first have sufficient military power to seize two fortified offshore military installations: Fort Sumter, on an island in the harbor of Charleston, South Carolina, garrisoned by a small force under Major Robert Anderson; and Fort Pickens, in the harbor of Pensacola, Florida. Buchanan refused to yield Fort Sumter when South

Confederacy Established Carolina demanded it. Instead, in January 1861, he ordered an unarmed merchant ship to proceed to Fort Sumter with additional troops and supplies. Confederate guns turned it back. Still, neither section was yet ready to concede that war had begun. And in Washington, efforts began once more to forge a compromise.

The Failure of Compromise

Crittenden Compromise Rejected Gradually, the compromise efforts came together around a proposal first submitted by Senator John J. Crittenden of Kentucky and known as the Crittenden Compromise. The heart of the plan was a proposal to reestablish the Missouri Compromise line and extend it westward to the Pacific coast. Slavery would be prohibited north of the line and permitted south of it. Southerners in the Senate seemed willing to accept the plan. But the compromise would have required the Republicans to abandon their most fundamental position—that slavery not be allowed to expand—and they rejected it.

And so nothing had been resolved when Abraham Lincoln arrived in Washington for his inauguration. In his inaugural address, Lincoln insisted that acts of force or violence to support secession were insurrectionary and that the government would "hold, occupy, and possess" federal property in the seceded states—a clear reference to Fort Sumter.

But Union forces at Fort Sumter were running short of supplies. So Lincoln sent a relief expedition to the fort and informed the South Carolina authorities that he would send no troops or munitions unless the supply ships met with resistance. The new Confederate government ordered General P. G. T. Beauregard, commander of

Fort Sumter Seized Confederate forces at Charleston, to take the fort. When Anderson refused to give up, the Confederates bombarded it for two days, April 12–13, 1861. On April 14, Anderson surrendered. The Civil War had begun.

Almost immediately, four more slave states seceded from the Union and joined the Confederacy: Virginia (April 17, 1861), Arkansas (May 6),

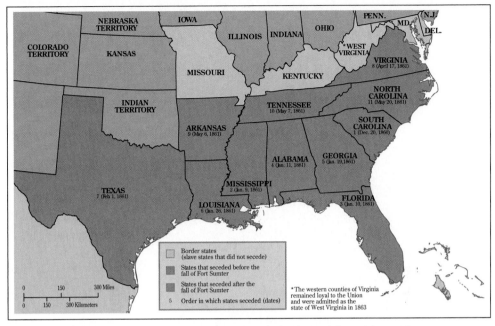

Border states
(slave states that did not secede)

States that seceded before the
fall of Fort Sumter

States that seceded after the
fall of Fort Sumter

5 Order in which states seceded (dates)

*The western counties of Virginia
remained loyal to the Union
and were admitted as the
state of West Virginia in 1863

THE PROCESS OF SECESSION The election of Lincoln, the candidate of the antislavery Republican party, to the presidency had the immediate result of inspiring many of the states in the deep South to secede from the Union, beginning with South Carolina only a little more than a month after the November election. Other states nearer the northern border of the slaveholding region remained in the Union for a time, but the U.S. attempt to resupply Fort Sumter (and the bombardment of the fort by the new Confederate army) mobilized the upper South to secede as well. Only enormous pressure from the federal government kept the slaveholding states of Maryland, Kentucky, and Missouri in the Union. ◆ *What accounted for the creation of the state of West Virginia during the Civil War?*

 For an interactive version of this map go to www.mhhe.com/unfinishednation4ch14maps

Tennessee (May 7), and North Carolina (May 20). The four remaining slave states, Maryland, Delaware, Kentucky, and Missouri—under heavy political pressure from Washington—remained in the Union.

The Opposing Sides

All the important material advantages for waging war lay with the North. It had an advanced industrial system and was able by 1862 to manufacture almost all its own war materials. The South had almost no industry at all.

The North's Material Advantage

In addition, the North had a much better transportation system than did the South, and in particular more and better railroads. During the war, the already inferior Confederate railroad system steadily deteriorated and by the beginning of 1864 had almost collapsed.

Abraham Lincoln, in his 1865 inaugural address, looked back at the beginning of the terrible war that was now nearing its end and said, "All knew [that slavery] was somehow the cause of the war." Few historians dispute that. But disagreement has been sharp over whether slavery was the only, or even the principal cause of the war.

The debate began even before the war itself. In 1858, Senator William H. Seward of New York took note of the two competing explanations of the sectional tensions that were then inflaming the nation. On one side, he said, stood those who believed the conflicts to be "accidental, unnecessary, the work of interested or fanatical agitators." Opposing them stood those (among them Seward himself) who believed there to be "an irrepressible conflict between opposing and enduring forces."

The "irrepressible-conflict" argument dominated historical discussion of the war from the 1860s to the 1920s. War was inevitable, some historians claimed, because there was no room for compromise on the central issue of slavery. Others de-emphasized slavery and pointed to the economic differences between the agrarian South and the industrializing North. Charles and Mary Beard, for example, wrote in 1927 of the "inherent antagonisms" between the interests of planters and those of industrialists. Still others cited social and cultural differences between the two sections as the source of an irrepressible conflict. Slavery, the historian Allan Nevins argued, was only one factor in the cultural divergence that was making residents of the North and South "separate peoples." There were fundamental differences in "assumptions, tastes, and cultural aim" that made it virtually impossible for the two societies to live together in peace.

More recent proponents of irrepressible-conflict arguments similarly emphasize culture and ideology but define the concerns of the North and the South in different terms. Eric Foner, writing in 1970, argued that the moral concerns of abolitionists and the economic concerns of industrialists were less important in explaining Northern hostility to the South than was the broad-based "free-labor" ideology of the region. Northerners opposed slavery because they feared it might spread into their own region and threaten the position of free white laborers.

Other historians have argued that the war was not inevitable, beginning with a group of scholars in the 1920s known as the revisionists. James G. Randall and Avery Craven were the two leading proponents of the view that the differences between the North and the South were not so great as to require a war, that only a "blundering generation" of leaders caused the conflict. Michael Holt revived the revisionist argument in a 1978 book, in which he too emphasized the partisan ambitions of politicians. But Holt also helped introduce another element to the debate. He was, along with Paul Kleppner, Joel Silbey, and William Gienapp, one of the creators of an "ethnocultural" interpretation of the war, which emphasizes that the collapse of the party system—which was central to the coming of the conflict—was a result less of the debate over slavery than of such ethnocultural issues as temperance and nativism. These scholars challenge the arguments of Eric Foner and others that the "free-labor ideal" of the North—and the challenge slavery and its possible expansion into the territories posed to that ideal—was the principal reason for the conflict.

(text continued from page 363)

But the South had advantages as well. The Southern armies were, for the most part, fighting a *Southern Advantages* defensive war on familiar land with local support. The Northern armies, on the other hand, were fighting mostly within the South amid hostile local populations; they had to maintain long lines of communication. The commitment of the white population of the South to the war was, with limited exceptions, clear and firm. In the North, opinion about the war was more divided, and support for it remained shaky until very near the end. A major Southern victory at any one of several crucial moments might have proved decisive by breaking the North's will to continue the struggle. Finally, the dependence of the English and French textile industries on American cotton inclined many leaders in those countries to favor the Confederacy; and Southerners hoped, with some reason, that one or both might intervene on their behalf.

THE MOBILIZATION OF THE NORTH

In the North, the war produced considerable discord, frustration, and suffering. But it also produced prosperity and economic growth. With the South now gone from Congress, the Republican Party had almost unchallenged supremacy. During the war, it enacted an aggressively nationalistic program to promote economic development.

Economic Nationalism

Two acts of 1862 assisted the rapid development of the West. The Homestead Act permitted any citi- *Homestead and Morrill Acts* zen or prospective citizen to purchase 160 acres of public land for a small fee after living on it for five years. The Morrill Act transferred substantial public acreage to the state governments, which could now sell the land and use the proceeds to finance public education. This act led to the creation of many new state colleges and universities, the so-called land-grant institutions. Congress also passed a series of tariff bills that by the end of the war had raised duties to the highest level in the nation's history—a great boon to domestic industries eager for protection from foreign competition, but a hardship for many farmers and other consumers.

Congress also moved to spur completion of a transcontinental railroad. It created two new federally chartered corporations: the Union Pacific Railroad Company, which was to build westward from Omaha, and the Central Pacific, which was to build eastward from California. The two projects were to meet in the middle and complete the link.

National Bank Acts   The National Bank Acts of 1863–1864 created a new national banking system. Existing or newly formed banks could join the system if they had enough capital and were willing to invest one-third of it in government securities. In return, they could issue United States Treasury notes as currency. The new system eliminated much (although not all) of the chaos and uncertainty in the nation's currency.

More difficult than promoting economic growth was financing the war itself. The government tried to do so in three ways: levying taxes, issuing paper currency, and borrowing. Congress levied new taxes on almost all goods and services; and in 1861 the government levied an income tax for the first time. But taxation raised only a small proportion of the funds necessary for financing the war, and strong popular resistance prevented the government from raising the rates.

At least equally controversial was the printing of paper currency, or "greenbacks." The new currency was backed not by gold or silver but simply by the good faith and credit of the government. The value of the greenbacks fluctuated according to the fortunes of *Financing the War*   the Northern armies. Early in 1864, with the war effort bogged down, a greenback dollar was worth only 39 percent of a gold dollar. Even at the close of the war, with confidence high, it was worth only 67 percent of a gold dollar.

By far the largest source of financing for the war was loans. The Treasury persuaded ordinary citizens to buy over $400 million worth of bonds. But public bond purchases constituted only a small part of the government's borrowing, which in the end totaled $2.6 billion, most of it from banks and large financial interests.

Raising the Union Armies

At the beginning of 1861, the regular army of the United States consisted of only 16,000 troops, many of them stationed in the West to protect white settlers from Indians. So the Union, like the Confederacy, had to raise its army mostly from scratch. Lincoln called for an increase of 23,000 in the regular army, but the bulk of the fighting, he knew, would have to be done by volunteers in state militias. When Congress convened in July 1861, it authorized enlisting 500,000 volunteers for three-year (as opposed to the customary three-month) terms.

This voluntary system of recruitment produced adequate forces only briefly, during the first flush of enthusiasm for the war. By March 1863, Congress was forced to pass a national draft law. Virtually all young adult males were eligible to be drafted, although a man could escape service by hiring someone to go in his place or by paying the government a fee of $300.

To many who were accustomed to a remote and inactive national government, conscription was strange and threatening. Opposition to the law was widespread, particularly among laborers, immigrants, and Democrats opposed to the war. Occasionally it erupted into violence. Demonstrators against the draft rioted in New York City for four days in July 1863. Over 100 people died. The riot- *New York City Draft Riots* ers lynched several African Americans and burned down black homes, businesses, and even an orphanage. It was the bloodiest riot in American history. Only the arrival of federal troops halted the violence.

Wartime Leadership and Politics

When Abraham Lincoln arrived in Washington early in 1861, many Republicans considered him a minor politician from the prairie who would be easily controlled by the real leaders of his party. The new president understood his own (and his party's) weaknesses, and he assembled a cabinet representing every faction of the Republican Party and every segment of Northern opinion. But Lincoln was not cowed by the distinguished figures around him. He moved boldly to use the war *Bold Use of* powers of the presidency, blithely ignoring incon- *Presidential Powers* venient parts of the Constitution because, he said, it would be foolish to lose the whole by being afraid to disregard a part.

He sent troops into battle without asking Congress for a declaration of war, arguing that the conflict was a domestic insurrection. He increased the size of the regular army without receiving legislative authority to do so. He unilaterally proclaimed a naval blockade of the South.

Lincoln's greatest political problem was the widespread popular opposition to the war, mobilized by those in the Democratic Party who were known as Peace Democrats (or, by their enemies, *"Copperheads"* "Copperheads"). Lincoln ordered military arrests of civilian dissenters and suspended the right of habeas corpus (the right of an arrested person to receive a speedy trial). At first, Lincoln used these methods only in sensitive areas such as the border states; but in 1862, he proclaimed that all persons who discouraged enlistments or engaged in disloyal practices were subject to martial law.

By the time of the presidential election of 1864, the North was in political turmoil. The Republicans had suffered heavy losses in 1862, and in response leaders of the party tried to create a broad coalition of all the groups that supported the war. They called the new organization the Union Party, but it was, in reality, little more than the Republican Party and a small faction of War Democrats. The Union Party nominated Lincoln for another term as president and Andrew Johnson of Tennessee, a War Democrat who had opposed his state's decision to secede, for the vice presidency.

The Democrats nominated George B. McClellan, *George B. McClellan* a celebrated former Union general, and adopted a platform denouncing the war and calling for a truce. McClellan repudiated that demand, but the Democrats were clearly the peace party in the campaign, trying to profit from growing war weariness. For a time, Lincoln's prospects for reelection seemed doubtful.

At this crucial moment, however, several Northern military victories, particularly the capture of Atlanta, Georgia, early in September, rejuvenated Northern morale and boosted Republican prospects. Lincoln won reelection comfortably, with 212 electoral votes to McClellan's 21.

The Politics of Emancipation

Despite their surface unity in supporting the war and their general agreement on most economic matters, the Republicans disagreed sharply with one another on the issue of slavery. Radicals—led in Congress by such men as Representative Thaddeus Stevens of Pennsylvania and Senators Charles Sumner of Massachusetts and Benjamin Wade of Ohio—wanted to use the war to abolish slavery immediately and completely. Conservatives favored a more cautious policy—in part so as to placate the border slave states that remained, precariously, within the Union.

Nevertheless, momentum began to gather behind emancipation early in the war. In 1861, Congress passed the Confiscation

Confiscation Act

Act, which declared that all slaves used for "insurrectionary" purposes (that is, in support of the Confederate military effort) would be considered freed. Subsequent laws in the spring of 1862 abolished slavery in the District of Columbia and in the western territories and provided for the compensation of owners. In July 1862, Radicals pushed through Congress the second Confiscation Act, which declared free the slaves of persons supporting the insurrection and authorized the president to employ African Americans as soldiers.

As the war progressed, many in the North seemed slowly to accept emancipation as a central war aim; nothing less, they believed, would justify the enormous sacrifices the struggle had required. As a result, the Radicals gained increasing influence within the Republican Party—a development that did not go unnoticed by the president, who decided to seize the leadership of the rising antislavery sentiment himself.

On September 22, 1862, after the Union victory at the Battle of Antietam, the president announced his intention to use his war powers to issue an executive order freeing all slaves in the Confederacy. And on Jan-

The Emancipation Proclamation

uary 1, 1863, he formally signed the Emancipation Proclamation, which declared forever free the slaves inside the Confederacy. The proclamation did not apply to the border slave states, which had never seceded from the Union; nor did it affect those parts of the Confederacy already under Union control (Tennessee, western Virginia, and southern Louisiana). It applied, in short, only to slaves over which the Union had no control. But the document was of great importance because it clearly and irrevocably established that the war was being fought not only to preserve the Union but also to eliminate slavery. Eventually, as federal armies occupied much of the South, the proclamation became a practical reality and led directly to the freeing of thousands of slaves.

AFRICAN-AMERICAN TROOPS Although most of the black soldiers who enlisted in the Union army during the Civil War performed noncombat jobs behind the lines, there were also black combat regiments—members of one of which are pictured here—that fought with great success and valor in critical battles. *(The Library of Congress)*

Even in areas not directly affected by the proclamation, the antislavery impulse gained *The Thirteenth Amendment* strength. By the end of the war, two Union slave states (Maryland and Missouri) and three Confederate states occupied by Union forces (Tennessee, Arkansas, and Louisiana) had abolished slavery. In 1865, finally, Congress approved and the states ratified the Thirteenth Amendment, which abolished slavery as an institution in all parts of the United States. After more than two centuries, legalized slavery finally ceased to exist in the United States.

African Americans and the Union Cause

About 186,000 emancipated blacks served as soldiers, sailors, and laborers for the Union forces. The services of African Americans to the Union military were significant in many ways, not least because of the substantial obstacles many blacks had to surmount in order to enlist.

In the first months of the war, blacks were largely excluded from the military. A few black reg- *Growing Black Enlistment* iments eventually took shape in some of the Union-occupied areas of the Confederacy. But once Lincoln issued the Emancipation Proclamation, black enlistment increased rapidly and the Union military began actively to recruit African-American soldiers and sailors in both the North and, where possible, the South.

Some of these men were organized into fighting units, of which the best known was probably the Fifty-fourth Massachusetts infantry which (like most black regiments) had a white commander: Robert Gould Shaw, a member of an aristocratic Boston family.

Low Status of Black Soldiers Most black soldiers, however, were assigned menial tasks behind the lines such as digging trenches and transporting water. Even though many fewer blacks than whites died in combat, the African-American mortality rate was actually higher than the rate for white soldiers because so many black soldiers died of disease from working long, arduous hours in unsanitary conditions. Conditions for blacks and whites were unequal in other ways as well. Black soldiers were paid a third less than were white soldiers (until Congress changed the law in mid-1864). Black fighting men captured by the Confederates were sent back to their masters (if they were escaped slaves) or executed. In 1864, Confederate soldiers killed over 260 black Union soldiers after capturing them in Tennessee.

Women, Nursing, and the War

The war thrust women into new and often unfamiliar roles. They took over positions vacated by men as teachers, salesclerks, office workers, and mill and factory hands. Above all, women entered nursing, a field previously dominated by men. The United States Sanitary Commission, an organization of civilian volunteers led by Dorothea Dix, mobilized large numbers of female nurses to serve in field hospitals. By the end of the war, women were the dominant force in nursing.

Traditional Gender Norms Reinforced Female nurses encountered considerable resistance from male doctors, many of whom thought it inappropriate for women to be taking care of male strangers. The Sanitary Commission countered such arguments by presenting nursing in domestic terms: as a profession that made use of the same maternal, nurturing roles women played as wives and mothers.

Some women came to see the war as an opportunity to win support for their own goals. Elizabeth Cady Stanton and Susan B. Anthony, who together founded the National Woman's Loyal League *National Woman's Loyal League* in 1863, worked simultaneously for the abolition of slavery and the awarding of suffrage to women.

THE MOBILIZATION OF THE SOUTH

Early in February 1861, representatives of the seven states that had seceded from the Union met at Montgomery, Alabama, to create a new Southern nation. When Virginia seceded several months later, the leaders of the Confederacy moved to Richmond.

There were, of course, important differences between the new Confederate nation and the nation it had left. But there were also important similarities between the Union and the Confederacy.

Confederate Government

The Confederate constitution was almost identical to the Constitution of the United States, with several significant exceptions. It explicitly acknowledged the sovereignty of the individual states (although not the right of secession). And it specifically sanctioned slavery and made its abolition (even by one of the states) practically impossible.

The constitutional convention at Montgomery named a provisional president and vice president: Jefferson Davis of Mississippi and Alexander H. Stephens of Georgia. *Jefferson Davis* They were later elected by the general public, without opposition, for six-year terms. Davis had been a moderate secessionist before the war. Stephens had argued against secession. The Confederate government, like the Union government, was dominated throughout the war by men of the political center.

Davis was a reasonably able administrator, and encountered little interference from the generally tame members of his unstable cabinet. But he rarely provided genuinely national leadership. He spent too much time on routine items, and unlike Lincoln, he displayed a punctiliousness about legal and constitutional requirements inappropriate to the needs of a new nation at war.

There were no formal political parties in the Confederacy, but its congressional and popular politics were badly divided nevertheless. Some white Southerners opposed secession and war altogether. Most white Southerners supported the war, but as in the North many were openly critical of the government and the military, particularly as the tide of battle turned against the South.

States' rights had become such a cult among many white Southerners that they resisted virtually all efforts to exert national authority, even those necessary to win the war. States' rights enthusiasts restricted Davis's ability to impose martial law and *Damaging Emphasis on States' Rights* suspend habeas corpus. They obstructed conscription. Governors such as Joseph Brown of Georgia and Zebulon M. Vance of North Carolina tried at times to keep their own troops apart from the Confederate forces. But the national government was not impotent. It experimented, successfully for a time, with a "food draft," which permitted soldiers to feed themselves by seizing crops from farms in their path. The government impressed slaves to work as laborers on military projects. The Confederacy seized control of the railroads and shipping; it imposed regulations on industry; it limited corporate profits. States' rights sentiment was a significant handicap, but the South nevertheless took dramatic steps in the direction of centralization.

Money and Manpower

Financing the Confederate war effort was a monumental task. The Confederate congress tried at first to requisition funds from the individual

CONFEDERATE VOLUNTEERS Smiling and apparently confident, young Southern soldiers pose for a photograph in 1861, shortly before the First Battle of Bull Run. The Civil War was one of the first military conflicts extensively chronicled by photographers. *(Cook Collection, Valentine Museum)*

states; but the states were as reluctant to tax their citizens as the congress was. In 1863, therefore, the congress enacted an income tax. But taxation produced only about 1 percent of the government's total income. Borrowing was not much more successful. The Confederate government issued bonds in such vast amounts that the public lost faith in them, and efforts to borrow money in Europe using cotton as collateral fared no better.

As a result, the Confederacy had to pay for the war through the least stable, most destructive form of financing: paper currency, which it began issuing in 1861. By 1864, the Confederacy had issued the staggering total of $1.5 billion in paper money. The result was a

Disastrous Inflation

disastrous inflation—a 9,000 percent increase in prices in the course of the war (in contrast to 80 percent in the North).

Like the United States, the Confederacy first raised armies by calling for volunteers. And as in the North, by the end of 1861 voluntary enlistments were declining. In April 1862, therefore, the congress enacted the

Conscription Act

Conscription Act, which subjected all white males between the ages of eighteen and thirty-five to military service for three years. As in the North, a draftee could avoid service if he furnished a substitute. But since the price of substitutes was high, the provision aroused such opposition from poorer whites that it was repealed in 1863.

Even so, conscription worked for a time, in part because enthusiasm for the war was intense and widespread among white men in most of the South. At the end of 1862, about 500,000 soldiers were in the Confederate army. That number did not include the many slave men and women recruited by the military to perform such services as cooking, laundry, and manual labor. Small numbers of slaves and free blacks enlisted in the Confederate army, and a few participated in combat.

After 1862, however, conscription began producing fewer men, and by 1864 the Confederate government faced a critical manpower shortage. The nation was suffering *Critical Manpower Shortage* from intense war weariness, and many had concluded that defeat was inevitable. Nothing could attract or retain an adequate army any longer. In a frantic final attempt to raise men, the congress authorized the conscription of 300,000 slaves, but the war ended before the government could attempt this incongruous experiment.

Economic and Social Effects of the War

The war cut off Southern planters and producers from markets in the North, and a Union blockade *Southern Economic Woes* of Confederate ports made the sale of cotton overseas much more difficult. The war robbed those farms and industries that did not have large slave populations of a male work force. In the North, production of all goods increased during the war; in the South, it declined by more than a third. Above all, the fighting itself wreaked havoc on the Southern landscape, destroying farmland, towns, cities, and railroads. As the war continued, the shortages, the inflation, and the carnage created increasing instability in Southern society. Resistance to conscription, food impressment, and taxation increased throughout the Confederacy, as did hoarding and black-market commerce.

The war forced many women (and some men) to question the prevailing assumption of their soci- *New Roles for Women* ety that females were not suited for the public sphere, since so many women had to perform untraditional, nondomestic tasks during the conflict. The war also decimated the male population. After the war, women outnumbered men in most Southern states by significant margins. The result was a large number of unmarried or widowed women who had no choice but to find employment.

Even before emancipation, the war had far-reaching effects on the lives of slaves. Confederate leaders enforced slave codes with particular severity. Even so, many slaves—especially those near the front—escaped their masters and crossed Union lines.

The American Civil War was an event largely rooted in conditions particular to the United States. But it was also a part of a worldwide movement in the nineteenth century to create large, consolidated nations. America's expansion into the western regions of the continent—and its efforts to incorporate those areas into the nation—was one of the principal causes of the controversies over slavery that led to the Civil War. A commitment to preserving the Union—to consolidating, rather than dismantling, the nation—was one of the principal motives for the North's commitment to fighting a war against the seceding states. Similar efforts at expansion, consolidation, and unification were occurring in many other nations at around the same time.

The consolidation of the nation states was, of course, not new to the nineteenth century. Spain, Britain, Russia, and other nations had united disparate states and regions into substantial nations in the fifteenth, sixteenth, and seventeenth centuries. But nationalism took on new force in the nineteenth century. That was partly because of growing sentiment among peoples who shared language, culture, ethnicity, and tradition and who came to believe that a consolidated nation was the best vehicle for strengthening their common bonds. Nationalism was also a product of the centralization of governments in many areas of the world, and the development within them of the ability to administer large territories from above. The revolutions in America and France in the late eighteenth century—and the subsequent strengthening of the French concept of nationhood under Napoleon in the early nineteenth century—inspired new nationalist enthusiasms in other parts of Europe.

In 1848, a wave of nationalist revolutions erupted in Italy, France, and Austria, challenging the imperial powers that many Europeans believed were subjugating national cultures. Those revolutions failed, but they helped lay the groundwork for the two most important national consolidations of nineteenth-century Europe.

One of them occurred in Germany, which was divided into numerous small, independent states in the early nineteenth century but where popular sentiment for German unification had been growing for decades. It was spurred in part by new histories of the German *volk* (people) and by newly constructed images of German traditions, visible in such literature as Grimm's fairy tales—an effort to record and popularize German folk traditions and make them the basis of a shared sense of a common past. In 1862, King Wilhelm I of Prussia—one of the most powerful of the scattered German states—appointed an aristocratic landowner, Otto von Bismarck, as his prime minister. Bismarck harnessed the growing nationalism throughout the various German states and helped develop a strong popular base for unification. He did so in part by launching Prussian wars against Denmark, Austria, and France—wars Prussia easily won, inspiring pride in German power that extended well beyond Prussia itself. The Franco-Prussian War of 1870 was particularly important, because Prussia fought it to take possession of the French provinces of Alsace and Lorraine—provinces the Prussians claimed were part of the German "national community" because its people, although legally French citizens, were ethnically and linguistically German. In 1871, capitalizing on the widespread nationalist sentiment the war had created throughout the German-speaking states, Bismarck persuaded the German king to proclaim himself emperor (or *Kaiser*) of a new empire that united all German peoples except those in Austria and Switzerland.

The second great European movement for national unification occurred in Italy, which had long been divided into regional kingdoms, city-states, and regions controlled by the Vatican. Some areas of Italy were at one time or another dominated by the French, the Spanish, and the Austro-Hungarian empire. Beginning in the early nineteenth century, Italian nationalists formed what became known as the Young Italy movement, under the leadership of Giuseppe Mazzini. The movement demanded an end of foreign control in Italy and the unification of the Italian people into a single nation. It promoted an idea of the nation as a kind of family, and of its territories as a family home. Peoples with common language, culture, and tradition, Mazzini believed, should be free to unite and govern themselves. But even greater than this growing popular nationalism as a cause of Italian unification were the efforts of powerful and ambitious leaders. The most powerful Italian state in the mid-nineteenth century was the kingdom of the Piedmont and Sardinia in the northwestern part of the peninsula. Its king, Victor Emmanuel II, appointed his own version of Bismarck—Camillo di Cavour—as prime minister in 1852. Cavour joined forces with nationalists in other areas of Italy in an effort to drive the Spanish and the Austrians out of Italian territory. Having first won independence for northern Italy, he joined forces with the southern nationalist leader Giuseppe Garibaldi, who helped win independence in the South and then agreed to a unification of the entire Italian nation under Victor Emmanuel in 1860.

Other nations in these years were also trying to create, preserve, and strengthen nation states. Some failed to do so—Russia, which despite the reform efforts of several tsars, never managed to create a stable nation state from among its broad and diverse peoples; Austria, whose empire could never consolidate its claim over a similarly diverse group of national groups; Turkey, whose Ottoman empire (known as "the sick man of Europe") remained frail despite the efforts of leaders to strengthen it; and China, which likewise tried and failed to produce reforms that would consolidate its vast lands effectively. But others succeeded. Meiji Japan, for example, instituted a series of reforms in the 1880s and 1890s that created a powerful new Japanese nation-state.

In fighting and winning the Civil War, the nationalists of the northern parts of the United States not only preserved the unity of their nation. They also became part of a movement toward the consolidation of national cultures and national territories that extended through many areas of the globe.

(text continued from page 373)

STRATEGY AND DIPLOMACY

The social and economic circumstances of the North and the South helped shape the outcome of the war. But much rested on the military and diplomatic strategies that the two sides employed.

The Commanders

The most important Union military commander was Abraham Lincoln, whose previous military experience consisted only of brief service in his state militia. Lincoln made many mistakes, but he was on the whole a successful commander in chief because he knew how to exploit the North's material advantages. He realized, too, that the proper objective of his armies was the destruction of the Confederate armies and not the occupation of Southern territory. It was fortunate for the North that Lincoln had a good grasp of strategy, because many of his generals did not.

From 1861 to 1864, Lincoln tried time and again to find a chief of staff capable of orchestrating the Union war effort. He turned first to General Winfield Scott, the aging hero of the Mexican War. But Scott was unprepared for the magnitude of the new conflict and soon retired. Lincoln then appointed the young George B. McClellan, who was the commander of the Union forces in the East, the Army of the Potomac; but the proud, arrogant McClellan had a wholly inadequate grasp of strategy and in any case returned to the field in March 1862. For most of the rest of the year, Lincoln had no chief of staff at all. And when he eventually appointed General Henry W. Halleck to the post, he found him an ineffectual strategist. Not until March 1864 did Lincoln finally

U.S. Grant find a general he trusted to command the war effort: Ulysses S. Grant, who shared Lincoln's belief in unremitting combat and in making enemy armies and resources, not enemy territory, the target of military efforts.

Lincoln's handling of the war effort faced constant scrutiny from the Committee on the Conduct of the War, a joint investigative committee of the two houses of Congress. Established in December 1861 and chaired by Senator Benjamin E. Wade of Ohio, it complained constantly of the inadequate ruthlessness of Northern generals, which Radicals on the committee attributed (largely inaccurately) to a secret sympathy among the officers for slavery. The committee's efforts often seriously interfered with the conduct of the war.

Davis's Ineffective Command Southern military leadership centered on President Davis, who was a trained soldier but who failed ever to create an effective central command system. Early in 1862, Davis named General Robert E. Lee as his principal military adviser. But in fact, Davis had no intention of sharing control of strategy with anyone. After a few months, Lee left Richmond to command forces in the field, and for the next two years Davis planned strategy alone. In February 1864, he named General Braxton Bragg as a military adviser, but Bragg never provided much more than technical advice.

At lower levels of command, men of markedly similar backgrounds controlled the war in both the North and the South. Many of the professional officers on both sides were graduates of the United States Military Academy at West Point and the United States Naval Academy at Annapolis. Amateur officers played an important role in both armies as command-

ULYSSES S. GRANT One observer said of Grant (seen here posing for a photograph during the Wilderness campaign of 1864): "He habitually wears an expression as if he had determined to drive his head through a brick wall, and was about to do it." It was an apt metaphor for Grant's military philosophy, which relied on constant, unrelenting assault. One result was that Grant was willing to fight when other Northern generals held back. Another was that Grant presided over some of the worst carnage of the Civil War. *(The Library of Congress)*

ers of volunteer regiments. In both North and South, such men were usually economic or social leaders in their communities who rounded up troops to lead. Sometimes this system produced officers of real ability; more often it did not.

The Role of Sea Power

The Union had an overwhelming advantage in naval power, and it gave its navy two important roles in the war. One was enforcing a blockade of the Southern coast. The other was assisting the Union armies in field operations.

Union Blockade

ROBERT E. LEE Lee was a moderate by the standards of Southern politics in the 1850s. He opposed secession and was ambivalent about slavery. But he could not bring himself to break with his region, and he left the U.S. army to lead Confederate forces beginning in 1861. He was (and remains) the most revered of all the white Southern leaders of the Civil War. For decades after his surrender at Appomattox, he was a symbol to white Southerners of the "Lost Cause." *(Bettmann/Corbis)*

The blockade of the South, which began in the first weeks of the war, kept most oceangoing ships out of Confederate ports, but for a time small blockade runners continued to slip through. Gradually, however, federal forces tightened the blockade by seizing the Confederate ports themselves. The last important port in Confederate hands—Wilmington, North Carolina—fell to the Union early in 1865.

The Confederates made a bold attempt to break the blockade with an ironclad warship, constructed by plating with iron a former United States frigate, the *Merrimac*. On March 8, 1862, the refit-ted *Merrimac*, renamed the *Virginia*, left Norfolk to attack a blockading squadron of wooden ships at nearby Hampton Roads. It destroyed two of the ships and scattered the rest. But the Union gov-

Monitor versus Merrimac

ernment had already built ironclads of its own. And one of them, the *Monitor*, arrived off the coast of Virginia only a few hours after the *Virginia's* dramatic foray. The next day, it met the *Virginia* in battle. Neither vessel was able to sink the other, but the *Monitor* put an end to the *Virginia's* raids and preserved the blockade.

The Union navy was particularly important in the western theater of the war, where the major rivers were navigable by large vessels. The navy transported supplies and troops and joined in attacking Confederate strong points. The South had no significant navy of its own and could defend against the Union gunboats only with ineffective fixed land fortifications.

Europe and the Disunited States

Judah P. Benjamin, the Confederate secretary of state for most of the war, was an intelligent but undynamic man who attended mostly to routine administrative tasks. William Seward, his counterpart *William Seward* in Washington, gradually became one of the outstanding American secretaries of state. He had invaluable assistance from Charles Francis Adams, the American minister to London. The gap between the diplomatic skills of the Union and the Confederacy proved to be a decisive factor in the war.

At the beginning of the conflict, the sympathies of the ruling classes of England and France lay largely with the Confederacy. That was partly because the two nations imported much Southern cotton; but it was also because they were eager to weaken the United States, an increasingly powerful rival to them in world commerce. But France was unwilling to take sides in the conflict unless England did so first. And in England, the government was reluctant to act because there was powerful popular support for the Union—particularly from the large and influential English antislavery movement. After Lincoln issued the Emancipation Proclamation, antislavery groups worked particularly avidly for the Union. Southern leaders hoped to counter the strength of the British antislavery forces by arguing that access to Southern cotton was vital to the English and French textile industries. But English manufacturers had a surplus of both raw cotton and finished goods on hand in 1861 and could withstand a temporary loss of access to American cotton. Later, as the supply of cotton began to diminish, both England and France managed to keep at least some of their mills open by importing cotton from Egypt, India, and other sources. Equally important, even the 500,000 English textile workers thrown out of jobs as a result of mill closings continued to support the North. In the end, therefore, no European nation offered diplomatic recognition to the Confederacy or intervened in the war. No nation wanted to antagonize the United States unless the Confederacy seemed likely to win, and the South never came close enough to victory to convince its potential allies to support it.

Tension with Britain

Even so, there was considerable tension, and on occasion near hostilities, between the United States and Britain. The Union government was angry when Great Britain, France, and other nations declared themselves neutral early in the war, thus implying that the two sides to the conflict had equal stature. Washington was insisting that the conflict was simply a domestic insurrection, not a war between two legitimate governments.

The Trent Affair

A more serious crisis, the so-called *Trent* affair, began in late 1861. Two Confederate diplomats, James M. Mason and John Slidell, had slipped through the then-ineffective Union blockade to Havana, Cuba, where they boarded an English steamer, the *Trent*, for England. Waiting in Cuban waters was the American frigate *San Jacinto*, commanded by the impetuous Charles Wilkes. Acting without authorization, Wilkes stopped the British vessel, arrested the diplomats, and carried them in triumph to Boston. The British government demanded the release of the prisoners, reparations, and an apology. Lincoln and Seward, aware that Wilkes had violated maritime law and unwilling to risk war with England, eventually released the diplomats with an indirect apology.

A second diplomatic crisis produced problems that lasted for years. Unable to construct large ships itself, the Confederacy bought six ships, known as commerce destroyers, from British shipyards. The United States protested that this sale of military equipment to a belligerent violated the laws of neutrality, and the protests became the basis, after the war, of a prolonged battle over damage claims (known as the *Alabama* claims, a name derived from one of the ships) by the United States against Great Britain.

CAMPAIGNS AND BATTLES

In the absence of direct intervention by the European powers, the two contestants in North America were left to resolve the conflict between themselves. They did so in four long years of bloody combat. More than

Staggering Casualties

618,000 Americans died in the course of the Civil War, far more than the 112,000 who perished in World War I or the 405,000 who died in World War II. There were nearly 2,000 deaths for every 100,000 of population during the Civil War. In World War I, the comparable figure was only 109; in World War II, 241.

The Technology of War

Much of what happened on the battlefield in the Civil War was a result of new technologies that transformed the nature of combat.

The most obvious change in the character of warfare in the 1860s was the nature of the armaments that both sides used in battle. Among the most important was the introduction of repeating weapons. Samuel Colt had patented a repeating pistol (the revolver) in 1835, but more important for military purposes was the repeating rifle, introduced in 1860 by Oliver Winchester. Also significant were greatly improved cannons and artillery, a result of advances in iron and steel technology of the previous decades.

It was now impossibly deadly to fight battles as they had been fought for centuries, with lines of infantry soldiers standing erect in the field firing volleys at their opponents until one side withdrew. Soldiers quickly learned that the proper position for combat was staying low to the ground and behind cover. For the first time in the history of organized warfare, therefore, infantry did not fight in formation, and the battlefield became a more chaotic place. Gradually, the deadliness of the new weapons encouraged armies on both sides *Deadlier Weaponry* to spend a great deal of time building elaborate fortifications and trenches to protect themselves from enemy fire. The sieges of Vicksburg and Petersburg, the defense of Richmond, and many other military events all produced the construction of vast fortifications around the cities and around the attacking armies. (They became the predecessors to the great network of trenches that became so central a part of World War I.)

Other weapons technologies were less central to the fighting of the war, but important nevertheless. There was sporadic use of the relatively new technology of hot-air balloons, employed intermittently to provide a view of enemy formations in the field. Ironclad ships such as the *Merrimac* (or *Virginia*) and the *Monitor* suggested the dramatic changes that would soon overtake naval warfare, but did not have a great impact on the fighting of the Civil War. Torpedoes and submarine technology also made a fleeting appearance in the 1860s, showing the way to future innovations in warfare but not playing a major role in the Civil War.

Critical to the conduct of the war, however, were two other relatively new technologies: the railroad and the telegraph. The railroad was particularly important in a war in *Military Importance of Railroads* which millions of soldiers were being mobilized and transferred to the front. Transporting such enormous numbers of soldiers, and the supplies necessary to sustain them, by land or by horse and wagon would have been almost impossible. Railroads made it possible for these large armies to be assembled and moved from place to place. However, they also limited the mobility of the armies. Commanders were forced to organize their campaigns at least in part around the location of the railroads rather than on the basis of the best topography or most direct land route to a destination. The dependence on the rails—and the resulting necessity of concentrating huge numbers of men in a few places—also encouraged commanders to prefer great battles with large armies rather than smaller engagements with fewer troops.

The impact of the telegraph on the war was limited both by the scarcity of qualified telegraph operators and by the difficulty of bringing telegraph wires into the fields where battles were being fought. Things improved somewhat after the new U.S. Military Telegraph Corps, headed by Thomas Scott and Andrew Carnegie, trained and employed over 1,200 operators. Gradually, too, both the Union and Confederate armies learned to string telegraph wires along the routes of their troops, so that field commanders were able to stay in close touch with one another during battles.

The Opening Clashes, 1861

The Union and the Confederacy fought their first major battle of the war in northern Virginia. A Union army of over 30,000 men under the command of General Irvin McDowell was stationed just outside Washington. About thirty miles away, at Manassas, was a slightly smaller Confederate army under P. G. T. Beauregard. If the Northern army could destroy the Southern one, Union leaders believed, the war might end at once. In mid-July, McDowell marched his inexperienced troops toward Manassas. Beauregard moved his troops behind Bull Run, a small stream north of Manassas, and called for reinforcements, which reached him the day before the battle.

First Battle of Bull Run On July 21, in the First Battle of Bull Run, or First Battle of Manassas, McDowell almost succeeded in dispersing the Confederate forces. But the Southerners managed to stop a last strong Union assault and then began a savage counterattack. The Union troops suddenly panicked, broke ranks, and retreated chaotically. McDowell was unable to reorganize them, and he had to order a retreat to Washington—a disorderly withdrawal complicated by the presence along the route of many civilians, who had ridden down from the capital, picnic baskets in hand, to watch the battle from nearby hills. The Confederates, as disorganized by victory as the Union forces were by defeat, did not pursue. The battle was a severe blow to Union morale and to the president's confidence in his officers.

Elsewhere, Union forces achieved some small but significant victories in 1861. Nathaniel Lyon, who commanded a small regular army force in St. Louis, moved his troops into southern Missouri to face secessionists trying to lead the state out of the Union. On August 10, at the Battle of Wilson's Creek, he was defeated and killed—but not before he had seriously weakened the striking power of the Confederates.

Meanwhile, a Union force under George B. McClellan moved east *West Virginia Established* from Ohio into western Virginia. By the end of 1861, it had "liberated" the antisecession mountain people of the region, who created their own state government loyal to the Union; the state was admitted to the Union as West Virginia in 1863.

THE WAR IN THE WEST, 1861–1863 While the Union armies in Virginia were meeting with repeated frustrations, the Union armies in the West were scoring notable successes in the first two years of the war. This map shows a series of Union drives in the western Confederacy. Admiral David Farragut's ironclads led to the capture of New Orleans—a critical Confederate port—in April 1862, while forces further north under the command of Ulysses S. Grant drove the Confederate army out of Kentucky and western Tennessee. These battles culminated in the Union victory at Shiloh, which led to Union control of the upper Mississippi River. ◆ *Why was control of the Mississippi so important to both sides?*

 For an interactive version of this map go to www.mhhe.com/unfinishednation4ch14maps

The Western Theater, 1862

After the battle at Bull Run, military operations in the East settled into a long and frustrating stalemate. The first decisive operations in 1862 occurred in the western theater. Here Union forces were trying to seize control of the southern part of the Mississippi River. Northern soldiers advanced on the southern Mississippi from both the north and south, moving down the river from Kentucky and up from the Gulf of Mexico toward New Orleans.

In April, a Union squadron of ironclads and wooden vessels commanded by David G. Farragut smashed past weak Confederate forts near the mouth of the Mississippi, and from there sailed up to New Orleans. The city was virtually defenseless because the Confederate high command had expected the attack to come from the north. The surrender of New Orleans on April 25, 1862, was an important turning point in the war. From then on, the mouth of the Mississippi was closed to Confederate trade, and the South's largest city and most important banking center was in Union hands.

New Orleans Seized

Farther north in the western theater, Confederate troops under the command of Albert Sidney Johnston were stretched out in a long defensive line around two forts in Tennessee, Fort Henry and Fort Donelson. Early in 1862, Ulysses S. Grant attacked Fort Henry, whose defenders, awed by the ironclad riverboats accompanying the Union army, surrendered with almost no resistance on February 6. Grant then moved both his naval and ground forces to Fort Donelson, where the Confederates put up a stronger fight but finally, on February 16, had to surrender. Grant thus gained control of river communications and forced Confederate troops out of Kentucky and half of Tennessee.

With about 40,000 men, Grant now advanced south along the Tennessee River. At Shiloh, Tennessee, he met a force almost equal to his own, commanded by Albert Sidney Johnston and P. G. T. Beauregard. The result was the Battle of Shiloh, April 6–7. In the first day's fighting (during which Johnston was killed), the Southerners drove Grant back to the river. But the next day, reinforced by 25,000 fresh troops, Grant recovered the lost ground and forced Beauregard to withdraw. After the narrow Union victory at Shiloh, Northern forces occupied Corinth, Mississippi, and took control of the Mississippi River as far south as Memphis.

Shiloh

Braxton Bragg, now in command of the Confederate army in the West, gathered his forces at Chattanooga, in eastern Tennessee, where he faced a Union army trying to capture Chattanooga. The two armies maneuvered for advantage inconclusively in northern Tennessee and southern Kentucky for several months until they finally met, on December 31–January 2, in the Battle of Murfreesboro, or Stone's River. Bragg was forced to withdraw to the South in defeat.

By the end of 1862, therefore, Union forces had made considerable progress in the West. But the major conflict remained in the East.

The Virginia Front, 1862

McClellan's Peninsular Campaign

During the winter of 1861–1862, George B. McClellan, commander of the Army of the Potomac, concentrated on training his army of 150,000 men

THE VIRGINIA THEATER, 1861–1863 Much of the fighting during the first two years of the Civil War took place in what became known as the Virginia theater—although the campaigns in this region eventually extended north into Maryland and Pennsylvania. The Union hoped for a quick victory over the newly created Confederate army. But as these maps show, the southern forces consistently thwarted those hopes. The map at top left shows the battles of 1861 and the first half of 1862, almost all of them won by the Confederates. The map at lower left shows the last months of 1862, during which the southerners again defeated the Union in most of their engagements—although northern forces drove the Confederates back from Maryland in September. The large map on the right shows the troop movements that led to the climactic battle of Gettysburg in 1863. ◆ *Why were the Union forces unable to profit more from material advantages during these first years of the war?*

 For an interactive version of this map go to www.mhhe.com/unfinishednation4ch14maps

near Washington. Finally, he designed a spring campaign to capture the Confederate capital at Richmond. But instead of heading overland directly toward Richmond, McClellan chose a complicated route that he thought would circumvent the Confederate defenses. The navy would carry his troops down the Potomac to a peninsula east of Richmond, between the York and James Rivers; the army would approach the city from there. The combined operations became known as the Peninsular campaign.

McClellan set off with 100,000 men, reluctantly leaving 30,000 members of his army behind, under General Irvin McDowell, to protect Washington. McClellan eventually persuaded Lincoln to send him the additional men. But before the president could do so, a Confederate army under Thomas J. ("Stonewall") Jackson staged a rapid march north through the Shenandoah Valley, as if preparing to cross the Potomac and attack Washington. Lincoln postponed sending reinforcements to McClellan, retaining McDowell's corps to head off Jackson. In the Valley campaign of May 4–June 9, 1862, Jackson defeated two separate Union forces and slipped away before McDowell could catch him.

Meanwhile, McClellan was battling Confederate troops under Joseph E. Johnston outside Richmond in the two-day Battle of Fair Oaks, or Seven Pines (May 31–June 1), and holding his ground. John-ston, badly wounded, was replaced by Robert E. Lee, *Robert E. Lee* who then recalled Stonewall Jackson from the Shenandoah Valley. With a combined force of 85,000 to face McClellan's 100,000, Lee launched a new offensive, known as the Battle of the Seven Days (June 25–July 1), in an effort to cut McClellan off from his base on the York River. But McClellan fought his way across the peninsula and set up a new base on the James.

McClellan was now only twenty-five miles from Richmond and in a good position to renew the campaign. But despite continuing pressure from Lincoln, he did not advance. The president finally ordered the army to move back to northern Virginia and join a smaller force under John Pope. The president hoped to begin a new offensive against Richmond on the direct overland route that he himself had always preferred. As the Army of the Potomac left the peninsula by water, Lee moved north with the Army of Northern Virginia to strike Pope before McClellan could join him. Pope was as rash as McClellan was cautious, and he attacked the approaching Confederates without waiting for the arrival of all of McClellan's troops. In the Second Battle of Bull Run, or Manassas (August 29–30), Lee threw back the assault and routed Pope's army, which fled to Washington. With hopes for an overland campaign against Richmond now in disarray, Lincoln removed Pope from command and put McClellan back in charge of all the federal forces in the region.

Lee soon went on the offensive again, heading north through western Maryland, and McClellan moved out to meet him. McClellan had the good luck to get a copy of Lee's orders, which revealed that a part of the Confederate army, under Stonewall Jackson, had separated from the rest to

SKIRMISH AT ANTIETAM The American public followed the course of the Civil War through newspaper reports and, at times, through published drawings of the battlefields by traveling artists who sketched important events for publication. Photographers chronicled the war as well. But cameras in the 1860s could not easily capture action scenes, and very few newspapers or magazines were technologically equipped to publish photographs. So drawings such as this one by A. R. Waud—of a Brooklyn, New York, regiment fighting Southern cavalry at the battle of Antietam—were much in demand. *(Bettmann/Corbis)*

attack Harpers Ferry. But instead of attacking quickly before the Confederates could recombine, McClellan stalled and gave Lee time to pull most of his forces together behind Antietam Creek, near the town of Sharpsburg. There, on September 17, *Antietam* McClellan's 87,000–man army repeatedly attacked Lee's force of 50,000, with staggering casualties on both sides. Late in the day, just as the Confederate line seemed ready to break, the last of Jackson's troops arrived from Harpers Ferry to reinforce it. McClellan might have broken through with one more assault. Instead, he allowed Lee to retreat into Virginia. Technically, Antietam was a Union victory; but in reality, McClellan had squandered an opportunity to destroy much of the Confederate army. In November, Lincoln finally removed McClellan from command for good.

McClellan's replacement, Ambrose E. Burnside, was a short-lived mediocrity. He tried to move toward Richmond by crossing the Rappahannock River at Fredericksburg. There, on December 13, he launched a series of attacks against Lee, all of them bloody, all of them hopeless. After losing a large part of his army, he withdrew to the north bank of the Rappahannock. He was relieved at his own request. The year 1862 ended, therefore, with a series of frustrations for the Union.

1863: Year of Decision

At the beginning of 1863, General Joseph Hooker was commanding the still-formidable Army of the Potomac, which remained north of the Rappahannock, opposite Fredericksburg. Taking part of his army, Hooker crossed the river above Fredericksburg and moved toward the town and Lee's army. But at the last minute, he drew back to a defensive position in a desolate area of brush and scrub trees known as the Wilderness. Lee divided his forces for a dual assault on the Union army. In the Battle of Chancellorsville, May 1–5, Stonewall Jackson attacked the Union right and Lee himself charged the front. Hooker barely managed to escape with his army. Lee had frustrated Union objectives, but he had not destroyed the Union army. And his ablest officer, Jackson, was fatally wounded in the course of the battle.

Chancellorsville

While the Union forces were suffering repeated frustrations in the East, they were winning some important victories in the West. In the spring of 1863, Ulysses S. Grant was driving at Vicksburg on the Mississippi River. Vicksburg was well protected on land and had good artillery coverage of the river itself. But in May, Grant boldly moved men and supplies—over land and by water—to an area south of the city, where the terrain was reasonably good. He then attacked Vicksburg from the rear. Six weeks later, on July 4, Vicksburg—whose residents were by then literally starving as a result of the prolonged siege—surrendered. At almost the same time, the other Confederate strong point on the river, Port Hudson, Louisiana, also surrendered to a Union force that had moved north from New Orleans. The Union had achieved one of its basic military aims: control of the whole length of the Mississippi. The Confederacy was split in two, with Louisiana, Arkansas, and Texas cut off from the other seceded states. The victories on the Mississippi were one of the great turning points of the war.

Vicksburg

During an early stage of the siege of Vicksburg, Lee proposed an invasion of Pennsylvania, which would, he argued, divert Union troops north. Further, he argued, if he could win a major victory on Northern soil, England and France might come to the Confederacy's aid. The war-weary North might even quit the war before Vicksburg fell.

In June 1863, Lee moved up the Shenandoah Valley into Maryland and then entered Pennsylvania. The Union Army of the Potomac, commanded first by Hooker and then (after June 28) by George C. Meade, moved north, too. The two armies finally encountered one another at the small town of Gettysburg, Pennsylvania. There, on July 1–3, 1863, they fought the most celebrated battle of the war.

Meade's army established a strong, well-protected position on the hills south of the town. Lee attacked, but his first assault on the Union forces on Cemetery Ridge failed. A day later, he ordered a second, larger effort. In what is remembered as Pickett's Charge, a force of 15,000 Confederate soldiers

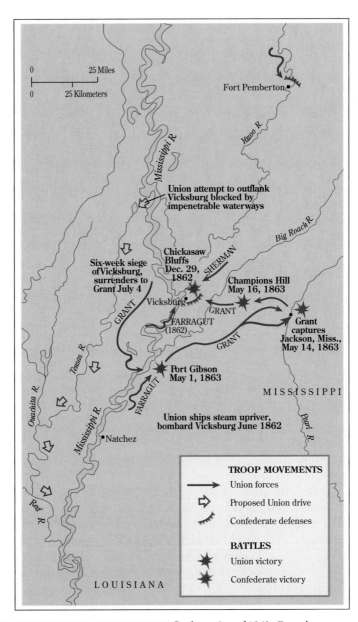

THE SIEGE OF VICKSBURG, MAY–JULY 1863 In the spring of 1863, Grant began a campaign to win control of the final piece of the Mississippi River still controlled by the Confederacy. To do that required capturing the southern stronghold at Vicksburg—a well-defended city sitting above the river. Vicksburg's main defenses were to its north, so Grant boldly moved men and supplies around the city and attacked it from the south. Eventually, he cut off the city's access to the outside world, and after a six-week siege, its residents finally surrendered. ◆ *What impact did the combined victories at Vicksburg and Gettysburg have on northern commitment to the war?*

 For an interactive version of this map go to www.mhhe.com/unfinishednation4ch14maps

GETTYSBURG, JULY 1–3, 1863 Gettysburg was the most important single battle of the Civil War. Had Confederate forces prevailed at Gettysburg, the future course of the war might well have been very different. The map on the left shows the distribution of Union and Confederate forces at the beginning of the battle, July 1, after Lee had driven the northern forces south of town. The map on the right reveals the pattern of the attacks on July 2 and 3. Note, in particular, Pickett's bold and costly charge, whose failure on July 3 was the turning point in the battle and, some have argued, the war. ◆ *Why did Robert E. Lee believe that an invasion of Pennsylvania would advance the Confederate cause?*

advanced for almost a mile across open country while being swept by Union fire. Only about 5,000 made it up the ridge, and this remnant finally had to surrender or retreat. By now, Lee had lost nearly a third of his army. On July 4, the same day as the surrender of Vicksburg, he withdrew from Get-

Gettysburg   tysburg. The retreat was another major turning point in the war. Never again were the weakened Confederate forces able seriously to threaten Northern territory.

Before the end of the year, there was another important turning point, this one in Tennessee. After occupying Chattanooga on September 9, Union forces under William Rosecrans began an unwise pursuit of Bragg's retreating Confederate forces. The two armies engaged in western Georgia, in the Battle of Chickamauga (September 19–20). Union forces could not break the Confederate lines and retreated back to Chattanooga.

Bragg now began a siege of Chattanooga itself, seizing the heights nearby and cutting off fresh supplies to the Union forces. Grant came to

Battle of Chattanooga   the rescue. In the Battle of Chattanooga (November 23–25), the reinforced Union army drove the

Confederates back into Georgia. Union forces had now achieved a second important objective: control of the Tennessee River.

The Last Stage, 1864–1865

By the beginning of 1864, Ulysses S. Grant had become general in chief of all the Union armies. Grant believed in using the North's great advantage in troops and material resources to overwhelm the South. He planned two great offensives for 1864. In Virginia, the Army of the Potomac would advance toward Richmond and force Lee into a decisive battle. In Georgia, the western army, under William T. Sherman, would advance east toward Atlanta and destroy the remaining Confederate force, now under the command of Joseph E. Johnston.

The northern campaign began when the Army of the Potomac, 115,000 strong, plunged into the *Grant's Northern Campaign* rough, wooded Wilderness area of northwestern Virginia in pursuit of Lee's 75,000-man army. After avoiding an engagement for several weeks, Lee turned Grant back in the Battle of the Wilderness (May 5–7). Without stopping to rest or reorganize, Grant resumed his march toward Richmond and met Lee again in the bloody, five-day Battle of Spotsylvania Court House, in which 12,000 Union troops and a large, but unknown, number of Confederates fell. Grant kept moving, but victory continued to elude him. Lee kept his army between Grant and the Confederate capital and on June 1–3 repulsed the Union forces again, just northeast of Richmond, at Cold Harbor.

Grant now moved his army east of Richmond and headed south toward the railroad center at Petersburg. If he could seize Petersburg, he could cut off the capital's communications with the rest of the Confederacy. But Petersburg had strong defenses; and once Lee came to the city's relief, the assault became a prolonged siege.

In Georgia, meanwhile, Sherman was facing less ferocious resistance. With 90,000 men, he confronted Confederate forces of 60,000 under Johnston. As Sherman advanced, Johnston tried to delay him by maneuvering. The two armies fought only one real battle—Kennesaw Mountain, northwest of Atlanta, on June 27—where Johnston scored an impressive victory. Even so, he was unable to stop the Union *Atlanta Taken* advance toward Atlanta. Sherman took the city on September 2 and burned it.

Hood now tried unsuccessfully to draw Sherman out of Atlanta by moving back up through Tennessee and threatening an invasion of the North. Sherman sent Union troops to reinforce Nashville. In the Battle of Nashville on December 15–16, 1864, Northern forces practically destroyed what was left of Hood's army.

Meanwhile, Sherman had left Atlanta to begin his soon-to-be-famous "March to the Sea." Living off the land, *"March to the Sea"* destroying supplies it could not use, his army cut

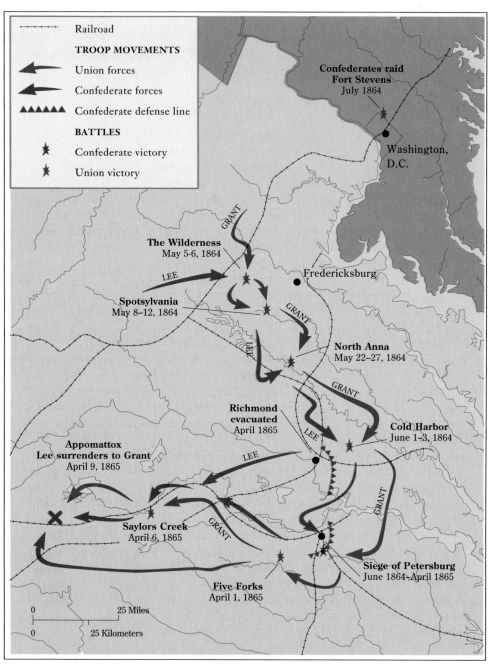

Map Legend:

- ┄┄┄┄ Railroad

TROOP MOVEMENTS
- ◄━━━ Union forces
- ◄━━━ Confederate forces
- ▲▲▲▲▲ Confederate defense line

BATTLES
- ✳ Confederate victory
- ✳ Union victory

Confederates raid
Fort Stevens
July 1864

Washington, D.C.

GRANT

The Wilderness
May 5-6, 1864

LEE

Fredericksburg

Spotsylvania
May 8–12, 1864

GRANT

LEE

North Anna
May 22–27, 1864

GRANT

Richmond evacuated
April 1865

LEE

Cold Harbor
June 1–3, 1864

Appomattox Lee surrenders to Grant
April 9, 1865

LEE

GRANT

Saylors Creek
April 6, 1865

GRANT

Five Forks
April 1, 1865

Siege of Petersburg
June 1864–April 1865

0   25 Miles
0   25 Kilometers

VIRGINIA CAMPAIGNS, 1864–1865 From the Confederate defeat at (and retreat from) Gettysburg until the end of the war, most of the eastern fighting took place in Virginia. By now, Ulysses S. Grant was commander of all Union forces and had taken over the Army of the Potomac. Although Confederate forces won a number of important battles during the Virginia campaign, the Union army grew steadily stronger and the southern forces steadily weaker. Grant believed that the Union strategy should reflect the North's greatest advantage: its superiority in men and equipment. ◆ *What effect did this decision have on the level of casualties?*

 For an interactive version of this map go to www.mhhe.com/unfinishednation4ch14maps

SHERMAN'S MARCH TO THE SEA, 1864–1865 While Grant was wearing Lee down in Virginia, General William Tecumseh Sherman was moving east across Georgia. After a series of battles in Tennessee and northwest Georgia, Sherman captured Atlanta and then marched unimpeded to Savannah, on the Georgia coast—deliberately devastating the towns and plantations through which his troops marched. Note that after capturing Savannah by Christmas 1864, Sherman began moving North through the Carolinas. A few days after Lee surrendered to Grant at Appomattox, Confederate forces further south surrendered to Sherman. ◆ *What did Sherman believe his devastating March to the Sea would accomplish?*

 For an interactive version of this map go to www.mhhe.com/unfinishednation4ch14maps

a sixty-mile-wide swath of desolation across Georgia. Sherman sought not only to deprive the Confederate army of war materials and railroad communications but also to break the will of the Southern people by burning towns and plantations along his route. By December 20, he had reached Savannah, which surrendered two days later. Early in 1865, Sherman continued his destructive march, moving northward through South Carolina. He was virtually unopposed until he was well inside North Carolina, where a small force under Johnston could do no more than cause a brief delay.

In April 1865, Grant's Army of the Potomac—still engaged in the prolonged siege at Petersburg—finally captured a vital railroad junction southwest of the town. Without rail access to the South, and plagued by heavy casualties and massive desertions, Lee informed the Confederate government that he could no longer defend Richmond. Within hours, Jefferson Davis, his cabinet, and as much of the white population as could find transportation fled. That night, mobs roamed the city, setting devastating fires. And the next morning, Northern forces entered the Confederate capital. With them was Abraham Lincoln, who walked through the streets of the burned-out city surrounded by black men and women cheering him as the "Messiah" and "Father Abraham." In one particularly stirring moment, the president turned to a former slave kneeling on the street before him and said: "Don't kneel to me. . . . You must kneel to God only, and thank Him for the liberty you will enjoy hereafter."

With the remnant of his army, now about 25,000 men, Lee began moving west in the forlorn hope of finding a way around the Union forces so that he could move south and link up with Johnston in North Carolina. But the Union army pursued him and blocked his escape route. Lee finally recognized that further bloodshed was futile. He arranged to meet Grant

Appomattox Courthouse   at a private home in the small town of Appomattox Courthouse, Virginia, where on April 9 he surrendered what was left of his forces. Nine days later, near Durham, North Carolina, Johnston surrendered to Sherman.

The long war was now effectively over. Jefferson Davis was finally captured in Georgia. A few Southern diehards continued to fight, but even their resistance collapsed before long.

CONCLUSION

The American Civil War began with high hopes and high ideals on both sides. In the North and the South alike, thousands of men enthusiastically enlisted in local regiments and went off to war. Four years later, over 600,000 of them were dead and many more maimed and traumatized for life. A fight for "principles" and "ideals"—a fight few people had thought would last more than a few months—had become one of the longest wars, and by far the bloodiest war, in American history, before or since.

During the first two years of fighting, the Confederate forces seemed to have all the advantages. They were fighting on their own soil. Their troops seemed more committed to the cause than those of the North. Their commanders were exceptionally talented, while Union forces were, for a time, erratically led. Gradually, however, the Union's advantages began to assert themselves. The North had a stabler political system led by one of the greatest leaders in the nation's history. It had a much larger population, a far more developed industrial economy, superior financial institutions, and a better railroad system. By the middle of 1863, the tide of the war had shifted; over the next two years, Union forces gradually wore down the Confederate armies before finally triumphing in 1865.

The war strengthened the North's economy, giving a spur to industry and railroad development. It greatly weakened the South's, by destroying millions of dollars of property and depleting the region's young male population. Southerners had gone to war in part because of their fears of growing northern dominance. The war itself, ironically, confirmed and strengthened that dominance.

But most of all, the Civil War was a victory for millions of African-American slaves. The war produced Abraham Lincoln's epochal Emancipation Proclamation and, later, the Thirteenth Amendment to the Constitution, which abolished slavery altogether. It also encouraged hundreds of thousands of slaves literally to free themselves, to desert their masters and seek refuge behind Union lines—at times to fight in the Union armies. The future of the freed slaves was not to be an easy one, but three and a half million people who had once lived in bondage emerged from the war as free men and women.

FOR FURTHER REFERENCE

James McPherson, *Battle Cry of Freedom* (1988) is a fine general history of the Civil War. Shelby Foote, *The Civil War: A Narrative,* 3 vols. (1958–1974) recounts the military history of the war with great literary power. David A. Mindell, *Technology and Experience aboard the USS Monitor* (2000) is an excellent study of the role of technology in major Civil War naval battles. David Herbert Donald, *Lincoln* (1995) is the best modern biography of the sixteenth president. Douglas Southall Freeman, *Robert E. Lee,* 4 vols. (1934–1935), William McFeely, *Grant* (1981), and Brooks D. Simpson, *Ulysses S. Grant: Triumph Over Adversity, 1822–1865* (2000) are significant biographies of the two most important Civil War generals. Philip Shaw Paludan, *"A People's Contest": The Union at War, 1861–1865* (1988) is a good account of the social impact of the war in the North. Iver Bernstein, *The New York City Draft Riots* (1990) examines an important event away from the battlefield. Alvin Josephy, *The Civil War in the West* (1992) remedies a long-neglected aspect of the war. Emory Thomas, *The Confederate Nation* (1979) is a fine one-volume history of the Confederacy. Ira Berlin et al., eds., *Free At Last: A Documentary History of Slavery, Freedom and the Civil War* (1992) is a superb compilation of primary sources from slaves and slaveowners relating to the demise of slavery during the Civil War years. Ira Berlin et al., *Slaves No More: Three Essays on Emancipation and the Civil War* (1992), the companion volume to the documents in *Free At Last,* argues that slaves and freedmen played an active role in destroying slavery and redefining freedom. Jeannie Attie, *Patriotic Toil: Northern Women and the American Civil War* (1998) examines the role of women. Catherine Clinton and Nina Silber, *Divided Houses* (1992) is a collection of essays in the "new social history" from various historians demonstrating the importance of gender to the history of the Civil War. *The Civil War* (1989), Ken Burns's outstanding popular and award-winning, nine-hour epic documentary has shaped the recent popular image of the conflict for many Americans.

For quizzes, Internet resources, references to additional books and films, and more, consult this book's Online Learning Center site at www.mhhe.com/unfinishednation4.

THE GENIUS OF FREEDOM This 1874 lithograph portrays a series of important moments in the history of African Americans in the South during Reconstruction—among them the participation of black soldiers in the Civil War, a speech by a black representative in the South Carolina legislature, and the movement of African-American workers from slavery into a system of free labor. It also portrays some of the white leaders (among them Lincoln and Charles Sumner) who had promoted the cause of the freedman. *(Chicago Historical Society)*

TIME LINE

1863	1864	1865	1866	1867	1868	1869
Lincoln announces Reconstruction plan	Lincoln vetoes Wade-Davis bill	Lincoln assassinated; Johnson is president	Republicans gain in congressional elections	Congressional Reconstruction begins	Grant elected president	Congress passes 15th Amendment
		Freedmen's Bureau			Johnson impeached and acquitted	
		Joint Committee on Reconstruction			14th Amendment ratified	

RECONSTRUCTION AND THE NEW SOUTH

The Problems of Peacemaking
Radical Reconstruction
The South in Reconstruction
The Grant Administration
The Abandonment of Reconstruction
The New South

Few periods in the history of the United States have produced as much bitterness or created such enduring controversy as the era of Reconstruction—the years following the Civil War during which Americans attempted to reunite their shattered nation. To many white Southerners, Reconstruction was a vicious and destructive experience—a period when vindictive Northerners inflicted humiliation and revenge on the prostrate South. Northern defenders of Reconstruction, in contrast, argued that their policies were the only way to prevent unrepentant Confederates from restoring Southern society to what it had been before the war.

To most African Americans at the time, and to many people of all races since, Reconstruction was notable for other reasons. Neither a vicious tyranny, as white Southerners charged, nor a thoroughgoing reform, as many Northerners hoped, it was, rather, a small but important first step in the effort to secure civil rights and economic power for the former slaves. Reconstruction did not provide African Americans with either the legal protections or the material resources to assure them anything like real equality. Most black men and women who continued to live in what came to be known as the New South had little power to resist their oppression for many decades.

And yet for all its shortcomings, Reconstruction did help African Americans create some new institutions and some important legal precedents that helped them survive and that ultimately, well into the twentieth century, became the basis of later efforts to win freedom and equality.

1872	1873	1875	1877	1883	1890s	1895	1896
Grant reelected	Panic and depression	"Whiskey ring" scandal	Hayes wins disputed election	Supreme Court upholds segregation	Jim Crow laws in South	Atlanta Compromise	*Plessy* v. *Ferguson*
			Compromise of 1877 ends Reconstruction				

THE PROBLEMS OF PEACEMAKING

In 1865, when it became clear that the war was almost over, no one in Washington was certain about what to do. Abraham Lincoln could not negotiate a treaty with the defeated government; he continued to insist that the Confederate government had no legal right to exist. Yet neither could he simply readmit the Southern states into the Union.

The Aftermath of War and Emancipation

The Devastated South   The South after the Civil War was a desolate place. Towns had been gutted, plantations burned, fields neglected, bridges and railroads destroyed. Many white Southerners—stripped of their slaves through emancipation and stripped of the capital they had invested in now worthless Confederate bonds and currency—had almost no personal property. More than 258,000 Confederate soldiers had died in the war, and thousands more returned home wounded or sick. Some white Southerners faced starvation and homelessness.

If conditions were bad for Southern whites, they were far worse for Southern blacks—the three and a half million men and women now emerging from bondage. As soon as the war ended, hundreds of thousands of them left their plantations in search of a new life in freedom. But most had nowhere to go, and few had any possessions except the clothes they wore.

Competing Notions of Freedom

For blacks and whites alike, Reconstruction became a struggle to define the meaning of freedom. But the former slaves and the defeated whites had very different conceptions of what freedom meant.

Some blacks believed the only way to secure freedom was to have the government take land away from white people, who owned virtually all of it, and give it to black people, who owned virtually none. Others asked only for legal equality, confident that they could advance successfully in American society once the formal obstacles to their advancement disap-

Black Desire for Independence   peared. But whatever their particular demands, virtually all former slaves were united in their desire for independence from white control. Throughout the post-Civil War South, African Americans separated themselves from white institutions—pulling out of white-controlled churches and establishing their own, creating clubs and societies for their own people, and in some cases starting their own schools.

For most white Southerners, freedom meant something very different. It meant the ability to control their own destinies without interference from the North or the federal government. And in the immediate af-

RICHMOND, 1865 By the time Union forces captured Richmond in early 1865, the Confederate capital had been under siege for months and much of the city lay in ruins, as this photograph reveals. On April 4, President Lincoln, accompanied by his son Tad, visited Richmond. As he walked through the streets of the shattered city, hundreds of former slaves emerged from the rubble to watch him pass. "No triumphal march of a conqueror could have equalled in moral sublimity the humble manner in which he entered Richmond," a black soldier serving with the Union army wrote. "It was a great deliverer among the delivered. No wonder tears came to his eyes." (*The Library of Congress*)

termath of the war, they attempted to exercise this version of freedom by trying to restore their society to its antebellum form. When these white Southerners fought for what they considered freedom, they were fighting above all to preserve local and regional autonomy and white supremacy.

In the immediate aftermath of the war, the federal government's contribution to solving the question of the future of the South was modest. Federal troops remained in the South to preserve order and protect the freedmen. And in March 1865, Congress established the Freedmen's Bureau, an agency of the army directed by General Oliver O. Howard. The Freedmen's Bureau distributed food to millions *The Freedmen's Bureau* of former slaves. It established schools, staffed by missionaries and teachers who had been sent to the South by Freedmen's Aid Societies and other private and church groups in the North. It made a modest effort to settle blacks on lands of their own. But the Freedmen's Bureau was not a permanent solution. It had authority to operate for only one year, and it was, in any case, far too small to deal effectively with the enormous problems facing Southern society. By the time the war ended, other proposals for reconstructing the defeated South were emerging.

A MONUMENT TO THE CONFEDERATE DEAD This monument in the town square of Greenwood, South Carolina, was typical of many such memorials erected all across the South in the aftermath of the Civil War. They served to commemorate the soldiers who had died in the struggle, but also to remind white Southerners of what was by the 1870s already widely known and romanticized as the "Lost Cause." *(Museum of the Confederacy, Richmond, Virginia)*

Plans for Reconstruction

Control of Reconstruction was in the hands of the Republicans, who were divided in their approach to the issue. Conservatives within the party insisted that the South accept the abolition of slavery, but they proposed few other conditions for the readmission of the seceded states. The Radicals,

Thaddeus Stevens and Charles Sumner

led by Representative Thaddeus Stevens of Pennsylvania and Senator Charles Sumner of Massachusetts, urged a much harsher course, including disenfranchising large numbers of Southern whites, protecting black civil rights, and confiscating the property of wealthy white Southerners who had aided the Confederacy and distributing the land among the freedmen. There was also a group of Republican Moderates, who rejected the most stringent demands of the Radicals but supported extracting at least some concessions from the South on black rights.

President Lincoln favored a lenient Reconstruction policy, and he believed that Southern Unionists (mostly former Whigs) could become the nucleus of new, loyal state governments in the South. Lincoln announced his Reconstruction plan in December 1863, more than a year before the war ended. It offered a general amnesty to white Southerners—other than high officials of the Confederacy—who would pledge an oath of loyalty to the government and accept the elimination of slavery. When 10 percent of a state's total number of voters in 1860 took the oath, those loyal voters could set up a state government. Lincoln also proposed extending suffrage to those African Americans who were educated, owned property, and had served in the Union army. Three Southern states—Louisiana, Arkansas, and Tennessee, all under Union occupation—reestablished loyal governments under the Lincoln formula in 1864.

The Radical Republicans were outraged at the mildness of Lincoln's program and refused to admit representatives from the three "reconstructed" states to Congress. In July 1864, they pushed their own plan through Congress in the form of the Wade-Davis *Wade-Davis Bill* Bill. It called for the president to appoint a provisional governor for each conquered state. When a majority of the white males of a state pledged their allegiance to the Union, the governor could summon a state constitutional convention, whose delegates were to be elected by voters who had never borne arms against the United States. The new state constitutions would be required to abolish slavery, disenfranchise Confederate civil and military leaders, and repudiate debts accumulated by the state governments during the war. Only then would Congress readmit the states to the Union. Like the president's proposal, the Wade-Davis Bill left the question of political rights for blacks up to the states.

Congress passed the bill a few days before it adjourned in 1864, and Lincoln disposed of it with a pocket veto. His action enraged the Radical leaders, and the pragmatic Lincoln realized he would have to accept at least some of the Radical demands.

The Death of Lincoln

What plan he might have produced no one can say. On the night of April 14, 1865, Lincoln and his wife attended a play at Ford's Theater in Washington. As they sat in the theater, John Wilkes Booth, an *John Wilkes Booth* actor fervently committed to the Southern cause, entered the presidential box from the rear and shot Lincoln in the head. Early the next morning, the president died.

ABRAHAM LINCOLN This haunting photograph of Abraham Lincoln, showing clearly the weariness and aging that four years as a war president had created, was taken in Washington only four days before his assassination in 1865. *(The Library of Congress)*

The circumstances of Lincoln's death earned him immediate martyrdom. They also produced something close to hysteria throughout the North, especially because it quickly became clear that Booth had been the leader of a conspiracy. One of his associates shot and wounded Secretary of State William Seward on the night of the assassination, and another abandoned at the last moment a scheme to murder Vice President Andrew Johnson. Booth himself escaped on horseback into the Maryland countryside, where, on April 26, he was cornered by Union troops and shot to death in a blazing barn. Eight other people were convicted by a military tribunal of participating in the conspiracy. Four were hanged.

To many Northerners, however, the murder of the president seemed evidence of an even greater conspiracy—one masterminded and directed by the unrepentant leaders of the defeated South. Militant Republicans exploited such suspicions relentlessly in the ensuing months.

Johnson and "Restoration"

Leadership of the Moderates and Conservatives fell to Lincoln's successor, Andrew Johnson of Tennessee. A Democrat until he had joined the Union ticket with Lincoln in 1864, he became president at a time of growing partisan passions.

Johnson revealed his plan for Reconstruction— *Johnson's Reconstruction Plan* or "Restoration," as he preferred to call it—soon after he took office, and he implemented it during the summer of 1865 when Congress was in recess. Like Lincoln, he offered some form of amnesty to Southerners who would take an oath of allegiance. In most other respects, however, his plan resembled the Wade-Davis Bill. The president appointed a provisional governor in each state and charged him with inviting qualified voters to elect delegates to a constitutional convention. In order to win readmission to Congress, a state had to revoke its ordinance of secession, abolish slavery and ratify the Thirteenth Amendment, and repudiate Confederate and state war debts.

By the end of 1865, all the seceded states had formed new governments— some under Lincoln's plan, some under Johnson's—and awaited congressional approval of them. But Radicals in Congress vowed not to recognize the Johnson governments, for, by now, Northern opinion had *Hardening Northern* become more hostile toward the South than it had *Attitudes* been a year earlier when Congress had passed the Wade-Davis Bill. Delegates to the Southern conventions had angered much of the North by their apparent reluctance to abolish slavery and by their refusal to grant suffrage to any blacks. Southern states had also seemed to defy the North by electing prominent Confederate leaders to represent them in Congress.

RADICAL RECONSTRUCTION

Reconstruction under Johnson's plan—often known as "presidential Reconstruction"—continued only until Congress reconvened in December 1865. At that point, Congress refused to seat the representatives of the "restored" states and created a new Joint Committee on Reconstruction to frame a Reconstruction policy of its own. The period of "congressional" or "Radical" Reconstruction had begun.

The Black Codes

Meanwhile, events in the South were driving Northern opinion in even more radical directions. Throughout the South in 1865 and early 1866, state legislatures were enacting sets of laws known as the Black Codes, which authorized local officials to apprehend unemployed blacks, fine

RECONSTRUCTION

Debate over the nature of Reconstruction has been unusually intense. Indeed, few issues in American history have raised such deep and enduring passions.

Beginning in the late nineteenth century and continuing well into the twentieth, a relatively uniform and highly critical view of Reconstruction prevailed among historians. William A. Dunning's *Reconstruction, Political and Economic* (1907) was the principal scholarly expression of this prevailing view. Dunning portrayed Reconstruction as a corrupt and oppressive outrage imposed on a prostrate South by a vindictive group of Northern Republican Radicals. Unscrupulous carpetbaggers flooded the South and plundered the region. Ignorant African Americans were thrust into political offices for which they were unfit. Reconstruction governments were awash in corruption and compiled enormous levels of debt. The Dunning interpretation dominated several generations of historical scholarship. It also helped shape such popular images of Reconstruction as those in the novel and film *Gone with the Wind*.

W. E. B. Du Bois, the great African-American scholar, offered one of the first alternative views in *Black Reconstruction* (1935). To Du Bois, Reconstruction was an effort by freed blacks (and their white allies) to create a more democratic society in the South, and it was responsible for many valuable social innovations. In the early 1960s, John Hope Franklin and Kenneth Stampp, building on a generation of work by other scholars, published new histories of Reconstruction that also radically revised the Dunning interpretation. Reconstruction, they argued, was a genuine, if flawed, effort to solve the problem of race in the South. Congressional Radicals were not saints, but they were genuinely concerned with protecting the rights of former slaves. Reconstruction had brought important, if temporary, progress to the South and had created no more corruption there than governments were creating in the North at the same time. What was tragic about Reconstruction, the revisionists claimed, was not what it did to Southern whites but what it failed to do for Southern blacks. It was, in the end, too weak and too short-lived to guarantee African Americans genuine equality.

In more recent years, some historians have begun to question the assessment of the first revisionists that, in the end, Reconstruction accomplished relatively little. Leon Litwack argued in *Been in the Storm So Long* (1979) that former slaves used the protections Reconstruction offered them to carve out a certain level of independence for themselves within Southern society: strengthening churches, reuniting families, and resisting the efforts of white planters to revive the gang labor system.

Eric Foner's *Reconstruction: America's Unfinished Revolution* (1988) also emphasized how far African Americans moved toward freedom and independence in a short time and how important they were in shaping the execution of Reconstruction policies. Reconstruction, he argues, "can only be judged a failure" as an effort to secure "blacks' rights as citizens and free laborers." But it "closed off even more oppressive alternatives. . . . The post-Reconstruction labor system embodied neither a return to the closely supervised gang labor of antebellum days, nor the complete dispossession and immobilization of the black labor force and coercive apprenticeship systems envisioned by white Southerners in 1865 and 1866. Nor were blacks, as in twentieth-century South Africa, barred from citizenship, herded into labor reserves, or prohibited by law from moving from one part of the country to another. . . . The doors of economic opportunity that had opened could never be completely closed."

(text continued from page 403)

them for vagrancy, and hire them out to private employers to satisfy the fine. Some of the codes forbade blacks to own or lease farms or to take any jobs other than as plantation workers or domestic servants.

Congress first responded to the Black Codes by passing an act extending the life of the Freedmen's Bureau and widening its powers so that it could nullify work agreements forced on freedmen under the Black Codes. Then, in April 1866, Congress passed the first Civil Rights Act, which declared blacks to be citizens of the United States and gave the federal government power to intervene in state affairs to protect the rights of citizens. Johnson vetoed both bills, but Congress overrode him on each of them.

Johnson's Vetoes

The Fourteenth Amendment

In April 1866, the Joint Committee on Reconstruction proposed a new amendment to the Constitution, which Congress approved in early summer and sent to the states for ratification. The Fourteenth Amendment offered the first constitutional definition of American citizenship. Everyone born in the United States, and everyone naturalized, was automatically a citizen and entitled to all the "privileges and immunities" guaranteed by the Constitution, including equal protection of the laws by both the state and national governments. There could be no other requirements for citizenship. The amendment also imposed penalties on states that denied suffrage to any adult male inhabitants. (The wording reflected the prevailing view in Congress and elsewhere that the franchise was properly restricted to men.) Finally, it prohibited former members of Congress or other former federal officials who had aided the Confederacy from holding any state or federal office unless two-thirds of Congress voted to pardon them.

Citizenship for African Americans

Congressional Radicals offered to readmit to the Union any state whose legislature ratified the Fourteenth Amendment. Only Tennessee did so. All the other former Confederate states, along with Delaware and Kentucky, refused, leaving the amendment temporarily without the necessary approval of three-fourths of the states.

But by now, the Radicals were growing more confident and determined. Bloody race riots in New Orleans and other Southern cities were among the events that strengthened their hand. In the 1866 congressional elections, Johnson actively campaigned for Conservative candidates, but he did his own cause more harm than good with his intemperate speeches. The voters returned an overwhelming majority of Republicans, most of them Radicals, to Congress. In the Senate, there were now 42 Republicans to 11 Democrats; in the House, 143 Republicans to 49 Democrats. Congressional Republicans were now strong enough to enact a plan of their own even over the president's objections.

Radicals Ascendant

The Congressional Plan

The Radicals passed three Reconstruction bills early in 1867 and overrode Johnson's vetoes of all of them. These bills finally established, nearly two years after the end of the war, a coherent plan for Reconstruction.

Under the congressional plan, Tennessee, which had ratified the Fourteenth Amendment, was promptly readmitted. But Congress rejected the Lincoln-Johnson governments of the other ten Confederate states and, instead, combined those states into five military districts. A military commander governed each district and had orders to register qualified voters (defined as all adult black males and those white males who had not participated in the rebellion). Once registered, voters would elect conventions to prepare new state constitutions, which had to include provisions for black suffrage. Once voters ratified the new constitutions, they could elect state governments. Congress had to approve a state's constitution, and the state legislature had to ratify the Fourteenth Amendment. Once that happened, and once enough states ratified the amendment to make it part of the Constitution, then the former Confederate states could be restored to the Union.

By 1868, seven of the ten former Confederate states (Arkansas, North Carolina, South Carolina, Louisiana, Alabama, Georgia, and Florida) had fulfilled these conditions (including ratification of the Fourteenth Amendment, which now became part of the Constitution) and were readmitted to the Union. Conservative whites held up the return of Virginia and Texas until 1869 and Mississippi until 1870. By then, Congress had added an additional requirement for readmission—ratification of another consti-

Fifteenth Amendment tutional amendment, the Fifteenth, which forbade the states and the federal government to deny suffrage to any citizen on account of "race, color, or previous condition of servitude." Ratification by the states was completed in 1870.

To stop the president from interfering with their plans, the congressional Radicals passed two remarkable laws of dubious constitutionality in

Tenure of Office Act 1867. One, the Tenure of Office Act, forbade the president to remove civil officials, including members of his own cabinet, without the consent of the Senate. The principal purpose of the law was to protect the job of Secretary of War Edwin M. Stanton, who was cooperating with the Radicals. The other law, the Command of the Army Act, prohibited the president from issuing military orders except through the commanding general of the army (General Grant), who could not be relieved or assigned elsewhere without the consent of the Senate.

The congressional Radicals also took action to stop the Supreme Court from interfering with their plans. In 1866, the Court had declared in the case of *Ex parte Milligan* that military tribunals were unconstitutional in places where civil courts were functioning. Radicals in Congress immediately proposed several bills that would require two-thirds of the justices to support any decision overruling a law of Congress, would deny

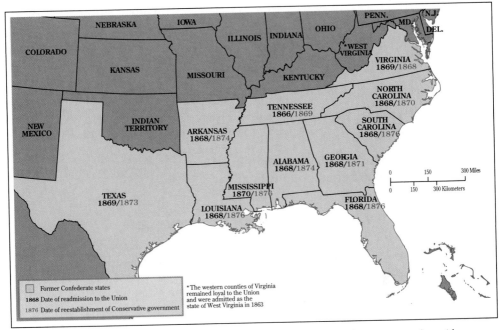

RECONSTRUCTION, 1866–1877 This map shows the former Confederate states and provides the dates when each was readmitted to the Union as well as a subsequent date when each state managed to return political power to traditional white, conservative elites—a process white southerners liked to call "redemption." ◆ *What had to happen for a state to be readmitted to the Union? What had to happen before a state could experience "redemption"?*

the Court jurisdiction in Reconstruction cases, would reduce its membership to three, and would even abolish it. The justices apparently took notice. Over the next two years, the Court refused to accept jurisdiction in any cases involving Reconstruction.

The Impeachment of the President

President Johnson had long since ceased to be a serious obstacle to the passage of Radical legislation, but he was still the official charged with administering the Reconstruction programs. As such, the Radicals believed, he remained a major impediment to their plans. Early in 1867, they began looking for a way to impeach him and remove him from office. A search for grounds for impeachment began. Republicans found them, they believed, when Johnson dismissed Secretary of War Stanton despite Congress's refusal to agree. Elated Radicals in the House quickly impeached the president and sent the case to the Senate for trial.

The trial before the Senate lasted throughout April and May 1868. The Radicals put heavy pressure on all the Republican senators, but the Moderates vacillated. On the first three charges to come to a vote, seven Republi-

The President Acquitted cans joined the Democrats and independents to support acquittal. The vote was 35 to 19, one short of the constitutionally required two-thirds majority. After that, the Radicals dropped the impeachment effort.

THE SOUTH IN RECONSTRUCTION

Reconstruction may not have accomplished what its framers intended, but it did have profound effects on the South.

The Reconstruction Governments

"Scalawags" and "Carpetbaggers" Critics labeled Southern white Republicans with the derogatory terms "scalawags" and "carpetbaggers." Many of the "scalawags" were former Whigs who had never felt comfortable in the Democratic Party or farmers who lived in remote areas where there had been little or no slavery. The "carpetbaggers" were white men from the North, most of them veterans of the Union army who looked on the South as a new frontier, more promising than the West. They had settled there at war's end as hopeful planters, businessmen, or professionals.

Freedmen The most numerous Republicans in the South were the black freedmen, most of whom had no previous experience in politics and tried, therefore, to build institutions through which they could learn to exercise their power. In several states, African-American voters held their own conventions to chart their future course. Freedmen had created their own churches after emancipation, and this religious independence also helped give them unity and self-confidence.

African Americans played a significant role in the politics of the Reconstruction South. They served as delegates to the constitutional conventions. They held public offices of practically every kind. Between 1869 and 1901, twenty blacks served in the United States House of Representatives, two in the Senate. They served, too, in state legislatures and in various other state offices. Southern whites complained loudly about "Negro rule" during Reconstruction, but in the South as a whole, the percentage of black officeholders was always far lower than the percentage of blacks in the population.

The record of the Reconstruction governments is mixed. Critics at the time and later denounced them for corruption and financial extravagance, and there is some truth to both charges. But the corruption in the South, real as it was, was hardly unique to the Reconstruction governments. Corruption had been rife in some antebellum and Confederate governments, and it was at least as rampant in the Northern states. And the large state expenditures of the Reconstruction years were huge only in

A CELEBRATION OF RECONSTRUCTION The celebrated cartoonist Thomas Nast—best known for his savage caricatures of machine politicians in New York's Tammany Hall—drew this celebratory, and optimistic, image of Reconstruction not long after the end of the Civil War: a classical goddess restoring the former Confederate states to their rightful place within a symbolic fasces that represented union. In fact, the Reconstruction process proved much more difficult than this hopeful image suggested. *(North Wind Picture Archives)*

comparison with the meager budgets of the antebellum era. They represented an effort to provide the South with desperately needed services that antebellum governments had never offered.

Education

Perhaps the most important of the accomplishments of the Reconstruction governments was a dramatic improvement in Southern education. In the first years of Reconstruction, much of the impetus for educational reform in the South came from outside groups—from the Freedmen's Bureau, from Northern private philanthropic organizations, from the many Northern white women who traveled to the South to teach in freedmen's schools—and from African Americans themselves. Over the opposition of many Southern whites, who feared that education *Establishment of Black Schools* would give blacks "false notions of equality," these reformers established a large network of schools for former slaves—4,000 schools by 1870, staffed by 9,000 teachers (half of them black), teaching 200,000 students. In the 1870s, Reconstruction governments began to build a comprehensive public school system in the South. By 1876, more than half of all white children and about 40 percent of all black children were attending schools in the South (although almost all such schools were racially segregated). Several black "academies," offering more advanced education, also began operating. Gradually, these academies grew into an important network of black colleges and universities.

Landownership and Tenancy

The most ambitious goal of the Freedmen's Bureau, and of some Republican Radicals in Congress, was to reform landownership in the South. The effort failed. By June 1865, the bureau had settled nearly 10,000 black families on their own land—most of it drawn from abandoned plantations in areas occupied by the Union armies. By the end of that year, however, Southern plantation owners were returning and demanding the restoration of their property. President Johnson supported their demands, and the government eventually returned most of the confiscated lands to their original white owners.

Land Reform Thwarted

Even so, the distribution of landownership in the South changed considerably in the postwar years. Among whites, there was a striking decline in landownership, from 80 percent before the war to 67 percent by the end of Reconstruction. Some whites lost their land because of unpaid debt or increased taxes; some left the marginal lands they had owned to move to more fertile areas, where they rented. Among blacks, during the same period, the proportion who owned land rose from virtually none to more than 20 percent.

Still, most blacks, and a growing minority of whites, did not own their own land during Reconstruction, and some who acquired land in the 1860s had lost it by the 1890s. Instead, they worked for others in one form or another. Many black agricultural laborers—perhaps 25 percent of the total—simply worked for wages. Most, however, became tenants of white landowners—that is, they worked their own plots of land and paid their landlords either a fixed rent or a share of their crop (hence the term "sharecropping"). As tenants and sharecroppers, blacks enjoyed at least a physical independence from their landlords and had the sense of working their own land, even if in most cases they could never hope to buy it. But tenantry also benefited landlords in some ways, relieving them of the cost of purchasing slaves and of responsibility for the physical well-being of their workers.

Rapid Growth of Sharecropping

Incomes and Credit

In some respects, the postwar years were a period of remarkable economic progress for African Americans in the South. The per capita income of blacks (when the material benefits of slavery are counted as income) rose 46 percent between 1857 and 1879, while the per capita income of whites declined 35 percent. African Americans were also able to work less than they had under slavery. Women and children were less likely to labor in the fields, and adult men tended to work shorter days. In all, the black labor force worked about one-third fewer hours during Reconstruction than it had been compelled to work under slavery—a reduction that brought the working schedule of blacks roughly into accord with that of white farm laborers.

But other developments were limiting these gains. While the black share of profits was increasing, the total profits of Southern agriculture were declining. Nor did the income redistribution of the postwar years lift many blacks out of poverty. Black per capita in- *Persistent Black Poverty* come rose from about one-quarter of white per capita income (which was itself low) to about one-half in the first few years after the war. After this initial increase, however, it rose hardly at all.

Blacks and poor whites alike often found themselves virtually imprisoned by the crop-lien system. Few of the traditional institutions of credit in the South—the "factors" and banks—returned after the war. In their stead emerged a new system of credit, centered in large part on local country stores—some of them owned by planters, others owned by independent merchants. Blacks and whites, landowners *The "Crop-lien System"* and tenants—all depended on these stores. And since farmers did not have the same steady cash flow as other workers, customers usually had to rely on credit from these merchants in order to purchase what they needed. Most local stores had no competition. As a result, they were able to set interest rates as high as 50 or 60 percent. Farmers had to give the merchants a lien (or claim) on their crops as collateral for the loans (thus the term "crop-lien system," generally used to describe Southern farming in this period). Farmers who suffered a few bad years in a row, as many did, could become trapped in a cycle of debt from which they could never escape.

One effect of this burdensome credit system was that some blacks who had acquired land during the early years of Reconstruction gradually lost it as they fell into debt. Another was that Southern farmers became almost wholly dependent on cash crops—and most of all on cotton—because only such marketable commodities seemed to offer any possibility of escape from debt. The relentless planting of cotton contributed to an exhaustion of the soil. The crop-lien system, in other words, was not only helping to impoverish small farmers; it was also contributing to a general decline in the Southern agricultural economy.

AFTER SLAVERY Although most freed slaves remained agricultural laborers after Emancipation, a considerable number moved off the land in search of new occupations and new homes. For many, that meant living for some time without stable employment or a permanent home. This photograph from the late 1860s shows a group of former slaves at a county almshouse in the South. *(Bettmann/Corbis)*

The African-American Family in Freedom

A major reason for the rapid departure of so many blacks from plantations was the desire to find lost relatives and reunite families. Thousands of African Americans wandered through the South looking for husbands, wives, children, or other relatives from whom they had been separated. Former slaves rushed to have their marriages, previously without legal standing, sanctified by church and law.

Families Reunited

Within the black family, the definition of male and female roles quickly came to resemble that within white families. Many women and children ceased working in the fields. Such work, they believed, was a badge of slavery. Instead, many women restricted themselves largely to domestic tasks. Still, economic necessity often compelled black women to engage in income-producing activities: working as domestic servants, taking in laundry, or helping their husbands in the fields. By the end of Reconstruction, half of all black women over the age of sixteen were working for wages.

THE GRANT ADMINISTRATION

American voters in 1868 yearned for a strong, stable figure to guide them through the troubled years of Reconstruction. They turned trustingly to General Ulysses S. Grant.

A CELEBRATION OF RECONSTRUCTION The celebrated cartoonist Thomas Nast—best known for his savage caricatures of machine politicians in New York's Tammany Hall—drew this celebratory, and optimistic, image of Reconstruction not long after the end of the Civil War: a classical goddess restoring the former Confederate states to their rightful place within a symbolic fasces that represented union. In fact, the Reconstruction process proved much more difficult than this hopeful image suggested. *(North Wind Picture Archives)*

comparison with the meager budgets of the antebellum era. They represented an effort to provide the South with desperately needed services that antebellum governments had never offered.

Education

Perhaps the most important of the accomplishments of the Reconstruction governments was a dramatic improvement in Southern education. In the first years of Reconstruction, much of the impetus for educational reform in the South came from outside groups—from the Freedmen's Bureau, from Northern private philanthropic organizations, from the many Northern white women who traveled to the South to teach in freedmen's schools—and from African Americans themselves. Over the opposition of many Southern whites, who feared that education *Establishment of Black Schools* would give blacks "false notions of equality," these reformers established a large network of schools for former slaves—4,000 schools by 1870, staffed by 9,000 teachers (half of them black), teaching 200,000 students. In the 1870s, Reconstruction governments began to build a comprehensive public school system in the South. By 1876, more than half of all white children and about 40 percent of all black children were attending schools in the South (although almost all such schools were racially segregated). Several black "academies," offering more advanced education, also began operating. Gradually, these academies grew into an important network of black colleges and universities.

Landownership and Tenancy

The most ambitious goal of the Freedmen's Bureau, and of some Republi-

Land Reform Thwarted

can Radicals in Congress, was to reform landownership in the South. The effort failed. By June 1865, the bureau had settled nearly 10,000 black families on their own land—most of it drawn from abandoned plantations in areas occupied by the Union armies. By the end of that year, however, Southern plantation owners were returning and demanding the restoration of their property. President Johnson supported their demands, and the government eventually returned most of the confiscated lands to their original white owners.

Even so, the distribution of landownership in the South changed considerably in the postwar years. Among whites, there was a striking decline in landownership, from 80 percent before the war to 67 percent by the end of Reconstruction. Some whites lost their land because of unpaid debt or increased taxes; some left the marginal lands they had owned to move to more fertile areas, where they rented. Among blacks, during the same period, the proportion who owned land rose from virtually none to more than 20 percent.

Still, most blacks, and a growing minority of whites, did not own their own land during Reconstruction, and some who acquired land in the 1860s had lost it by the 1890s. Instead, they worked for others in one form or another. Many black agricultural laborers—perhaps 25 percent of the total—simply worked for wages. Most, however, became tenants of white landowners—that is, they worked their own plots of land and paid

Rapid Growth of Sharecropping

their landlords either a fixed rent or a share of their crop (hence the term "sharecropping"). As tenants and sharecroppers, blacks enjoyed at least a physical independence from their landlords and had the sense of working their own land, even if in most cases they could never hope to buy it. But tenantry also benefited landlords in some ways, relieving them of the cost of purchasing slaves and of responsibility for the physical well-being of their workers.

that William W. Belknap, secretary of war, had accepted bribes to retain an Indian-post trader in office (the so-called Indian ring). Other, lesser scandals added to the growing impression that "Grantism" had brought rampant corruption to government.

The Greenback Question

Compounding Grant's, and the nation's, problems was a financial crisis, known as the Panic of 1873. It began with the failure of a leading investment banking firm, Jay Cooke and Company, which had invested too heavily in postwar railroad building. There had been panics before—in 1819, 1837, and 1857—but this was the worst one yet.

Debtors now pressured the government to redeem federal war bonds with greenbacks, which would increase the amount of money in circulation. But Grant and most Republicans wanted a "sound" currency—based solidly on gold reserves—which would favor the interests of banks and other creditors. There was approximately $356 million in paper currency issued during the Civil War that was still in circulation. In 1873, the Treasury issued more in response to the panic. But in 1875, Republican leaders

Specie Resumption Act — in Congress passed the Specie Resumption Act. It provided that after January 1, 1879, the greenback dollars would be redeemed by the government and replaced with new certificates, firmly pegged to the price of gold. The law satisfied creditors, who had worried that debts would be repaid in paper currency of uncertain value. But "resumption" made things more difficult for debtors, because the gold-based money supply could not easily expand.

National Greenback Party — In 1875, the "greenbackers" formed their own political organization: the National Greenback Party. It failed to gain widespread support, but it did keep the money issue alive. The question of the proper composition of the currency was to remain one of the most controversial and enduring issues in late-nineteenth-century American politics.

Republican Diplomacy

The Johnson and Grant administrations achieved their greatest successes in foreign affairs. The accomplishments were the work not of the presidents themselves but of two outstanding secretaries of state: William H. Seward and Hamilton Fish.

An ardent expansionist, Seward acted with as much daring as the demands of Reconstruction politics and the Republican hatred of President

Purchase of Alaska — Johnson would permit. Seward accepted a Russian offer to sell Alaska to the United States for $7.2 million, despite criticism from many who derided the purchase as "Seward's Folly." In 1867, Seward also engineered the American annexation of the tiny Midway Islands, west of Hawaii.

The Soldier President

Grant could have had the nomination of either party in 1868. But believing that Republican Re- *Grant Elected* construction policies were more popular in the North, he accepted the Republican nomination. The Democrats nominated former governor Horatio Seymour of New York. The campaign was a bitter one, and Grant's triumph was surprisingly narrow. Without the 500,000 new black Republican voters in the South, he would have had a minority of the popular vote.

Grant entered the White House with no political experience, and his performance was clumsy and ineffectual from the start. Except for Hamilton Fish, whom Grant appointed secretary of state, most members of the cabinet were ill-equipped for their tasks. Grant relied chiefly on established party leaders—the group most ardently devoted to patronage, and his administration used the spoils system even more blatantly than most of its predecessors. Grant also alienated the many Northerners who were growing disillusioned with the Radical Reconstruction policies, which the president continued to support. Some Republicans suspected, correctly, that there was also corruption in the Grant administration itself.

By the end of Grant's first term, therefore, members of a substantial faction of the party—who referred to themselves as Liberal Republicans—had come to oppose what *Liberal Republicans* they called "Grantism." In 1872, hoping to prevent Grant's reelection, they bolted the party and nominated their own presidential candidate: Horace Greeley, veteran editor and publisher of the *New York Tribune*. The Democrats, somewhat reluctantly, named Greeley their candidate as well, hoping that the alliance with the Liberals would enable them to defeat Grant. But the effort was in vain. Grant won a substantial victory, polling 286 electoral votes to Greeley's 66.

The Grant Scandals

During the 1872 campaign, the first of a series of political scandals came to light that would plague Grant and the Republicans for the next eight years. It involved the French-owned Crédit Mobilier construction company, which had helped build the Union Pacific Railroad. The heads of Crédit Mobilier had used their positions as Union Pacific stockholders to steer large fraudulent contracts to their construction company, thus bilking the Union Pacific of millions. To prevent investigations, the directors had given Crédit Mobilier stock to key members of Congress. But in 1872, Congress did conduct an investigation, which revealed that some highly placed Republicans—including Schuyler Colfax, now Grant's vice president—had accepted stock.

One dreary episode followed another in Grant's second term. Benjamin H. Bristow, Grant's third Treasury secretary, discovered that some of his officials and a group of distillers operating as a "whiskey ring" were cheating the government *The "Whiskey Ring"* out of taxes by filing false reports. Then a House investigation revealed

Hamilton Fish's first major challenge was resolving the longstanding controversy with England over the American claims that it had violated neutrality laws during the Civil War by permitting English shipyards to build ships (among them the *Alabama*) for the Confederacy. American demands that England pay for the damage these vessels had caused became known as the "*Alabama* claims." In 1871, after a number of failed efforts, Fish forged an agreement, *"Alabama Claims" Resolved* the Treaty of Washington, which provided for international arbitration.

THE ABANDONMENT OF RECONSTRUCTION

As the North grew increasingly preoccupied with its own political and economic problems, interest in Reconstruction began to wane. By the time Grant left office, Democrats had taken back seven of the governments of the former Confederate states. For three other states—South Carolina, Louisiana, and Florida—the end of Reconstruction had to wait for the withdrawal of the last federal troops in 1877.

The Southern States "Redeemed"

In the states where whites constituted a majority—the states of the upper South—overthrowing Republican control was relatively simple. By 1872, all but a handful of Southern whites had regained suffrage. Now a clear majority, they needed only to organize and elect their candidates.

In other states, where blacks were a majority or where the populations of the two races were almost equal, whites used intimidation and violence to undermine the Reconstruction regimes. Secret societies—the Ku Klux Klan, the Knights of the *Ku Klux Klan* White Camellia, and others—used terrorism to frighten or physically bar blacks from voting. Paramilitary organizations—the Red Shirts and White Leagues—armed themselves to "police" elections and worked to force all white males to join the Democratic Party. Strongest of all, however, was the simple weapon of economic pressure. Some planters refused to rent land to Republican blacks; storekeepers refused to extend them credit; employers refused to give them work.

The Republican Congress responded to this wave of repression with the Enforcement Acts of 1870 and 1871 (better known as the Ku Klux Klan Acts), which prohibited states from discriminating against voters on the basis of race and gave the national government the authority to prosecute crimes by individuals under federal law. The laws also authorized the president to use federal troops to protect civil rights—a provision President Grant used in 1871 in nine counties of South Carolina. The Enforcement Acts, although seldom enforced, discouraged Klan violence, which declined by 1872.

Waning Northern Commitment

But this Northern commitment to civil rights in the South did not last very long. After the adoption of the Fifteenth Amendment in 1870, some reformers convinced themselves that their long campaign on behalf of black people was now over, that with the vote blacks ought to be able to take care of themselves. Former Radical leaders such as Charles Sumner and Horace Greeley now began calling themselves Liberals, cooperating with the Democrats, and denouncing what they viewed as black-and-carpetbag misgovernment. Within the South itself, many white Republicans now moved into the Democratic Party.

Flagging Interest in Civil Rights

The Panic of 1873 further undermined support for Reconstruction. In the congressional elections of 1874, the Democrats won control of the House of Representatives for the first time since 1861. Grant reduced the use of military force to prop up the Republican regimes in the South.

By the end of 1876, only three states were left in the hands of the Republicans—South Carolina, Louisiana, and Florida. In the state elections that year, Democrats (after using terrorist tactics) claimed victory in all three. But the Republicans claimed victory as well and were able to remain in office because of the presence of federal troops.

The Compromise of 1877

Grant had hoped to run for another term in 1876, but most Republican leaders—shaken by recent Democratic successes and the scandals with which Grant was associated—resisted. Instead, they settled on Rutherford B. Hayes, three-time governor of Ohio and a champion of civil service reform. The Democrats united behind Samuel J. Tilden, the reform governor of New York, who had been instrumental in overthrowing the corrupt Tweed Ring of New York City's Tammany Hall.

Although the campaign was a bitter one, there were few differences of principle between the candidates. The November election produced an apparent Democratic victory. Tilden carried the South and several large Northern states, and his popular margin over Hayes was nearly 300,000 votes. But disputed returns from Louisiana, South Carolina, Florida, and Oregon, whose electoral votes totaled 20, threw the election in doubt. Hayes could still win if he managed to receive all 20 disputed votes.

Disputed Election

The Constitution had established no method to determine the validity of disputed returns. The decision clearly lay with Congress, but it was not clear with which house or through what method. (The Senate was Republican, and the House was Democratic.) Members of each party naturally supported a solution that would yield them the victory. Finally, late in January 1877, Congress tried to break the deadlock by creating a special electoral commission composed of five senators, five representatives, and five justices of the Supreme

Special Electoral Commission

AFRICAN-AMERICAN WORK AFTER SLAVERY Black men and women engaged in a wide range of economic activities in the aftermath of slavery. But discrimination by white Southerners and the former slaves' own lack of education limited most of them to relatively menial jobs. Many black women (including this former slave) earned money for their families by working as "washer women," doing laundry for white people. *(Historic New Orleans Collection)*

Court. The congressional delegation would consist of five Republicans and five Democrats. The Court delegation would include two Republicans, two Democrats, and the only independent, Justice David Davis. But when the Illinois legislature elected Davis to the United States Senate, the justice resigned from the commission. His seat went instead to a Republican justice. The commission voted along straight party lines, 8 to 7, awarding every disputed vote to Hayes.

Behind the resolution of the deadlock, however, lay a series of elaborate compromises among leaders of both parties. When a Democratic filibuster threatened to derail the commission's report, Republican Senate leaders met secretly with Southern Democratic leaders to work out terms by which the Democrats would support Hayes. As the price of their cooperation, the Southern Democrats exacted several pledges from the Republicans: the appointment of at least one Southerner to the Hayes cabinet, control of federal patronage in their areas, generous internal improvements, federal aid for the Texas and Pacific Railroad, and withdrawal of the troops. Many powerful Southern Democrats believed that Republican programs of federal support for business and industry would help their region develop economically.

In his inaugural address, Hayes announced that the South's most pressing need was the restoration of "wise, honest, and peaceful local self-

Federal Troops Withdrawn government," and he soon withdrew the troops and let white Democrats take over the remaining southern state governments. That produced charges that he was paying off the South for acquiescing in his election. But the election had already created such bitterness that not even Hayes's promise to serve only one term could mollify his critics.

The president and his party hoped to build up a "new Republican" organization in the South committed to modest support for black rights. But although many white Southern leaders sympathized with Republican economic policies, resentment of Reconstruction was so deep that supporting the party was politically impossible. The "solid" Democratic South, which would survive until the mid-twentieth century, was taking shape.

The Legacy of Reconstruction

Reconstruction made important contributions to the efforts of former slaves to achieve dignity and equality in American life. There was a significant redistribution of income. There was a more limited but not unimportant redistribution of landownership. Perhaps

Lasting Contributions most important, there was a large, and largely successful, effort by African Americans themselves to carve out a society and culture of their own and to create or strengthen their own institutions.

Reconstruction was not as disastrous an experience for Southern white elites as most believed at the time. Within little more than a decade after the end of a devastating war, the white South had regained control of its own institutions and, to a great extent, restored its traditional ruling class to power. The federal government imposed no drastic economic reforms on the region, and indeed few lasting political changes of any kind other than the abolition of slavery.

Reconstruction was notable, finally, for its limitations. For in those years the United States failed in its first serious effort to resolve its oldest and deepest social problem—the problem of race. What was more, the experience so disillusioned white Americans that it would be nearly a century before they would try again to combat racial injustice. *Limits of Reconstruction*

Given the odds confronting them, however, African Americans had reason for considerable pride in the gains they were able to make during Reconstruction. And future generations could be grateful for two great charters of freedom—the Fourteenth and Fifteenth Amendments to the Constitution—which, although widely ignored at the time, would one day serve as the basis for a "Second Reconstruction" that would renew the drive to bring freedom to all Americans.

THE NEW SOUTH

The agreement between southern Democrats and northern Republicans that helped settle the disputed election of 1876 was supposed to be the first step toward developing a stable, permanent Republican Party in the South. In that respect, at least, it failed. In the years following the end of Reconstruction, white southerners established the Democratic Party as the only viable political organization for the region's whites. Even so, the South did change in some of the ways the framers of the Compromise of 1877 had hoped.

The "Redeemers"

Many white southerners rejoiced at the restoration of what they liked to call "home rule." But in reality, political power in the region was soon more restricted than at any time since the Civil War. Once again, most of the South fell under the control of a powerful, conservative oligarchy, whose members were known variously as the "Redeemers" or the "Bourbons." *"Home Rule"*

In some places, this post-Reconstruction ruling class was much the same as the ruling class of the antebellum period. In Alabama, for example, the old planter elite retained much of its former power. In other areas, however, the Redeemers constituted a genuinely new ruling class. They were merchants, industrialists, railroad developers, and financiers. Some of them were former planters, some of them northern immigrants, some of them ambitious, upwardly mobile white southerners from the region's lower social tiers. They combined a commitment to "home rule" and social conservatism with a commitment to economic development.

The various Bourbon governments of the New South behaved in many respects quite similarly. Virtually all the new Democratic regimes lowered taxes, reduced spending, and drastically diminished state services. One state after another eliminated or reduced its support for public school systems.

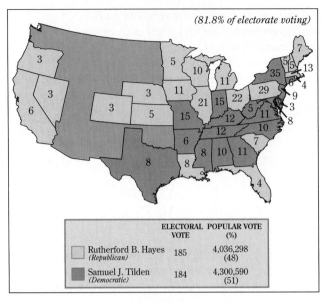

THE ELECTION OF 1876 The election of 1876 was one of the most controversial in American history. As in the elections of 1824, 1888, and 2000, the winner of the popular vote—Samuel J. Tilden—was not the winner of the electoral college, which he lost by one vote. The final decision as to who would be president was not made until the day before the official Inauguration in March. ◆ *How did the Republicans turn this apparent defeat into a victory?*

For an interactive version of this map go to www.mhhe.com/unfinishednation4ch15maps

Industrialization and the "New South"

Many white southern leaders in the post-Reconstruction era hoped to see their region become the home of a vigorous industrial economy, a "New

Henry Grady

South." Henry Grady, editor of the *Atlanta Constitution*, and other New South advocates seldom challenged white supremacy, but they did promote the virtues of thrift, industry, and progress—qualities that prewar southerners had often denounced in northern society.

Southern industry did expand dramatically in the years after Reconstruction. Most visible was the growth in textile manufacturing. In the past, southern planters had usually shipped their cotton out of the region to manufacturers in the North or in Europe. Now textile factories appeared in the South itself—many of them drawn to the region from New England by the abundance of water power, the ready supply of cheap labor, the low taxes, and the accommodating conservative governments. The tobacco-processing industry, similarly, established an important foothold in the region. In the lower South, and particularly in Birmingham, Alabama, the iron (and, later, steel) industry grew rapidly.

Substantial Railroad Development

Railroad development also increased substantially in the post-Reconstruction years. Between 1880 and 1890, trackage in the South more than doubled. And in 1886, the South changed the gauge (width) of its trackage to correspond with the standards of the North. No longer would it be necessary for cargoes heading into the South to be transferred from one train to another at the borders of the region.

Yet southern industry developed within strict limits, and its effects on the region were never even remotely comparable to the effects of industrialization on the North. The southern share of national manufacturing doubled in the last twenty years of the century, but it was still only 10 percent of the total. The region's per capita income increased 21 percent in the same period, but average income in the South was still only 40 percent of that in the North; in 1860 it had been more than 60 percent. And even in those industries where development had been most rapid—textiles, iron, railroads—much of the capital had come from, and many of the profits thus flowed to, the North.

The growth of industry in the South required the region to recruit a substantial industrial work force for the first time. From the beginning, a high percentage of the factory workers were women. Heavy male casualties in the Civil War had helped create a large population of unmarried women who desperately needed employment. *Worker Exploitation* Hours were long (often as much as twelve hours a day), and wages were far below the northern equivalent; indeed, one of the greatest attractions of the South to industrialists was that employers were able to pay workers there as little as one-half what northern workers received. Life in most mill towns was rigidly controlled by the owners and managers of the factories. They rigorously suppressed attempts at protest or union organization. Company stores sold goods to workers at inflated prices and issued credit at exorbitant rates (much like country stores in agrarian areas), and mill owners ensured that no competing merchants were able to establish themselves in the community.

Some industries, such as textiles, offered virtually no opportunities to African-American workers. Others—tobacco, iron, and lumber, for example—did provide some employment for blacks. Some mill towns, therefore, were places where the black and white cultures came into close contact. This juxtaposition of cultures inhibited the growth of racial harmony and increased the determination of white leaders to take additional measures to protect white supremacy.

Tenants and Sharecroppers

The most important economic reality in the post-Reconstruction South was the impoverished state of agriculture. The *Impoverished Agriculture* 1870s and 1880s saw an acceleration of the process that had begun in the immediate postwar years: the imposition of systems of tenantry and debt peonage on much of the region; the reliance on a few cash crops rather than on a diversified agricultural system; and increasing absentee ownership of valuable farmlands. During Reconstruction, perhaps a third or more of the farmers in the South were tenants; by 1900 the figure had increased to 70 percent.

Tenantry took several forms. Farmers who owned tools, equipment, and farm animals usually paid an annual cash rent for their land. But many farmers (including most black ones) had no money or equipment at all. Landlords would supply them with land, a crude house, a few tools, seed, and sometimes a mule. In return, the farmers would promise the landlord a large share of the annual crop. After paying their landlords and their local furnishing merchants (who were often the same people), these "sharecroppers" seldom had anything left to sell on their own.

African Americans and the New South

The "New South creed" was not the property of whites alone. Many African Americans were attracted to the vision of progress and self-improvement as well. Some blacks succeeded in elevating themselves into a distinct middle class. These were former slaves (and, as the decades passed, their offspring) who managed to acquire property, establish small businesses, or enter professions. This rising group of African Americans believed strongly that education was vital to the future of their people, and they expanded the network of black colleges and institutes that had taken root during Reconstruction into an important educational system.

Booker T. Washington

The chief spokesman for this commitment to education was Booker T. Washington, founder and president of the Tuskegee Institute in Alabama. Born into slavery, Washington had worked his way out of poverty after acquiring an education (at Virginia's Hampton Institute). He urged other blacks to follow the same road to self-improvement.

Washington's message was both cautious and hopeful. African Americans should attend school, learn skills, and establish a solid footing in agriculture and the trades. Industrial, not classical, education should be their goal. Blacks should, moreover, refine their speech, improve their dress, and adopt habits of thrift and personal cleanliness; they should, in short, adopt the standards of the white middle class. Only thus, he claimed, could they win the respect of the white population.

In a famous speech in Georgia in 1895, Washington outlined a controversial philosophy of race relations that became widely known as the Atlanta Compromise. Blacks, he said, should forgo agitating for political rights and concentrate on self-improvement and preparation for equality. Washington offered a powerful challenge to those whites who wanted to discourage African Americans from acquiring an education or winning any economic gains. But his message was also intended to assure whites that blacks would not challenge the system of segregation, which southern governments were in the process of creating.

Atlanta Compromise

"IS THIS A REPUBLICAN FORM OF GOVERNMENT?" The New York artist and cartoonist
Thomas Nast marked the end of Reconstruction in 1876 with this biting cartoon in *Harper's
Weekly*, expressing his dismay at what he considered the nation's betrayal of the former slaves,
who still had not received adequate guarantees of their rights. The caption of the cartoon
continued: "Is *this* protecting life, liberty, or property? Is *this* equal protection of the laws?"
(The Newberry Library, Chicago, Illinois)

The Birth of Jim Crow

Few white southerners had ever accepted the idea of racial equality. That
the former slaves acquired any legal and political rights at all after emancipation was in large part the result of their own efforts and critical federal
support. That outside support all but vanished after 1877, when federal
troops withdrew and the Supreme Court stripped the Fourteenth and Fifteenth Amendments of much of their significance. In the so-called civil
rights cases of 1883, the Court ruled that the Fourteenth Amendment prohibited state governments from discriminating against people because of
race but did not restrict private organizations or individuals from doing so.

Eventually, the Court also validated state legislation that institutionalized
the separation of the races. In *Plessy v. Ferguson*
(1896), a case involving a Louisiana law that required   *Plessy v. Ferguson*

TUSKEGEE INSTITUTE, 1881 From these modest beginnings, Booker T. Washington's Tuskegee Institute in Alabama became the preeminent academy offering technical and industrial training to black men. It deliberately de-emphasized the traditional liberal arts curricula of most colleges. Washington considered such training less important than developing practical skills. *(Bettmann/Corbis)*

separate seating arrangements for the races on railroads, the Court held that separate accommodations did not deprive blacks of equal rights if the accommodations were equal. In *Cumming* v. *County Board of Education* (1899), the Court ruled that communities could establish schools for whites only, even if there were no comparable schools for blacks.

Even before these decisions, white southerners were working to separate the races to the greatest extent possible. They were particularly determined to strip African Americans of the right to vote. In some states, disenfranchisement had begun almost as soon as Reconstruction ended. But in other areas, black voting continued for some time after Reconstruction—largely because conservative whites believed they could control the black electorate and use it to beat back the attempts of poor white farmers to take control of the Democratic Party.

In the 1890s, however, franchise restrictions became much more rigid. During those years, some small white farmers began to demand complete *Black Disenfranchisement* black disenfranchisement—because they objected to the black vote being used against them by the Bourbons. At the same time, many members of the conservative elite began to fear that poor whites might unite politically with poor blacks to challenge them.

In devising laws to disenfranchise black males, the southern states had to find ways to evade the Fifteenth Amendment, which prohibited states from denying anyone the right to vote because of race. Two devices emerged before 1900 to accomplish this goal. One was the poll tax or some form of property qualification; few blacks were prosperous enough to meet such requirements. Another was the "literacy" or "understanding" test, which required voters to demonstrate an ability to read and to interpret the Constitution. Even those African Americans who could read had a hard time passing the difficult test white officials gave them. The laws affected poor white voters as well as blacks. By the late 1890s, the black vote had decreased by 62 percent, the white vote by 26 percent.

Laws restricting the franchise and segregating schools were only part of a network of state and local statutes—known as the Jim Crow laws—that by the first years of the *Jim Crow Laws* twentieth century had institutionalized an elaborate system of segregation reaching into almost every area of southern life. Blacks and whites could not ride together in the same railroad cars, sit in the same waiting rooms, use the same washrooms, eat in the same restaurants, or sit in the same theaters. Blacks had no access to many public parks, beaches, or picnic areas; they could not be patients in many hospitals. Much of the new legal structure did no more than confirm what had already been widespread social practice in the South. But the Jim Crow laws also stripped blacks of many of the modest social, economic, and political gains they had made in the late nineteenth century.

More than legal efforts were involved in this process. The 1890s witnessed a dramatic increase in white violence against blacks, which, along with the Jim Crow laws, served to inhibit black agitation for equal rights. The worst such violence—lynching of blacks by white mobs—reached appalling levels. In the nation as a whole in the 1890s, there was an average of 187 lynchings each year, more than 80 percent of them in the South. The vast majority of victims were black. Those who participated in lynchings often saw their actions as a legitimate form of law enforcement, and some victims of lynchings had in fact committed crimes. But lynchings were also a means by which whites controlled the black population through terror and intimidation.

The rise of lynchings shocked the conscience of many white Americans in a way that other forms of racial injustice did not. In 1892 Ida B. Wells, a committed black journalist, *Ida B. Wells* launched what became an international anti-lynching movement with a series of impassioned articles after the lynching of three of her friends in Memphis, Tennessee, her home. The movement gradually gathered strength in the first years of the twentieth century, attracting substantial support from whites in both the North and South (particularly from white women). Its goal was a federal anti-lynching law, which would allow the national government to do what state and local governments in the South were generally unwilling to do: punish those responsible for lynchings.

But the substantial southern white opposition to lynchings stood as an exception to the general white support for suppression of African Americans. Indeed, just as in the antebellum period, the shared commitment to white supremacy helped dilute class animosities between poorer whites and the Bourbon oligarchies. Economic issues tended to play a secondary role to race in southern politics, distracting people from the glaring social inequalities that afflicted blacks and whites alike.

CONCLUSION

Reconstruction was a profoundly important moment in American history. Despite the bitter political battles in Washington and throughout the South, culminating in the unsuccessful effort to remove President Andrew Johnson from office, the most important result of the effort to reunite the nation after its long and bloody war was a reshaping of the lives of ordinary people in all regions of the nation.

In the North, Reconstruction solidified the power of the Republican Party. The rapid expansion of the northern economy continued and accelerated, drawing more and more of its residents into a burgeoning commercial world.

In the South, Reconstruction fundamentally rearranged the relationship between the region's white and black citizens. Only for a while did Reconstruction permit African Americans to participate actively and effectively in southern politics. After a few years of widespread black voting and significant black officeholding, the forces of white supremacy forced most African Americans to the margins of the southern political world, where they would mostly remain until the 1960s.

In other ways, the lives of southern blacks changed dramatically and permanently. Overwhelmingly, they left the plantations. Some sought work in towns and cities. Some left the region altogether. But the great majority began farming on small farms of their own—not as landowners, except in rare cases, but as tenants and sharecroppers on land owned by whites. The result was a form of economic bondage, driven by debt, only scarcely less oppressive than the legal bondage of slavery. Within this system, however, African Americans managed to carve out a much larger sphere of social and cultural activity than they had ever been able to create under slavery. Black churches proliferated in great numbers. African-American schools emerged in some communities, and black colleges began to operate in the region. Some former slaves owned businesses and flourished.

Strenuous efforts by "New South" advocates to advance industry and commerce in the region produced significant results in a few areas. But the South on the whole remained what it had always been: an overwhelmingly rural society with a sharply defined class structure. It was also a region with a deep commitment among its white citizens to the subordination of African Americans—a commitment solidified in the 1890s and the early twentieth century when white southerners erected an elaborate legal system of segregation (the "Jim Crow" laws). The promise of the great Reconstruction amendments to the Constitution—the Fourteenth and Fifteenth—remained largely unfulfilled in the South as the century drew to its close.

FOR FURTHER REFERENCE

Eric Foner, *Reconstruction: America's Unfinished Revolution, 1863–1877* (1988), the most important modern synthesis of Reconstruction scholarship, emphasizes the radicalism of Reconstruction and the agency of freed people in the process of political and economic renovation. David W. Blight, *Race and Reunion: The Civil War in American Memory* (2001) is an excellent study of the ways in which Americans reinterpreted the Civil War in the late nineteenth century. Amy Dru Stanley, *From Bondage to Contract: Wage Labor, Marriage, and the Market in the Age of Slave Emancipation* (1998) and Jeffrey R. Kerr-Ritchie, *Freedpeople in the Tobacco South: Virginia, 1860–1900* (1999) are important examinations of African-American labor during and after Emancipation. Thomas Holt, *Black over White: Negro Political Leadership in South Carolina During Reconstruction* (1977) examines Reconstruction in the state where black political power reached its apex. C. Vann Woodward, *Origins of the New South* (1951), a classic work on the history of the South after Reconstruction, argues that a rising middle class defined the economic and political transformation of the New South. Edward Ayers, *The Promise of the New South* (1992) offers a rich portrait of social and cultural life in the New South. Jacqueline Jones, *Labor of Love, Labor of Sorrow* (1985) examines the lives of African-American women after Emancipation. Mia Bay, *The White Image in the Black Mind: African-American Ideas about White People, 1830–1925* (2000) is a valuable study of African-American attitudes toward white society. Leon Litwack, *Been in the Storm So Long: The Aftermath of Slavery* (1979) is a major study of the experiences of freed slaves. C. Vann Woodward, *The Strange Career of Jim Crow* (rev. 1974) claims that segregation emerged only gradually across the South after Reconstruction. The "Woodward Thesis" has been challenged by, among others, Joel Williamson, *After Slavery: The Negro in South Carolina During Reconstruction* (1965); John W. Cell, *The Highest Stage of White Supremacy: The Origins of Segregation in South Africa and the American South* (1982); and Howard N. Rabinowitz, *Race Relations in the Urban South, 1865–1890* (1978).

For quizzes, Internet resources, references to additional books and films, and more, consult this book's Online Learning Center site at www.mhhe.com/unfinishednation4.

APPENDICES

Documents and Tables

THE UNITED STATES

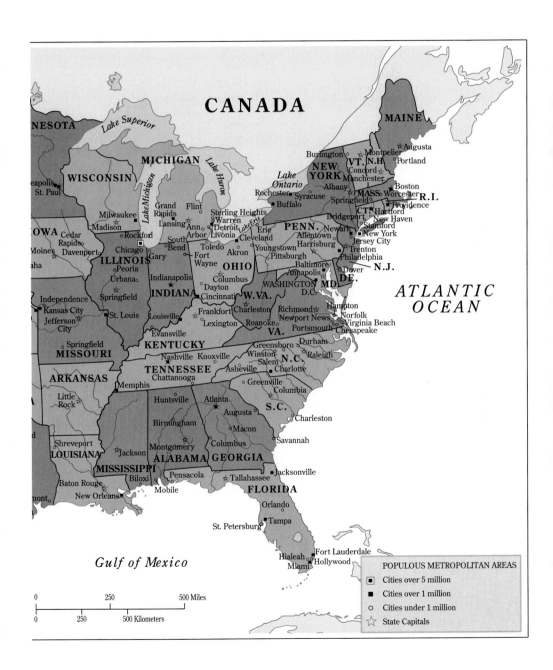

CANADA

MAINE

UNITED STATES TERRITORIAL EXPANSION, 1783–1898

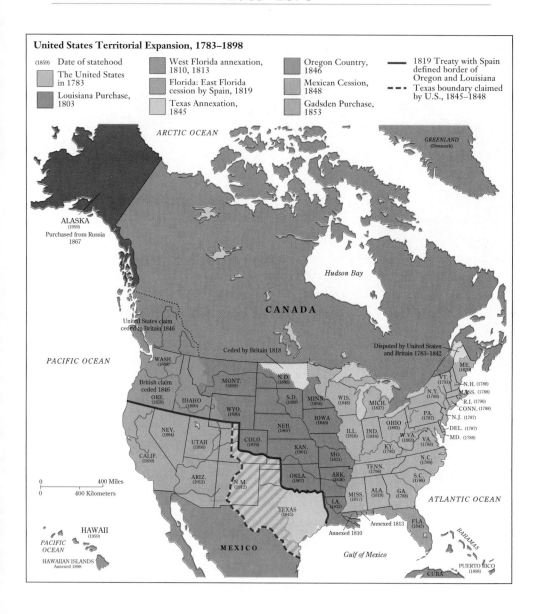

United States Territorial Expansion, 1783–1898

(1859) Date of statehood

The United States in 1783

Louisiana Purchase, 1803

West Florida annexation, 1810, 1813

Florida: East Florida cession by Spain, 1819

Texas Annexation, 1845

Oregon Country, 1846

Mexican Cession, 1848

Gadsden Purchase, 1853

—— 1819 Treaty with Spain defined border of Oregon and Louisiana

– – – Texas boundary claimed by U.S., 1845–1848

THE DECLARATION OF INDEPENDENCE

In Congress, July 4, 1776,

The Unanimous Declaration of the Thirteen United States of America

When, in the course of human events, it becomes necessary for one people to dissolve the political bands which have connected them with another, and to assume, among the powers of the earth, the separate and equal station to which the laws of nature and of nature's God entitle them, a decent respect to the opinions of mankind requires that they should declare the causes which impel them to the separation.

We hold these truths to be self-evident, that all men are created equal; that they are endowed by their Creator with certain unalienable rights; that among these, are life, liberty, and the pursuit of happiness. That, to secure these rights, governments are instituted among men, deriving their just powers from the consent of the governed; that, whenever any form of government becomes destructive of these ends, it is the right of the people to alter or to abolish it, and to institute a new government, laying its foundation on such principles, and organizing its powers in such form, as to them shall seem most likely to effect their safety and happiness. Prudence, indeed, will dictate that governments long established, should not be changed for light and transient causes; and, accordingly, all experience hath shown, that mankind are more disposed to suffer, while evils are sufferable, than to right themselves by abolishing the forms to which they are accustomed. But, when a long train of abuses and usurpations, pursuing invariably the same object, evinces a design to reduce them under absolute despotism, it is their right, it is their duty, to throw off such government and to provide new guards for their future security. Such has been the patient sufferance of these colonies, and such is now the necessity which constrains them to alter their former systems of government. The history of the present King of Great Britain is a history of repeated injuries and usurpations, all having, in direct object, the establishment of an absolute tyranny over these States. To prove this, let facts be submitted to a candid world:

He has refused his assent to laws the most wholesome and necessary for the public good.

He has forbidden his governors to pass laws of immediate and pressing importance, unless suspended in their operation till his assent should be obtained; and, when so suspended, he has utterly neglected to attend to them.

He has refused to pass other laws for the accommodation of large districts of people, unless those people would relinquish the right of representation in the legislature; a right inestimable to them, and formidable to tyrants only.

He has called together legislative bodies at places unusual, uncomfortable, and distant from the depository of their public records, for the sole purpose of fatiguing them into compliance with his measures.

He has dissolved representative houses repeatedly for opposing, with manly firmness, his invasions on the rights of the people.

He has refused, for a long time after such dissolutions, to cause others to be elected; whereby the legislative powers, incapable of annihilation, have returned to the people at large for their exercise; the state remaining, in the meantime, exposed to all the danger of invasion from without, and compulsions within.

He has endeavored to prevent the population of these States; for that purpose, obstructing the laws for naturalization of foreigners, refusing to pass others to encourage their migration hither, and raising the conditions of new appropriations of lands.

He has obstructed the administration of justice, by refusing his assent to laws for establishing judiciary powers.

He has made judges dependent on his will alone, for the tenure of their offices, and the amount and payment of their salaries.

He has erected a multitude of new offices, and sent hither swarms of officers to harass our people, and eat out their substance.

He has kept among us, in time of peace, standing armies, without the consent of our legislatures.

He has affected to render the military independent of, and superior to, the civil power.

He has combined, with others, to subject us to a jurisdiction foreign to our Constitution, and unacknowledged by our laws; giving his assent to their acts of pretended legislation:

For quartering large bodies of armed troops among us:

For protecting them by a mock trial, from punishment, for any murders which they should commit on the inhabitants of these States:

For cutting off our trade with all parts of the world:

For imposing taxes on us without our consent:

For depriving us, in many cases, of the benefit of trial by jury:

For transporting us beyond seas to be tried for pretended offences:

For abolishing the free system of English laws in a neighboring province, establishing therein an arbitrary government, and enlarging its boundaries, so as to render it at once an example and fit instrument for introducing the same absolute rule into these colonies:

For taking away our charters, abolishing our most valuable laws, and altering, fundamentally, the powers of our governments:

For suspending our own legislatures, and declaring themselves invested with power to legislate for us in all cases whatsoever.

He has abdicated government here, by declaring us out of his protection, and waging war against us.

He has plundered our seas, ravaged our coasts, burnt our towns, and destroyed the lives of our people.

He is, at this time, transporting large armies of foreign mercenaries to complete the works of death, desolation, and tyranny, already begun, with circumstances of cruelty and perfidy scarcely paralleled in the most barbarous ages, and totally unworthy the head of a civilized nation.

He has constrained our fellow citizens, taken captive on the high seas, to bear arms against their country, to become the executioners of their friends, and brethren, or to fall themselves by their hands.

He has excited domestic insurrections amongst us, and has endeavored to bring on the inhabitants of our frontiers, the merciless Indian savages, whose known rule of warfare is an undistinguished destruction of all ages, sexes, and conditions.

In every stage of these oppressions, we have petitioned for redress, in the most humble terms; our repeated petitions have been answered only by repeated injury. A prince, whose character is thus marked by every act which may define a tyrant, is unfit to be the ruler of a free people.

Nor have we been wanting in attention to our British brethren. We have warned them, from time to time, of attempts made by their legislature to extend an unwarrantable jurisdiction over us. We have reminded them of the circumstances of our emigration and settlement here. We have appealed to their native justice and magnanimity, and we have conjured them, by the ties of our common kindred, to disavow these usurpations, which would inevitably interrupt our connections and correspondence. They, too, have been deaf to the voice of justice and consanguinity. We must, therefore, acquiesce in the necessity which denounces our separation, and hold them as we hold the rest of mankind, enemies in war, in peace, friends.

We, therefore, the representatives of the United States of America, in general Congress assembled, appealing to the Supreme Judge of the world for the rectitude of our intentions, do, in the name, and by the authority of the good people of these colonies, solemnly publish and declare, that these united colonies are, and of right ought to be, free and independent states: that they are absolved from all allegiance to the British Crown, and that all political connection between them and the state of Great Britain is, and ought to be, totally dissolved; and that, as free and independent states, they have full power to levy war, conclude peace, contract alliances, establish commerce, and to do all other acts and things which independent states may of right do. And, for the support of this declaration, with a firm reliance on the protection of Divine Providence, we mutually pledge to each other our lives, our fortunes, and our sacred honor.

The foregoing Declaration was, by order of Congress, engrossed, and signed by the following members:

John Hancock

New Hampshire
Josiah Bartlett
William Whipple
Matthew Thornton

Connecticut
Roger Sherman
Samuel Huntington
William Williams
Oliver Wolcott

New York
William Floyd
Philip Livingston
Francis Lewis
Lewis Morris

New Jersey
Richard Stockton
John Witherspoon
Francis Hopkinson
John Hart
Abraham Clark

Massachusetts Bay
Samuel Adams
John Adams
Robert Treat Paine
Elbridge Gerry

Pennsylvania
Robert Morris
Benjamin Rush
Benjamin Franklin
John Morton
George Clymer
James Smith
George Taylor
James Wilson
George Ross

Delaware
Caesar Rodney
George Read
Thomas M'Kean

Maryland
Samuel Chase
William Paca
Thomas Stone
Charles Carroll,
    of Carrollton

Rhode Island
Stephen Hopkins
William Ellery

Virginia
George Wythe
Richard Henry Lee
Thomas Jefferson
Benjamin Harrison
Thomas Nelson, Jr.
Francis Lightfoot Lee
Carter Braxton

North Carolina
William Hooper
Joseph Hewes
John Penn

South Carolina
Edward Rutledge
Thomas Heyward, Jr.
Thomas Lynch, Jr.
Arthur Middleton

Georgia
Button Gwinnett
Lyman Hall
George Walton

Resolved, That copies of the Declaration be sent to the several assemblies, conventions, and committees, or councils of safety, and to the several commanding officers of the continental troops; that it be proclaimed in each of the United States, at the head of the army.

THE CONSTITUTION OF THE UNITED STATES[1]

We the People of the United States, in Order to form a more perfect Union, establish Justice, insure domestic Tranquility, provide for the common defence, promote the general Welfare, and secure the Blessings of Liberty to ourselves and our Posterity, do ordain and establish this CONSTITUTION for the United States of America.

Article I

Section 1.
All legislative Powers herein granted shall be vested in a Congress of the United States, which shall consist of a Senate and House of Representatives.

Section 2.
The House of Representatives shall be composed of Members chosen every second Year by the People of the several States, and the Electors in each State shall have the Qualifications requisite for Electors of the most numerous Branch of the State Legislature.

No Person shall be a Representative who shall not have attained to the Age of twenty-five Years, and been seven Years a Citizen of the United States, and who shall not, when elected, be an Inhabitant of that State in which he shall be chosen.

[Representatives and direct Taxes[2] shall be apportioned among the several States which may be included within this Union, according to their respective Numbers, which shall be determined by adding to the whole Number of free Persons, including those bound to Service for a Term of Years, and excluding Indians not taxed, three fifths of all other Persons.][3] The actual Enumeration shall be made within three Years after the first Meeting of the Congress of the United States, and within every subsequent Term of ten Years, in such Manner as they shall by Law direct. The Number of Representatives shall not exceed one for every thirty Thousand, but each State shall have at Least one Representative; and until such enumeration shall be made, the State of New Hampshire shall be entitled to chuse three, Massachusetts eight, Rhode-Island and Providence Plantations one, Connecticut five, New York six, New Jersey four, Pennsylvania eight, Delaware one, Maryland six, Virginia ten, North Carolina five, South Carolina five, and Georgia three.

When vacancies happen in the Representation from any State, the Executive Authority thereof shall issue Writs of Election to fill such Vacancies.

The House of Representatives shall chuse their Speaker and other Officers; and shall have the sole Power of Impeachment.

---

[1]This version, which follows the original Constitution in capitalization and spelling, was published by the United States Department of the Interior, Office of Education, in 1935.
[2]Altered by the Sixteenth Amendment.
[3]Negated by the Fourteenth Amendment.

Section 3.

The Senate of the United States shall be composed of two Senators from each State, chosen by the Legislature thereof, for six Years; and each Senator shall have one Vote.

Immediately after they shall be assembled in Consequence of the first Election, they shall be divided as equally as may be into three Classes. The Seats of the Senators of the first Class shall be vacated at the Expiration of the second Year, of the second Class at the Expiration of the fourth Year, and of the third Class at the Expiration of the sixth Year, so that one-third may be chosen every second Year; and if Vacancies happen by Resignation, or otherwise, during the Recess of the Legislature of any State, the Executive thereof may make temporary Appointments until the next Meeting of the Legislature, which shall then fill such Vacancies.

No Person shall be a Senator who shall not have attained to the Age of thirty Years, and been nine Years a Citizen of the United States, and who shall not, when elected, be an Inhabitant of that State for which he shall be chosen.

The Vice President of the United States shall be President of the Senate, but shall have no vote, unless they be equally divided.

The Senate shall chuse their other Officers, and also a President pro tempore, in the absence of the Vice President, or when he shall exercise the Office of President of the United States.

The Senate shall have the sole Power to try all Impeachments. When sitting for that purpose they shall be on Oath or Affirmation. When the President of the United States is tried, the Chief Justice shall preside: And no person shall be convicted without the Concurrence of two thirds of the Members present.

Judgment in Cases of Impeachment shall not extend further than to removal from Office, and disqualification to hold and enjoy any Office of honor, Trust, or Profit under the United States: but the Party convicted shall nevertheless be liable and subject to Indictment, Trial, Judgment, and Punishment, according to Law.

Section 4.

The Times, Places and Manner of holding Elections for Senators and Representatives, shall be prescribed in each State by the Legislature thereof; but the Congress may at any time by Law make or alter such Regulations, except as to the Places of Chusing Senators.

The Congress shall assemble at least once in every Year, and such Meeting shall be on the first Monday in December, unless they shall by Law appoint a different Day.

Section 5.

Each House shall be the Judge of the Elections, Returns and Qualifications of its own Members, and a Majority of each shall constitute a Quorum to do Business; but a smaller number may adjourn from day to day, and may be authorized to compel the Attendance of absent Members, in such Manner, and under such Penalties, as each House may provide.

Each House may determine the Rules of its Proceedings, punish its Members for disorderly Behaviour, and, with the Concurrence of two thirds, expel a Member.

Each House shall keep a Journal of its Proceedings, and from time to time publish the same, excepting such Parts as may in their Judgment require Secrecy; and the Yeas and Nays of the Members of either House on any question shall, at the Desire of one fifth of those Present, be entered on the Journal.

Neither House, during the Session of Congress, shall, without the Consent of the other, adjourn for more than three days, nor to any other Place than that in which the two Houses shall be sitting.

Section 6.

The Senators and Representatives shall receive a Compensation for their Services, to be ascertained by Law, and paid out of the Treasury of the United States. They shall in all Cases, except Treason, Felony, and Breach of the Peace, be privileged from Arrest during their Attendance at the Session of their respective Houses, and in going to and returning from the same; and for any Speech or Debate in either House, they shall not be questioned in any other Place.

No Senator or Representative shall, during the Time for which he was elected, be appointed to any civil Office under the Authority of the United States, which shall have been created, or the Emoluments whereof shall have been increased, during such time; and no Person holding any Office under the United States shall be a Member of either House during his continuance in Office.

Section 7.

All Bills for raising Revenue shall originate in the House of Representatives; but the Senate may propose or concur with Amendments as on other bills.

Every Bill which shall have passed the House of Representatives and the Senate, shall, before it become a Law, be presented to the President of the United States; If he approve he shall sign it, but if not he shall return it, with his Objections, to that House in which it shall have originated, who shall enter the Objections at large on their Journal, and proceed to reconsider it. If after such Reconsideration two thirds of that House shall agree to pass the bill, it shall be sent, together with the objections, to the other House, by which it shall likewise be reconsidered, and if approved by two thirds of that House, it shall become a Law. But in all such Cases the Votes of both Houses shall be determined by Yeas and Nays, and the Names of the Persons voting for and against the Bill shall be entered on the Journal of each House respectively. If any Bill shall not be returned by the President within ten Days (Sundays excepted) after it shall have been presented to him, the Same shall be a Law, in like Manner as if he had signed it, unless the Congress by their Adjournment prevent its Return, in which Case it shall not be a Law.

Every Order, Resolution, or Vote to which the Concurrence of the Senate and House of Representatives may be necessary (except on a question of Adjournment) shall be presented to the President of the United States; and before the Same shall take Effect, shall be approved by him, or being disapproved by him, shall be repassed by two thirds of the Senate and House of Representatives, according to the Rules and Limitations prescribed in the Case of a Bill.

Section 8.

The Congress shall have Power To lay and collect Taxes, Duties, Imposts and Excises, to pay the Debts and provide for the common Defence and general Welfare of the United States; but all Duties, Imposts and Excises shall be uniform throughout the United States;

To borrow money on the credit of the United States;

To regulate Commerce with foreign Nations, and among the several States, and with the Indian Tribes;

To establish an uniform rule of Naturalization, and uniform Laws on the subject of Bankruptcies throughout the United States;

To coin Money, regulate the Value thereof, and of foreign Coin, and fix the Standard of Weights and Measures;

To provide for the Punishment of counterfeiting the Securities and current Coin of the United States;

To establish Post Offices and post Roads;

To promote the Progress of Science and useful Arts, by securing for limited Times to Authors and Inventors the exclusive Right to their respective Writings and Discoveries;

To constitute Tribunals inferior to the Supreme Court;

To define and punish Piracies and Felonies committed on the high Seas, and Offenses against the Law of Nations;

To declare War, grant Letters of Marque and Reprisal, and make Rules concerning Captures on Land and Water;

To raise and support Armies, but no Appropriation of Money to that Use shall be for a longer Term than two Years;

To provide and maintain a Navy;

To make Rules for the Government and Regulation of the land and naval forces;

To provide for calling forth the Militia to execute the Laws of the Union, suppress Insurrections and repel Invasions;

To provide for organizing, arming, and disciplining the Militia, and for governing such Part of them as may be employed in the Service of the United States, reserving to the States respectively, the Appointment of the Officers, and the Authority of training the Militia according to the discipline prescribed by Congress;

To exercise exclusive Legislation in all Cases whatsoever, over such District (not exceeding ten Miles square) as may, by Cession of particular States, and the acceptance of Congress, become the Seat of the Government of the United States, and to exercise like Authority over all Places purchased by the Consent of the Legislature of the State in which the Same shall be, for the Erection of Forts, Magazines, Arsenals, Dock-yards, and other needful Buildings;—And

To make all Laws which shall be necessary and proper for carrying into Execution the foregoing Powers, and all other Powers vested by this Constitution in the Government of the United States, or in any Department or Officer thereof.

Section 9.

The Migration or Importation of such Persons as any of the States now existing shall think proper to admit, shall not be prohibited by the Congress prior to the Year one thousand eight hundred and eight, but a tax or duty may be imposed on such Importation, not exceeding ten dollars for each Person.

The privilege of the Writ of Habeas Corpus shall not be suspended, unless when in Cases of Rebellion or Invasion the public Safety may require it.

No bill of Attainder or ex post facto Law shall be passed.

No capitation, or other direct, Tax shall be laid unless in Proportion to the Census or Enumeration herein before directed to be taken.

No Tax or Duty shall be laid on Articles exported from any State.

No Preference shall be given by any Regulation of Commerce or Revenue to the Ports of one State over those of another: nor shall Vessels bound to, or from, one State, be obliged to enter, clear, or pay Duties in another.

No Money shall be drawn from the Treasury, but in Consequence of Appropriations made by Law; and a regular Statement and Account of the Receipts and Expenditures of all public Money shall be published from time to time.

No Title of Nobility shall be granted by the United States: And no Person holding any Office of Profit or Trust under them, shall, without the Consent of the Congress, accept of any present, Emolument, Office, or Title, of any kind whatever, from any King, Prince, or foreign State.

Section 10.

No State shall enter into any Treaty, Alliance, or Confederation; grant Letters of Marque and Reprisal; coin Money; emit Bills of Credit; make any Thing but gold and silver Coin a Tender in Payment of Debts; pass any Bill of Attainder, ex post facto Law, or Law impairing the Obligation of Contracts, or grant any Title of Nobility.

No State shall, without the Consent of the Congress, lay any Imposts or Duties on Imports or Exports, except what may be absolutely necessary for executing its inspection Laws; and the net Produce of all Duties and Imposts, laid by any State on Imports or Exports, shall be for the use of the Treasury of the United States; and all such Laws shall be subject to the Revision and Control of the Congress.

No state shall, without the Consent of Congress, lay any duty of Tonnage, keep Troops, or Ships of War in time of Peace, enter into any Agreement or Compact with another State, or with a foreign Power, or engage in War, unless actually invaded, or in such imminent Danger as will not admit of delay.

Article II

Section 1.

The executive Power shall be vested in a President of the United States of America. He shall hold his Office during the Term of four years, and, together with the Vice President, chosen for the same Term, be elected, as follows:

Each State shall appoint, in such Manner as the Legislature thereof may direct, a Number of Electors, equal to the whole Number of Senators and Representatives to which the State may be entitled in the Congress: but no Senator or Representative, or Person holding an Office of Trust or Profit under the United States, shall be appointed an Elector.

[The Electors shall meet in their respective States, and vote by Ballot for two persons, of whom one at least shall not be an Inhabitant of the same State with themselves. And they shall make a List of all the Persons voted for, and of the Number of Votes for each; which List they shall sign and certify, and transmit sealed to the Seat of the Government of the United States, directed to the President of the Senate. The President of the Senate shall, in the Presence of the Senate and House of Representatives, open all the Certificates, and the Votes shall then be counted. The Person having the greatest Number of Votes shall be the President, if such Number be a Majority of the whole Number of Electors appointed; and if there be more than one who have such Majority, and have an equal Number of Votes, then the House of Representatives shall immediately chuse by Ballot one of them for President; and if no Person have a Majority, then from the five highest on the List the said House shall in like Manner chuse the President. But in chusing the President, the Votes shall be taken by States, the Representation from each

State having one Vote; a quorum for this Purpose shall consist of a Member or Members from two-thirds of the States, and a Majority of all the States shall be necessary to a Choice. In every Case, after the Choice of the President, the Person having the greatest Number of Votes of the Electors shall be the Vice President. But if there should remain two or more who have equal votes, the Senate shall chuse from them by Ballot the Vice President.]⁴

The Congress may determine the Time of chusing the Electors, and the Day on which they shall give their Votes; which Day shall be the same throughout the United States.

No person except a natural-born Citizen, or a Citizen of the United States, at the time of the Adoption of this Constitution, shall be eligible to the Office of President; neither shall any Person be eligible to that Office who shall not have attained to the Age of thirty-five years, and been fourteen Years a Resident within the United States.

In Case of the Removal of the President from Office, or of his Death, Resignation, or Inability to discharge the Powers and Duties of the said Office, the same shall devolve on the Vice President, and the Congress may by Law provide for the Case of Removal, Death, Resignation, or Inability, both of the President and Vice President, declaring what Officer shall then act as President, and such Officer shall act accordingly, until the disability be removed, or a President shall be elected.

The President shall, at stated Times, receive for his Services a Compensation, which shall neither be increased nor diminished during the Period for which he shall have been elected, and he shall not receive within that Period any other Emolument from the United States, or any of them.

Before he enter on the execution of his Office, he shall take the following Oath or Affirmation:—"I do solemnly swear (or affirm) that I will faithfully execute the Office of President of the United States, and will, to the best of my Ability, preserve, protect, and defend the Constitution of the United States."

Section 2.
The President shall be Commander in Chief of the Army and Navy of the United States, and of the Militia of the several States, when called into the actual Service of the United States; he may require the Opinion, in writing, of the principal Officer in each of the executive Departments, upon any subject relating to the Duties of their respective Offices, and he shall have Power to Grant Reprieves and Pardons for Offenses against the United States, except in Cases of Impeachment.

He shall have Power, by and with the Advice and Consent of the Senate, to make Treaties, provided two-thirds of the Senators present concur; and he shall nominate, and by and with the Advice and Consent of the Senate, shall appoint Ambassadors, other public Ministers and Consuls, Judges of the supreme Court, and all other Officers of the United States, whose Appointments are not herein otherwise provided for, and which shall be established by Law: but the Congress may by Law vest the Appointment of such inferior Officers, as they think proper, in the President alone, in the Courts of Law, or in the Heads of Departments.

The President shall have Power to fill up all Vacancies that may happen during the Recess of the Senate, by granting Commissions which shall expire at the End of their next Session.

⁴Revised by the Twelfth Amendment.

Section 3.

He shall from time to time give to the Congress Information of the State of the Union, and recommend to their Consideration such Measures as he shall judge necessary and expedient; he may, on extraordinary occasions, convene both Houses, or either of them, and in Case of Disagreement between them, with respect to the Time of Adjournment, he may adjourn them to such Time as he shall think proper; he shall receive Ambassadors and other public Ministers; he shall take care that the Laws be faithfully executed, and shall Commission all the Officers of the United States.

Section 4.

The President, Vice President and all civil Officers of the United States, shall be removed from Office on Impeachment for, and Conviction of, Treason, Bribery, or other high Crimes and Misdemeanors.

Article III

Section 1.

The judicial Power of the United States, shall be vested in one supreme Court, and in such inferior Courts as the Congress may from time to time ordain and establish. The Judges, both of the supreme and inferior Courts, shall hold their Offices during good Behaviour, and shall, at stated Times, receive for their Services, a Compensation, which shall not be diminished during their Continuance in Office.

Section 2.

The judicial Power shall extend to all Cases, in Law and Equity, arising under this Constitution, the Laws of the United States, and Treaties made, or which shall be made, under their Authority;—to all Cases affecting ambassadors, other public ministers and consuls;—to all cases of admiralty and maritime Jurisdiction;—to Controversies to which the United States shall be a Party;—to Controversies between two or more States;—between a State and Citizens of another State;[5]—between Citizens of different States—between Citizens of the same State claiming Lands under Grants of different States, and between a State, or the Citizens thereof, and foreign States, Citizens, or Subjects.

In all Cases affecting Ambassadors, other public Ministers and Consuls, and those in which a State shall be Party, the supreme Court shall have original Jurisdiction. In all the other Cases before mentioned, the supreme Court shall have appellate Jurisdiction, both as to Law and Fact, with such Exceptions, and under such Regulations as the Congress shall make.

The trial of all Crimes, except in Cases of Impeachment, shall be by Jury; and such Trial shall be held in the State where the said Crimes shall have been committed; but when not committed within any State, the Trial shall be at such Place or Places as the Congress may by Law have directed.

Section 3.

Treason against the United States, shall consist only in levying War against them, or in adhering to their Enemies, giving them Aid and Comfort. No Person shall be convicted of Treason unless on the Testimony of two Witnesses to the same overt Act, or on Confession in open Court.

---

[5]Qualified by the Eleventh Amendment.

The Congress shall have power to declare the Punishment of Treason, but no Attainder of Treason shall work Corruption of Blood, or Forfeiture except during the Life of the Person attained.

Article IV

Section 1.
Full Faith and Credit shall be given in each State to the public Acts, Records, and judicial Proceedings of every other State. And the Congress may by general Laws prescribe the Manner in which such Acts, Records and Proceedings shall be proved, and the Effect thereof.

Section 2.
The Citizens of each State shall be entitled to all Privileges and Immunities of Citizens in the several States.

A Person charged in any State with Treason, Felony, or other Crime, who shall flee from Justice, and be found in another State, shall on demand of the executive Authority of the State from which he fled, be delivered up, to be removed to the State having Jurisdiction of the crime.

No Person held to Service or Labour in one State, under the Laws thereof, escaping into another, shall, in Consequence of any Law or Regulation therein, be discharged from such Service or Labour, but shall be delivered up on Claim of the Party to whom such Service or Labour may be due.

Section 3.
New States may be admitted by the Congress into this Union; but no new State shall be formed or erected within the Jurisdiction of any other State; nor any State be formed by the Junction of two or more States, or parts of States, without the Consent of the Legislatures of the States concerned as well as of the Congress.

The Congress shall have Power to dispose of and make all needful Rules and Regulations respecting the Territory or other Property belonging to the United States; and nothing in this Constitution shall be so construed as to Prejudice any Claims of the United States, or of any particular State.

Section 4.
The United States shall guarantee to every State in this Union a Republican Form of Government, and shall protect each of them against Invasion; and on Application of the Legislature, or of the Executive (when the Legislature cannot be convened) against domestic Violence.

Article V

The Congress, whenever two-thirds of both Houses shall deem it necessary, shall propose Amendments to this Constitution, or, on the Application of the Legislatures of two-thirds of the several States, shall call a Convention for proposing Amendments, which, in either Case, shall be valid to all Intents and Purposes, as part of this Constitution, when ratified by the Legislatures of three-fourths of the several States, or by Conventions in three-fourths thereof, as the one or the other Mode of Ratification may be proposed by the Congress; Provided that no Amendment which may be made prior to the Year One thousand eight hundred and eight shall in any Manner affect the first and fourth Clauses in the Ninth Section of the first Article; and that no State, without its Consent, shall be deprived of its equal Suffrage in the Senate.

Article VI

All Debts contracted and Engagements entered into, before the Adoption of this Constitution, shall be as valid against the United States under this Constitution, as under the Confederation.

This Constitution, and the Laws of the United States which shall be made in Pursuance thereof; and all Treaties made, or which shall be made, under the Authority of the United States, shall be the supreme Law of the Land; and the Judges in every State shall be bound thereby, any Thing in the Constitution or Laws of any State to the Contrary notwithstanding.

The Senators and Representatives before mentioned, and the Members of the several State Legislatures, and all executive and judicial Officers, both of the United States and of the several States, shall be bound by Oath or Affirmation to support this Constitution; but no religious Tests shall ever be required as a qualification to any Office or public Trust under the United States.

Article VII

The Ratification of the Conventions of nine States shall be sufficient for the Establishment of this Constitution between the States so ratifying the same.

Done in Convention by the Unanimous Consent of the States present the Seventeenth Day of September in the Year of our Lord one thousand seven hundred and Eighty seven, and of the Independence of the United States of America the Twelfth. In Witness whereof We have hereunto subscribed our Names.[6]

George Washington
President and deputy from Virginia

New Hampshire
John Langdon
Nicholas Gilman

Massachusetts
Nathaniel Gorham
Rufus King

Connecticut
William Samuel Johnson
Roger Sherman

New York
Alexander Hamilton

New Jersey
William Livingston
David Brearley
William Paterson
Jonathan Dayton

Pennsylvania
Benjamin Franklin
Thomas Mifflin
Robert Morris
George Clymer
Thomas FitzSimons
Jared Ingersoll
James Wilson
Gouverneur Morris

Delaware
George Read
Gunning Bedford, Jr.
John Dickinson
Richard Bassett
Jacob Broom

Maryland
James McHenry
Daniel of
    St. Thomas Jenifer
Daniel Carroll

Virginia
John Blair
James Madison, Jr.

North Carolina
William Blount
Richard Dobbs
    Spaight
Hugh Williamson

South Carolina
John Rutledge
Charles Cotesworth
    Pinckney
Charles Pinckney
Pierce Butler

Georgia
William Few
Abraham Baldwin

[6]These are the full names of the signers, which in some cases are not the signatures on the document.

Articles in Addition to, and Amendment of, the Constitution of the United States of America, Proposed by Congress, and Ratified by the Legislatures of the Several States, Pursuant to the Fifth Article of the Original Constitution.[7]

[Article I]

Congress shall make no law respecting an establishment of religion, or prohibiting the free exercise thereof; or abridging the freedom of speech, or of the press; or the right of the people peaceably to assemble, and to petition the Government for a redress of grievances.

[Article II]

A well regulated Militia, being necessary to the security of a free State, the right of the people to keep and bear Arms shall not be infringed.

[Article III]

No Soldier shall, in time of peace, be quartered in any house, without the consent of the Owner, nor in time of war, but in a manner to be prescribed by law.

[Article IV]

The right of the people to be secure in their persons, houses, papers, and effects, against unreasonable searches and seizures, shall not be violated, and no Warrants shall issue, but upon probable cause, supported by Oath or affirmation, and particularly describing the place to be searched, and the persons or things to be seized.

[Article V]

No person shall be held to answer for a capital or otherwise infamous crime, unless on a presentment or indictment of a Grand Jury, except in cases arising in the land or naval forces, or in the Militia, when in actual service in time of War or public danger; nor shall any person be subject for the same offence to be twice put in jeopardy of life or limb; nor shall be compelled in any criminal case to be a witness against himself, nor be deprived of life, liberty, or property, without due process of law; nor shall private property be taken for public use, without just compensation.

[Article VI]

In all criminal prosecutions, the accused shall enjoy the right to a speedy and public trial, by an impartial jury of the State and district wherein the crime shall have been committed, which district shall have been previously ascertained by law, and to be informed of the nature and cause of the accusation; to be confronted with the witnesses against him; to have compulsory process for obtaining witnesses in his favour, and to have the Assistance of Counsel for his defense.

[Article VII]

In suits at common law, where the value in controversy shall exceed twenty dollars, the right of trial by jury shall be preserved, and no fact tried by a jury, shall be otherwise reexamined in any Court of the United States, than according to the rules of the common law.

---

[7]This heading appears only in the joint resolution submitting the first ten amendments.

[Article VIII]

Excessive bail shall not be required, nor excessive fines imposed, nor cruel and unusual punishments inflicted.

[Article IX]

The enumeration of the Constitution, of certain rights, shall not be construed to deny or disparage others retained by the people.

[Article X]

The powers not delegated to the United States by the Constitution, nor prohibited by it to the States, are reserved to the States respectively, or to the people. [Amendments I–X, in force 1791.]

[Amendment XI][8]

The Judicial power of the United States shall not be construed to extend to any suit in law or equity, commenced or prosecuted against one of the United States by Citizens of another State, or by Citizens or Subjects of any Foreign State.

[Amendment XII][9]

The Electors shall meet in their respective States and vote by ballot for President and Vice-President, one of whom, at least, shall not be an inhabitant of the same State with themselves; they shall name in their ballots the person voted for as President, and in distinct ballots the person voted for as Vice-President, and they shall make distinct lists of all persons voted for as President, and of all persons voted for as Vice-President, and of the number of votes for each, which lists they shall sign and certify, and transmit sealed to the seat of the government of the United States, directed to the President of the Senate;—The President of the Senate shall, in the presence of the Senate and House of Representatives, open all the certificates and the votes shall then be counted;—The person having the greatest number of votes for President, shall be the President, if such number be a majority of the whole number of Electors appointed; and if no person have such majority, then from the persons having the highest numbers not exceeding three on the list of those voted for as President, the House of Representatives shall choose immediately, by ballot, the President. But in choosing the President, the votes shall be taken by states, the representation from each state having one vote; a quorum for this purpose shall consist of a member or members from two-thirds of the states, and a majority of all the states shall be necessary to a choice. And if the House of Representatives shall not choose a President whenever the right of choice shall devolve upon them, before the fourth day of March next following, then the Vice-President shall act as President, as in the case of the death or other constitutional disability of the President.—The person having the greatest number of votes as Vice-President, shall be the Vice-President, if such number be a majority of the whole number of Electors appointed, and if no person have a majority, then from the two highest numbers on the list, the Senate shall choose the Vice-President; a quorum for the purpose shall consist of two-thirds of the whole number of Senators, and a majority of the whole number shall be necessary to a choice. But no person constitutionally ineligible to the office of President shall be eligible to that of Vice-President of the United States.

---

[8]Adopted in 1798.
[9]Adopted in 1804.

[Amendment XIII][10]

Section 1.
Neither slavery nor involuntary servitude, except as a punishment for crime whereof the party shall have been duly convicted, shall exist within the United States, or any place subject to their jurisdiction.

Section 2.
Congress shall have power to enforce this article by appropriate legislation.

[Amendment XIV][11]

Section 1.
All persons born or naturalized in the United States, and subject to the jurisdiction thereof, are citizens of the United States and of the State wherein they reside. No State shall make or enforce any law which shall abridge the privileges or immunities of citizens of the United States; nor shall any State deprive any person of life, liberty, or property, without due process of law; nor deny to any person within its jurisdiction the equal protection of the laws.

Section 2.
Representatives shall be apportioned among the several States according to their respective numbers, counting the whole number of persons in each State, excluding Indians not taxed. But when the right to vote at any election for the choice of electors for President and Vice-President of the United States, Representatives in Congress, the Executive and Judicial officers of a State, or the members of the Legislature thereof, is denied to any of the male inhabitants of such State, being twenty-one years of age, and citizens of the United States, or in any way abridged, except for participation in rebellion, or other crime, the basis of representation therein shall be reduced in the proportion which the number of such male citizens shall bear to the whole number of male citizens twenty-one years of age in such State.

Section 3.
No person shall be a Senator or Representative in Congress, or elector of President and Vice-President, or hold any office, civil or military, under the United States, or under any State, who, having previously taken an oath, as a member of Congress, or as an officer of the United States, or as a member of any State legislature, or as an executive or judicial officer of any State, to support the Constitution of the United States, shall have engaged in insurrection or rebellion against the same, or given aid or comfort to the enemies thereof. But Congress may by a vote of two-thirds of each House, remove such disability.

Section 4.
The validity of the public debt of the United States, authorized by law, including debts incurred for payment of pensions and bounties for services in suppressing insurrection or rebellion, shall not be questioned. But neither the United States

[10]Adopted in 1865.
[11]Adopted in 1868.

nor any State shall assume or pay any debts or obligation incurred in aid of insurrection or rebellion against the United States, or any claim for the loss or emancipation of any slave; but all such debts, obligations, and claims shall be held illegal and void.

Section 5.
The Congress shall have the power to enforce, by appropriate legislation, the provisions of this article.

[Amendment XV][12]

Section 1.
The right of citizens of the United States to vote shall not be denied or abridged by the United States or by any State on account of race, color, or previous condition of servitude—

Section 2.
The Congress shall have power to enforce this article by appropriate legislation.

[Amendment XVI][13]

The Congress shall have power to lay and collect taxes on incomes, from whatever source derived, without apportionment among the several States, and without regard to any census or enumeration.

[Amendment XVII][14]

The Senate of the United States shall be composed of two Senators from each State, elected by the people thereof, for six years; and each Senator shall have one vote. The electors in each State shall have the qualifications requisite for electors of the most numerous branch of the State legislatures.

When vacancies happen in the representation of any State in the Senate, the executive authority of such State shall issue writs of election to fill such vacancies: *Provided*, That the legislature of any State may empower the executive thereof to make temporary appointments until the people fill the vacancies by election as the legislature may direct.

This amendment shall not be so construed as to affect the election or term of any Senator chosen before it becomes valid as part of the Constitution.

[Amendment XVIII][15]

Section 1.
After one year from the ratification of this article the manufacture, sale, or transportation of intoxicating liquors within, the importation thereof into, or the exportation thereof from the United States and all territory subject to the jurisdiction thereof for beverage purposes is hereby prohibited.

[12]Adopted in 1870.
[13]Adopted in 1913.
[14]Adopted in 1913.
[15]Adopted in 1918.

Section 2.

The Congress and the several States shall have concurrent power to enforce this article by appropriate legislation.

Section 3.

This article shall be inoperative unless it shall have been ratified as an amendment to the Constitution by the legislatures of the several States, as provided in the Constitution, within seven years from the date of the submission hereof to the States by the Congress.

[Amendment XIX][16]

The right of citizens of the United States to vote shall not be denied or abridged by the United States or by any State on account of sex.

Congress shall have power to enforce this article by appropriate legislation.

[Amendment XX][17]

Section 1.

The terms of the President and Vice-President shall end at noon on the 20th day of January, and the terms of Senators and Representatives at noon on the 3d day of January, of the years in which such terms would have ended if this article had not been ratified; and the terms of their successors shall then begin.

Section 2.

The Congress shall assemble at least once in every year, and such meeting shall begin at noon on the 3d day of January, unless they shall by law appoint a different day.

Section 3.

If, at the time fixed for the beginning of the term of the President, the President elect shall have died, the Vice-President elect shall become President. If a President shall not have been chosen before the time fixed for the beginning of his term or if the President elect shall have failed to qualify, then the Vice-President elect shall act as President until a President shall have qualified; and the Congress may by law provide for the case wherein neither a President elect nor a Vice-President elect shall have qualified, declaring who shall then act as President, or the manner in which one who is to act shall be selected, and such person shall act accordingly until a President or Vice-President shall have qualified.

Section 4.

The Congress may by law provide for the case of the death of any of the persons from whom the House of Representatives may choose a President whenever the right of choice shall have devolved upon them, and for the case of the death of any of the persons from whom the Senate may choose a Vice-President whenever the right of choice shall have devolved upon them.

Section 5.

Sections 1 and 2 shall take effect on the 15th day of October following the ratification of this article.

[16]Adopted in 1920.
[17]Adopted in 1933.

Section 6.
This article shall be inoperative unless it shall have been ratified as an amendment to the Constitution by the legislatures of three-fourths of the several States within seven years from the date of its submission.

[Amendment XXI][18]

Section 1.
The eighteenth article of amendment to the Constitution of the United States is hereby repealed.

Section 2.
The transportation or importation into any State, Territory, or possession of the United States for delivery or use therein of intoxicating liquors, in violation of the laws thereof, is hereby prohibited.

Section 3.
This article shall be inoperative unless it shall have been ratified as an amendment to the Constitution by conventions in the several States, as provided in the Constitution, within seven years from the date of the submission hereof to the States by the Congress.

[Amendment XXII][19]

No person shall be elected to the office of the President more than twice, and no person who has held the office of President, or acted as President, for more than two years of a term to which some other person was elected President shall be elected to the office of the President more than once.

But this Article shall not apply to any person holding the office of President when this Article was proposed by the Congress, and shall not prevent any person who may be holding the office of President, or acting as President, during the term within which this Article becomes operative from holding the office of President or acting as President during the remainder of such term.

This article shall be inoperative unless it shall have been ratified as an amendment to the Constitution by the legislatures of three-fourths of the several states within seven years from the date of its submission to the states by the Congress.

[Amendment XXIII][20]

Section 1.
The District constituting the seat of Government of the United States shall appoint in such manner as the Congress may direct:

A number of electors of President and Vice-President equal to the whole number of Senators and Representatives in Congress to which the District would be entitled if it were a State, but in no event more than the least populous State; they shall be in addition to those appointed by the States, but they shall be considered,

[18]Adopted in 1933.
[19]Adopted in 1961.
[20]Adopted in 1961.

for the purposes of the election of President and Vice-President, to be electors appointed by a State; and they shall meet in the District and perform such duties as provided by the twelfth article of amendment.

Section 2.

The Congress shall have power to enforce this article by appropriate legislation.

[Amendment XXIV][21]

Section 1.

The right of citizens of the United States to vote in any primary or other election for President or Vice President, for electors for President or Vice President, or for Senator or Representative in Congress, shall not be denied or abridged by the United States or any state by reason of failure to pay any poll tax or other tax.

Section 2.

The Congress shall have the power to enforce this article by appropriate legislation.

[Amendment XXV][22]

Section 1.

In case of the removal of the President from office or of his death or resignation, the Vice President shall become President.

Section 2.

Whenever there is a vacancy in the office of the Vice President, the President shall nominate a Vice President who shall take office upon confirmation by a majority vote of both Houses of Congress.

Section 3.

Whenever the President transmits to the President Pro Tempore of the Senate and the Speaker of the House of Representatives his written declaration that he is unable to discharge the powers and duties of his office, and until he transmits to them a written declaration to the contrary, such powers and duties shall be discharged by the Vice President as Acting President.

Section 4.

Whenever the Vice President and a majority of either the principal officers of the executive departments or of such other body as Congress may by law provide, transmit to the President Pro Tempore of the Senate and the Speaker of the House of Representatives their written declaration that the President is unable to discharge the powers and duties of his office, the Vice President shall immediately assume the powers and duties of the office as Acting President.

[21]Adopted in 1964.
[22]Adopted in 1967.

Thereafter, when the President transmits to the President Pro Tempore of the Senate and the Speaker of the House of Representatives his written declaration that no inability exists, he shall resume the powers and duties of his office unless the Vice President and a majority of either the principal officers of the executive departments or of such other body as Congress may by law provide, transmit within four days to the President Pro Tempore of the Senate and the Speaker of the House of Representatives their written declaration that the President is unable to discharge the powers and duties of his office. Thereupon Congress shall decide the issue, assembling within forty-eight hours for that purpose if not in session. If the Congress, within twenty-one days after receipt of the latter written declaration, or, if Congress is not in session, within twenty-one days after Congress is required to assemble, determines by two-thirds vote of both Houses that the President is unable to discharge the powers and duties of his office, the Vice President shall continue to discharge the same as Acting President; otherwise, the President shall resume the powers and duties of his office.

[Amendment XXVI][23]

Section 1.
The right of citizens of the United States, who are eighteen years of age or older, to vote shall not be denied or abridged by the United States or by any State on account of age.

Section 2.
The Congress shall have power to enforce this article by appropriate legislation.

[Amendment XXVII][24]

No law varying the compensation for the services of the Senators and Representatives shall take effect until an election of Representatives shall have intervened.

[23]Adopted in 1971.
[24]Adopted in 1992.

PRESIDENTIAL ELECTIONS

Year	Candidates	Parties	Popular Vote	Percentage of Popular Vote	Electoral Vote	Percentage of Voter Participation
1789	GEORGE WASHINGTON (VA.)*				69	
	John Adams				34	
	Others				35	
1792	GEORGE WASHINGTON (VA.)				132	
	John Adams				77	
	George Clinton				50	
	Others				5	
1796	JOHN ADAMS (MASS.)	Federalist			71	
	Thomas Jefferson	Democratic Republican			68	
	Thomas Pinckney	Federalist			59	
	Aaron Burr	Dem.-Rep.			30	
	Others				48	
1800	THOMAS JEFFERSON (VA.)	Dem.-Rep.			73	
	Aaron Burr	Dem.-Rep.			73	
	John Adams	Federalist			65	
	C. C. Pinckney	Federalist			64	
	John Jay	Federalist			1	
1804	THOMAS JEFFERSON (VA.)	Dem.-Rep.			162	
	C. C. Pinckney	Federalist			14	
1808	JAMES MADISON (VA.)	Dem.-Rep.			122	
	C. C. Pinckney	Federalist			47	
	George Clinton	Dem.-Rep.			6	

Year	Candidate	Party	Popular Vote	% Popular Vote	Electoral Vote	% Voter Participation
1812	**James Madison (Va.)**	Dem.-Rep.			128	
	De Witt Clinton	Federalist			89	
1816	**James Monroe (Va.)**	Dem.-Rep.			183	
	Rufus King	Federalist			34	
1820	**James Monroe (Va.)**	Dem.-Rep.			231	
	John Quincy Adams	Dem.-Rep.			1	
1824	**John Q. Adams (Mass.)**	Dem.-Rep.	108,740	30.5	84	26.9
	Andrew Jackson	Dem.-Rep.	153,544	43.1	99	
	William H. Crawford	Dem.-Rep.	46,618	13.1	41	
	Henry Clay	Dem.-Rep.	47,136	13.2	37	
1828	**Andrew Jackson (Tenn.)**	Democratic	647,286	56.0	178	57.6
	John Quincy Adams	National Republican	508,064	44.0	83	
1832	**Andrew Jackson (Tenn.)**	Democratic	687,502	55.0	219	55.4
	Henry Clay	National Republican	530,189	42.4	49	
	John Floyd	Independent			11	
	William Wirt	Anti-Mason	33,108	2.6	7	
1836	**Martin Van Buren (N.Y.)**	Democratic	765,483	50.9	170	57.8
	W. H. Harrison	Whig			73	
	Hugh L. White	Whig	739,795	49.1	26	
	Daniel Webster	Whig			14	
	W. P. Magnum	Independent			11	
1840	**William H. Harrison (Ohio)**	Whig	1,274,624	53.1	234	80.2
	Martin Van Buren	Democratic	1,127,781	46.9	60	
	J. G. Birney	Liberty	7,069		—	

*State of residence at time of election.

(continued)

Year	Candidates	Parties	Popular Vote	Percentage of Popular Vote	Electoral Vote	Percentage of Voter Participation
1844	JAMES K. POLK (TENN.)	Democratic	1,338,464	49.6	170	78.9
	Henry Clay	Whig	1,300,097	48.1	105	
	J. G. Birney	Liberty	62,300	2.3	—	
1848	ZACHARY TAYLOR (LA.)	Whig	1,360,967	47.4	163	72.7
	Lewis Cass	Democratic	1,222,342	42.5	127	
	Martin Van Buren	Free-Soil	291,263	10.1	—	
1852	FRANKLIN PIERCE (N.H.)	Democratic	1,601,117	50.9	254	69.6
	Winfield Scott	Whig	1,385,453	44.1	42	
	John P. Hale	Free-Soil	155,825	5.0	—	
1856	JAMES BUCHANAN (PA.)	Democratic	1,832,955	45.3	174	78.9
	John C. Frémont	Republican	1,339,932	33.1	114	
	Millard Fillmore	American	871,731	21.6	8	
1860	ABRAHAM LINCOLN (ILL.)	Republican	1,865,593	39.8	180	81.2
	Stephen A. Douglas	Democratic	1,382,713	29.5	12	
	John C. Breckinridge	Democratic	848,356	18.1	72	
	John Bell	Union	592,906	12.6	39	
1864	ABRAHAM LINCOLN (ILL.)	Republican	2,213,655	55.0	212	73.8
	George B. McClellan	Democratic	1,805,237	45.0	21	
1868	ULYSSES S. GRANT (ILL.)	Republican	3,012,833	52.7	214	78.1
	Horatio Seymour	Democratic	2,703,249	47.3	80	
1872	ULYSSES S. GRANT (ILL.)	Republican	3,597,132	55.6	286	71.3
	Horace Greeley	Democratic; Liberal Republican	2,834,125	43.9	66	

Year	Candidate	Party	Popular Vote	Electoral Vote	%
1876	**RUTHERFORD B. HAYES (OHIO)**	Republican	4,036,298	185	48.0
	Samuel J. Tilden	Democratic	4,300,590	184	51.0
1880	**JAMES A. GARFIELD (OHIO)**	Republican	4,454,416	214	48.5
	Winfield S. Hancock	Democratic	4,444,952	155	48.1
1884	**GROVER CLEVELAND (N.Y.)**	Democratic	4,874,986	219	48.5
	James G. Blaine	Republican	4,851,981	182	48.2
1888	**BENJAMIN HARRISON (IND.)**	Republican	5,439,853	233	47.9
	Grover Cleveland	Democratic	5,540,309	168	48.6
1892	**GROVER CLEVELAND (N.Y.)**	Democratic	5,556,918	277	46.1
	Benjamin Harrison	Republican	5,176,108	145	43.0
	James B. Weaver	People's	1,041,028	22	8.5
1896	**WILLIAM MCKINLEY (OHIO)**	Republican	7,104,779	271	51.1
	William J. Bryan	Democratic People's			
1900	**WILLIAM MCKINLEY (OHIO)**	Republican	6,502,925	176	47.7
	William J. Bryan	Dem.-Populist	7,207,923	292	51.7
			6,358,133	155	45.5
1904	**THEODORE ROOSEVELT (N.Y.)**	Republican	7,623,486	336	57.9
	Alton B. Parker	Democratic	5,077,911	140	37.6
	Eugene V. Debs	Socialist	402,283	—	3.0
1908	**WILLIAM H. TAFT (OHIO)**	Republican	7,678,908	321	51.6
	William J. Bryan	Democratic	6,409,104	162	43.1
	Eugene V. Debs	Socialist	420,793		2.8
1912	**WOODROW WILSON (N.J.)**	Democratic	6,293,454	435	41.9
	Theodore Roosevelt	Progressive	4,119,538	88	27.4
	William H. Taft	Republican	3,484,980	8	23.2
	Eugene V. Debs	Socialist	900,672	—	6.0

(continued)

Year	Candidates	Parties	Popular Vote	Percentage of Popular Vote	Electoral Vote	Percentage of Voter Participation
1916	**WOODROW WILSON (N.J.)**	Democratic	9,129,606	49.4	277	61.6
	Charles E. Hughes	Republican	8,538,221	46.2	254	
	A. L. Benson	Socialist	585,113	3.2	—	
1920	**WARREN G. HARDING (OHIO)**	Republican	16,152,200	60.4	404	49.2
	James M. Cox	Democratic	9,147,353	34.2	127	
	Eugene V. Debs	Socialist	919,799	3.4	—	
1924	**CALVIN COOLIDGE (MASS.)**	Republican	15,725,016	54.0	382	48.9
	John W. Davis	Democratic	8,386,503	28.8	136	
	Robert M. LaFollette	Progressive	4,822,856	16.6	13	
1928	**HERBERT HOOVER (CALIF.)**	Republican	21,391,381	58.2	444	56.9
	Alfred E. Smith	Democratic	15,016,443	40.9	87	
	Norman Thomas	Socialist	267,835	0.7	—	
1932	**FRANKLIN D. ROOSEVELT (N.Y.)**	Democratic	22,821,857	57.4	472	56.9
	Herbert Hoover	Republican	15,761,841	39.7	59	
	Norman Thomas	Socialist	881,951	2.2	—	
1936	**FRANKLIN D. ROOSEVELT (N.Y.)**	Democratic	27,751,597	60.8	523	61.0
	Alfred M. Landon	Republican	16,679,583	36.5	8	
	William Lemke	Union	882,479	1.9	—	
1940	**FRANKLIN D. ROOSEVELT (N.Y.)**	Democratic	27,244,160	54.8	449	62.5
	Wendell L. Willkie	Republican	22,305,198	44.8	82	
1944	**FRANKLIN D. ROOSEVELT (N.Y.)**	Democratic	25,602,504	53.5	432	55.9
	Thomas E. Dewey	Republican	22,006,285	46.0	99	

Year	Candidate	Parties	Popular Vote	Percentage of Popular Vote	Electoral Vote	Percentage of Voter Participation
1948	HARRY S. TRUMAN (MO.)	Democratic	24,105,695	49.5	304	53.0
	Thomas E. Dewey	Republican	21,969,170	45.1	189	
	J. Strom Thurmond	State-Rights Democratic	1,169,021	2.4	38	
	Henry A. Wallace	Progressive	1,156,103	2.4	—	
1952	DWIGHT D. EISENHOWER (N.Y.)	Republican	33,936,252	55.1	442	63.3
	Adlai E. Stevenson	Democratic	27,314,992	44.4	89	
1956	DWIGHT D. EISENHOWER (N.Y.)	Republican	35,575,420	57.6	457	60.6
	Adlai E. Stevenson	Democratic	26,033,066	42.1	73	
	Other		—		1	
1960	JOHN F. KENNEDY (MASS.)	Democratic	34,227,096	49.9	303	62.8
	Richard M. Nixon	Republican	34,108,546	49.6	219	
	Other		—		15	
1964	LYNDON B. JOHNSON (TEX.)	Democratic	43,126,506	61.1	486	61.7
	Barry M. Goldwater	Republican	27,176,799	38.5	52	
1968	RICHARD M. NIXON (N.Y.)	Republican	31,770,237	43.4	301	60.6
	Hubert H. Humphrey	Democratic	31,270,533	42.7	191	
	George Wallace	American Independent	9,906,141	13.5	46	
1972	RICHARD M. NIXON (N.Y.)	Republican	47,169,911	60.7	520	55.2
	George S. McGovern	Democratic	29,170,383	37.5	17	
	Other		—		1	
1976	JIMMY CARTER (GA.)	Democratic	40,828,587	50.0	297	53.5
	Gerald R. Ford	Republican	39,147,613	47.9	241	
	Other		1,575,459	2.1	—	

(continued)

Year	Candidates	Parties	Popular Vote	Percentage of Popular Vote	Electoral Vote	Percentage of Voter Participation
1980	RONALD REAGAN (CALIF.)	Republican	43,901,812	50.7	489	52.6
	Jimmy Carter	Democratic	35,483,820	41.0	49	
	John B. Anderson	Independent	5,719,722	6.6	—	
	Ed Clark	Libertarian	921,188	1.1	—	
1984	RONALD REAGAN (CALIF.)	Republican	54,455,075	59.0	525	53.3
	Walter Mondale	Democratic	37,577,185	41.0	13	
1988	GEORGE BUSH (TEX.)	Republican	47,946,422	54.0	426	50.2
	Michael S. Dukakis	Democratic	41,016,429	46.0	112	
1992	WILLIAM J. CLINTON (ARK.)	Democratic	43,728,375	43.0	370	55.0
	George Bush	Republican	38,167,416	38.0	168	
	Ross Perot	Independent	19,237,247	19.0	0	
1996	WILLIAM J. CLINTON (ARK.)	Democratic	47,401,185	49.3	379	49.0
	Robert Dole	Republican	39,197,469	40.7	159	
	Ross Perot	Reform	8,085,294	8.4	—	
2000	GEORGE W. BUSH (TEXAS)	Republican	50,459,211	47.89	271	51.0
	Albert Gore, Jr.	Democratic	51,003,894	48.41	266	
	Ralph Nader	Green	2,834,410	2.69	—	

POPULATION OF THE UNITED STATES, 1790–2000

Year	Population	Percent Increase	Population per Square Mile	Percent Urban/ Rural	Percent White/ Nonwhite	Median Age
1790	3,929,214		4.5	5.1/94.9	80.7/19.3	NA
1800	5,308,483	35.1	6.1	6.1/93.9	81.1/18.9	NA
1810	7,239,881	36.4	4.3	7.3/92.7	81.0/19.0	NA
1820	9,638,453	33.1	5.5	7.2/92.8	81.6/18.4	16.7
1830	12,866,020	33.5	7.4	8.8/91.2	81.9/18.1	17.2
1840	17,069,453	32.7	9.8	10.8/89.2	83.2/16.8	17.8
1850	23,191,876	35.9	7.9	15.3/84.7	84.3/15.7	18.9
1860	31,443,321	35.6	10.6	19.8/80.2	85.6/14.4	19.4
1870	39,818,449	26.6	13.4	25.7/74.3	86.2/13.8	20.2
1880	50,155,783	26.0	16.9	28.2/71.8	86.5/13.5	20.9
1890	62,947,714	25.5	21.2	35.1/64.9	87.5/12.5	22.0
1900	75,994,575	20.7	25.6	39.6/60.4	87.9/12.1	22.9
1910	91,972,266	21.0	31.0	45.6/54.4	88.9/11.1	24.1
1920	105,710,620	14.9	35.6	51.2/48.8	89.7/10.3	25.3
1930	122,775,046	16.1	41.2	56.1/43.9	89.8/10.2	26.4
1940	131,669,275	7.2	44.2	56.5/43.5	89.8/10.2	29.0
1950	150,697,361	14.5	50.7	64.0/36.0	89.5/10.5	30.2
1960	179,323,175	18.5	50.6	69.9/30.1	88.6/11.4	29.5
1970	203,302,031	13.4	57.4	73.5/26.5	87.6/12.4	28.0
1980	226,545,805	11.4	64.0	73.7/26.3	86.0/14.0	30.0
1990	248,709,873	9.9	70.3	77.5/22.5	80.3/19.7	32.9
2000	281,421,906	13.0	79.6	NA/NA	83.0/17.0	35.3

NA = Not available.

EMPLOYMENT, 1870–2000

Year	Number of Workers (in millions)	Male/Female Employment Ratio	Percentage of Workers in Unions
1870	12.5	85/15	—
1880	17.4	85/15	—
1890	23.3	83/17	—
1900	29.1	82/18	3
1910	38.2	79/21	6
1920	41.6	79/21	12
1930	48.8	78/22	7
1940	53.0	76/24	27
1950	59.6	72/28	25
1960	69.9	68/32	26
1970	82.1	63/37	25
1980	108.5	58/42	23
1985	108.9	57/43	19
1990	118.8	55/45	16
2000	134.3	53/47	13.5

PRODUCTION, TRADE, AND FEDERAL SPENDING/DEBT, 1790–2000

Year	Gross National Product (GNP) (in billions $)	Balance of Trade (in millions $)	Federal Budget (in billions $)	Federal Surplus/ Deficit (in billions $)	Federal Debt (in billions $)
1790	—	–3	.004	+0.00015	.076
1800	—	–20	.011	+0.0006	.083
1810	—	–18	.008	+0.0012	.053
1820	—	–4	.018	–0.0004	.091
1830	—	+3	.015	+0.100	.049
1840	—	+25	.024	–0.005	.004
1850	—	–26	.040	+0.004	.064
1860	—	–38	.063	–0.01	.065
1870	7.4	–11	.310	+0.10	2.4
1880	11.2	+92	.268	+0.07	2.1
1890	13.1	+87	.318	+0.09	1.2
1900	18.7	+569	.521	+0.05	1.2
1910	35.3	+273	.694	–0.02	1.1
1920	91.5	+2,880	6.357	+0.3	24.3
1930	90.7	+513	3.320	+0.7	16.3
1940	100.0	–3,403	9.6	–2.7	43.0
1950	286.5	+1,691	43.1	–2.2	257.4
1960	506.5	+4,556	92.2	+0.3	286.3
1970	992.7	+2,511	196.6	+2.8	371.0
1980	2,631.7	+24,088	579.6	–59.5	914.3
1985	4,087.7	–148,480	946.3	–212.3	1,827.5
1990	5,764.9	–101,012	1,251.8	–220.5	4,064.6
2000	9,860.8	–369.7	1,789.6	+237.0	5,674.2

Index

Note: Page numbers followed by the letter "*i*" refer to illustrations and by the letter "*m*" refer to maps.

MAINE

★Augusta

NEW
HAMPSHIRE
Concord   •Portland
    ★.Manchester
     ★ Boston
MASSACHUSETTS
     ↘Providence
★   RHODE
artford   ISLAND
    CONNECTICUT
w York
ark
on

Y

RE

YLAND

*ATLANTIC
OCEAN*

Land Elevation

Feet		Meters
10,000		3,000
7,000		2,000
3,000		1,000
700		200
Level) 0		0 (Sea Level)
ea Level		Below Sea Level

150	300 Miles
150	300 Kilometers

AHAMAS

HAITI

For more helpful study tools, visit

our Online Learning Center at

www.mhhe.com/unfinishednation4

YOU'LL FIND

● materials to help you review

chapter content

● interactive maps with exercises

● quizzes for every chapter

● links to interesting history sites,

organized by chapter and much

more!

ISBN 0-07-287725-1

TIME LINE

1947
- Truman Doctrine
- Marshall Plan proposed
- Levittown construction begins

1948
- Berlin blockade
- Hiss case begins

1949
- NATO established
- Soviet Union explodes A-bomb

1950
- Korean War begins
- McCarthy's anticommunism campaign begins

1952
- Eisenhower elected president

1953
- Korean War ends

1954
- *Brown* v. *Board of Education*
- Army-McCarthy hearings

1955
- Montgomery bus boycott

1957
- *Sputnik* launched
- Little Rock desegregation crisis

1959
- Castro seizes power in Cuba

1960
- U-2 incident
- Kennedy elected president

1961
- First American in space
- Freedom rides
- Bay of Pigs
- Berlin Wall erected

1962
- Cuban missile crisis

1963
- March on Washington
- Kennedy assassinated; Johnson becomes president

1964
- Johnson launches war on poverty
- Civil Rights Act
- Gulf of Tonkin resolution

1965
- Malcolm X assassinated
- Voting Rights Act
- U.S. troops in Vietnam

1966
- National Organization for Women founded

1968
- Tet offensive
- Martin Luther King, Jr. assassinated
- Robert Kennedy assassinated
- Nixon elected president

1969
- Americans land on moon

1970
- Cambodian incursion

1972
- Nixon visits China
- SALT I
- Watergate burglary

1973
- U.S. withdraws from Vietnam
- Arab oil embargo
- Supreme Court decides *Roe* v. *Wade*

1974
- Nixon resigns; Ford becomes president
- Ford pardons Nixon

1976
- Carter elected president

1977
- Apple introduces first personal computer

1978-1979
- Camp David accords
- American hostages in Iran
- Soviet Union invades Afghanistan
- U.S. and China restore relations

1980
- Reagan elected president

1981
- American hostages in Iran released
- AIDS first reported in U.S.

1986
- Iran-contra scandal revealed

1988
- Bush elected president

1989
- Berlin Wall dismantled
- Communist regimes collapse

1991
- Collapse of Soviet regime
- Persian Gulf War

1992
- Los Angeles race riots
- Clinton elected president

1995
- O. J. Simpson trial

1998
- Clinton impeached by House

1999
- Clinton aquitted by Senate

2000
- G.W. Bush loses popular vote, but wins presidency

2001
- Sept. 11th terrorist attacks

2003
- Coalition forces invade Iraq

TIME LINE

- **1812** — U.S. d... war on ... Britain
- **1814** — Hartford Conven..., Treaty of Ghent
- **1815** — Battle of ... Orleans; U.S. ta... western ... from Ind...
- **1816** — Secon... of U.S.; Monroe elected presiden...
- **1817-1...**
- **1820** — Erie Ca... construc...
- **1822** — Missou... Compro...
- **1823** — Denma... Vesey's conspira...
- **1824** — Monroe Doctrine
- **1828** — John Q... Adams e... presiden...; Jackso... elected presiden...

- **1793** — Eli Whitney invents cotton gin
- **1796** — John Adams elected president
- **1797**
- **1800** — Jefferson elected president; Alien and Sedition Acts
- **1801** — Marshall chief justice of Supreme Court
- **1803** — Louisiana Purchase; *Marbury v. Madison*
- **1804-1806** — Lewis and Clark expedition
- **1807** — Embargo
- **1808** — Madison elected president; Slave importation banned

- **1777** — Articles of Confederation adopted
- **1781** — Articles of Confederation ratified; Cornwallis surrenders at Yorktown
- **1783** — Treaty of Paris
- **1786** — Shays's Rebellion
- **1787** — Constitutional Convention; Northwest Ordinance adopted
- **1787-1788** — Constitution adopted; States ratify Constitution
- **1789** — Washington becomes first president
- French Revolution
- **1791** — First Bank of U.S. chartered; Bill of Rights adopted

- **1763** — Peace of Paris; Proclamation of 1763
- **1764** — Sugar Act
- **1765** — Stamp Act
- **1767** — Townshend Duties
- **1770** — Most Townshend Duties repealed; Boston Massacre
- **1773** — Tea Act; Boston Tea Party
- **1774** — First Continental Congress in Philadelphia
- **1775** — Battles of Lexington and Concord; American Revolution begins; Second Continental Congress begins
- **1776** — Washington commands American forces; Paine's *Common Sense*; Declaration of Independence

- **1636** — Roger Williams founds Rhode Island
- **1637** — Pequot War
- **1663** — Carolina chartered
- **1664** — English capture New Netherlands
- **1675** — King Philip's War
- **1676** — Bacon's Rebellion
- **1681** — Pennsylvania chartered
- **1692** — Salem witchcraft trials
- **1732** — Georgia chartered
- **1734** — Great Awakening begins
- **1754** — Beginning of French and Indian War
- **1756** — Seven Years' War begins

- **16,000-14,000 B.C.** — Asians migrate to North America
- **1492** — Columbus discovers America
- **1502** — African slaves arrive in Spanish America
- **1518-1530** — Smallpox ravages Indians
- **1608** — French establish Quebec
- **1609** — Spanish found Santa Fe
- **1619** — First African workers in Virginia
- **1620** — Pilgrims found Plymouth Colony
- **1624** — Dutch settle Manhattan
- **1630** — Puritans establish Massachusetts Bay Colony
- **1634** — Maryland founded

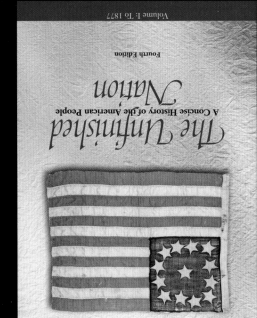

Volume I: To 1877

Fourth Edition

The Unfinished Nation

A Concise History of the American People

ALAN BRINKLEY

Volume II: From 1865

Fourth Edition

The Unfinished Nation

A Concise History of the American People

ALAN BRINKLEY

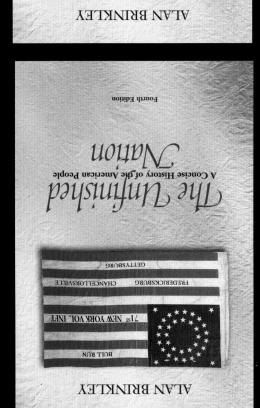

Fourth Edition

The Unfinished Nation

A Concise History of the American People

ALAN BRINKLEY

ALAN BRINKLEY

THE UNFINISHED NATION

A CONCISE HISTORY OF THE AMERICAN PEOPLE

AMERICAN HISTORY AT A GLANCE
QUICK REFERENCE TO ACCOMPANY